Reforming Britain's Economic and Financial Policy

Reforming Britain's Economic and Financial Policy

Towards Greater Economic Stability

HM TREASURY

Foreword by Gordon Brown,
Chancellor of the Exchequer

Edited by Ed Balls and Gus O'Donnell

First published 2002 by
PALGRAVE
Houndmills, Basingstoke, Hampshire RG21 6XS and
175 Fifth Avenue, New York, N.Y. 10010
Companies and representatives throughout the world

PALGRAVE is the new global academic imprint of
St. Martin's Press LLC Scholarly and Reference Division and
Palgrave Publishers Ltd (formerly Macmillan Press Ltd).

ISBN 0–333–96610–4 hardback
ISBN 0–333–96611–2 paperback

This book is printed on paper suitable for recycling and made from fully managed and sustained forest sources.

A catalogue record for this book is available from the British Library.

Library of Congress Cataloging-in-Publication Data
Reforming Britain's economic and financial policy / HM Treasury.
     p. cm.
   Includes index.
   ISBN 0–333–96610–4
     1. Great Britain—Economic policy. 2. Fiscal
   policy—Great Britain. 3. Great Britain. Treasury.
   HC256.65 .R44 2001
   338.941—dc21
                                              2001021739

10   9   8   7   6   5   4   3   2   1
11   10   09   08   07   06   05   04   03   02

Printed and bound in Great Britain by
Antony Rowe Ltd, Chippenham, Wiltshire

Contents

List of Tables   vi
List of Figures   viii

Foreword by Gordon Brown, Chancellor of the Exchequer   x

Introduction   1
  1 Lessons from Past Policy Experience   4
  2 Overview: Key Principles for Policy Making in an
      Open Economy   27
  3 The New Monetary Policy Framework   44
  4 The Benefits of Maintaining Low and Stable Inflation   58
  5 The Specification of the Inflation Target   71
  6 The UK Model of Central Bank Independence: An Assessment 85
  7 Reforms to Financial Regulation   110
  8 An Overview of the New Fiscal Policy Framework   132
  9 Understanding the Fiscal Rules   155
10 Analysing UK Fiscal Policy   182
11 The Public Finances and the Economic Cycle   203
12 Planning and Controlling Public Spending   230
13 Resource Accounting and Budgeting   239
14 Assessing Long-Term Sustainability   249
15 The Public Sector Balance Sheet   263
16 Debt Management: Theory and Practice   280
17 Reforming the International Financial Architecture   299
18 The EU Macroeconomic Framework   317
19 An Assessment of the New Macroeconomic Policy
      Framework   332

Notes   355
Glossary of Monetary and Fiscal Policy Terms   361
Bibliography   372
Index   386

List of Tables

1.1	Monetary policy targets (1979–97)	13
1.2	Change in interest rates, structural deficit and output gap, 1985–86 to 1989–90	25
1.3	Post-Budget interest rate changes	25
4.1	Recent studies of the impact of inflation on growth	61
4.2	Recent studies of the impact of inflation on the level of GDP	65
4.3	Net welfare benefit of reducing inflation from 2 per cent to zero	66
4.4	Income of the poor and inflation in 19 OECD countries	68
4.5	Inequality and inflation in 19 OECD countries	68
5.1	Years taken for price level to increase given various annual inflation rates	73
5.2	Boskin Report estimates of bias in the US consumer price index	76
5.3	Sacrifice ratios for the UK	78
5.4	International comparison of inflation targets	84
10.1	Using the key fiscal aggregates	193
10.2	Summary of Budget 2001	194
10.A1	Public sector primary balance required to stabilise net public debt at 40 per cent of GDP	202
11.1	Historical growth in trend output	210
11.2	Contributions to annual trend growth	218
11.3	Treasury 'ready reckoners' for estimating cyclically adjusted fiscal indicators	220
11.A1(a)	General government expenditure and the cycle	225
11.A1(b)	Total managed expenditure and the cycle	225
11.A1(c)	Public sector current expenditure and the cycle	226
11.A2	Cyclical social security and the cycle	226
11.A3	Debt interest and the cycle	226
11.A4(a)	Aggregate tax burden and the cycle: Occasional Paper results	227
11.A4(b)	Aggregate tax burden and the cycle: new results	227
11.A5(a)	Tax bases and the cycle: Occasional Paper results	228
11.A5(b)	Tax bases and the cycle: new results	228

11.A6(a)	Receipts and the tax base: Occasional Paper results	229
11.A6(b)	Receipts and the tax base: new results	229
14.1	Long-term economic assumptions	254
15.1	Public sector balance sheet, end 1999	265
15.2	Public sector net worth and the current balance	274
18.1	Key characteristics of the euro-area as at the start of EMU Stage III	321
19.1	Range of inflation expectations, 1997 and 2001	344

List of Figures

1.1	Three decades of high inflation	6
1.2	G7 average inflation rates and volatility (1980–97)	6
1.3	Inflation expectations 10 years ahead	9
1.4	Inflation and unemployment	11
1.5	The output gap and interest rates: late 1980s and early 1990s	15
1.6	UK base rates (1980–97)	16
1.7	G7 countries interest rate volatility (1985–98)	17
1.8	Successive projections of real GDP	20
1.9	Published public sector net cash requirement projections and outturn	21
1.10	Public sector net borrowing	24
4.1	Average inflation and inflation volatility	62
5.1	Real short-term interest rates in the UK, Germany and the US	82
6.1	Central bank independence and inflation in the 1980s: Cukierman index	89
6.2	Central bank independence and inflation between 1961 and 1992: GMT index	90
6.3	Nordhaus model policy game	103
8.1	The new fiscal framework	133
9.1	Public sector net investment	161
9.2	Surplus on current budget	163
9.3	Public sector net wealth	165
9.4	Primary budget surplus required to stabilise the public debt ratio	172
9.5	Public debt in the UK	176
9.6	General government financial liabilities	177
9.7	Net public debt	179
9.8	General government net financial liabilities	180
10.1	Public sector net debt and net worth	195
10.2	Public sector net borrowing – actual and cyclically adjusted	197
10.3	Meeting the golden rule – cautious assumptions	200
11.1	CBI survey of capacity utilisation in manufacturing	209

11.2	Non-oil GDP – actual and trend (quarterly)	211
11.3	Average population growth until 2005 and the current employment rate	213
11.4	Annual and smoothed labour productivity rates	216
11.5	Surplus on current budget – actual and cyclically adjusted	223
11.6	Public sector net borrowing – actual and cyclically adjusted	224
13.1	Linkages between the fiscal framework, the spending control framework and RAB	242
14.1(a)	UK population by age and sex, 2000	251
14.1(b)	UK population by age and sex, 2036	251
14.2	Baseline projections	256
14.3	Effects of higher labour market participation rate	257
15.1	Public sector net worth	267
15.2	Net worth by level of government	268
15.3	Public sector net worth by type of asset	269
15.4	Net worth versus net debt	273
18.1	Organisational structure of the ESCB as of 1 January 2001	323
19.1	Inflation performance and expectations against target	333
19.2	The output gap and interest rates	336
19.3	The output gap and inflation	337
19.4	UK–German 5-year forward rate differential	340
19.5(a)	UK forward nominal interest rates	341
19.5(b)	German forward nominal interest rates	341
19.6	Inflation expectations 10 years ahead	343
19.7	Average of independent forecasts of RPIX inflation one year ahead	345
19.8	Surplus on current budget – actual and cyclically adjusted	350
19.9	Net public debt	352

Foreword

Gordon Brown

My first words from the Treasury, as I became Chancellor and announced the independence of the Bank of England, were to reaffirm for this government our commitment to the goal first set out in 1944 of high and stable levels of growth and employment, and to state that from 1997 onwards the attainment of this goal would require a wholly new monetary and fiscal framework.

This book, written by those whose expertise shaped the detail of the new policy, traces the intellectual journey to the new economic and financial policy framework.

In 1997, as in 1944, a new paradigm was required. Our analysis indicated that a radical reform of the institutions of policy making was essential if we were to deliver growth and employment and that the key to success was fiscal and monetary stability, not as an end in itself, but as a foundation for growth.

Neither the old 'fine tuning' of the past, which appeared to trade off inflation for growth, nor the rigid monetary targets of the 1980s, made sense in newly liberalised capital markets. We recognised too that the discretion necessary for effective economic policy could only be possible within an institutional framework that commanded market credibility and public trust. That credibility depends upon a long-term approach to policy making, openness, transparency and clear and accountable divisions of responsibility: the fundamental principles of the new macro-economic framework.

So the new monetary and fiscal framework Britain needed had to be based on clear policy rules, well established procedures, and an openness and transparency not seen in the past. Hence the independence of the Bank of England, the new fiscal rules, the Open Letter system, the symmetrical inflation target and our new Code for Fiscal Stability: institutional changes that broke new ground but were firmly rooted in British values and could lay claim to a clear democratic legitimacy.

The reforms are built on three pillars: first, a monetary policy framework with an independent Monetary Policy Committee responsible for setting interest rates to meet the Government's inflation target; second, a fiscal policy framework which is delivering sound public finances through a Code for Fiscal Stability, firm fiscal rules and better planned public spending which focuses on the quality of public service provision; and third, new institutions such as the Financial Services Authority to ensure financial stability through transparency, responsibility and clear lines of accountability.

It is the conclusion of this book that the new macroeconomic framework is already producing real benefits. At the time of writing unemployment had fallen to levels not seen for over two decades, while inflation is at its lowest level since the 1960s. A sustained track record of stability is the best foundation upon which the Government can deliver its wider goals of high levels of growth and employment, and so deliver rising living standards and better public services. So the true test of the macroeconomic framework will come not just in attaining long-term stability but also in higher living standards and finding the resources to deliver world-class public services to an educated and employed population.

The book makes clear that the prosperity brought about by the new macroeconomic framework is not just for Britain.

Just as in the mid 1940s a new British economic policy was matched by the high ideals that brought the creation of the World Bank and the IMF, so too at the turn of the century the same high ideals are driving change from debt relief to major reforms in the international financial architecture.

We must, at an international level, build a new consensus, with a new and broader emphasis on the conditions for high and stable levels of growth and employment, ensuring countries have in place the macroeconomic, financial, structural and social policies for long-term success in the global economy.

For this reason we have been active in international institutions such as the G8, the IMF and World Bank. Here we have been sharing our experiences and encouraging the development of transparent macroeconomic frameworks to avoid the crises of the past and to reduce poverty and injustice throughout the world. Our proposals include new codes and standards for monetary policy and fiscal policy, corporate behaviour and social policy as the building blocks of the international economic system; far more effective mechanisms for crisis prevention and crisis resolution; a far greater attention to financial stability; and action to meet the 2015 development targets – that all children have primary education, that infant mortality is reduced by two-thirds and that poverty is halved. Here again the attainment of stability is the precondition of economic prosperity but stability has a purpose: the opportunity of prosperity for all.

And while much remains to be done before a new international financial architecture is in place, I believe we are making progress. Britain will continue to contribute to a prosperous world and will actively participate in institutions addressing poverty and injustice. History has taught us that peace, prosperity and justice are indivisible and intertwined. We learned at tremendous cost in the twentieth century how poverty and injustice drove the world to cycles of war and hatred. Our goal, in the twenty-first century, to build prosperity and a more inclusive world, is proof that we are learning from the past and building for the future.

Chancellor of the Exchequer

Introduction

This book provides a comprehensive guide to the macroeconomic and certain key financial reforms implemented following the change of administration in May 1997. It is intended for all those who wish to understand the economic foundations of these policies and how they have been implemented in practice. It should be useful for those working in private sector financial institutions and public sector bodies, both here and abroad, who wish to understand UK monetary, fiscal and certain aspects of financial policy. At various points, UK policy is contrasted with macroeconomic policies operated elsewhere, especially in the European Union.

We should add that there are of course many aspects of Government economic policy, particularly in terms of structural reform, that are not covered in this book. Interested readers should consult the Treasury web page (www.hm-treasury.gov.uk) for many relevant papers.

The book will also be of interest to economics students, undergraduates or postgraduates. It is most suitable for second- or third-year students and should be read in conjunction with a more traditional macroeconomics textbook such as Romer (2001) or Miles and Scott (2002). This book differs from traditional textbooks in that all the policies described here are actually being implemented. Hence there is much more detail on *how* to achieve certain objectives which those interested only in the theory might choose to skip.

Chapter 1 explains why the new government decided in 1997 to embark on a radical overhaul of monetary and fiscal policy. It explains its diagnosis of the perceived policy mistakes of earlier periods. Chapter 2 describes the underlying principles which guided the choice of solutions. Chapters 3–6 then explain in detail the new monetary policy framework built around an independent Monetary Policy Committee at the Bank of England with responsibility for setting interest rates to hit a symmetrical inflation target.

At the same time, in order to improve the UK's system of financial regulation and help the Bank concentrate on monetary policy, a new single regulator, the Financial Services Authority, was set up. This is described in Chapter 7 which also covers other aspects of Government policy towards financial regulation, including the benchmarking of financial services and stakeholder pensions.

Chapters 8–16 describe various aspects of fiscal policy. It is an unfortunate consequence of the fact that monetary policy decisions are usually made monthly whereas budgets or 'green' budgets come only once or twice a year that monetary policy is analysed much more than fiscal policy. It is also the belief of the editors that fiscal policy is much more complicated as there are multiple objectives and multiple instruments. This explains why this part of the book is much longer. It covers not just judgements about how far fiscal policy should stimulate the economy at any point in the cycle but other crucial aspects that are often ignored in the textbooks such as how to plan and control public spending, how to determine whether the public sector is financially viable over the longer term and how best to borrow to finance any gap between revenue and spending.

Chapter 17 explains how the government has applied the same principles, such as openness and transparency, to the reform of international financial 'architecture'. We should explain that the term 'architecture' refers to the relationship between the various international financial institutions, their methods of operation and their guiding principles. It seems that in almost every area of life 'experts' develop special terms or give ordinary words special meanings in order to communicate with other experts. It is unfortunately necessary to understand this jargon which is why we have included a lengthy glossary at the end of the book.

Chapter 18 looks at the macroeconomic framework, that is the monetary and fiscal policies and their coordination, that governs the European Union, with particular emphasis on the euro area. It explains how the European Central Bank conducts monetary policy, and how the Stability and Growth Pact affects fiscal policy.

Finally, Chapter 19 gives an assessment of how the new macroeconomic policy framework is operating. No doubt in the years to come as the UK economy experiences various shocks it will be possible to assess in more detail the strengths and weaknesses of the new system. Our hope is that this book will provide the authoritative description of why the Government undertook this set of radical policy changes so others can assess for themselves the degree of success that has been achieved.

It is expected that many readers will use this book as a work of reference. Such readers will want to dip into various chapters without necessarily reading all the preceding ones. For this reason, we have tried to make the chapters as self-contained as possible. This means that there may be a degree of overlap in the material covered. For example, having read Chapters 1 and 2, it should be possible to skip parts of Chapters 3–6.

The editors would like to thank all Treasury officials past and present, and too numerous to mention by name, who have worked on developing and implementing these policies over the last four years. Many of the same officials have been responsible for various chapters of this book. But we would like to register our particular thanks to Ashok Bhundia, Roland Clarke, Darren Gibbs and Andrew Kilpatrick for their assistance in bringing all this work together. We would also like to express our thanks to officials of the FSA and the Bank of England for comments on earlier drafts of this book. As usual we should add that the opinions expressed in the book are those of HM Treasury, not necessarily of the Bank or the FSA.

1
Lessons from Past Policy Experience

This chapter examines some of the issues and problems in the UK's past monetary and fiscal policy which motivated the reforms discussed in the remainder of this book.

Introduction

This chapter draws out some of the issues in the design and conduct of monetary and fiscal policy which were central to the proposals to reform the macroeconomic framework in 1997. While it is not possible to provide here a detailed history of monetary and fiscal policy over the last 30 years, the analysis highlights some of the key lessons from past policy experience.

A broad consensus now exists that price stability is an essential precondition for achieving the Government's central economic objective of high and stable levels of growth and employment. It is clear that tolerating higher rates of inflation does not lead to higher employment or output over the long term.

A similar consensus has emerged in support of sound public finances as the principal medium-term objective of fiscal policy. This consensus grew out of the experience of the 1970s and 1980s which saw a relaxation of fiscal discipline, with consequent sharp increases in public sector indebtedness across many industrial economies.

The UK's monetary policy experience prior to the Government's reforms

The need for a new monetary policy framework

In order to understand why it was necessary to overhaul the way in which monetary policy was conducted, it is instructive to examine the UK's past inflation record. As Figure 1.1 shows, for most of the 30 years prior to the introduction of the new framework, this record was very poor. During the 1970s, annual inflation averaged 13 per cent, peaking at almost 27 per cent in August 1975. During the 1980s, annual inflation averaged 7 per cent (compared with 3 per cent in Germany and 5 per cent in the US), while in the early 1990s inflation peaked again at a high level of over 9 per cent.

Inflation was not only high in the past, but was also highly volatile. As Figure 1.2 shows, between 1980 and 1997, the UK had the second highest average inflation rate among the G7 countries, with only France and Italy having greater variability in inflation. Figure 1.2 also illustrates a positive relationship between the level of inflation and its variability. Volatile inflation increases uncertainty and thus increases the costs of unanticipated inflation.

In the post-war period there have been significant changes in the prevailing monetary regimes (see Box 1.1). These arrangements reflected a process of learning and adaptation to the problems generated by previous regimes and changing institutional and external environments.

Following the departure of sterling from the Exchange Rate Mechanism in September 1992, there was a noticeable downward shift in the average level of inflation. It coincided with reconstructed monetary arrangements introduced in October 1992 in which inflation was targeted directly for the first time. Details of the new arrangements were outlined in a letter by the then Chancellor (Norman Lamont) to the Treasury Select Committee. The inflation target was not, however, precise in either its value or horizon. The letter set an 'objective of keeping underlying inflation within the range 1–4 per cent ... [B]y the end of the parliament we need to be in the lower half of that range' (Lamont 1992).

While rejecting a specific exchange rate target it was also emphasised that interest rates would not be set by purely domestic criteria. In addition a target range of 0–4 per cent was retained for the narrow monetary aggregate M0 and a 'monitoring range' for the broad monetary aggregate M4.

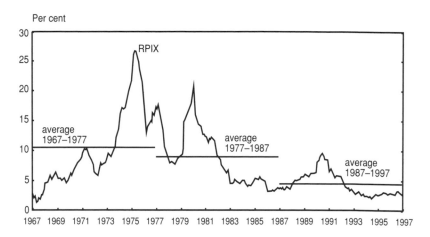

Figure 1.1   Three decades of high inflation

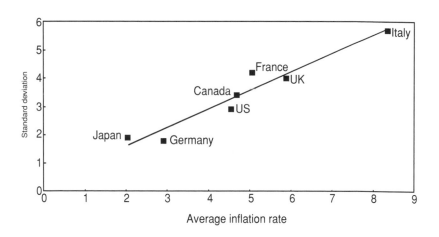

Source: OECD.

Figure 1.2   G7 average inflation rates and volatility (1980–97)

Box 1.1   Post-war monetary policy regimes prior to 1997

In the post-war period it is possible to identify five broad monetary policy regimes, each with different institutional constraints and external environments, prior to the introduction of the new monetary framework in 1997. The regimes are as follows:

Fixed Exchange Rates (Bretton Woods) 1948–71. Direct controls on domestic credit, strong foreign exchange controls on capital account, relatively passive monetary policy aiming to raise growth and employment. Current account and exchange rate and acted as a discipline on policy. Results: Stop-Go policy, balance of payments crises, devaluation and gradually increasing inflation and unemployment.

Floating exchange rate, no monetary anchor 1971–76. Credit controls and exchange controls, monetary policy targets growth and employment. Results: rapidly accelerating inflation, volatile growth rates.

Monetary targets: 1976–87. From 1979 exchange and credit controls liberalised. Monetary policy directed at controlling different monetary aggregates in order to reduce inflation. Results: behaviour of monetary aggregates is unpredictable; complications due to financial liberalisation. Inflation reduced at expense of output volatility and unemployment.

Exchange rate targeting: 1987–92. No exchange and capital controls. Increasingly globalised markets. Monetary policy constrained by exchange rate target. Results: inappropriate monetary policy for domestic conditions, overvalued exchange rate, recession and ejection from Exchange Rate Mechanism (ERM) due to capital movements and lack of credibility of policy.

Inflation targeting (post-ERM): 1992–97. Open economy, floating exchange rate. Monetary policy directed mainly at inflation, but still managed by the Chancellor. Some transparency introduced. Results: inflation falls, but framework is not fully credible as expectations of inflation remain above official targets.

The post-ERM framework implicitly recognised the past problems of targeting intermediate monetary aggregates or the exchange rate, but could not reject these completely. A role for transparency was included and this was gradually expanded with the introduction of the Bank of England's Inflation Report in 1993 and regular meetings between the Chancellor and the Governor of the Bank of England with minutes published from 1995.

One factor behind the comparatively low inflation that was recorded in the period between 1992 and early 1997 was the presence of a negative output gap (GDP below potential). In particular, the recession of 1991–92 created a large degree of spare capacity in the economy, reducing the inflation rate sharply. This situation persisted for several years, preventing any build-up in inflationary pressures. As was pointed out by the Bank of England's Deputy Governor, Mervyn King,

> from 1992 to 1996, the ability to grow at above-trend rates without an increase in inflationary pressure was made possible by using up the margin of spare capacity created by the deep recession of the early 1990s. (King 1999a)

Despite the clarification of the RPIX inflation in 1995 to 2½ per cent or less for the next parliament, inflation expectations remained close to 4 per cent. As Figure 1.3 shows, there was a large 'credibility gap' between what policy makers were aiming for and what markets expected to happen.

The failure of inflation expectations to fall during this period suggests a lack of confidence in the arrangements to deliver the target in the long term. This contrasts with the marked fall in inflation expectations following the introduction of the new monetary framework in 1997, as discussed in greater detail in Chapter 19.

Inflation did fall after the introduction of a target in 1992, but for 48 out of the 52 months prior to the change of the monetary framework in May 1997, it remained above 2½ per cent. Of more immediate concern in early 1997 was that there were strong signs that inflation was poised to pick up again. The UK economy was expanding rapidly to a point where capacity pressures had become evident. Consumer spending was growing at an unsustainable rate and inflation was set to rise above target. For example, in early 1997, independent forecasters, on average, were expecting inflation to increase to almost 3½ per cent the following year, reflecting a lack of confidence in the ability of the then existing framework to maintain price stability. Further action was needed.

A key problem that the post-ERM arrangements had not addressed was the political economy of interest rate decisions made by any Chancellor who could not avoid the suspicion that decisions were made or deferred due to short-term political considerations. This problem was latent until the economy recovered and began to require significant interest rate rises, *prior* to an acceleration of inflation. It was likely that this was one of the reasons that expectations of future inflation failed to fall. Thus

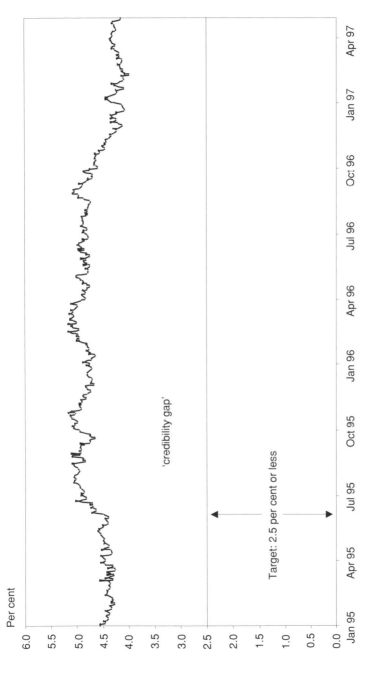

Figure 1.3 Inflation expectations 10 years ahead

despite the advances of the 1992–97 arrangements, they did not carry full credibility. The objectives remained unclear, roles and responsibilities were still poorly defined, and the influence of short-term political factors had not been resolved.

Lessons from past policy experience

Although there are many reasons for the UK's poor inflation record in recent decades, one key factor was poor institutional arrangements. Monetary policy, if set correctly, should be a stabilising force for the economy. However, serious mistakes were made, which often meant that inflation was higher and more volatile than it would otherwise have been. This, in turn, created substantial economic instability that harmed the long-term performance of the UK economy. Many of these policy mistakes were made because the aims and procedures of monetary policy were not properly defined. The purpose of this discussion is not to criticise previous policy decisions (which is always easy with the benefit of hindsight); rather, the aim is to identify several lessons from this experience.

Inappropriate objectives

It is now widely accepted that price stability is an essential precondition for achieving high and stable levels of growth and employment. Price stability, therefore, is the best contribution monetary policy can make towards meeting this goal. However, for part of the last 30 years, monetary policy was not directed at maintaining price stability. Indeed, for a long time it was thought that tolerating higher inflation actually enhanced rather than damaged long-term growth and employment.

The UK's poor inflation record can be traced initially to a fundamental misunderstanding about the relationship between inflation and unemployment. Prior to 1976, policy makers attempted to use monetary policy to exploit an apparent relationship between these variables, hoping that unemployment could be lowered by stimulating demand and trading off an increase in inflation. As Figure 1.4 shows, attempts to hold unemployment down during this period not only failed in the long term, but were also associated with accelerating inflation.

Although in the short term, such a trade-off often was possible, it could only work because the private sector did not anticipate the higher future inflation. Once people revised their expectations of inflation, the trade-off would disappear, with unemployment rising again. This had the long-term effect of ratcheting up the levels of both inflation and unemployment.

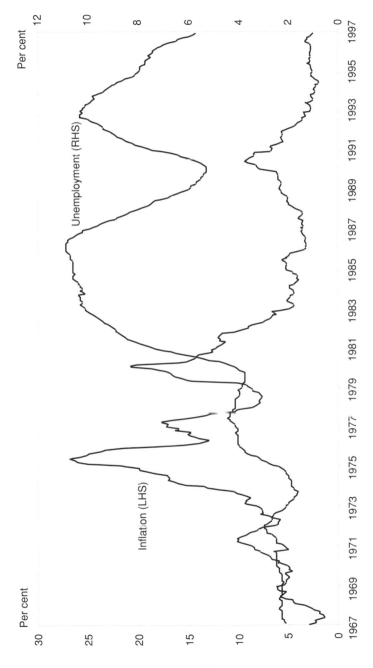

Figure 1.4 Inflation and unemployment

11

Another period in which monetary policy was directed at an inappropriate objective was from 1987 to 1992, when policy makers attempted to use monetary policy to target the exchange rate. This approach was often at the expense of price and output stability. For example interest rates were prevented from being reduced quickly enough in 1991 and 1992 as a consequence of the UK's ERM membership. It was only following sterling's exit from the ERM in September 1992 that monetary policy was first explicitly used to target inflation directly.

Poorly specified objectives

The goal of monetary policy should be price stability. However, this is not enough. It is also important to ensure that this goal is specified properly. For example, in the 1980s policy makers believed that low inflation could be achieved by rigidly targeting various monetary aggregates. While the attempt to control inflation was laudable, money supply targets reflected a theory of how monetary policy operated which neglected the impact of institutional changes on the relationship between prices and money supply. Factors such as the development of global capital markets, financial deregulation and changing technology led to significant and unanticipated changes in the velocity of circulation of money. As a result, there was no clear and stable relationship between money demand and inflation over this period, making it impossible to rely on fixed monetary rules to deliver price stability.

This experience highlights a key shortcoming of targeting intermediate variables, rather than the inflation rate. Intermediate targets can lead policy makers to focus too much on the variable they are targeting at the expense of the wide variety of other important indicators of inflationary pressures. On a number of occasions, it became clear to policy makers that the intermediate targets they had set were not delivering the results expected. However, rather than abandoning this approach, policy makers instead tried to modify it by setting different target ranges or by targeting different indicators, including the exchange rate. As Table 1.1 shows, this happened on an almost annual basis during the 1980s and early 1990s.

These frequent changes created uncertainty, damaged the credibility of policy makers and led to policy mistakes. These problems were a direct result of not specifying the goal of monetary policy precisely. If the goal of policy makers is price stability, it is best to specify that goal directly in terms of an inflation target. This allows policy makers to take into account all factors that affect inflation and also enables the objective of monetary policy to be expressed in terms that are stable and well understood.

Table 1.1 Monetary policy targets (1980–97)

Target year[1]	*M3*[8]	*(Annual % change unless stated otherwise)* *M4*[8]	*M0*[8]	*£ exchange*	*RPIX*
1980–81	7–11	–	–	–	–
1981–82	6–10	–	–	–	–
1982–83[2]	8–12	–	–	–	–
1983–84[2]	7–11	–	–	–	–
1984–85	6–10	–	4–8	–	–
1985–86	5–9	–	3–7	–	–
1986–87	11–15	–	2–6	–	–
1987–88[3]	–	–	2–6	–	–
1988–89	–	–	1–5	–	–
1989–90	–	–	1–5	–	–
1990–91	–	–	1–5	DM2.95[4]	–
1991–92[4]	–	–	0–4	DM2.95	–
1992–93[5]	–	4–8[6]	0–4	DM2.95[5]	–
1993–94	–	3–9	0–4	–	1–4[5]
1994–95	–	3–9	0–4	–	1–4
1995–96[7]	–	3–9	0–4	–	1–4
1996–97	–	3–9	0–4	–	2½ or less
1997–98	–	3–9	0–4	–	2½ or less

Notes:
[1] As set in the Medium-Term Financial Strategy (MTFS).
[2] Targets were also set for PSL2 and M1 in the 1982 and 1983 MTFS.
[3] 1987–88 MTFS said: 'Monetary conditions are assessed in the light of movements in narrow and broad money, and the behaviour of other financial indicators, in particular the exchange rate.' There was no formal target for broad money. Similar references are to be found in the MTFS in 1988–89, 1989–90 and 1990–91.
[4] The UK joined the Exchange Rate Mechanism (ERM) of the European Monetary System in October 1990. The 1991–92 MTFS said, 'Interest rate decisions must now be set consistently with keeping sterling within its announced bands.'
[5] The UK left the ERM in September 1992. The new framework was based on an inflation target for RPIX of 1 to 4 per cent, with inflation in the lower part of the range by the end of the Parliament. Medium-term monitoring ranges for M4 and M0 were also announced.
[6] Announced in the Autumn Statement in 1992 after the UK left the ERM.
[7] In June 1995 the 1 to 4 range for RPIX was confirmed by the Chancellor and a new target of 2½ per cent or less was announced for beyond the end of this Parliament.
[8] M0, M3 and M4 are three different definitions of monetary supply.

Insufficiently forward-looking

A lack of clear, stable objectives was also one of the main reasons why the authorities were sometimes slow to react to changing circumstances. Without a well-defined objective, policy makers find it more difficult to be proactive. Inflationary pressures were thus often allowed to build unnecessarily before corrective action was taken. In turn, this meant that interest rates were eventually higher and more volatile than they otherwise would have been.

In the late 1980s, for example, the economy was allowed to grow at a rate well above its sustainable level, pushing up inflation past 9 per cent. This eventually forced the authorities to raise interest rates to extremely high levels, peaking at 15 per cent, after which a severe recession followed. Had monetary policy been tightened earlier, rates may not have needed to have been raised so high, and the recession might have been less severe or may have been avoided altogether.

Figure 1.5 illustrates what happened over this period, showing clearly how interest rates consistently lagged the output gap profile.

- From January 1986 to May 1988, interest rates were reduced by 5 percentage points, from 12½ per cent to 7½ per cent, yet the estimated output gap moved from just below trend, –½ per cent, to far above trend, +3½ per cent.
- A belated realisation in June 1988 that the economy was overheating led to four base rate increases in that month alone – a total of 2 percentage points – and by the end of the year rates had risen a further 3½ percentage points to 13 per cent. Rates finally peaked at 15 per cent in October 1989 and remained at that level for a year.
- Policy was also changed too late on the downswing. Interest rates were still at 14 per cent at the beginning of 1991, even though the output gap had turned negative; and interest rate reductions were delayed throughout 1991 and the first half of 1992, partly as a result of ERM membership.

A failure to act promptly during this period meant that interest rates eventually had to rise by more than they would otherwise have done. As Figures 1.6 and 1.7 show, rates frequently rose to very high levels during the 1980s and early 1990s, with the UK's interest rate volatility the highest among G7 countries.

Even the post-ERM monetary framework suffered from this problem, since there was no clear mechanism to ensure that a Chancellor would anticipate inflation and raise interest rates before inflation accelerated.

Roles and responsibilities were not clear and consistent

In monetary policy regimes prior to 1997, the Government was responsible both for designing the monetary policy framework and for taking policy decisions to meet the stated target. In addition to advising on and implementing the Government's monetary policy decisions, the Bank of England was also responsible for managing the Government's debt, as well as the regulation and supervision of the financial sector.

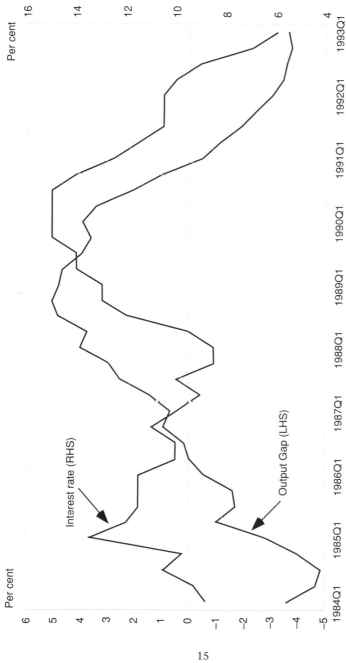

Per cent

16
14
12
10
8
6
4

1993Q1
1992Q1
1991Q1
1990Q1
1989Q1
1988Q1
1987Q1
1986Q1
1985Q1
1984Q1

Interest rate (RHS)

Output Gap (LHS)

Per cent

6
5
4
3
2
1
0
-1
-2
-3
-4
-5

Source: ONS and HM Treasury.

Figure 1.5   The output gap and interest rates: late 1980s and early 1990s

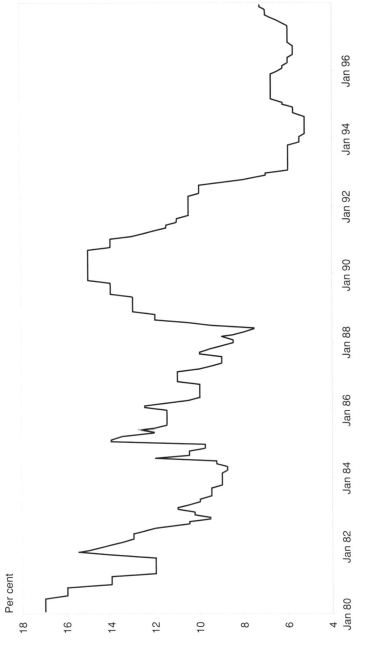

Figure 1.6 UK base rates (1980–97)

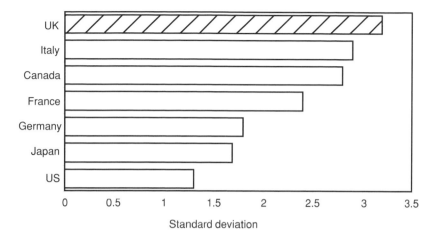

Figure 1.7   G7 countries interest rate volatility (1985–98)

The specific nature of the Government's responsibilities remained less than clear due to the ambiguous specification of its objectives. Moreover, by giving the Bank multiple responsibilities, it was not always obvious which activity was of paramount importance to the Bank.

Decisions made by politicians, not experts

For most of the period until the 1990s, monetary policy had generally been conducted on an ad hoc basis. Although a range of informal conventions were in place, no specific guidelines were set out to govern how decisions should be made. There was not even a precise and regular timetable for monetary policy decisions to be made and announced. There was often little consistency in monetary policy over time, and outsiders were unable to examine the process by which decisions were made.

This problem was compounded by the fact that monetary policy decisions were made in the context of a political process where short-term pressures were often paramount.[1] Although the politicians had access to the advice of independent experts, they would not always follow that advice, making monetary policy even more difficult to predict.

The mere fact that monetary policy decisions were made by politicians created the suspicion that they could be based on short-term political considerations, rather than the economy's long-term interests. As has been pointed out by Mervyn King, Deputy Governor of the Bank of England:

[L]ong-term interest rates contained a risk premium to reflect the possibility that the timing and magnitude of interest changes might reflect political considerations. (King 1999a)

A lack of transparency and accountability harmed credibility

Monetary policy also lacked transparency. Policy makers operated behind closed doors, and decisions were often made with little or no explanation.

This lack of transparency meant it was not easy to hold policy makers accountable for their performance. But more importantly, it also meant that policy makers were unable to build credibility with markets and with the general public. Because people did not have a clear idea of what policy makers were trying to achieve, and how they were operating, they did not have confidence that policy makers would be able to deliver long-term price stability.

From 1992 successive Chancellors did make attempts to introduce more transparency through such mechanisms as the publication of new arrangements for monetary policy in a letter from the Chancellor to the Treasury Select Committee (Lamont 1992), monthly monetary reports, inflation reports, regular meetings between the Chancellor and the Governor of the Bank of England, and later the publication of minutes of these meetings. However this greater transparency was not combined with clear accountability, a well defined target of inflation and separation of responsibilities, and thus failed to lower inflation expectations prior to 1997.

The UK's fiscal policy experience prior to the Government's reforms

The problems of macroeconomic instability in the last 30 years cannot be attributed to the monetary framework alone. The numerous changes in monetary arrangements were paralleled by changing fiscal arrangements as successive governments sought to lower taxation and expenditure as a proportion of GDP, while often being overoptimistic about future trends. This was particularly true with respect to assessments of the impact of the economic cycle on the fiscal position.

Fiscal policy contributed to instability

The consequences of failing adequately to take account of the impact of the economic cycle when setting policy can be seen readily by reviewing the UK's experience in the late 1980s and early 1990s. (For more details, see HM Treasury 1997b.)

In the early 1980s, growth turned out to be higher than assumed as the economy rebounded from recession and inflation fell. Growth continued to exceed expectations and the assumed trend or average growth rate published in the *Financial Statement and Budget Report* (FSBR) was raised progressively, from 2¼ per cent in 1984 to 3 per cent by the March 1988 Budget. Fiscal and monetary policies were thus loosened, based on the conclusion that the higher rate of growth could be sustained.

With the benefit of hindsight, however, it is clear that this policy action was inappropriate – the economy had in fact moved significantly above trend and was on an unsustainable path. The loosening of macroeconomic policy exacerbated this imbalance. The output gap continued to widen, and peaked at nearly 5 per cent above trend in 1988 89.[2]

A sharp tightening in monetary policy was required to combat the associated strong rise in inflationary pressures. However, when the necessary tightening in monetary policy did occur, it was too severe and lasted too long, as noted above. As Figure 1.8 shows, the consequences of this policy error were not realised until it was too late, and the economy slid into recession.

The errors in forecasting the economy were directly translated into errors in forecasting the health of the public finances. Figure 1.9 shows the Budget projections and actual outturns for the preferred fiscal indicator of the time – the public sector borrowing requirement (PSBR) (now known as the public sector net cash requirement (PSNCR)). As can be seen, the Government underestimated the deterioration that would take place as the economy returned to trend. This happened because the structural position of the public finances was much poorer than believed.

The deterioration in the fiscal position over this period contributed to higher net Government debt, which rose from 31 per cent of GDP in 1988–89 to 44 per cent of GDP in 1996–97.

Had a more cautious approach to trend growth been adopted in the above trend phase of the cycle, fiscal and monetary policies might not have been relaxed. Consequently, the rise in economic activity would have been less intense, permitting a less painful adjustment as the economy returned to trend.

Lessons from past experience

There are a number of lessons to be learnt from the fiscal policy experience of the last cycle. The following stand out.

Figure 1.8 Successive projections of real GDP

20

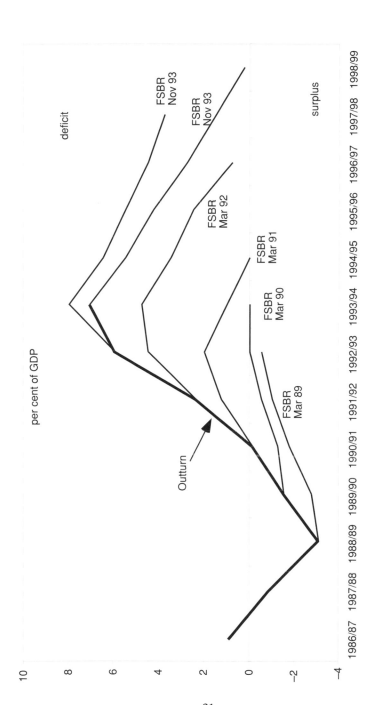

Figure 1.9 Published public sector net cash requirement projections and outturn

Adjust for the cycle and build in a margin for uncertainty

At the end of the 1980s the authorities underestimated the role of cyclical expansion in generating the fiscal surpluses. The UK was only able to repay part of its public debt because output was significantly above its trend level. With hindsight, had policy been set on the basis of cautious estimates of the cyclically adjusted position there was no case for relaxing policy.

However, it needs to be recognised that forming accurate estimates of the cyclically adjusted position is difficult. Cyclical adjustment requires estimates of the current level of output and of the trend level of output, both of which are uncertain. Overoptimism about the trend level of output at the end of the 1980s was a critical factor for the deterioration of the public finances over the last cycle. In the early stages of recovery it is possible to observe above trend growth without an immediate increase in inflation. Thus it can be tempting to conclude that the underlying growth which the economy can sustain without increasing inflation is higher than is actually the case. This points to taking a cautious view of the underlying trend rate of growth.

Moreover, the Treasury's estimates of the cyclicality of the public finances are based on a stylised average cycle, so can give only a broad indication of the underlying fiscal position rather than a precise estimate. So although forecasts of the cyclically adjusted deficits are key indicators for assessing the appropriate fiscal stance, they are themselves bound to be subject to some margins of error over and above the uncertainty about the output gap.

Finally, the two components of the fiscal balance – revenues and expenditures – are in themselves difficult to forecast with accuracy. For example, outturns for value added tax (VAT) receipts were consistently below the forecasts published in successive FSBRs since 1989–90. Therefore, policy should recognise the significant uncertainty inherent in the forecasting of the public finances.

The experience of fiscal policy over the last economic cycle demonstrates that it is easier to reduce revenue and increase expenditure than to do the reverse. So when things go wrong with the public finances it is difficult to put them right, particularly since it can take a long time even to recognise the problem. Moreover, when public borrowing turns out higher than expected, debt interest costs also rise, intensifying the problem.

All of this underlines the value of a deliberately cautious approach. If, in the event, the caution turns out to have been unnecessary – because events turned out as expected, or even better than expected – it is not difficult to deal with the resulting bonus. Therefore a lesson from past mistakes is that policy makers should err on the side of caution.

Set stable fiscal rules and explain clearly fiscal policy

Over the last full economic cycle, the stated fiscal policy objectives changed on a number of occasions. However, with a lack of constancy of stated objectives, policy is never obliged to compensate for past slippages since the objective can be changed according to circumstances. Further, objectives tended to be set over 'the medium term', an imprecise time horizon. Estimates of trend output and cyclically adjusted fiscal indicators were not published.

Objective evaluation of policy was thus made more difficult. Clear fiscal rules or objectives, which remain stable over the economic cycle, allow objective ex post evaluation, particularly when relevant information is published to explain fiscal policy decisions. With this approach, a commitment to meeting stated fiscal objectives can be strengthened. A more credible and predictable fiscal policy can contribute to producing a stable macroeconomic environment.

The current Government has made clear that it is determined not to repeat these mistakes of the past. Of course, it is not possible to remove all sources of uncertainty. But by taking a prudent approach, including using cautious assumptions and publishing cyclically adjusted estimates of the key fiscal indicators, the risk of mistakes can be minimised. Figure 1.10 shows public sector net borrowing, both in actual and cyclically adjusted terms.

Coordination of monetary and fiscal policy

For most of the last 30 years, the operation of both monetary and fiscal policy was directed by one person. On the advice of HM Treasury and the Bank of England, the Chancellor of the Exchequer had responsibility for both the public finances and the setting of interest rates.

Although it could be expected that such an arrangement would facilitate a high degree of coordination between both arms of policy, in practice this was often not the case. A lack of clear goals, and a failure to act in a forward-looking manner, often meant that monetary and fiscal policy were not working in the same direction.

The experience of the late 1980s again provides a good illustration of this point. During this period, fiscal policy was loosened just as the economy was overheating. Fiscal policy was relaxed, for example, with

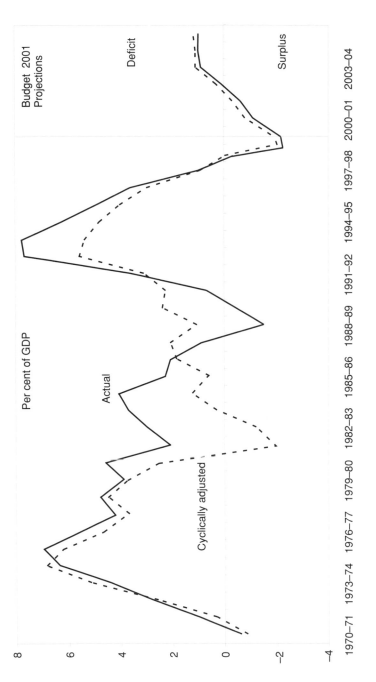

Figure 1.10 Public sector net borrowing

Table 1.2   Change in interest rates, structural deficit and output gap, 1985–86 to 1989–90

Change in:		1985/86–1987/88	1987/88–1989/90
Output gap[2]		4	1¼
Interest rates		–2¾	5¼
Structural deficit[3]		1½	¼
	1985–86	1987–88	1989–90[1]
Memo item:			
Output gap level[2]	–1½	2½	3¾

Notes:
[1]   One year after peak of output gap.
[2]   As percentage of potential GDP.
[3]   Cyclically adjusted public sector net borrowing as percentage of GDP.

Table 1.3   Post-Budget interest rate changes (percentage points)

Budget date	Interest rate movements	
	Rate change	Decision
12 Jun 1979	15 Jun	up 2 pps
26 Mar 1980		
10 Mar 1981	11 Mar	down 2 pps
9 Mar 1982	12 Mar	down ½ pp
15 Mar 1983	15 Mar	down ½ pp
13 Mar 1984	7 Mar	down ¼ pp
	15 Mar	down ¼ pp
19 Mar 1985	20 Mar	down ½ pp
	29 Mar	down ½ pp
18 Mar 1986	19 Mar	down 1 pp
17 Mar 1987	10 Mar	down ½ pp
	19 Mar	down ½ pp
15 Mar 1988	17 Mar	down ½ pp
14 Mar 1989		
20 Mar 1990		
19 Mar 1991	22 Mar	down ½ pp
10 Mar 1992		
16 Mar 1993		
30 Nov 1993	23 Nov	down ½ pp
29 Nov 1994	7 Dec	up ½ pp
28 Nov 1995	13 Dec	down ¼ pp
26 Nov 1996		

tax cuts of £6 billion in the March 1988 Budget and £3.5 billion in the March 1989 Budget. The overall structural deficit – defined as cyclically adjusted public sector net borrowing (PSNB) – moved from an estimated small deficit of 1 per cent of GDP in 1985–86 to a deficit of 2½ per cent of GDP in 1989–90. When monetary policy was finally tightened, interest rates had to be increased by more than would otherwise have been necessary to offset the cumulative loosening of fiscal policy. Table 1.2 provides further details.

Another feature of monetary and fiscal policy during the 1980s was that budgets were frequently followed within days by interest rate cuts. As Table 1.3 shows, this happened on eight out of ten occasions. On three of these occasions, the interest rate cuts were followed by rises within six months.

Conclusion

This chapter has demonstrated that monetary and fiscal policy for a long time failed to make an adequate contribution to high and stable levels of growth and employment. Indeed, monetary and fiscal policy were sometimes a source of instability. The post-1992 monetary framework addressed some but not all of the past problems by introducing inflation targeting and greater transparency. As a result it was only partially successful and did not provide a durable solution. The substantial reforms that have been put in place recently to strengthen the macro-economic policy framework built on these foundations are discussed in the remainder of this book.

2
Overview: Key Principles for Policy Making in an Open Economy

This chapter, which draws heavily from a lecture given by Ed Balls, Chief Economic Adviser to the Treasury, to the Scottish Economic Society in October 1997, provides an overview of the key principles underpinning the Government's approach to policy making in an open economy.

Introduction

There are three pillars to the Government's approach to economic policy· delivering macroeconomic stability, tackling the supply-side barriers to growth and delivering employment and economic opportunities to all. This chapter elaborates on the Government's economic goals and then sets out four principles for macroeconomic policy making which flow from changes in the world economy and the world of economic ideas over the past 20 or 30 years. These are:

- the principle of stability through constrained discretion
- the principle of credibility through sound, long-term policies
- the principle of credibility through maximum transparency
- the principle of credibility through pre-commitment.

These principles underpin the reforms discussed throughout the remainder of this book.

The Government's economic approach – stability, growth, opportunity

The institutional changes which have been introduced over the last few years at the Treasury and the Bank of England add up to what is now probably one of the most open and accountable systems of economic policy making in the world. Changes in both the world economy and our economic understanding of it over the past 20 years mean that policy makers must adjust to new ways of making decisions. Gone are the days of fixed policy rules announced in public and of private deliberations behind closed finance ministry doors, with little or no justification or explanation about policy decisions or mistakes.

Instead, new principles must guide decision making and institutional design. This chapter explains how these principles underpin the Government's macroeconomic policy reforms – in monetary and fiscal policy. In a world of global capital markets in which policy making by fixed rules has been discredited in theory and practice, governments must take a different route to ensuring macroeconomic credibility.

Credibility in modern open economies requires three ingredients:

- a reputation for following sound long-term policies
- maximum openness and transparency
- and new institutional arrangements which guarantee a long-term view.

These principles, which stress the importance of open macroeconomic policy making, apply to any small or medium-sized open economy. Indeed, this is why the UK was at the forefront in proposing that the International Monetary Fund (IMF) draw up codes of good practice on openness and transparency covering several aspects of economic and social policy – a proposal which was supported by other finance ministers (Chancellor of the Exchequer 1997d). Chapter 17 discusses these initiatives further.

Macroeconomic stability – low and stable inflation and sound public finances – is only a means to an end. The aim of the Government's economic thinking, as set out in the Chancellor's 6 May 1997 letter to the Governor of the Bank of England (Chancellor of the Exchequer 1997a) was not simply to ensure low and stable inflation and sound public finances but to deliver high and stable levels of growth and employment by ensuring economic and employment opportunities for all. Growth, jobs and fairness are the tests against which the Government will be judged.

Delivering on these objectives depends not simply on one policy pillar, but three – delivering macroeconomic stability, tackling the supply-side barriers to growth and delivering employment and economic opportunities to all. The Chancellor's first Mansion House and Budget speeches made clear that stability – low inflation and sound public finances – is an essential precondition for achieving higher levels of growth and employment (Chancellor of the Exchequer 1997b, 1997c; *Red Book* 1997).

As discussed in Chapter 1, the unstable economic cycles of the past 30 or so years have been more severe than in any other major developed economy. They have had a serious negative impact on long-term interest rates, on the employability of the long-term unemployed, and on the capacity of the economy and the willingness of companies to make long-term investment commitments.

Long-term stability is necessary for investment. But a strong economy is also necessary to entrench stability. The UK will only be able to deliver and sustain stable economic growth and employment if it has a strong, productive, wealth-creating economy which can generate both jobs and rising incomes. The inflation of the late post-war period was as much a symptom of a depressed growth potential, and the struggle to get a share of a slower growing cake, as it was of macroeconomic policy errors.

So while stability is the first pillar of the Government's economic policies, supply-side action to make the economy more dynamic and remove barriers to growth is the second pillar. That means understanding that the proper role for government in economic policy making goes well beyond macroeconomic policy making.

It means a new role for government – not picking winners or responding to market failures by trying to replace the market in its entirety – but using the proper role of government to tackle short-termism and market failures by making markets work more dynamically and encouraging investment in the broadest sense: not just in machines, but in technology and innovation, skills and infrastructure – the fuel for growth in the modern economy.

The new growth agenda goes beyond public spending into all areas where either the wrong kind of government or the absence of government creates barriers to growth. Over the past ten years, following the pioneering work of Paul Romer, the theory of economic policy has been replacing the old idea of exogenous technological change as the main driver of economic growth with a much more sophisticated role for governments: in tax policy, competition policy, corporate governance, support for small business, regional development agencies and education and training (Romer 1986, Boltho and Holtham 1992).

Without stability, this long-term project of raising the economy's growth potential cannot get off the ground. But only by taking action to tackle barriers to growth can the UK avoid the mistakes of the past – attempts at maintaining stability which led to conflict and unemployment. The unemployed have lost most from the instability and slow growth of recent decades.

The third pillar of the new Government's economic policy has been to actively increase employment opportunity and reform the welfare state so that it promotes work not dependency. Only by providing the skills for work, a tax and benefit system which rewards work, and new opportunities for the long-term unemployed to return to work can government translate stability and growth into high levels of employment.

Four principles of open macroeconomic policy

While macroeconomic stability may not be sufficient to deliver the Government's growth and employment objectives, it is certainly a necessary goal – and one which has eluded British governments for over three decades.

The institutional changes to macroeconomic policy making which the Government has taken represent an important advance towards ensuring long-term stability. As Chapter 19 explains, so far the results of the reforms are very encouraging. For example:

- the Government is on track to meet both its fiscal rules and the public finances have been returned to a sustainable long-term position
- inflation has been close to the Government's target level and is expected to remain so
- Britain has avoided a return to the instability of the past.

The remainder of the chapter describes and analyses the implications of the four principles discussed in the introduction.

Stability through constrained discretion

Despite the failure of monetarism in the 1980s, the economics profession owes a debt of gratitude towards Milton Friedman, one of the great US post-war economists. This reflects his work on consumption functions in the 1950s, but also his 1968 American Economic Association Presidential lecture in which, with his vertical expectations-augmented Phillips curve, he demolished the idea of a long-run trade-off between inflation and unemployment.

This is not, of course, to agree with those who concluded in the 1970s that, because people's expectations are entirely rational and forward-looking, there is not even a short-run trade-off between the unemployment and inflation, or that there is a 'natural rate' of unemployment which is not affected by macroeconomic policy. What clearer evidence could there be of the short-run trade-off between reducing inflation and rising unemployment, or the persistent effect this can have in the form of long-term unemployment, than Britain's 1980–81 recession? So severe a long-term cost, indeed, that when inflation accelerated in the late 1980s boom, long-term unemployment remained twice as high as at the previous cyclical peak.

In fact, the experience of the late 1970s and 1980s – persistent mass unemployment alongside accelerating inflation – serves to make Friedman's 1968 point: an expansionary monetary and fiscal policy mix cannot, in and of itself, deliver, let alone sustain, full employment. Indeed, excessive macroeconomic expansions – which allow inflation to run out of control and then be forcibly restrained – end up involving a long-term price in higher unemployment, a 'hysteresis' effect as it was called in the late 1980s (Blanchard and Summers 1990).

With hindsight, the story of the early 1980s is simple enough. What had seemed to be a stable relationship between money and inflation collapsed with the beginning of financial deregulation in 1979. The growth rate of M3 shot out of its target range and stayed there, even after inflation had begun to fall (Britton 1991). But the then government persisted with a policy of high interest rates and high exchange rate, in a continuing attempt to meet its rigid monetary targets, at the expense of a deep recession. With hindsight, it is clear that by 1982 monetary targets were not a useful guide for monetary policy, although the government persisted in setting targets for a range of indicators until 1985. The experience with exchange rate targets in 1987 and 1988 and Britain's membership of the Exchange Rate Mechanism (ERM) both had similar narrow monetarist undertones – attempts to achieve low inflation by clinging to intermediate indicators which appeared to have been associated with inflation in past times or places, but which now implied perverse policy mixes.

Maintaining low and stable inflation – not too high, not too low – is an increasingly accepted goal of monetary policy around the developed world. Indeed, an increasing number of governments and central banks now adopt inflation targets. But using fixed intermediate monetary targets to achieve this low inflation goal is no longer common practice. No major central bank now uses money supply targets as rigid policy rules, as opposed to using them as one source among a number of sources of economic information. Economic judgement now rules the day, not blind observance of monetary or exchange rate rules.

First, fixed intermediate monetary targets rely on stable money demand functions. But financial deregulation, changing technology and widening consumer choice have delivered such instability in money demand functions that fixed monetary rules have proved unworkable – not just in the UK, but in the US and Germany too. For, while modern open economy macroeconomics says that demand shocks should not be accommodated – the underlying case for fixed intermediate policy rules – these rules break down as a guide to the correct policy response if the money demand function itself breaks down. No one could accuse the government of accommodating inflationary pressures in 1979 and 1980. In retrospect, domestic monetary policy was too tight during this period. But, according to the government's own monetary targets which were consistently overshot by the accelerating demand for broad money, policy was too loose. If monetary targets had ever been a reliable guide to policy making in the UK, they had certainly become redundant by the time they were put to the test.

Second, fixed intermediate targets rely not only on stable money demand but also on the assumption that demand shocks are predominant while shocks to supply are both infrequent and easily recognisable. While standard macroeconomics recommends keeping money supply growth steady in the face of demand shocks, assuming a stable money demand function, to do so in the face of a large supply shock would mean a heavy and unnecessary price in terms of lost output – which is why the standard economic response to a supply shock is to use monetary and fiscal policy to accommodate its direct effects on the price level, again overriding any fixed intermediate monetary target. If the aim of policy is to stick to the policy rule, then stick to the policy rule. But if the aim of policy is to keep inflation low and stable, and growth as high and stable as possible, then the policy rule is again redundant.

This is the first principle, *stability through constrained discretion*: stability and low inflation is a necessary condition for achieving and sustaining high and stable levels of growth and employment, but achieving stability requires the discretionary ability for macroeconomic policy to respond flexibly to different economic shocks – constrained, of course, by the need to meet the low inflation objective or target over time.

But if the need for discretion was so straightforward, then why the attraction in fixed monetary targets in the first place? Were monetarist governments in the early 1980s simply putting faith in an empirical relationship which had by then broken down? In which case, if the monetarist belief in fixed policy rules can simply be replaced by our first principle, then macroeconomic policy making would once more become a straightforward – if technical – task. The Chancellor could sit back, take the advice of his officials and perhaps other experts in private, then simply make decisions which outsiders could observe and, if they so desired, try to rationalise – stability, if you like, through private discretion.

The answer is that governments were trying to achieve something more than a simple and automatic rule for monetary policy making. That extra something was *credibility*. Credibility is the elusive elixir of modern macroeconomics.

In a 1995 lecture, Mervyn King, Deputy Governor of the Bank of England, defines credibility as 'a question of whether announced intentions are believable' (King 1995). It is not simply a matter of trust – 'read my lips: no more inflationary booms' – but, he says, of whether the monetary authorities face an *incentive* to pursue low inflation. Or, in the language of economics, to make policy making 'time consistent' by ensuring that the government actually has an incentive to achieve the goals in the future what it says now it wants to achieve in the future.

Monetarism, then, was not simply an empirical fact at one extreme, or a free market dogma at the other. It was also a reaction against post-war discretionary macroeconomic policy making which became popular in the academic literature in the late 1970s and early 1980s in the guise of the 'new classical' or 'rational expectations' movement in macroeconomics which followed Friedman's seminal presidential lecture (Kydland and Prescott 1976, Lucas 1976).

An incoming government might declare that it wanted to achieve low inflation, but this goal was 'time inconsistent' – when it came to pre-election time, the government's incentive would always be to cheat and dash for growth, knowing that the resulting recession would only come along later. But, as Friedman pointed out, the result of trying to exploit this short-term trade-off between unemployment and inflation was simply to build in higher inflation expectations (and therefore higher long-term interest rates) with no long-term gain in terms of output or employment; indeed, possibly higher unemployment and lower investment if the resulting recession had lasting effects.

So policy makers needed to look for ways to deny themselves the temptation of using 'discretion' to cheat on electorates by saying they were committed to low inflation, but then privately trading a little more inflation for a little less unemployment. The monetarist answer to this problem of 'time inconsistency' was to buy credibility – and therefore lower inflation expectations and lower long-term interest rates – by 'tying the government's hands' and removing discretion from policy making – thereby increasing both trust in the government's long-term goals and in the government's commitment to operate policy to achieve those goals.

The problem was that the actual result was quite the opposite. As the UK experience shows, persisting with fixed monetary rules as monetary aggregates ran out of control was disastrous. Because the government had staked its anti-inflationary credentials on following these rules, it – and the economy – was immediately faced with paying a heavy price for breaking them – not simply in lost output but also lost credibility. As one rule after another proved unsustainable and was replaced by the next, not only were the government's anti-inflationary credentials weakened, but it took its eye off the ball to such an extent that the information that the double-digit growth of M4 did transmit from the mid-1980s onwards was not given the attention it was due.

Nor did the attempt, at the beginning of the 1990s, to maintain credibility though the ERM fare much better. Linking the anti-inflationary commitment to a fixed exchange rate target at a time when German reunification supply shock was pulling the anchor currency – the Deutsche Mark – in a direction which most other countries and certainly Britain were not in a position to go, guaranteed that the right economic decisions were not taken. Then when economic pressures proved too much and the nominal anchor broke, the government was left with the credibility of its long-term goals undermined.

This is the lesson of the ERM failure: trying to achieve credibility through sticking to fixed and rigid intermediate policy rules is destabilising, as the principle of *stability through constrained discretion* suggests. But that does not mean that one can reject the need for credibility in the Government's commitment to its declared goals or ignore the conflict between credibility and discretion which Friedman and his followers highlighted. So what is the modern route to credibility which preserves discretion? The remaining three principles pick up three different ways in which the world makes private discretion more difficult or costly – and focuses on how long-term, open, transparent and devolved decision making provides a better alternative route to goal credibility than fixed monetary or exchange rate rules.

Credibility through sound long-term policies

The rapid globalisation of the world economy has made achieving credibility more rather than less important. This process of globalisation has many dimensions – technological change, capital market liberalisation and the growth and global reach of international trade – all of which have profound implications for domestic economic policy. A discussion of the Government's economic policy cannot avoid a lengthy discussion of how technological change and the growth of world trade have affected labour market outcomes. While macroeconomic policy errors are one central cause of the rise and persistence of unemployment in the 1980s, the concentration of long-term unemployment among the unskilled demonstrates that changes in the global pattern of demand and supply are another.

For macroeconomic policy making, there can be no doubt that the most significant change in the world economy is the globalisation of international capital markets which began before the collapse of the Bretton Woods system of global fixed exchange rates and, spurred on by liberalisation and technological change, has accelerated apace since.

Global capital markets have intensified the 'time inconsistency' problem. In a closed economy, the issue is whether governments can fool their electorates into believing higher growth is sustainable for a while before domestic price inflation rises and the value of their real wages falls. But in an open economy, with capital mobility, discretion also gives the government the ability to fool international investors into believing that growth will be sustained before the exchange rate – and therefore the profitability of their investments – falls.

Do governments have this power? Some despair about the power of 'the markets', arguing that it renders governments impotent in the face of market judgement, making discretion impossible, full employment unattainable, slow growth inevitable (see, for example, Marr 1995). The time inconsistency problem is solved because governments cannot afford to cheat even for a short while, because markets immediately punish any government which strays from the macroeconomic straight and narrow.

The problem is that this argument is not borne out by either theory or the international evidence: it ignores the theoretical point that, even with free capital markets and perfect information, the existence of nominal wage and price rigidities means that there is still a short-term Phillips curve trade-off which governments can try to exploit; but it also enormously overrates the rationality and omnipotence of financial markets. It is precisely because markets can sometimes be misinformed, short-termist, irrational, speculative and herd-like that governments do retain the power of discretion – for good or bad.

In retrospect, what is surprising about the financial market turbulence in the 1990s; for example, in the UK or in various emerging markets, is not that exchange rates came under pressure but that governments were able to get away with unsustainable policies for so long before their soundness came into question. Far from the markets homogenising economic policies by preventing electorates from choosing different economic policies, what remains striking is the diversity of economic policy across developed economies. As a survey of the views of market participants shows, market investors take a strong view of a relatively narrow range of macroeconomic indicators, of which the current and projected inflation rates and fiscal deficits are the most monitored (Mosley 1997). But these are just a few of the many variables upon which economic policy acts and across which there is wide variation even between European countries: the tax/spending share of GDP, the corporate tax rate, the level of the minimum wage or the toughness of competition law, to name but four.

Far from rendering governments impotent or rewriting the laws of economics, global capital markets actually render governments more powerful in their ability to do bad or good. The main dimensions on which they have influence are scale and speed rather than direction. As many of the emerging market crises of the past have shown, governments which pursue monetary and fiscal policies which are not seen to be sustainable in the long term, and, worse, attempt to conceal the fact through short-term diversion or deceit while delaying the necessary corrective action, are punished hard these days; and much more rapidly than 30 or 40 years ago.

When these crises hit, the effects can be hard and painful: high interest rates and fiscal retrenchment to stabilise the macro economy; low investment, fewer jobs and slower growth as a result; a halt to structural reform and the wider economic agenda as the crisis consumes time, energy and confidence; and contagion effects as – perhaps irrationally – confidence slumps in the wider economic area or region. But there is also a longer-term effect to be paid. Once such a mistake occurs, it can take a long time to repair the damage, in terms of lost credibility, and so rebuild the ability to deliver stability through discretion.

Recent examples are illustrative:

- The UK's attempt to maintain its ERM parity in 1992 proved unsustainable, in the face of growing evidence from the traded sector and the domestic economy that the exchange rate and the level of interest rates it demanded could not be maintained; while the speeches made by government ministers that the policy was central to the government's economic strategy, and the attempt to sell DM-denominated bonds to increase the fiscal cost of failure to maintain the parity, only served to demonstrate the degree of desperation and made it much harder to regain credibility once the policy failed.

- Mexico's attempt to have simultaneously a strong exchange rate and low interest rates was unsustainable; selling short-term dollar-denominated bonds to boost confidence probably accelerated the crisis, and certainly made it worse when it hit.

- Similarly, Thailand ran into balance of payments difficulties because it tried to maintain an unsustainable exchange rate, compounded first by excessive credit expansion in a financial sector which was not sufficiently regulated and supervised so that non-performing loans accumulated, and then by an undeclared policy of intervening heavily in the forward market to try to sustain the exchange rate to preserve flagging credibility and confidence in the long-term sustainability of policy. Ironically, when the authorities were finally forced to publish their forward book, the crisis was deepened in the short term because only then did it become clear quite how unsustainable policy had become.

But governments which pursue, and are judged by the markets to be pursuing, sound monetary and fiscal policies, can attract inflows of investment capital at higher speed, in greater volume and at a lower cost than even ten years ago.

Moreover, if governments are judged to be pursuing sound, long-term macroeconomic policies and institutional procedures, then they can use discretionary monetary, or indeed fiscal, policy to deal with macroeconomic shocks which need to be accommodated in the short term. It was the fact that German economic policy making institutions were judged to be credible in the long-term that enabled the Bundesbank to accommodate the supply shock of unification and effectively ignore its favoured money supply targets.

All of the above leads to the second principle, *credibility through sound long-term policies*: in a world of rapidly mobile capital, governments can have policy credibility and maintain constrained policy discretion if they pursue, and are seen to be pursuing, monetary and fiscal policies which are well understood and sustainable over the long term and where problems are spotted and tackled promptly rather than disguised, while the government clings to intermediate indicators to prop up credibility.

The problem with this second principle is that, while a step in the right direction, it still rather begs the question of how credibility can be achieved and the 'time inconsistency' problem solved. Of course, it would be much better to be a government which preserves its power of discretion in macroeconomic policy, has low long-term interest rates and has time and space to focus on structural reform. Being truly credible means facing 'time inconsistency' down over time. The longer the track record, the greater the cost of breaking that record and therefore the greater the belief that discretion is being used wisely. But how does a new government establish such a track record? Does it simply have to wait, pay a short-term cost and prove its intentions are genuine? Or are there actions it can take to build credibility, short of fixed policy rules?

Credibility through maximum transparency

At the heart of the 'time inconsistency' problem is imperfect information – about the true state of the macroeconomy and, more importantly, about the true motivations of policy makers.

Economics requires perfect information – about prices today and in the future and about the quality of the goods you buy – in order to produce first-best outcomes. But, as the US economist Joseph Stiglitz has argued in numerous articles over the past two decades, if that information is partial, and can be manipulated, then often quite perverse outcomes can result (Stiglitz and Weiss 1981, Stiglitz 1994). The consequences of imperfect information underpin much of the new Keynesian research agenda, from failures in insurance or credit markets through job signalling and efficient wage explanations of unemployment. At its simplest, it is captured in the classic prisoners' dilemma, where two isolated prisoners cannot trust each other to cooperate and plead guilty, which would make them both better off, because of the risk that one pleads guilty while the other cheats and pleads not guilty. So they both plead not guilty and remain in jail – the worst outcome.

How does imperfect and asymmetric information affect macroeconomic policy making?

First, at the heart of the time-inconsistency problem is inevitable uncertainty about the true motivations of policy makers – about whether their claims to be pursuing long-term sustainable macroeconomic policies are genuine. But this problem is compounded by imperfect information about the state of the economy and policy actions which are being taken. Discretion for macro policy makers would be straight-forward if it were always immediately clear what discretionary action was needed and why and when action was being taken. If it was always clear what the level of the output gap was, or the underlying rate of pro-ductivity growth, or whether a particular shock was a supply shock to be accommodated rather than a demand shock to be countered, life would be easier.

The problem is that the suspicion that the government is manipulat-ing information or policy for short-term motives is as damaging to credibility and the economy as evidence that it has done so. Even if macroeconomic errors begin as mistakes rather than deliberate deception, the more suspicion there is about motivation, and the greater the asymmetry of information between government and the investing public, the higher short-term cost that is paid in lost credibility and the heavier the blow to credibility when things go wrong.

There can be no doubt that the UK paid a price in lost credibility because of previous macroeconomic mistakes. But there is no need to suggest that this was the result of deceit. Hubris is as serious a risk. Who can be surprised that, after declaring that an 'economic miracle' was occurring for some years, a government came to believe its own rhetoric and overestimate the capacity of the economy to sustain higher levels of growth – only to find the miracle to be rather less significant than hoped for and inflation accelerating once again?

Recent history shows that credibility in macroeconomic policy making is a valuable commodity – once promises on tax, borrowing or interest rates are broken it is hard to rebuild credibility in future promises. And without it, the economy pays a higher price in terms of higher long-term interest rates, slower growth and a constrained ability to use discretion when it is really needed.

But the less the public knows about how decisions are taken, the more suspicious it will be about motivation and the more the risk of the kinds of market turbulence that can occur when information is incomplete and policies are not well understood. The more economic information that the government withholds from public scrutiny, the greater the suspicion that there is a truth which is being withheld and the books are being cooked. And when discretionary action is needed, the less the public is taken into the confidence of policy makers about the nature of the policy dilemma, and the associated risks, the harder it will be to maintain credibility and support if things do not turn out as anticipated.

This information problem is compounded when the possibility of bail-out by international institutions exists. It is clear that the willingness of the IMF to provide rapid financial assistance to crisis-hit countries, helped to stabilise crises and limit the domestic damage.

But the willingness of the IMF to play this 'bail-out' role also has a cost. The more the IMF is willing to step in to bail out failure, the less private capital and national governments have to suffer when problems occur, and the less vigilant they need to be in avoiding crises in the first place. This moral hazard problem reduces the risk premium which investors demand from potentially vulnerable countries at the expense of a greater risk borne by those who finance the international institutions. Which is why the international institutions, and their developed countries financiers, have an interest in greater transparency in all countries so that proper surveillance can occur and unsustainable problems are not hidden from view. This is one motivation behind the code of good practices referred to earlier.

So the third principle is *credibility through maximum transparency*: the greater the degree of transparency about the government's objectives and the reasons why decisions are taken, the more information about outcomes that is published as a matter of routine, and the more checks on the ability of government to manipulate the flow of information, the less likely is it that investors will be suspicious of the government's intentions, the greater the flexibility of policy to react to real crises and the easier it is to build a consensus for difficult decisions.

This principle takes us part, but not all of the way, to credible discretion. It helps guard against the hubris trap. And by making more information available to the public and the markets not only about long-term objectives, but also about the short-term state of the economy and policy, it makes 'cheating' on policy mistakes less likely, and more costly – so helping to ease the time inconsistency problem. But it does not alone solve the problem. Indeed, cynics would argue that the more the government does to persuade the markets and the public that it can be trusted, the more it has to gain *in the short term* from cheating. Which is why we have to turn to a further strand of economic theory, implicit in the preceding discussion of credibility and discretion, which underpins the final principle.

Credibility through pre-commitment

The existence of asymmetric information about the government's motives explains only half of the problem which central bank independence is designed to solve. The other is that we live in a dynamic world in which reputation matters. The tragedy of the prisoners' dilemma is not simply that they choose the second-best outcome, but that they cannot learn from their mistakes. Each time they are offered the opportunity to gamble on mutual cooperation, it is a gamble they dare not take for fear that the other will continue to cheat. If only there was a way in which they could both pre-commit to plead guilty, then the dilemma would be solved.

The same applies to governments. The problem is that the government can get away with cheating once, by claiming that discretion is needed to respond to a shock when all that is intended is a short-term pre-election dash for growth. For it does so at the cost of its reputation in the future. You can only fool people once. But once you have, the public and markets expect it again. And again.

The problems which continued to undermine the credibility of economic policy after the UK left the ERM make this point. The government tried to focus on the long term – by setting an inflation target against which it could be judged. It tried to be more open in the provision of information – the minutes of the new monthly meetings between the Chancellor and the Governor of the Bank of England were published, and the Bank produced a new, quarterly *Inflation Report* which provided much more information about the state of the economy and the stance of policy. Yet, once the Governor and the Chancellor began to disagree, it harmed the credibility of the new regime.

The answer has been to put in place institutional mechanisms which mean it is clearly the government's intention to do the right thing – to make a strategic pre-commitment. Part of the solution, as the third principle suggests, is to give information about the government's objectives and whether it is meeting them, to such an extent that it makes failure to take a long-term view too costly to contemplate. But it is also possible to go further – to pre-commit not to cheat and dash for growth while retaining the discretion which is lost with fixed policy rules.

This is the heart of the case for central bank independence as a solution to the time inconsistency problem, as made by Robert Barro and Robert Gordon in the early 1980s and more recently and most eloquently by Stan Fischer, the First Deputy Managing Director of the IMF (Barro and Gordon 1983, Fischer 1994a). The government, by legislating to make the central bank independent in setting policy to deliver low inflation, can strategically pre-commit policy to meeting that objective while still preserving the discretion for monetary policy to respond flexibly to shocks. Central to the ability of the Bundesbank and the US Federal Reserve to use discretion in the late 1980s was the fact that they could do so without suspicion that they were manipulating information or policy for short-term political reasons.

This leads to the final principle, *credibility through pre-commitment*: the more institutional arrangements can demonstrate that policy is truly trying to achieve its declared objectives, and the more difficult it is for the government to cheat by breaking promises or aiming for different objectives, the more the public and investors will believe that decisions are being taken for sound long-term reasons.

There are, of course, a range of types of 'independence' depending on how the bank is constituted, whether the government or the central bank sets the targets for policy and the degree of openness in its deliberations. These arguments are discussed further in Chapter 6. Credibility through maximum transparency applies at least as much when the central bank is independent. Putting aside the more political arguments about the need for democratic legitimacy, and the need to ensure that the government and central bank are seen to be united on objectives, the argument for maximising discretion by explaining to the markets and the public why decisions are being taken and for what purpose strengthens credibility of policy whether in the hands of the government or the central bank.

The same institutional arguments apply also to fiscal policy – but necessarily to a lesser extent. The goal of monetary policy is relatively easy to codify: governments can sensibly set the inflation target but then devolve decision making over interest rates to an arm's-length monetary agency which is charged with achieving that goal. But setting targets for public borrowing and then asking a fiscal agency to make the necessary decisions to meet those targets would be much more difficult. The reason, of course, is that public borrowing is the difference between two much larger variables – taxes and public spending. And decisions about how much and who to tax and how much and how to spend affect not simply the level of public borrowing, but a much wider set of economic and social objectives, not least the distribution of income and wealth across society and between generations. It is precisely to make these choices and trade-offs, about ends and means, for which governments are elected – trade-offs which, unlike the supposed long-run trade-off between unemployment and inflation, are not spurious but real. But there are ways in which a government can preserve its ability to make these fiscal choices and yet also buy credibility by making pre-commitments to long-run targets, open procedures and institutional constraints. The approach of the UK Government is set out Chapter 8.

Conclusion

This chapter has discussed the broad principles underpinning the Government's approach to macroeconomic policy in an open economy context. Further chapters discuss the reforms that the Government has put in place based on these principles. Will these reforms make for better policy? Only time will tell. But clear principles, sound institutional reforms, and a genuine commitment to transparency and accountability, create the conditions for better policy making.

3
The New Monetary Policy Framework

This chapter describes the key features of the new monetary framework, as set out in the Bank of England Act 1998 and in the Government's remit for the Monetary Policy Committee.

Introduction

In May 1997 the Government announced the establishment of a new monetary policy framework for the UK, with operational responsibility for meeting its monetary policy objectives transferred to the newly created Monetary Policy Committee (MPC) of the Bank of England. Details of the new framework were contained in a letter from the Chancellor to the Governor of the Bank of England, and in a statement to Parliament by the Chancellor later that month.

On 12 June 1997 the Government published its remit for the MPC, in which it specified an inflation target and outlined the measures by which the MPC would be held to account for meeting the target. After operating on a de facto basis for 12 months, the new monetary policy framework was formalised by the Bank of England Act, which came into force in June 1998.

The objectives of monetary policy

The Government's central economic objective is to achieve high and stable levels of growth and employment. Based on its conviction that low and stable inflation is a key condition for meeting this goal, the Government's primary objective for monetary policy is to deliver price stability. As specified in Section 11 of the Act, therefore, the maintenance of price stability is the Bank's chief responsibility. Subject to this primary objective, Section 11 also requires the Bank to support the Government's economic policy objectives, including those for growth and employment. This makes it clear that price stability is not considered to be an end in itself, but is instead regarded as necessary to meet the Government's other economic objectives.

The new framework, therefore, explicitly rejects the idea that price stability can only be achieved at the expense of growth and employment. Instead, it is based on the conviction that the best contribution that monetary policy can make to long-term growth and employment is to deliver price stability. There are a number of ways in which high and variable inflation severely damages the long-term performance of an economy.

- In a market economy, prices act as a signal for the allocation of resources. If the price of a product or asset rises, this encourages producers to provide more of that product or asset, while consumers are encouraged to spend their money elsewhere. If, however, all prices are rising due to excessive demand in the economy, producers and consumers find it hard to make relative price comparisons, leading to an inefficient allocation of resources.
- High inflation prompts people to protect themselves from its effects or to engage in speculative activities, rather than concentrating on the creation of new wealth.
- High inflation can also have serious social effects and creates arbitrary changes in wealth. The economic instability associated with high inflation also results in substantial deterioration in the skills of those made unemployed, particularly those on low incomes.
- More generally, high and variable inflation makes it difficult for individuals and businesses to plan for the future. This is particularly harmful for the investment, both in human and physical capital, that is necessary for long-term prosperity.

As noted in Chapter 1, it is not only important to recognise that the goal of monetary policy should be price stability, but it is also necessary to ensure that this goal is specified properly. In particular, it is best to specify that goal directly in terms of an inflation target, rather than using intermediate targets, such as monetary aggregates, since the latter have an uncertain relationship with the ultimate goal of maintaining price stability. By targeting the policy objective of price stability directly, the new framework removes the risk that hitting an intermediate target may be inconsistent with achieving the ultimate objective.

It is also important that the inflation target should be clear and stable over time. This ensures that policy makers know what is expected of them. It also provides an effective anchor for inflation expectations. This should make the task of maintaining price stability easier, allowing the benefits of price stability to be maximised. In addition, such a target allows both the Government and the general public to assess policy makers' performance objectively by comparing outturns with target.

These considerations also suggest that it is preferable to express the target in terms of a point target, rather than as a range. Since the scale and nature of the shocks hitting an economy are impossible to predict, it is very difficult to determine how wide a target range should be. A narrow target range gives a misleading impression of what monetary policy can and cannot achieve given the uncertainties which surround it. A wide range, however, does not provide an effective anchor for inflation expectations and would make it difficult to hold policy makers to account.

These requirements are met in the new monetary policy framework. Section 12 of the Act requires the Government to specify on an annual basis what the objective of price stability is to be a requirement that is met in the remit that is renewed each year and confirmed in the Budget. In the remit, the price stability objective is explicitly specified and defined by the Government to be an inflation target of 2½ per cent annual increase in the retail price index, excluding mortgage interest payments (RPIX).

The inflation target is expressed in terms of RPIX, rather than RPI, as the latter is unsuitable as a target due to a perverse short-run effect on it when interest rates are changed. Using RPIX avoids this problem without jeopardising the integrity of the measure, as it is well understood and widely accepted.

The optimal target for inflation is uncertain. It is likely to differ between countries and over time, reflecting differences in the extent of measurement bias in price indices, institutional structures and historical experiences, which affect the extent of rigidities in the setting of wages and prices. The academic debate is inconclusive. However, the target chosen by the Government lies in a similar range to those of other industrial countries that have explicit inflation targets.

It is also important to note that the MPC is required to aim to meet the inflation target at all times. In particular, the MPC is not to aim to achieve 2½ per cent on average over some particular time period. Crude averaging over a rigid period would be arbitrary and unhelpful in assessing the MPC's performance. Any economy can at some point be subject to external events or temporary difficulties which can cause inflation to depart from the desired level. Thus attempts to meet the inflation target on average could lead to sharp, destabilising policy changes towards the end of the period covered or, alternatively, could mean that the MPC would aim for something other than 2½ per cent at the end of the period.

The inflation target is not only clear, but is also stable. It is important to have a good track record of achieving a target once it has been set. For example, the Treasury Committee concluded in July 1999:

> We agree with the Chancellor's view that keeping to the same inflation target for a period of time makes it clear that the Government is pursuing a consistent aim and adds to the credibility of its anti-inflation policy. (Treasury Committee 1999)

Another important feature of the inflation target is that it is symmetrical, so that deviations below the target are treated in the same way as deviations above the target. This helps to ensure that monetary policy not only delivers price stability, but also supports growth and employment. If the target was not symmetrical – for example, if it was 2½ per cent or less – policy makers could have an incentive to drive inflation as low as possible to ensure they met their target comfortably, even if there were detrimental consequences for output and employment. The symmetrical target means that monetary policy is neither unnecessarily loose nor unnecessarily tight. In effect, it allows policy makers to aim for the highest level of growth and employment consistent with keeping RPIX inflation at 2½ per cent.

The Government has on several occasions made it clear that it views undershooting of the target just as seriously as overshooting. This point has also been made by the Governor of the Bank of England, Eddie George:

> We have made it clear by our actions that we are just as vigorous in relaxing policy when the risks to inflation are on the downside as we are in tightening policy when the risks to inflation are on the upside. (George 1999)

A symmetrical inflation target, designed to support growth and employment, also helps policy makers to be more forward-looking. By acting promptly, policy makers can prevent a buildup in inflationary pressures, thereby reducing volatility in both inflation and output. Under the new framework, monetary policy is proactive with the MPC acting pre-emptively to meet the target.

Although it is the MPC's responsibility at all times to meet the inflation target, the monetary policy framework does recognise that the actual inflation rate will on occasions depart from its target as a result of various shocks and disturbances. Attempts to restore inflation back to target too rapidly in such circumstances might cause undesirable volatility in output. For example, if the economy were subject to a large supply shock that pushed inflation temporarily above or below its target, the new framework would not require the MPC to overreact to keep inflation at its target level at the expense of substantial instability in output and employment. Rather, the MPC might choose to accommodate the first-round impact of the shock on the price level, while ensuring that this temporary deviation was not translated into a more permanent departure of inflation from the target.

While the new framework recognises the need for flexibility, it does not give the MPC a free hand. The framework makes clear that when inflation does deviate from target as a result of economic shocks, the onus is on the MPC to justify its actions. Further, if inflation is more than 1 percentage point below or above the inflation target, the Governor is required to write an open letter to the Chancellor, setting out:

- the reasons why inflation has moved so far away from the target
- the policy action that is being taken to deal with it
- the period in which inflation is expected to return to target
- how this approach meets the Government's objectives for growth and employment.

Another letter is required after three months if inflation remains more than 1 percentage point below or above target. It is important to note that an open letter would not necessarily be a sign of failure. For example, if the deviation was the result of an economic shock, the open letter provides a further, and immediate, means by which the MPC can explain the reasons behind its decisions.

The relationship between the Government and the MPC

In the new monetary policy framework set out in the Act, there is a clear distinction between the roles of the Government and the MPC. This means that all parties are aware of what each is required to achieve, promoting transparency and accountability.

- The Government is responsible for designing the framework, including setting the objectives which the MPC must achieve. The Government is also responsible for monitoring the success of the new framework and for keeping the MPC accountable for its performance.
- The MPC has operational responsibility for meeting the objectives specified by the Government.

Under these arrangements, the Government retains overall responsibility for monetary policy. Most importantly, it is the Government that sets the inflation target. However, once this target is set, it becomes primarily a technical issue as to what level of interest rates is appropriate to meet that target. As such technical decisions are best made by independent but fully accountable experts, it is the MPC that has responsibility for setting interest rates under the new framework. Such an arrangement also ensures that monetary policy decisions are unencumbered by short-term political considerations.

One potential concern with the new monetary policy framework is that central bank independence may lead to less effective coordination of fiscal and monetary policy. Some commentators have suggested that by separating responsibility for monetary and fiscal policy, the two sets of policy makers would find it more difficult to have both arms of policy working in the same direction.

This view, however, is too simplistic. First, it fails to recognise that even if monetary and fiscal policy decisions are made by the same set of policy makers, they may not be well coordinated. In the case of the UK, the IMF concluded in a recent report that, 'experience before 1997 shows that having both policy instruments under the control of the government provides no guarantee of effective policy coordination' (IMF 1999b).

The view that central bank independence is likely to hinder monetary and fiscal policy coordination also fails to take into account the procedures in place to prevent this from happening. The new macroeconomic policy framework addresses the potential coordination problem in three main ways.

- Most importantly, coordination is achieved because the Government sets the objectives for both monetary and fiscal policy. Indeed, both arms of policy have the same fundamental objective of helping to achieve long-term growth and employment by delivering economic stability. Monetary policy does this by aiming to deliver price stability, while fiscal policy aims to deliver sound public finances.
- Because the objectives of both arms of policy are clear, and their procedures transparent, both sets of policy makers are aware of what the other is trying to achieve and how the other will react to their policy decisions.
- This process is also aided by the presence at MPC meetings of a representative from HM Treasury, who is able, in particular, to provide information on fiscal policy. This includes detailed presentations on the Budget and *Pre-Budget Report*.

Although the Act gives the Bank responsibility for the conduct of monetary policy, it grants the Treasury reserve powers in certain exceptional circumstances. In particular, the Treasury may give the Bank directions with respect to monetary policy if it is satisfied that they are required in the public interest and by 'extreme economic circumstances'. A more detailed discussion on the theory and practice of monetary–fiscal coordination can be found in Chapter 6.

The introduction of the new monetary policy framework was accompanied by the transfer of certain other functions away from the Bank of England. This allows the Bank to focus its attention on making the best monetary policy decisions, backed up by quality economic analysis. Under the new arrangements, the Debt Management Office is responsible for managing the Government's debt, while the Financial Services Authority is responsible for financial regulation and supervision.

The Monetary Policy Committee

The composition of the MPC is set out in detail in the Act. In particular, the Act specifies that the MPC consists of the Governor and two Deputy Governors of the Bank, two other Bank members, and four external members. The Governor and Deputy Governor are appointed, under statute, for a period of five years, while the other two Bank members are appointed by the Governor after consultation with the Chancellor. The four external members are appointed by the Chancellor for three-year terms which are renewable. These external members may work on either a full-time or a part-time basis.

The two members appointed by the Bank are the Bank officials responsible for monetary policy analysis and monetary policy operations, while the four members appointed by the Chancellor must have knowledge or experience relevant to the MPC's functions. This ensures that the MPC consists of individuals who are best qualified to make the decisions necessary to achieve the Government's monetary policy objectives. In addition to the nine MPC members, the Act also allows for a representative of HM Treasury to attend and speak at MPC meetings, but this representative has no vote.

There is also a stable and well organised process by which monetary policy is conducted. The MPC is required by the Act to meet at least once a month. At these meetings the MPC must decide whether official interest rates need to be raised, lowered or kept unchanged in order to meet the inflation target. The MPC therefore goes about its business according to a regular monthly cycle, augmented by the quarterly *Inflation Report* in which the Bank assesses recent economic developments and provides forecasts. This regular process helps to ensure that the MPC's decisions are consistent and well thought out, and it also allows all relevant information to be taken into account when policy decisions are made. This is done in a number of ways.

- The MPC benefits from having access to a substantial number of professional staff from the Bank of England who provide reports and analyses on all relevant factors.
- The MPC is required to consider regional and sectoral issues, and a comprehensive network of twelve regional agents has been established for this purpose. The main role of these agents is to report back on local business conditions and sectoral developments.
- The MPC also has access to a representative from HM Treasury at its meetings to ensure that it is well briefed on fiscal policy and other issues.
- To improve its access to timely and accurate data, the Bank has established a formal Service Level Agreement with the Office for National Statistics.

The MPC's decisions also reflect a considerable amount of research on monetary policy issues, conducted by MPC members with the assistance of Bank staff. In November 1999 this process was formalised with the adoption of new arrangements for determining the Bank's research agenda. Under these new arrangements, the MPC meets six times a year to determine research priorities. Four of these meetings are related to the quarterly *Inflation Report*, with the other two concerned with longer-term issues (the first, at the start of the year, to set priorities for the year ahead, and the second, half-way through the year, to review those priorities). In addition, each external member has access to dedicated research assistance.

Importantly, the MPC publishes the dates of its meetings well in advance.[1] Together with its reporting obligations and other transparency measures (discussed below), these procedures mean that monetary policy is conducted in a regular and predictable fashion. Meetings are held on the Wednesday and Thursday following the first Monday of each month and are preceded with detailed consideration of recent economic developments and how they affect prospects for inflation over the coming two years. Special attention is given to issues where interpretation of the latest data is unclear or where there has been significant departure from previous expectations.

Once preliminary discussions are complete, the MPC decides whether the current interest rate remains appropriate. Each member has one vote, with the Governor retaining a casting vote if there is no majority. Decisions on interest rates are announced immediately after the monthly meeting.

In addition to setting interest rates, the MPC is also able to conduct monetary policy by intervening directly in financial markets (but only where this furthers the achievement of the price stability objective). As part of the changes introduced with the Act, the Bank can now manage its own pool of foreign exchange reserves, separately from those it manages on behalf of HM Treasury. These reserves are available for use in operations related to monetary policy, subject to limits authorised by the Bank's Court of Directors.

Another means by which the Bank has been able to intervene in financial markets is via the weekly tender of Treasury bills. In April 1998, however, the newly formed Debt Management Office (DMO) took over responsibility for the management of the Government's debt and the oversight of the gilt market. Responsibility for the overall management of the Government's cash requirements was transferred to the DMO in April 2000.

If the MPC decides that the Bank should intervene in financial markets, that decision will normally be announced immediately after the meeting, unless the MPC considers that immediate publication would impede or frustrate the achievement of the intervention's purpose.

Transparency and accountability

The granting of operational independence to the Bank in the Act is accompanied by the introduction of a range of measures aimed at improving the transparency and accountability of monetary policy. These measures are designed to ensure that the public is well informed of what the MPC is trying to achieve, what it is doing to meet its objectives, and how well it is performing. To the extent that this helps to deliver lower inflationary expectations, it will also reduce the costs of maintaining low inflation. Greater transparency also makes monetary policy more consistent and predictable, thereby helping people to make better long-term decisions.

The Act imposes a range of reporting requirements on the MPC. These requirements not only improve the transparency and accountability of monetary policy, but also provide the means for the MPC to explain the reasoning behind its decisions and the factors that need to be considered. As a result, the public are able to examine the arguments and issues that lie behind monetary policy decisions and are given a thorough explanation of those decisions.

The primary reporting obligation contained in the Act is the requirement that the MPC publishes the minutes of its meetings within six weeks. These minutes report the discussions that took place at the meeting, record how individual members voted on particular decisions, and also present, in an annex, a summary of the data presented by Bank staff to the MPC. If there is disagreement within the MPC about the appropriate decision, these differing views will all be published, thereby giving the public more information about the range of factors that need to be considered, as well as giving them an opportunity to judge for themselves whether or not the MPC made the right decision.

The minutes must also contain a record of decisions to intervene in financial markets, unless the MPC considers that publication would be likely to impede or frustrate the achievement of the intervention's purpose.

Provided it meets its statutory deadline of six weeks, the Act states that timing of the release of the minutes is a matter for the MPC to decide. In October 1998, the MPC decided to publish the MPC minutes two weeks after the meetings take place. By improving the timeliness with which information is made available, the MPC has further enhanced the public's ability to scrutinise and understand the conduct of monetary policy.

The Bank is also obliged under the Act to publish a report every three months that reviews recent monetary policy decisions, assesses developments in inflation, and indicates the expected approach to meeting the Bank's objectives. This requirement is met in the quarterly *Inflation Report*. This report serves two purposes – its preparation provides a comprehensive and forward-looking framework for discussion among MPC members, while its publication allows them to explain the reasons for their decisions. Preparation of the *Inflation Report* is supported by a statutory power to collect information for monetary policy purposes given to the Bank under the Act.

In addition to the material that it is obliged to contain, the *Inflation Report* also typically includes a detailed discussion of economic developments, including sections on money and financial markets, demand and output, the labour market, and costs and prices. The report also includes the minutes of recent MPC meetings and a record of MPC announcements.

Accountability measures are also crucial in the new framework. Authorities with responsibility for decisions that affect the daily lives of most people in the UK must be held accountable to the public for their performance. The main measures are as follows.

- The MPC is directly accountable to the Government for its performance. It is responsible for meeting the target and must provide an open explanation to the Chancellor and the public if inflation deviates more than 1 percentage point above or below target.
- In addition, the MPC is responsible to the Bank's Court of Directors who are required to ensure that the MPC collects the regional, sectoral and other information needed to formulate monetary policy. In turn, the MPC is obliged to submit a monthly report on its activities to the Court of Directors.
- The Act also requires the Bank to submit to the Chancellor of the Exchequer an annual report on its activities. This must include a report by the sub-committee of Non-Executive Directors on the activities of the MPC. The Chancellor is obliged to lay copies of the annual reports before Parliament.
- The MPC is also responsible to Parliament. The main avenue through which this scrutiny is exercised is the Treasury Committee, which has at least two sessions a year dedicated to monetary policy

following publication of two of the four *Inflation Reports*. These sessions give Members of Parliament the opportunity to question Bank officials and MPC members on their decisions and their performance. Further opportunities for parliamentary scrutiny of the MPC's performance are provided by the House of Lords Select Committee on the MPC, additional hearings of the Treasury Committee, and by debates on the Bank's annual report.

Other aspects of the Act

In addition to formalising the new monetary policy framework, the Bank of England Act introduced a number of other measures. Most significantly, the Act provided for the transfer to the newly established Financial Services Authority of the Bank's supervisory functions. A more detailed discussion of these changes is contained in Chapter 7.

The Act also makes a number of changes to the Bank's administration and finances. In particular, the Act specifies that the Bank's Court of Directors is to consist of the Governor, two Deputy Governors, and sixteen Non-Executive Directors. The Act also provides for the formal creation of a Committee of all Non-Executive Directors, with a Chairman designated by the Chancellor. While the Court as a whole is responsible for managing the affairs of the Bank, including setting its objectives and strategy, the Committee of Non-Executive Directors is responsible for reviewing the Bank's performance in relation to the strategy, and its financial affairs.

APPENDIX: THE GOVERNMENT'S REMIT FOR THE MPC

Following the announcement that a new monetary policy framework would be established, the Chancellor wrote a letter to the Governor of the Bank of England detailing the MPC's remit. Under the Bank of England Act 1998, the remit for the MPC is to be updated on an annual basis. Below is the original remit for the MPC, which has been confirmed annually.

12 June 1997

Eddie George Esq
Governor
Bank of England
Threadneedle Street
LONDON EC2R 8AH

REMIT FOR THE MONETARY POLICY COMMITTEE

In my letter of 6 May I said that the monetary policy objective of the Bank of England will be to deliver price stability (as defined by the inflation target) and, without prejudice to this objective, to support the Government's economic policy, including its objectives for growth and employment. Tonight, at the Mansion House, I will explain how I intend the new framework for monetary policy to work. This letter sets out the Government's remit for the Monetary Policy Committee and explains how the MPC will be held to account for meeting the target.

The Open Letter system

My intention is to lock into our policy making system a commitment to consistently low inflation in the long term. The real stability that we need will be achieved not when we meet the inflation target one or two months in succession but when we can confidently expect inflation to remain low and stable for a long period of time. To this end, I propose a new more rigorous and more precise framework for achieving the inflation target.

Of course, I have to take into account that any economy at some point can suffer from external events or temporary difficulties, often beyond its control. The framework I propose is based on the recognition that the actual inflation rate will on occasions depart from its target as a result of shocks and disturbances. Attempts to keep inflation at the inflation target in these circumstances may cause undesirable volatility in output.

But if inflation moves away from the target by more than 1 percentage point in either direction I shall expect you to send an open letter to me, following the meeting of the Monetary Policy Committee and referring as necessary to the Bank's Inflation Report, setting out:

- the reasons why inflation has moved away from the target by more than 1 percentage point;
- the policy action which you are taking to deal with it;
- the period within which you expect inflation to return to the target;
- how this approach meets the Bank's monetary policy objectives.

You would send a further letter after three months if inflation remained more than 1 percentage point above or below the target. In responding to your letter, I shall, of course, have regard to the circumstances prevailing at the time.

The thresholds *do not* define a target range. Their function is to define the points at which I shall expect an explanatory letter from you because the actual inflation rate is appreciably away from its target.

The operational target for monetary policy is an underlying inflation rate (measured by the 12-month increase in the RPI excluding mortgage interest payments) of 2½ per cent.

In setting in place this new framework, I believe we have a better chance of achieving consistently low inflation.

Accountability

The Monetary Policy Committee will be accountable to the Government for the remit set out in this letter. The Committee's performance and procedures will be reviewed by the reformed Court on an ongoing basis (with particular regard to ensuring the Bank is collecting proper regional and sectoral information). The Bank will be accountable to the House of Commons through regular reports and evidence given to the Treasury Select Committee. Finally, through the publication of the minutes of the Monetary Policy Committee meetings and the Inflation Report, the Bank will be accountable to the public at large.

Restatement of the Remit

The inflation target will be confirmed in each Budget. There is a value in continuity and I will have proper regard to that. But I will also need to consider the case for a revised target at these times on its merits. Any changes to the remit will be set out in the Budget.

GORDON BROWN

4
The Benefits of Maintaining Low and Stable Inflation

This chapter explains why maintaining low and stable inflation is the best contribution that monetary policy can make to the goal of high and stable levels of growth and employment.

Introduction

This chapter considers the benefits of maintaining low inflation. The evidence confirms there is no long-run trade-off between growth and inflation. The possibility of raising growth at the cost of higher inflation only exists in the short run. In fact, the evidence suggests that low inflation may bring benefits in terms of higher growth or a higher level of output in the long run and benefits in terms of reducing poverty.

The chapter is split into three sections:

- the theoretical channels through which inflation may affect the real economy
- recent empirical evidence on the inflation-growth trade-off
- empirical evidence on the effect of low inflation on poverty.

Channels of influence

The literature on the costs of inflation has blossomed over the past decade or so. The costs of inflation can be grouped into two categories: those associated with fully anticipated inflation (that is, they occur even when future inflation is known) and those associated with unanticipated inflation (that is, they occur due to uncertainty about the future inflation rate).

Costs of anticipated inflation

There are four key costs associated with fully anticipated inflation:

- costs arising from the interaction of inflation with the tax system: inflation-linked increases in nominal incomes incur a higher real tax burden. Although this effect can be reduced by index-linking the tax system, applying this to complex systems will itself carry a cost
- 'shoe leather' costs resulting from peoples' efforts to economise on money balances: economic agents will not want to hold onto cash balances if they are losing their value rapidly and this will change their behaviour from what was previously optimal by, for instance, making more frequent trips to the bank and trying to synchronise receipts of cash income with cash expenditures
- 'menu' costs due to the need to quote revised prices and contracts: prices have to be revised more often with high and variable inflation and this leads to costs arising from changing menus, vending machines, re-advertising prices, and so on
- the 'front-end loading' of nominal debt contracts: higher inflation means the real value of fixed nominal debt repayments is high early in the contract but then declines with inflation. This may be a sub-optimal time path for debt repayments and could distort economic decisions even if the total real value of the loan repayments remains the same over the life of the loan.

Of these costs, operating a less than perfectly indexed tax system and 'shoe leather' costs have perhaps received the most academic attention. Although many studies have tended to suggest that the costs of fully anticipated inflation is small, Bakhshi et al. (1998) have argued that these findings fail to capture the total costs of anticipated inflation.

Firstly, although lower inflation *per se* may not lead to higher economic growth, the increase in the level of GDP could still be significant. Second, aggregate time series, on which many of these studies are based upon, may be a blunt tool to assess the dynamic costs and benefits of a change in average inflation.

Finally, the interaction of distortions to the tax system and positive inflation can act to turn second-order distortions in the tax system into first-order welfare losses.

Costs of unanticipated inflation

There is a well documented positive relationship between the level of inflation and its variability. For instance, Chowdhury (1991) looked at 66 countries over the period 1955–85 and found a significant positive relationship between the rate of inflation and its variability. Figure 4.1 illustrates the relationship clearly for the OECD countries.

More volatile inflation is harder to predict, and additional costs arise from unanticipated inflation:

- The price mechanism works less effectively if consumers and firms find it more difficult to discern relative price changes when all prices are increasing regularly. Furthermore, unanticipated inflation can *distort the allocation of resources*, because greater uncertainty makes real assets more attractive as a hedge against inflation, diverting resources from nominal assets.
- Unanticipated inflation can also lead to *arbitrary redistributions of income and wealth*, in particular from creditors to debtors (if inflation is higher than expected). This may be very costly for certain individuals and sectors of the economy and may undermine confidence in property rights.
- Uncertainty about inflation *makes long-term investment more difficult*, by discouraging agents from entering into long-term monetary contracts. It creates a tendency for investment to be biased towards short-term assets.
- Savers and lenders may respond to inflation uncertainty by demanding a risk premium, leading to *higher long-term interest rates* than otherwise would have been the case.
- Finally, *monetary policy makers are more likely to make mistakes*. High and volatile inflation makes it harder for the authorities to set policy and can lead to an increase in the volatility of output and employment.

Some of these costs can be offset at least partly by indexation of institutionalised economic arrangements, but this itself is costly and can impair the workings of the price mechanism.

Benefits of low inflation

Set against these costs of inflation it has been suggested that *moderate* rates of inflation may confer two main benefits:

- With moderate inflation *nominal rigidities in the economy become less important*.

- Moderate inflation might also *make monetary policy more effective.*

These arguments are discussed in more detail in Chapter 5 which considers the specification of the Government's inflation target.

Empirical evidence

There have been numerous studies trying to quantify the effect of inflation on growth. These fall into several categories. This section looks at (a) the impact of inflation on growth, (b) the impact of inflation on the level of GDP, and (c) the evidence for nominal rigidities in the economy.

The impact of inflation on growth

Table 4.1 summarises some of the main results of cross-country studies of the impact of inflation on growth.

Table 4.1 Recent studies of the impact of inflation on growth

Author	Detail of study	Inflation coefficient[1]	Significant?
Jarrett and Selody (1982)	Canada	−0.3	✓
Grimes (1991)	21 industrialised countries. Single-country time series	Negative for 13 countries	✓
Stanners (1993)	9 industrialised countries. Single-country time series	Negative	✗
Fischer (1993)	80 countries panel	−0.04	✓
Englander and Gurney (1994)	OECD countries panel	−0.06	✓
Barro (1995)	100 countries panel	−0.025	✓
Fry, Goodhart and Almeida (1996)	45 developing countries panel	−0.05	✓
Judson and Orphanides (1996)	119 countries panel	−0.05	✓
Andrés and Hernando (1997)	OECD panel countries	−0.08	✓
Ghosh and Phillips (1998)	145 countries panel	−0.03 to −0.04	✓

Note: [1] Impact on annual growth of an increase in inflation of 1 percentage point.

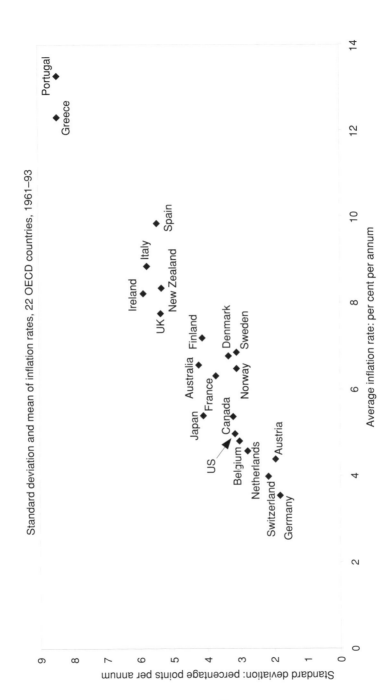

Figure 4.1 Average inflation and inflation volatility

62

Two approaches have been used:

- *Single-country time series approach* – output is simply regressed on current and lagged inflation. These studies may underestimate the negative impact of inflation[1] on long-run growth, yet Grimes (1991) still found evidence of a significant negative relationship.
- *Panel data* – long-run growth of a set of countries is explained in terms of a base set of regressors including long-run trends in physical and human capital accumulation and initial income. Macroeconomic factors such as inflation, the budget deficit and the exchange rate, are then added to determine whether they have a separate effect on growth other than what would be captured already through their effect on the stock of capital. The results of these studies imply that the inflation–growth relationship is predominantly negative.

Table 4.1 shows that the negative effect of inflation on growth is small in any one year. An increase in the average inflation rate by 10 percentage points per year may lower the growth rate by 0.25 to 0.8 percentage points per year. But such small changes in the average growth rate imply important gains in the longer term from reducing inflation. Taking –0.05 as an illustrative example, if inflation was reduced permanently by just 1 percentage point the level of GDP would be around 1½ per cent higher after 20 years. For a 10 percentage point reduction the gain would amount to 16¾ per cent of initial GDP after 20 years.

A caveat to this evidence is that the panel data used in these studies includes few examples of countries with very low inflation. Barro (1995) found that the benefits from inflation reduction on growth are smaller when inflation is being reduced from a lower initial rate. Sarel (1996) argues that although high inflation has a powerful negative effect on economic growth, when inflation is low it has no significant negative effect on growth. Hess and Morris (1996) acknowledge that the gains to growth from reducing inflation may be very small when inflation is already low. However, they argue that it is still justifiable to pursue lower inflation because of other benefits, namely reductions in inflation uncertainty, real growth variability and relative price variability.

Similarly, Levine and Zervos (1993) suggest that inflation–growth findings can depend on a very few countries with high inflation, and Bruno and Easterly (1996) show that excluding all countries with inflation above 40 per cent can make inflation lose statistical significance. Ghosh and Phillips (1998) contend that there is a convex relationship between inflation and growth and suggest that imposing linearity gives a large downward bias in the inflation–growth slope.

Impact of lower inflation on the level of GDP

A second set of studies looks at the effect of inflation on the level of GDP. These are summarised in Table 4.2.

In addition to the main results reported in Table 4.2, both Feldstein (1996) and Bakhshi et al. (1998) allow for short-term disinflation costs. Feldstein (1996) estimates that the transitional costs of disinflating from 2 per cent to zero inflation would be about 5 per cent of current GDP. Feldstein concludes that the benefits of price stability exceed the transitional costs within six to nine years for the 'most plausible' parameter values.

Following the lead of Feldstein (1996), several authors have attempted to estimate the net welfare benefit (excluding the output costs associated with the disinflation process) that would accrue by reducing the distortions to decisions on consumption and savings, housing demand and money demand (that is, shoe-leather costs). The welfare loss from the need to raise tax to replace the inflation tax on government debt is also considered. Table 4.3, drawn partially from Bonato (1998), summarises the results of five studies examining the welfare benefits of lowering the true inflation rate from 2 per cent to zero.

The variation in the estimated net welfare gains is due to the differing characteristics of the tax systems in each country and differing assumptions about, for example, the interest elasticity of savings and the deadweight loss associated with a given increase in taxes. The estimated welfare gain for the UK – 0.21 per cent of GDP per annum – reflects Bakhshi et al.'s preferred estimate based on assumptions backed by a range of studies. However, Bakhshi et al. report gains of up to 0.37 per cent of GDP given a higher interest elasticity of savings than assumed in their central projection. The abolition of mortgage interest relief at source (MIRAS) means that the distortion due to housing demand is likely to decline significantly. Therefore, assuming that this distortion falls to the same level as in New Zealand (which also has no mortgage interest relief), a realistic range of estimates for the net welfare gain from reducing inflation to zero may be about 0.14 to 0.30 per cent of GDP per annum. The significance of such gains in present value terms is quite significant.[2]

Evidence on the menu cost savings from eliminating inflation is scant. While positive rates of inflation should raise the likelihood of price setters changing their prices, it is not clear whether this is reflected in a

Table 4.2   Recent studies of the impact of inflation on the level of GDP

Author	Reduction in inflation	Welfare benefits	Detail
Fischer (1981)	10 pps	0.3 to 2% income gain	Study looks at tax on money balances or shoe leather costs (0.3%) and interaction of inflation and taxation (2%). US.
Lucas (1981)	10 pps	0.9% income gain	Tax on money balances. US.
Cooley and Hansen (1991)	10 pps	0.6% income gain	Tax on money balances and interaction with income taxation. US.
Black, Macklem and Poloz (1993)	10 pps	2% to 8% income gain	Canada. Tax on money balances (2%) and interaction of inflation and taxation (8%).
Feldstein (1996)	From 2% to 0%	1% increase in level of GDP (present value 35% of initial GDP)	Paper looks at the benefits from eliminating annual deadweight loss from non-indexed tax system. Does not look at other costs of inflation.
Bakhshi, Haldane and Hatch (1998)	2 pps	0.2% increase in level of GDP (present value 6.5% of initial GDP)	Paper looks at costs of anticipated inflation. Does not look at costs of unanticipated inflation. The authors say their estimates 'provide a strict lower bound on the benefits of reducing inflation'.

greater number of price changes or larger price changes (the former being necessary to generate additional costs as a result of inflation).

Bakhshi, Haldane and Hatch (1998) find that even with high estimates of the output costs of disinflation – such as 4 to 6 per cent of a year's output lost for a 2 percentage point reduction in inflation – the welfare benefits of reducing inflation exceed the output costs of doing so. However, as the authors note, the paper looks only at a subset of the benefits which come from lower inflation and does not look at the possibly much larger benefits from reducing the likelihood of unanticipated inflation. This strengthens the significance of the conclusion.

Table 4.3   Net welfare benefit of reducing inflation from 2 per cent to zero (% of GDP)

	UK	US	Germany	Spain	NZ
Consumption/saving	0.21	0.67	1.48	0.72	0.39
Housing demand	0.11	0.22	0.09	0.11	0.04
Money demand	–0.02	–0.03	–0.04	–0.02	–0.01
Government debt	–0.09	–0.10	–0.12	–0.10	–0.03
Total	0.21	0.76	1.41	1.64	0.39

Sources: Bonato (1998); UK (Bakhshi et al. 1998), US (Feldstein 1997), Germany (Tödter and Ziebarth 1997), Spain (Dolado et al. 1997) and NZ (Bonato 1998).

Summary of empirical evidence

Overall, despite a number of shortcomings, the available evidence provides strong support for a negative relationship between inflation and growth in the long run, consistent with the predictions of the theoretical literature. So efforts to keep inflation low should be expected to raise growth and the level of output.

It is not possible yet to draw any firm conclusion as to the relationship between inflation and growth at the very low inflation rates current in G7 countries. There is little evidence of a significant *positive* association between inflation and growth even at these inflation rates. However, the data leave open the possibility that there is a negative relationship between inflation and growth, even at rates of inflation as low as 1 to 3 per cent.

Low inflation and its effect on poverty

Most of the literature on inflation and growth looks at how inflation affects economy-wide growth without tackling distributional issues. If people in the lower strata of the income distribution were not benefiting from low inflation then, even if income in the economy as a whole was higher, social welfare might not have increased (depending on society's welfare function). The distributional costs of inflation have long been recognised by economists – Keynes wrote in 1939:

> A rising cost of living puts an equal proportionate burden on every one, irrespective of his level of income, from the old-age pensioner upwards, and is a cause, therefore, of great social injustice. (Keynes 1978, p. 44)

Recent work has found some evidence that stable macroeconomic policies which deliver low inflation do in fact help reduce poverty and inequality as well as delivering higher income for the economy as a whole.

Romer and Romer (1998) look at the influence of monetary policy on poverty and inequality. First they examine the short-run effects monetary policy can have on poverty using data for the US in the period 1969–94. They find that monetary policy can produce a cyclical expansion which reduces unemployment and increases inflation. Lower unemployment reduces poverty as measured by the number of people below a fixed cut-off income but has no noticeable effect on the income distribution. They also find that higher inflation has little direct impact on poverty, but may narrow the income distribution slightly. Thus an expansionary monetary policy leads to a temporary period of below-normal poverty at the cost of permanently higher inflation.

The authors suggest that policy makers are likely to adopt contractionary policies to bring inflation back down to its initial level, with a period of below-normal output and above-normal unemployment and poverty resulting. In this case, policy has had no impact on the average level of poverty, it has only rearranged its timing. Moreover the evidence suggests that the inflation–output trade-off is asymmetric, and so the contraction needed to reduce inflation is larger than the expansion that increased it; and so 'the boom–bust cycle raises average poverty'.

Romer and Romer also look at the long-run effect of monetary policy on poverty and inequality. The authors look at cross-country performance to determine how the poorest segment of society fares in countries where monetary policy has kept inflation low and demand stable relative to countries where policy has produced high inflation and unstable demand.

Romer and Romer first look at the average income of the poorest quintile of a country's population. They find that, for the 66 countries for which data are available, a 1 percentage point rise in average inflation is associated with a reduction in the poor's average income of about 1½ per cent, although this is not precisely estimated. For the 19 OECD countries they find that a 1 percentage point rise in average inflation is associated with a 7 per cent fall in the poor's average income (see Table 4.4), and that the null of no relationship between the two variables is overwhelmingly rejected.

Table 4.4   Income of the poor and inflation in 19 OECD countries

y *variable*	*Constant*	*Average inflation*	*Sample size*	R^2	*s.e.*[*]
Average income of lowest quintile	8.87 (64.51)	−6.74 (5.79)	19	0.66	0.31

Note: [*] Equation standard error.
Source: Romer and Romer (1998; table 6).

Second, Romer and Romer use Gini coefficients for 76 countries to see how inequality is affected by monetary policy. They find that the distribution of income is less equal in countries with higher average inflation and greater macroeconomic volatility. A 1 percentage point rise in average inflation is associated with a rise in the Gini coefficient of 0.2 points and the null of no association is rejected.

For the 19 OECD countries (see Table 4.5) the authors also find a statistically significant positive association between inequality and average inflation. A 1 percentage point rise in average inflation is associated with a rise in the Gini coefficient of 0.46 points.

Table 4.5   Inequality and inflation in 19 OECD countries

y *variable*	*Constant*	*Average inflation*	*Sample size*	R^2	*s.e.*[*]
Gini coefficient	0.29 (19.07)	0.46 (3.41)	21	0.38	0.04

Note: [*] Equation standard error.
Source: Romer and Romer (1998; table 9).

Al-Marhubi (1997) also finds a positive correlation between inequality and average inflation. Although Al-Marhubi looks for causality in the opposite direction using a regression of inflation on inequality, he finds the relationship is robust to controlling for political stability, central bank independence and openness to trade.

Romer and Romer point out that the correlation found may not prove causation. It is possible, as Sachs (1989) argues, that low incomes for the poor and greater inequality may lead to distributional conflicts which lead to fiscal policy problems and force monetary financing of spending. But, allowing for this, they draw two main conclusions from their empirical work:

- Expansionary monetary policy can create a boom and reduce poverty temporarily but this leads to permanently higher inflation. There is evidence to suggest there is an asymmetric output–inflation trade off increases economic instability and raises average poverty.
- The evidence suggests an important relationship between the long-run performance of monetary policy and the well-being of the poor. Romer and Romer conclude that, 'On average, the poor are much better off in countries where monetary policy has kept inflation low and aggregate demand growth stable.'

Conclusion

In summary, the studies discussed above suggest that the gross benefits of low inflation may be larger than previously thought. The benefits include, in the long term, reductions in poverty and inequality, as a stable macroeconomic framework provides the basis for economic growth and development. The costs to the poor come from policy fluctuations arising from intermittent and inconsistent attempts to fight inflation, and the fact that inflation is often a reflection of distributional struggles within the economy in which those with less power and resources are likely to be most adversely affected.

In addition, inflation introduces a number of direct welfare costs to the economy including inefficiencies in the tax system, shoe leather and menu costs. Through its effect on nominal interest rates inflation introduces distortions into debt contracts. These distortions also encourage rent seeking activities at the expense of productive investment. To the extent that inflation is unanticipated the price mechanism will be less efficient at allocating resources, and this may introduce cumulative dynamic inefficiencies into the economy.

Empirical studies clearly show a long run negative relationship between inflation and growth, consistent with theoretical predictions.

However, it is difficult to draw a firm conclusion on the relationship between inflation and growth at the current low inflation rates prevailing in G7 countries.

Against these benefits it is important to note that inflation very close to zero may also have costs, particularly if there are nominal rigidities in the price mechanism. The other cost is that monetary policy may become less effective due to a lower bound on nominal interest rates.

Thus while it is not possible to determine an optimal numerical target for inflation, it would appear that the evidence would support a target for low positive inflation, such as the current 2.5 per cent target set for the MPC of the Bank of England, rather than an objective of zero inflation.

5
The Specification of the Inflation Target

This chapter discusses issues relevant to the choice of inflation target once the decision to direct monetary policy towards achieving low and stable inflation has been made.

Introduction

As explained in Chapter 3, the framework for determining the inflation target to be achieved by the Bank of England's Monetary Policy Committee (MPC) is set out in the Bank of England Act 1998. Section 11 of the Act requires the Bank 'to maintain price stability', while Section 12 requires the Treasury to specify 'what price stability is taken to consist of'.

Pursuant to the Act, the Treasury wrote to the Bank's Governor in April 2001, reconfirming the remit first given to the MPC when the new framework was unveiled in May 1997. Specifically, the remit (a copy of which is appended to Chapter 3) states:

> The operational target for monetary policy remains an underlying inflation rate (measured by the 12-month increase in the RPI excluding mortgage interest payments) of 2½ per cent.

The remit defines both the level of the inflation target and the index against which achievement of the target is to be judged. This chapter considers some of the issues that were considered when deciding upon the specification of the inflation target. Specifically, the chapter asks:

- Why an explicit inflation target and not some other target?
- Which index should the Government target?
- At what level should the inflation target be set?

Why an explicit inflation target?

An inflation target or an intermediate target?

As explained in Chapter 1, intermediate targets can lead policy makers to focus too much on the variable they are targeting at the expense of the wide variety of other important indicators of inflationary pressures. And because the relationships between intermediate targets and the final objective are uncertain, policy makers have frequently resorted to setting different target ranges or targeting different indicators. Such frequent changes create uncertainty, damaging the credibility of policy makers and leading to policy mistakes.

Over recent years a number of countries – New Zealand, Canada, Sweden, the UK – have moved towards inflation targeting and away from targeting intermediate variables, such as the money supply.[1] An explicit target for inflation has a number of desirable properties:

- it ensures that the focus of policy remains firmly on achieving the final objective
- it provides a clear anchor for inflation expectations, making it easier to attain and maintain price stability
- it makes it easy for the public and Parliament to monitor how successful the central bank is in achieving the target set.

Given the above, the Government believes that explicit inflation targets are superior to intermediate targets, and the new monetary policy framework reflects this conclusion. Of course, it remains important for the Bank to consider a wide range of data, including the monetary aggregates, when assessing the future prospects for inflation.

An inflation target or a price level target?

Table 5.1 shows the number of years required for the *measured* price level to increase by a multiple of 50 per cent and 100 per cent respectively, given a range of possible average inflation rates.

Table 5.1 Years taken for price level to increase given various annual inflation rates

Increase in price level	Inflation rate					
	0.5	1.0	1.5	2.0	2.5	3.0
50 per cent	81	41	27	21	17	14
100 per cent	139	70	47	35	28	24

All of the inflation rates considered in the table are very low. However, the cumulative impact of inflation over many years means that meeting the current inflation target would still lead to a 50 per cent increase in the measured price level after 17 years and a 100 per cent increase after 28 years.[2] A 1 per cent inflation target would see the *measured* price level increase by 50 per cent after 41 years, and 100 per cent after 70 years. This raises the question of whether the Government should target the price level, rather than the more conventional target of the rate of inflation. A price level target would mean that bygones would not be bygones following a period of inflation; prices would be required to fall so as to return the price level to its target.[3] In a recent paper, King (1999b) emphasises that the difference between price level and inflation targeting is a matter of degree. If the target is expressed as an *average* inflation rate, then it corresponds to setting a predetermined path for the price level. The key issue then is to decide over what horizon the price level is to brought back to its predetermined target path. This would limit any price level drift from period to period by anchoring it to a predetermined path and would make the variance of the price level bounded.

A consideration of the merits of price level versus inflation targeting requires an assessment of the nature of the costs of inflation and the costs of disinflation (as would be required from time to time given a price level target). Eliminating price level drift may be welfare maximising if the costs of inflation originate from uncertainty about the underlying price level. In this case, targeting zero inflation may be an inferior proxy for the ultimate goal of making prices more predictable. However, if prices and wages are subject to rigidities (as discussed further below, pp. 81–2), striving to achieve a price level target may lead to greater volatility in real variables (such as output and employment) than would occur under an inflation target. This suggests that there may be a trade-off between the benefits of achieving price level stability and the costs of doing so.

There are relatively few empirical studies that have looked explicitly at this issue. Fillion and Tetlow (1994) conduct stochastic simulations with a model calibrated to fit Canadian data to compare the output costs of price level versus inflation targeting in the face of shocks to demand, supply and the exchange rate. The results from their base case scenario suggest that a zero inflation targeting regime is superior to a price level targeting regime, more so as the variance of demand and supply shocks increases.

Which price index should the Government target?

There are many price indices that the Government could choose as its target. This section explains why the Government chose to target the retail price index (RPI) excluding mortgage interest rates (RPIX).

The RPI, RPIX and RPIY

A significant advantage of basing the formal inflation target on the RPI is that it is well understood and statistically respected. This characteristic was judged to be crucial to building the credibility of monetary policy, especially in the context of a radically new monetary policy framework. The RPI is also available quickly and on a monthly basis and is not subject to revision. It closely corresponds to the measures targeted by other countries.

But the RPI has characteristics which reduce its suitability as an inflation target. The RPI includes mortgage interest payments within its regimen. This has a perverse short-run effect when interest rates change. For example, if the MPC raises interest rates to combat rising pressures on inflation this action will itself lead to an increase in the RPI. It is therefore necessary to exclude mortgage interest payments from the target index so as to avoid a situation where the MPC could, in effect, be asked to chase its own tail. This calculation can be done without affecting the credibility of the inflation target.

A further alternative is RPIY – that is, RPIX less indirect taxes. Like RPI and RPIX, RPIY is published by the Office for National Statistics (ONS). Specifying the target in terms of RPIY means that the first-round effect of changes in indirect taxes (for example, a change in VAT) are excluded. In principle, this means that RPIY should be a better guide to 'underlying inflation'. There are, however, significant disadvantages associated with RPIY. First and foremost, RPIY does not measure actual 'prices in the shops'. In practice it is an artificial measure of prices which assumes that the indirect taxes are passed on to consumer prices straight away. In fact, this is often not the case. Depending on demand conditions, there can be a delay in passing on changes in indirect taxes. If so, the calculated

RPIY would initially fall by more than the reality. Second, because RPIY is an artificial measure, and is not widely understood or universally accepted as a better measure of underlying inflation, it is likely to lack the credibility of the RPIX target. This of course does not rule out using RPIY as an indicator of future trends in RPIX.

Other price indices: the GDP Deflator, PPIs and the HICP

There are a variety of other price indices that might also serve as inflation targets. Two further possibilities are set out below.

National accounts-based measures

One alternative is national accounts-based measures such as the GDP deflator. This captures the price of all goods and services produced, though not necessarily consumed, in the UK. Such an index includes the prices of the UK's exports, but not UK's imports. A domestic price index can be obtained by simply looking at gross domestic expenditure, which excludes the prices of exports but includes the prices of imports.

The advantage of these indicators is that they are very broad, covering a wider basket of prices across the economy than the RPI. However, there are significant disadvantages that more than offset the advantages. In particular, these measures are reported only quarterly, with a lag, and are subject to revision. Importantly, they are also less well understood than measures based on the RPI, and are thus likely to be less credible in the eyes of the public.

The Harmonised Index of Consumer Prices

Harmonised Indices of Consumer Prices (HICPs) for each EU member state have been developed by the statistical offices of the member states, in conjunction with Eurostat. The construction of the HICPs was intended to facilitate inflation comparisons between EU countries. They were used to check whether member states passed one of the convergence criteria for EMU membership.

The UK HICP has been calculated from the same raw price data as the RPI. There are, however, a number of methodological and coverage differences. First, expenditure weights in the HICP are based on the purchasing patterns of all private households. The RPI excludes the expenditure of the top 4 per cent of households by income and pensioner households that derive over three-quarters of their income from state benefits. Second, the HICP aggregates prices at the elementary level (below which expenditure weights are not available) by taking the geometric mean of individual price quotes for items within each group. The RPI uses alternative formulae – the so-called average of relatives and the ratio of averages. Third, there are also differences in product coverage. The major difference is the exclusion of several main components of housing costs from the HICP: specifically, mortgage interest payments, council tax and housing depreciation, which have a weight of just over 10 per cent in the RPI and 6.5 per cent in RPIX. Some health series, such as NHS prescriptions and dental charges, are also excluded from the HICP, whilst there are alternative methodological treatments for both insurance and new cars.

The HICPs are still under development and are subject to revision. However, the European Central Bank (ECB) uses the HICP for the eurozone as the price measure for assessing its price stability objective.

At what level should the inflation target be set?

This section discusses the factors which were taken into consideration in setting the inflation target at its current level of 2½ per cent.

Price index measurement bias

There is good reason to believe that deficiencies in price index calculations means that movements in the *measured* price level overstate the *true* movement in the price level. Interest into the possibility of bias in consumer price indices was stimulated by the publication of the Boskin Report (Boskin et al. 1996) on the US consumer price index (CPI). This concluded that the US CPI was upwardly biased by about 1.1 percentage points per year, compared with a cost of living index (Table 5.2).

Table 5.2   Boskin Report estimates of bias in the US consumer price index

	Estimate (percentage points)
Commodity substitution	0.15
Formula effect	0.25
Outlet substitution	0.10
New items/Quality change	0.60
Total	1.10

Bias is usually classified under five headings:

- Commodity substitution: consumers shift spending from expenditure groups where prices are rising rapidly to those where prices are rising more slowly or falling, a failure to update expenditure weights regularly would lead to inflation being overstated.

- Formula Effect: to aggregate individual price quotes at the elementary level (below which expenditure weights are not available) requires the use of either an arithmetic or geometric mean. The use of an arithmetic mean (as in the UK RPI) assumes that there is no substitution within a specific weighting group in reaction to a change in relative prices. In contrast, the geometric mean formula allows for substitution – assuming an elasticity of substitution of –1. The appropriate formulae would depend on views of the degree of substitution which takes place.
- Outlet Substitution: the bias resulting from a switch in expenditure patterns from outlets where prices are high and rising to those where they are not.
- New Items: the bias resulting from non-inclusion or delayed inclusion of new goods and services.
- Quality adjustment: if a product improves in quality, purchasers get more for their money and hence true price increases are less than apparent ones. A bias would result if appropriate adjustments are not made for quality changes.

In the US, the Bureau of Labor Statistics has moved to implement some of the recommendations from the Boskin Report. In the UK, the annual updating of expenditure weights and basket of goods should help minimise the bias related to commodity substitution and new items. Nevertheless, to the extent that bias exists, this provides one argument for setting the inflation target greater than zero.

How low should the inflation target be?

Chapter 4 discussed the gross benefits of a low inflation environment compared with a high inflation environment. The chapter concluded that there was very strong evidence that, all things being equal, low (single-digit) inflation rates are associated with better economic performance than high inflation rates. But how low should the inflation target be set? Economists have also identified a number of potential costs which must be set against the benefits of moving to a very low – perhaps zero – inflation target. The three main costs are:

- the output loss associated with disinflation to the new target due to the absence of complete credibility in policy (the so-called sacrifice ratio) and hysteresis effects

- the possibility that nominal rigidities in wage and price setting lead to *ongoing* output costs at lower inflation rates
- less effective macroeconomic stabilisation due to the inability to engineer negative real interest rates when inflation falls to zero (because nominal interest rates can't fall below zero).

The sacrifice ratio and hysteresis effects

Unless an announced reduction in inflation is fully credible, a policy of moving to a lower inflation rate is certain to lead to a loss of output as monetary policy tightens to reduce actual inflation and inflation expectations. This loss of output is a cost of the disinflation process and needs to be set against the long-term output and/or welfare gains from sustaining a lower average inflation rate. A number of authors have calculated sacrifice ratios for the UK, defined as the cumulative loss of output needed to reduce inflation by 1 percentage point. Table 5.3 presents estimates taken from Ball (1994) and Bakhshi et al. (1998).

Table 5.3   Sacrifice ratios for the UK

Period concerned	RPI inflation at beginning of period	Ball (1994)	Bakhshi et al. (1998)
1961Q1 to 1963Q3	2.6	1.9	–
1965Q2 to 1966Q3	5.2	0.0	–
1975Q1 to 1978Q2	20.2	0.9	–
1980Q2 to 1983Q3	21.6	0.3	0.8
1984Q2 to 1986Q3	5.1	0.9	–
1990Q2 to 1994Q4	9.6	–	2.8

Estimates of the sacrifice ratio are very uncertain. For example, it can be difficult to disentangle the output cost of disinflationary policies from that due to, say, structural reforms. Moreover, as Table 5.3 shows, the sacrifice ratio can vary from period to period, ranging from an estimate of zero for the 1965Q2–1966Q3 disinflation to 2.8 for the 1990Q2 to 1994Q4 disinflation (the latter estimate more in keeping with results from US studies). The average estimate over the six periods concerned is 1.2.

Some authors (for example, Layard et al. 1991) have suggested that disinflation may be also be associated with permanent effects on output due to hysteresis effects (that is, a permanent upward shift in the non-accelerating inflation rate of unemployment, or NAIRU). Empirical evidence for such effects is not conclusive. Using US data, Ball (1996) estimates that a 1 percentage point decrease in inflation leads to a 0.42 percentage point rise in the NAIRU. This impact seems implausibly large. Bakhshi et al. suggest that a 0.1 percentage point rise in the NAIRU might be more plausible, based on estimates of movements in the UK NAIRU during the 1980s. Translating this estimate to an impact on the output gap requires an assumption to be made about the Okun coefficient. Given a plausible range of 2 to 3, hysteresis effects could mean that a 1 percentage point reduction in inflation leads to a permanent reduction in output by 0.2 to 0.3 percentage points. Of course, it is quite possible that hysteresis effects are not permanent at all, but merely highly persistent, in which case the long-term significance would be much lower.

Nominal price and wage rigidities

There are reasons to believe that previous estimates of the sacrifice ratio may understate the costs of disinflating when inflation is already low. Table 5.3 provides some support to this proposition, especially with regard to the period 1961Q1 to 1963Q3, althought the evidence is not conclusive.

Several empirical studies have found evidence supporting the prevalence of nominal rigidities in the economy. Laxton, Meredith and Rose (1995) find strong evidence of convexity in the short-run Phillips curve amongst G7 countries, that is, greater output costs are incurred for successive reductions in inflation. However, Dupasquier and Ricketts (1997) argue that the source of non-linearity is as important as the presence of non-linearity, with models linking the sacrifice ratio to the level of inflation having different policy implications to those that link the ratio to the sign of the output gap. They argue that the models favoured by empirical studies tend to be those based on short-run capacity constraints, in which the costs of disinflation are independent of the initial level of inflation.

Akerloff et al. (1996) have suggested that the lower levels of inflation may be associated with a higher NAIRU. They argue that nominal wage rigidities mean that a positive rate of inflation is required to facilitate real wage adjustments in the economy. A very low inflation rate is thought to impede such adjustments, thus raising the NAIRU.

Card and Hyslop (1997), looking at the US, found that a 1 per cent increase in the rate of inflation reduces the proportion of workers with nominal wage rigidities by about 0.8 per cent, which allows real wages to decline 0.06 per cent faster. This provides weak evidence that real wage adjustments occur faster when inflation is higher.

However, other studies have found evidence against the prevalence of nominal rigidities (for example, Parkin 1997). Crawford and Harrison (1997) looked at changes in *total* compensation in Canada. They found that in adjusting to external shocks firms find it easier to reduce or modify non-wage compensation (for example, bonuses) as a way of reducing total labour costs. McLaughlin (1994) also found a relatively high degree of downward flexibility in total labour compensation for the US. Laidler (1997) argued that the evidence for downward nominal wage rigidity is drawn either from a period of medium to high inflation or from a period when high inflation was still a recent memory. Resistance to nominal wage cuts might diminish or disappear once expectations adjust to a low-inflation environment.

Yates (1998), looking at data for the UK (and other countries), found no correlation between lower wage inflation and greater skewness of the wage distribution. Yates also used Granger causality tests and found no evidence of causality running from mean wage inflation to skewness. Yates concluded that 'the evidence for downward nominal rigidity is unpersuasive'. Smith (1998) used the British Household Panel Study to examine changes in self-reported 'usual' gross pay. Smith found self-reported nominal pay cuts were common, with 30 per cent of respondents reporting a fall in nominal pay in each year between 1991 and 1995.

Asymmetries may exist due to nominal rigidities in wage and price setting in the economy, for example, if, for psychological reasons, employees are reluctant to take nominal wage cuts, even if they would accept lower real wages as a result of higher than expected inflation. However, it seems likely that such rigidities are largely a function of the inflation regime. Bakshi et al. estimate the short-run Phillips curve for the UK over the period 1932–1942, a period of relative price stability in the UK economy. Although they find some evidence of convexity, the degree of curvature is quite modest. Even if nominal wages are sticky, firms can adjust non-wage components of remuneration (for example, bonuses and perks).

It is possible that after several years of low inflation, the increased inflation-fighting credibility of central banks and governments means that the costs of further disinflation would be less than indicated by historical experience. However, at such an early stage, it is not possible to verify this empirically.

Non-negative real interest rates

A further argument against very low inflation rates, often credited to Summers (1991), is that very low levels of inflation restrict the ability of central banks to engineer negative real interest rates. Given non-negative nominal interest rates, real interest rates can only be negative if inflation (strictly speaking, inflation expectations) is positive and higher than the prevailing nominal rate. A target of zero inflation, therefore, places a lower bound of zero on the real interest rate. The current situation in Japan in which real interest rates cannot be lowered due to price deflation and zero nominal rates, provides a lesson in the risks of inflation falling too low. Summers argues that this constraint may be costly in terms of conducting stabilisation policy, and therefore the optimal inflation rate is positive, and perhaps as high as 2 to 3 per cent (Summers also argues that an inflation target of zero would simply not be credible, because there is no consensus that a slightly higher rate would be detrimental).

Although this argument is appealing at an intuitive level, there is little empirical evidence to suggest that Summers' constraint binds in a costly way. Fuhrer and Madigan (1997) find that non-negative real interest rates are only costly in rare cases. Black, Coletti and Monnier (1998) simulate the Bank of Canada's economic model and find that a lower bound of zero on the nominal interest rate has only minor implications for an inflation target range with a mid-point as low as zero. Orphanides and Wieland's (1998) US study concludes that the zero bound on nominal interest rates has a significant detrimental impact on economic performance if policy makers strive to target inflation below 1 per cent (recessions are more frequent and last longer). Reifschneider and Williams' (1998) US study using the Federal Reserve's model also finds that the zero bound becomes important for inflation targets less than 1 per cent.

At a more practical level, real interest rates are but one channel through which monetary stimulus can be transmitted, with asset prices and the exchange rate also important. Provided that the public finances remain in sound long-term shape, fiscal policy can also play a role in stabilising the economy though discretionary means.

Negative real interest rates only occurred in the period 1971–80 in the UK, Germany and the US (see Figure 5.1). These negative interest rates mainly reflected inflation rising rapidly and monetary policy failing to control inflation, rather than monetary policy deliberately engineering negative real interest rates to counter a recession.

Point targets versus ranges

One issue that must be confronted is whether to specify the target as a single point (for example 2½ per cent as in the UK) or as a range (for

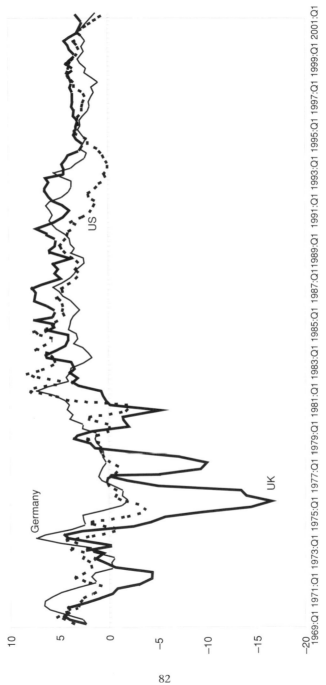

Figure 5.1 Real short-term interest rates in the UK, Germany and the US

example, 0 to 3 per cent as in New Zealand). Arguments that favour selecting a point target include:

- it provides a stronger focus for inflation expectations and makes it easy for the public to monitor how successful the central bank is in achieving the target over time
- since the scale and nature of the shocks hitting the economy are impossible to predict, it is very difficult to determine how wide a target range should be. A tight target range would give a misleading impression of what monetary policy can and cannot achieve given the uncertainties which surround the forecasting of inflation and uncertainties about the monetary policy transmission mechanism. At the same time, a wide target range does not provide an effective anchor for inflation expectations and would make it difficult to hold the central bank to account.

The importance of symmetry

Price stability is a means to an end, but is not an end in itself. The new monetary policy framework makes it clear that the MPC should support the Government's objective of high and stable levels of growth and employment.

One way in which the framework can do this is by specifying a symmetric inflation target, so that deviations below the target are treated just as seriously as deviations above. The Government's target of 2½ per cent annual movements in the RPIX is an example of a symmetric target. If the target was not symmetric – for example, if the target was 2 per cent *or less* annual movements in the RPIX – policy makers could have an incentive to drive inflation as low as possible to ensure they met their target comfortably, even if this had detrimental consequences for output and employment.

The symmetric target means that monetary policy is neither unnecessarily loose nor unnecessarily tight. In effect, it allows policy makers to aim for the highest level of growth and employment consistent with keeping inflation at the Government's target.

Conclusion

This chapter has considered the specification of the inflation target. To summarise, although there is a wide consensus that achieving low inflation should be the primary objective of monetary policy, there is little agreement about the optimal rate of inflation. Given the potential transitional and permanent costs associated with moving to a new, lower target, convincing evidence would needed in order for the Government to consider a change in the inflation target. Moreover, once set, it is important that the Government establish a record of meeting its inflation target.

Therefore the chapter concludes that the current target – a symmetric annual inflation target of 2½ per cent based on the RPIX series – is the most appropriate target for the UK in the current circumstances. This does not rule out the possibility of a change to the target at some point in the future.

Table 5.4 compares the UK's inflation target with a selection of other countries that pursue explicit inflation targets. It is apparent that the UK's inflation target falls within the range of experience elsewhere.

Table 5.4   International comparison of inflation targets

Country/area	Quantitative target (12-month increase)[1]	Index targeted
UK	2.5 per cent	RPIX
Eurozone	2 per cent or less	HICP
Canada	1 to 3 per cent	CPI
New Zealand	0 to 3 per cent	CPI (excl. interest costs)
Australia	2 to 3 per cent over the economic cycle	CPI (excl. interest costs)
Sweden	2 per cent ±1 per cent	Looks at CPI and CPI excluding direct taxes and interest costs
Switzerland	1 to 2 per cent considered to be consistent with price stability	Not specified

Note: [1] Excluding Australia which is over the economic cycle.

6
The UK Model of Central Bank Independence: An Assessment

This chapter examines the UK model of central bank independence and its roots in the analysis of past economic policy failures, as well as recent theoretical developments. It draws heavily on a lecture given by Ed Balls, chief Economic Adviser to the Treasury, to the Oxford University Business School Alumni Association in June 2001 (Balls 2001) and a forthcoming paper co-authored by Gus O'Donnell, the Treasury's representative on the Bank of England's Monetary Policy Committee, and Ashok Bhundia.

In recent years the institutions and practice of UK economic policy have gone through a process of radical economic change and overhaul. The most decisive change in the institutional practice of UK economic policy was granting operational independence to the Bank of England to set UK interest rates.

The decision to go for independence had very substantial implications for both the Treasury and the Bank of England and it overturned decades of practice and tradition. It was also a very significant constitutional change. A Chancellor and a government choosing to cede such a significant power as setting national interest rates to an unelected agency was politically and constitutionally innovative. As reported in *The Times* the next morning: 'Mr Brown has signalled the most fundamental shake-up of the Bank of England since its formation nearly 303 years ago.' It also constituted – as the House of Lords Select Committee concluded two years later – 'a radical new departure in economic policymaking', establishing a new and distinctive UK model of central bank independence.

Different countries and regions have chosen and succeeded with different routes to stability, depending on their economic circumstances, history and traditions. The US, and particularly the Federal Reserve Chairman, Alan Greenspan, has established a daunting reputation for stability and far-sightedness based on the Federal Reserve model. And in Europe, the introduction of the euro offers the prospect of a new stability, with the Maastricht Treaty basing the European Central Bank model closely along the lines of the Bundesbank which had established a highly impressive track record of stability over 50 years.

But for the UK, facing formidable obstacles to entry into the first wave of the euro, both a new route to stability and a new model of central bank independence were needed. The model had to be one suited to a medium-sized open economy operating in a fast-moving open global capital market. It also had to be compatible with a strong tradition of parliamentary, public and press accountability in economic policy making, and take account of a track record of instability and previous policy making failures.

This chapter sets out in more detail the background to this decision, why it was felt that central bank independence was the right route to stability for the UK and why changes in the global economy and the history of economic policy making in the UK led to this particular model of central bank independence.

Theoretical arguments for central bank independence

The main theoretical argument in favour of central bank independence is based on the problem of the time inconsistency of optimal monetary policy. This was first discussed in an article by Kydland and Prescott (1977).

Dynamic inconsistency as applied to monetary policy arises when the optimal monetary policy in the long term (low inflation) may not be optimal at a particular time in the short run. These models assume that the government – reflecting the preferences of the electorate – desires both low inflation and high employment.

The government realises that in the long term the best way to deliver these objectives is for monetary policy to aim at low inflation. However, in the short term if the government promises low inflation, once pay settlements and nominal contracts have been entered into, the government has an incentive to renege on its promise. The government can lower interest rates to generate higher inflation which reduces real wages and temporarily boosts output and employment until agents can renegotiate their wage settlements and nominal contracts.

The problem is that economic agents understand the government's incentive to renege and therefore do not believe the government's announcement in the first place. As a result the monetary authority is tempted to inflate to temporarily reduce unemployment but this will

---

Box 6.1   Pre-commitment through rules

We assume the economy has the following social welfare function (S), where society likes higher output (y) but dislikes higher inflation (π), y* is the equilibrium level of output:

$$S(\pi) = b(y - y^*) - a\pi^2 \tag{1}$$

The model also assumes that output is equal to its equilibrium level plus an amount determined by unanticipated inflation. Higher-than-expected inflation gives output a temporary boost above its equilibrium level:

$$y = y^* + c(\pi - E(\pi)) \tag{2}$$

Substituting (2) into (1) the y*'s cancel out and we have:

$$S(\pi) = bc\pi - bcE(\pi) - a\pi^2 \tag{3}$$

As described above, the government takes inflation expectations as given in the short term and so treats $E(\pi)$ as a constant. Differentiating to find the government's desired inflation rate we get:

$$dS(\pi)/d\pi = bc - 2a\pi = 0 \tag{4}$$

This gives the result that $\pi = bc/2a$, and $y = y^* + bc^2/2a$. However, rational economic agents will expect the government to do this ($E(\pi) = \pi$) and as a result there will be no effect on output but inflation will be higher.

By contrast if the monetary policy maker follows a policy rule which takes into account that inflation expectations will adjust, then we substitute $E(\pi) = \pi$ into (3) and the authority has to maximise:

$$S(\pi) = -a\pi^2 \tag{5}$$

$$dS(\pi)/d\pi = -2a\pi = 0 \tag{6}$$

Thus once the monetary authority allows for the change in inflation expectations, the optimal inflation rate is lower at zero and output is also at its equilibrium level. This is a Pareto improvement on the previous case (that is, all parties can be made better off).

have no effect other than to permanently increase inflation as agents quickly adjust their expectations and raise their wages and prices to maintain their real value, thus offsetting the effects of the inflationary policy on output and employment. So policy makers are more likely to achieve their own goals by removing this temptation to inflation in the short term. Kydland and Prescott (1977) argued that the solution to this problem was for policy to be constrained by rules rather than set with discretion. This point is illustrated by a model shown in Box 6.1.

Barro and Gordon (1983) argued that an announced rule not to use monetary policy to boost output in the short term was not enough to constrain policy as a policy maker could renege on it. There needed to be a credible commitment to follow the rule. Devices such as central bank independence and inflation targeting could improve credibility and raise welfare by lowering steady state inflation.

Several economists have questioned whether the government could not overcome the dynamic inconsistency problem itself. McCallum (1997) argued that to improve on the Kydland–Prescott outcome all it requires is that a policy maker recognises the futility of trying to exploit a non-existent trade-off. Blinder (1997) also points out that in the 1980s governments did not need rules or binding commitments to reduce inflation, they just did it. Minford (1995) also says that elections provide an opportunity for the punishment of a policy maker who has not kept inflation low and give an incentive to governments not to exploit the short-term trade-off.

Empirical evidence

Empirical work in this area has tended to look at the correlation between indices of central bank independence and inflation. Most studies have found that, on average, inflation is lower in countries with more independent central banks. Eijffinger and De Haan (1996) found that all but two of the 20 separate studies of the link between central bank independence and inflation that they looked at reached this conclusion. Grilli et al. (1991) found that the three most independent central banks (Germany, the US and Switzerland) averaged inflation of less than 6 per cent a year in the 1980s, while the three least independent (Greece, Portugal and New Zealand) averaged inflation of more than 12 per cent.

In two separate studies Cukierman, Webb and Neyapti (CWN) (1992) and Grilli, Masciandrao and Tabellini (GMT) (1991) attempted to correlate the degree of Central Bank independence with inflation rate. Figures 6.1 and 6.2 show the results of the CWN index (1980–89) and

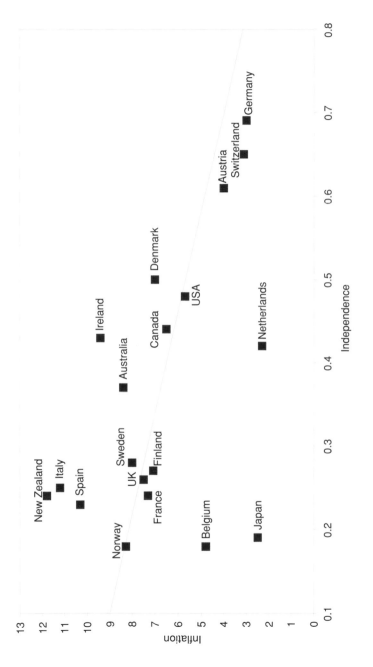

Figure 6.1 Central bank independence and inflation in the 1980s: Cukierman index

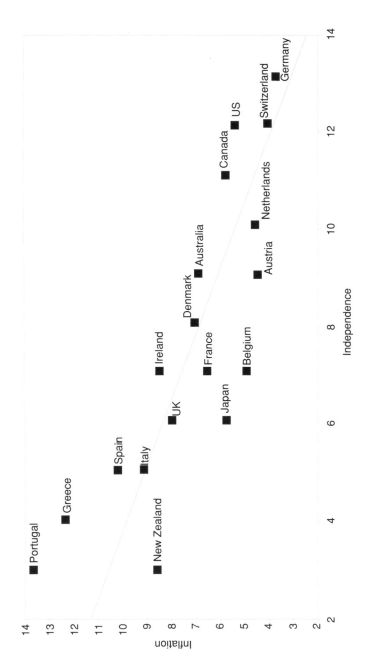

Figure 6.2 Central bank independence and inflation between 1961 and 1992: GMT index

the GMT index (1961–92) respectively. For both indices and periods there is a significant negative relationship between the average rate of inflation and central bank independence. As reflected in the number of studies which have confirmed this relationship, this correlation is robust to changes in the sample period and countries examined.

The political economy of independence

The decision to go for independence in 1997 was a long-term economic policy decision based on clear economic policy principles, as well as on theoretical arguments in favour of central bank independence. It is important to explain why this decision was taken. But first it is necessary to discuss some of the incorrect theses about why the Government decided to move to establish the independence of the Bank of England.

It has been suggested that the decision to grant independence would allow the Chancellor to duck responsibility for difficult decisions. However, it was always likely that the Chancellor who made the Bank independent would be held ultimately responsible for what happened subsequently to the economy, with less ability to influence it directly month by month.

Nor was it an admission that national economic policies, in a global economy, can no longer be either effective or distinctive – that governments are impotent in the face of market judgements; or that national governments do not have the power to make their own decisions about economic policy, making full employment unattainable and slower growth inevitable.

The evidence of the past decade in the UK and also, for example, of emerging markets shows that governments which pursue monetary and fiscal policies which are not seen to be sustainable in the long term, are punished hard by markets – and much more rapidly than 30 or 40 years ago. However, those developed and emerging country governments which have pursued, and been judged by the markets to be pursuing, transparent and credible monetary and fiscal policies have attracted inflows of investment capital at higher speed, in greater volume and at a lower cost than even ten years ago.

A final mistaken view was that the decision was made in order to avoid the potential for conflict between a new Chancellor and the Governor of the Bank of England. In the new model of central bank independence there is a continuing close relationship between the Chancellor and Governor, with the Chancellor setting the inflation target and making key appointments to the central bank. And in practice, a very close relationship, by historical standards, has been built between the Chancellor and Treasury, on the one hand, and the Governor and Deputy Governors of the Bank of England, on the other.

Central bank independence provided three important benefits for the UK. First, it represented a decisive break with previous short-term approaches to policy making and provided a clear commitment to a new long-term approach to UK economic policy making. It had a decisive impact, not only on the international reputation of the Government, but also on the credibility of the commitment by the Treasury to take a long-term perspective across a much wider range of policy areas.

Second, central bank independence liberated the Treasury. Handing over the monthly process of decision making on interest rates – to meet a target set by the Government – created the time, space and long-term credibility for the Chancellor and senior Treasury management to concentrate on other levers of economic policy and the Government's wider economic objectives.

Setting interest rates, and all the short-term activity which comes with that task, was a substantial drain on the time and energy of past Chancellors. That time could have been available for work on fiscal policy, public spending, reforming the welfare state and the productivity agenda, for example.

The other large benefit has been an improvement in relations between the Bank and the Treasury which is partly the result of having greater clarity of roles and responsibilities. Each institution is now concentrating on its area of comparative advantage, exploring its distinctive capabilities. It has recently been argued that this is the route to success for companies. We shall see over the next few years whether it also applies to institutions like the Bank and the Treasury.

But while stability is only a means to wider ends, it is a necessary condition. After the failures of past decades, building a stable economy and a credible and forward-looking macroeconomic policy was an essential precondition for achieving these wider goals. So the third, and most important, reason for the move to independence was that it provided a unique opportunity to reshape the objectives, institutions and practice of UK macroeconomic policy making and establish, for the first time for decades, a credible platform of stability for the UK economy.

The economic cycles of the past 30 or so years (with greater volatility than in any other major developed economy) had a serious negative impact on long-term interest rates because of higher inflation expectations, on the employability of the long-term unemployed, and on the capacity of the economy and the willingness of companies to make long-term investment commitments. Instability thus lowered the long-term rate of growth of the economy.

Given the UK's history, a return to short-termism and instability in macroeconomic policy making would have quickly undermined any chance of focusing on long-term supply-side reform.

The radical institutional reforms after the instability and uncertainty of the previous three decades provided a great opportunity to learn from history and analyse the changes in the global economy that had occurred over that time and establish a modern, stable, but post-monetarist macroeconomic framework for the UK.

Credibility, flexibility and legitimacy

The challenge for policy makers in the 1990s was to create the necessary ingredients of a modern macroeconomic framework based upon an analysis of the failures of UK economic policy in the preceding 30 years.

Chapters 1 and 2 provide a detailed account of how policy makers searched for the technical instruments to manage policy and achieve stable growth. Amid the changes of targets (different measures of money, exchange rates, ambiguous inflation targets) and regimes, it was not appreciated that technical solutions could not solve the problems of the political economy of policy making. In particular, policy regimes suffered from an accumulated credibility deficit which could only be addressed by fundamental institutional reforms.

The new framework endeavoured to meet three objectives. The first was credibility. A policy framework in which the government's commitment to long-term stability commanded trust from the public, business and markets was required. Establishing credibility was essential given the poor track record of UK economic policy under governments of both major political parties – not simply because a credible commitment to long-term stability has a direct financial gain, but also because it makes it possible for the Government to plan a long-term course without the expectation that the Government is about to veer off in response to short-term pressures.

The second objective was flexibility. A framework within which policy makers could take early and decisive action in both monetary and fiscal policy was needed. The framework had to respond to economic shocks and the economic cycle without jeopardising the credibility of its long-term goals. That would require not rigid monetarist rules but rather a combination of institutional reform and greater transparency and accountability, and the ability to maintain the right balance between monetary and fiscal policy.

The third objective was legitimacy. The new framework had to be capable of rebuilding and then entrenching public support and a new cross-party political and parliamentary consensus for long-term stability. It required a new consensus about goals: striking the right balance between delivering low and stable inflation and supporting the Government's wider objectives for sustainable growth and employment without the previous deflationary mistakes. It also required a new consensus about institutions and methods, so that policy makers would be able to take difficult decisions, when necessary, in the public interest without paying a heavy cost in terms of public and political support.

It is clear from their description that these three objective are intimately related. Being able to respond flexibly and decisively to surprise economic events is critical for establishing a track record for delivering long-term stability without huge swings in inflation, output and unemployment. Insufficient flexibility to respond as the economic circumstances change implies big swings in output and unemployment which can quickly undermine legitimacy as well as credibility.

Without a credible framework which commands trust and a track record for making the right decisions, it is hard for policy to respond flexibly without immediately raising the suspicion that the Government is about to sacrifice its long-term goals for monetary or fiscal stability and make a short-term dash for growth at the expense of inflation later.

Different routes to stability

There is, of course, more than one route to stability for countries and regions – depending on their history, institutions and track record. And just as there are different routes to stability, so there are different successful models of central bank independence.

In the US, Alan Greenspan has established credibility through his track record of monetary policy making. This credibility has allowed the Federal Reserve to maintain great policy flexibility without setting explicit targets for monetary policy – either for inflation or for any other intermediate targets.

The Bundesbank also had a highly successful history. Credibility was established over a 50-year track record of stability. It could respond flexibly because long-term credibility enabled the Bundesbank regularly to turn a blind eye to its publicly announced money supply targets, not least in the early 1990s as it accommodated the supply-shock of German reunification. Finally legitimacy grew from the apolitical approach to monetary policy making shared by the Bundesbank, the government and the German people for historical reasons.

The drafters of the Maastricht Treaty had this Bundesbank model at the centre of their thinking when they established the European Central Bank. Indeed, the Maastricht Treaty establishes, in the ECB, the most independent central bank in the world. But legal independence from political interference is only part of the story. The fundamental question the Treaty designers had to decide – and which the ECB's track record will establish – is whether the ECB could inherit the credibility and reputation of the Bundesbank or whether, like the UK, it was starting from scratch in building a reputation for long-term stability.

A Bundesbank-style approach would not have worked for the UK in 1997. Such an approach to objectives and transparency can only work where there is a strong track record of successful stability-orientated policy making and a long-established tradition of central bank independence. The UK had no such tradition. Indeed, the 1980s UK experience had discredited fixed monetary or exchange rate targeting as a credible commitment to stability. UK economic policy and institutions were discredited further by a lack of transparency. In effect, policy was made through a regime of private deliberations behind closed finance ministry or central bank doors, with no justification or explanation about policy decisions and mistakes being made public.

The UK was instead starting from scratch in establishing a reputation and public trust. In this new world of global capital markets in which policy making by fixed rules has been discredited in theory and practice, a new post-monetarist model was needed – a model based on 'Constrained Discretion'. This new model had recognised that in an open economy rigid monetary rules that assume a fixed relationship between money and inflation do not produce reliable targets for achieving long-term stability; rather, the *discretion* necessary for effective economic policy – short-term flexibility to meet credible long-term goals – is possible only within an institutional framework that commands market credibility and public trust with the government *constrained* to deliver clearly defined long-term policy objectives and maximum openness and transparency.

Thus a newly independent UK central bank could not hope to command market credibility, respond flexibly to shocks, successfully coordinate monetary and fiscal policy or sustain wider public legitimacy without a more clearly defined inflation target, proper procedures and commitment to transparency and accountability to Parliament.

This commitment to transparency is critical for countries starting from scratch to establish credibility, flexibility and legitimacy in a post-monetarist world because long-term credibility and short-term constrained discretion to respond flexibly in the face of economic shocks are only consistent if policy makers pursue and are seen to be pursuing long-term goals when they make short-term changes.

The greater the degree of transparency about the Government's objectives and the reasons why decisions are taken, the more information about outcomes that is published as a matter of routine, and the more checks on the ability of government to manipulate the flow of information, the less likely it is that the public and investors would be suspicious of the Government's intentions. This then allows greater flexibility for policy to react to real crises and makes it easier to build a consensus for difficult decisions.

The new UK model

Meeting these objectives for credibility, flexibility and legitimacy required, in each area, a radical departure both from past UK practice and from standard models of central bank independence. In order to strike the right balance between a credible commitment to long-term goals, flexibility in responding to shocks and the transparency and accountability needed to build the track record upon which legitimacy depends, it was recognised that the new UK model needed five key features:

1. *Strategic ownership*: with a clear division of responsibilities between the Government and the central bank so that the elected government sets the wider economic strategy including the objectives for monetary policy, while monthly decisions to meet the target are passed over to the central bank, thereby pre-committing the Government to long-term stability
2. *A single symmetric inflation target*: with no ambiguity about the inflation target and no deflationary bias, and no dual targeting of inflation and the short-term exchange rate
3. *Independent expert decisions*: with monthly decisions to meet the Government's inflation target and support its wider objectives being taken by an independent Monetary Policy Committee within the Bank of England made up of both existing Bank staff and four outside experts appointed directly by the Chancellor

4. *Built-in flexibility*: an explicit mechanism – the Open Letter system – to allow the necessary flexibility so that policy can respond in the short-term to surprise economic events without jeopardising long-term goals. In addition, fiscal rules and a Treasury representative at the MPC ensure proper coordination of monetary and fiscal policy within the new and parallel medium-term framework for fiscal policy

5. *Maximum transparency and accountability*: monthly minutes published and individual votes attributed and with a strengthened role for Parliament, so that the public and markets could see that decisions were being taken for sound long-term reasons.

These features will be discussed in turn. First, *strategic ownership*. The division of responsibilities between the Treasury and the Bank of England – with the Treasury responsible for setting the objectives each year and the Bank required to support them – was a change from the normal model of central bank independence. The Federal Reserve, Bundesbank and ECB are all 'goal independent' – charged in legislation with delivering price stability, and responsible for both defining the precise target for policy as well as making monthly decisions to meet that target.

Why did the UK choose a different path? Partly, as discussed below, in order to shift to a symmetric target. But also to reinforce the understanding that the stability the MPC was asked to deliver by the Government was not only consistent with but critical to achieving the Government's wider goals for high and stable growth and employment.

Some feared that this would lead to a less independent central bank, with a weaker commitment to achieving low inflation. But if it is accepted that there is no long-term trade-off between higher inflation and higher unemployment, then there would be nothing to gain and everything to lose from a weaker target.

In fact, far from weakening independence, having the Government set the target strengthens the operational independence of the central bank. Having set the target for the central bank, it is then very hard indeed for the Government to question the decisions of the MPC. To doubt their decisions is either to doubt that the target is right, which is not its fault, or doubt its expertise, which is hard for the Government to do, especially if it has appointed the experts to make those expert decisions. Instead, the incentive for the Government of the day is publicly to back the MPC's decisions rather than throw into question its wider economic strategy. From the central bank's point of view, as well as having the Government firmly alongside it in making difficult and sometimes controversial decisions, it is able to spend its time each month debating how best to meet the inflation target rather than debating and disagreeing over what price stability should mean in practice.

At no time has the Government ever cast any doubt on the sagacity of the MPC's individual decisions. Indeed, while backing its strategy in public speeches, the Chancellor has been careful to avoid ever commenting on individual decisions – although the Treasury publicly reviews the MPC's performance against target.

But the second reason for setting the target was to institute a further, critical, departure from past practice on monetary policy making – from an asymmetric to a *single symmetric inflation target*. This was done in June 1997, changing from the previous inflation target of 2.5 per cent or less to a symmetrically defined inflation target of 2.5 per cent.

The commitment to stability rests on a rejection of the idea that there is a long-run trade-off between unemployment and inflation and that it was possible to fine-tune policy to achieve sustainable lower unemployment at the expense of higher inflation. But the rejection of the old approach to fine-tuning means recognising that there is no long-term gain to be had from trying to trade higher inflation for more output or jobs.

So the shift to a stable and symmetric target removes possible deflationary bias from policy. It requires that deviations below target are taken as seriously as those above. It is the key innovation which ensures that monetary policy does support the goals of high levels of growth and employment.

In discussions prior to the decision, some feared at the time that dropping the aspiration to an inflation level lower than 2.5 per cent would damage the credibility of UK monetary policy. In fact, the role of the symmetric target as the sole target for monetary policy is critical to credibility, flexibility and legitimacy of UK monetary policy making.

A clearly defined and symmetric target gives much greater clarity and credibility to policy. It is much more straightforward for the MPC to publicly justify its decisions and be held to account for its record. But, importantly, it ensures that the MPC takes an explicitly forward-looking as well as symmetric view of the risks to the UK economy.

The MPC has made clear that it views inflation below target as seriously as inflation above target. As Eddie George said to the TUC Congress in September 1998:

The inflation target we have been set is symmetrical. A significant, sustained, fall below 2½% is to be regarded just as seriously as a significant, sustained, rise above it. And I give you my assurance that we will be just as rigorous in cutting interest rates if the overall evidence begins to point to our undershooting the target as we have been in raising them when the balance of risks was on the upside. (George 1998)

The rapid response of the MPC in cutting interest rates in the autumn and winter of 1998 as the world economy slowed was explained publicly by the downside risks to meeting the 2.5 per cent target.

The setting of the symmetric target, by the government, as the sole target for monetary policy also removed any suspicion that the government or the MPC might be trying – covertly or otherwise – to target the exchange rate as well as inflation. As the Chancellor's 6 May 1997 statement set out, the symmetric inflation target as the sole target for monetary policy is the right way for monetary policy to contribute to delivering a 'stable and competitive pound in the medium-term, consistent with price stability'.

For an open economy with open capital markets, successfully trying to run dual targets for inflation and the exchange rate is flawed in theory and has proved disastrous in practice. The UK's economic history suggests that trying to deliver an exchange rate target can only be achieved at the expense of wider instability in inflation and output.

The strength of the current system is that a return to previous ambiguity is out of the question. The government both sets the inflation target and is responsible for exchange rate policy and intervention. Therefore the MPC cannot be held responsible for the strength of sterling in recent years.

The third new departure, to achieve *independent expert decisions*, was the establishment of the new Monetary Policy Committee – a reform which did away with the old personalised approach to policy making seen in the 1980s. The role of the Chancellor in appointing the four outsiders was part of the delicate constitutional balance that was struck in a move towards a legitimate model of central independence consistent with British-style ministerial accountability to Parliament.

Some doubted whether the commitment to appoint genuine and independent experts was real. However, the quality and independence of all the appointments speak for themselves. They are not only important for their expertise – the Bank of England already has many acknowledged experts; outside appointments demonstrated that it was perfectly acceptable and indeed desirable for independent experts to disagree in public over difficult monetary policy judgements.

The fourth departure in the new UK model is the *built-in flexibility* provided by the Open Letter system, which allows the MPC to respond flexibly in the face of economic shocks as well as to instigate institutional reform to permit the effective coordination of monetary and fiscal policy.

If inflation goes more than 1 percentage point either side of 2.5 per cent, the legislation requires the Governor to write to the Chancellor, on behalf of the MPC, to explain why it has happened, what the MPC has done about it, how long it will take for inflation to come back to target, and how the MPC's response is consistent with the Government's economic objectives of both price stability and high and stable levels of growth and employment.

The Open Letter system has not yet been used, despite fears that it would be used many times. There are misconceptions about its importance. Some have assumed it exists for the Chancellor to discipline the MPC if inflation goes outside the target range. In fact the opposite is true. In the face of a supply-shock, such as a big jump in the oil price, which pushes inflation way off target, for the MPC to strive to get inflation back to 2.5 per cent immediately would involve a draconian interest rate response at the expense of stability, growth and jobs. Any sensible monetary policy maker would want a more measured and more sensible stability-orientated strategy to get inflation back to target. The Open Letter system not only allows a more sensible approach to be explained but also allows the Chancellor publicly to endorse it.

Regarding the fifth departure, *maximum transparency and accountability*, as the Treasury Select Committee concluded in its report on Bank of England accountability in July 1998: 'We agree with the conclusion by the Organisation for Economic Co-operation and Development (OECD) in its country survey of the UK that "In international comparison the United Kingdom's framework is among the strongest in terms of accountability and transparency".'

Meanwhile, the practice of the past four years has confounded those who claimed that central bank independence would make it impossible for proper coordination of monetary and fiscal policy. In fact, monetary and fiscal policy are much more coordinated now than they ever were when the sole decision maker was the Chancellor for both interest rates and fiscal policy. To understand this it is important to examine theoretical models of coordination and see how they apply to the UK.

Central bank independence and policy coordination

In their work on the subject, Alesina and Tabellini (1987) conclude that the benefits of central bank independence depend on the degree of coordination between the fiscal and monetary authority. The literature approaches the subject by setting a policy game between the fiscal authority (FA) and monetary authority (MA) and concludes that the cost of independence is less policy coordination. What is surprising is the lack of attention paid to institutional design and how this can overcome the potential difficulty of coordinating the actions of the MA and FA. Here it is shown that the generic policy game played out in the literature between the FA and the MA misrepresents the actual practice of macroeconomic policy making in the UK. In particular, the design of the UK's macroeconomic framework means that policy coordination has improved since independence.

Modelling policy coordination

Policy coordination is modelled using game theory which requires some motivation for strategic behaviour between the players, in this case the FA and the MA. This is achieved by giving each a different set of preferences over macroeconomic variables such as inflation and the fiscal deficit. In a repeated game involving two players, cooperation (or coordination) is always Pareto superior to non-coordination. Credibility is the key: each player should be able to make a credible pre-commitment to cooperate ex ante.

In the typical policy game neither the MA nor the FA is able make a credible pre-commitment to cooperate but behaves strategically to maximise its own welfare. Below, we use the Nordhaus (1994) model of a policy game to critically examine the assumptions of the model and to show how, once they are modified to reflect the UK institutional design, policy coordination is achieved. It is argued that in the UK, because the Treasury and the Bank of England MPC have a principal–agent relationship in which the Government sets both the fiscal rules and the inflation target, it is the Government's preferences which determine both the MPC's and the Treasury's objectives, removing any tension found in the policy games.

An overview of the Nordhaus (1994) model

The model is a deterministic one-shot game in which the FA and the MA do not try to stabilise the economy in the face of random shocks, but instead bargain over steady-state inflation, output and the fiscal surplus.

The MA and the FA are assumed to have different preferences over macroeconomic outcomes – inflation, growth potential of the economy and unemployment.

Figure 6.3 captures the essential elements of the Nordhaus model. The axes are policy instruments: the fiscal surplus (*s*) and the real interest rate (*r*). Each authority desires levels of unemployment and inflation that are lower than are simultaneously feasible given the structure of the economy, and so each minimises its losses subject to this constraint. The solution to this is given by their 'bliss' points (see figure). Note that the FA is assumed to have a desire for higher deficits (lower surplus) reflecting political economy incentives such as re-election, whilst the MA has no intrinsic interest in the government surplus other than its effect on its own ability to deliver its preferred inflation rate.

The *F* and *M* lines trace out combinations of the policy instruments for the FA and the MA that give them the same level of aggregate demand as their respective bliss points – their optimal level of aggregate demand. Moving in the north-east direction, aggregate demand is lower (both the fiscal surplus and real interest rates are higher). The MA has a lower optimal level of aggregate demand than the FA because it desires a lower rate of inflation, whereas the FA is more worried about unemployment.

The reaction function of the MA coincides with line *M* as it only cares about output and inflation and not the fiscal surplus. The FA also cares about the fiscal surplus (preferring a lower surplus) and so its reaction function is less steep because it is willing to forgo some output and inflation for a lower fiscal surplus (higher deficit).

In this game information is assumed to be *complete and symmetric*. With no mechanism for a credible pre-commitment to cooperate, bargaining between the FA and the MA inevitably leads to a Nash (or non-cooperative) solution given by point *N* where interest rates are higher and the fiscal surplus is lower than desired by each authority. This is because for a combination of *r,S* below that at *N*, the FA's optimal reaction is to set a lower fiscal surplus than desired by the MA. Note, however, that both the FA and the MA are responding to the state of the economy and not to each other's policy response which is taken as given.

Both could do better by cooperating (policy coordination) along the contract curve *CC*. Exactly where on the *CC* curve a bargain is struck will depend on the relative bargaining power of the MA and the FA. Below we argue that because in the UK the Government sets both the monetary and fiscal objectives, there is no difference in preferences and the monetary bliss point 'collapses' onto the fiscal bliss point – policy is set

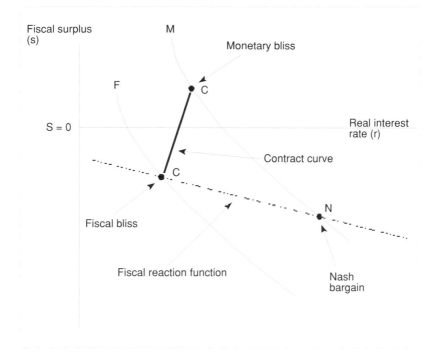

Figure 6.3 Nordhaus model policy game

jointly. In the Nordhaus model this is equivalent to the MA and the FA being able to make a credible pre-commitment to cooperate (coordinate) but with the FA having full bargaining power.

Policy coordination in the UK's new framework

Preferences are determined by the Government

Fischer (1990) distinguishes between two types of independence: goal and instrument. Goal independence allows the MA to set its own objectives, whereas instrument independence is more limited and allows the MA to set its policy instrument to meet the objectives delegated to it by the Government.

In the UK the Government sets both the monetary policy goal defined as an inflation target and the fiscal objectives underpinned by the fiscal rules. The Treasury acts as the principal in this relationship and the Bank of England Monetary Policy Committee acts as the agent. It makes no

logical sense for the Government to set an inflation target that is inconsistent with its fiscal objectives because the MPC will stand ready to
counteract any fiscal impulse that puts at risk the inflation target.

In the UK's case, it would also be wrong to give the FA and the MA
different preferences because the MPC has operational independence but
not goal independence. If the MA is able to set its own goal then
arguably there may be scope for preferences across the MA and FA to
differ, although it can also be argued that if the MA sets a goal that does
not have wider public support then it is unlikely to be sustainable. If the
Government sets the operational goals for both fiscal and monetary
policy then preferences should be mutually consistent and there is no
tension and no policy game. In the Nordhaus model this would be
equivalent to the monetary authority's (the MPC's) bliss point collapsing
onto the FA's (the Treasury's) bliss point emphasising that as the agent,
the MPC's preferences are determined by the Treasury. In fact, illustrat-
ing fiscal and monetary coordination in the UK using a policy game is
the wrong approach because there is no tension (or game) in the first
place between the Treasury's and the MPC's objectives.

The Government's pre-commitment to policy coordination

We know from the analysis of strategic behaviour that by being able to
credibly commit in advance of playing a game both players have much
to gain (Fudenberg and Tirole 1991). In the Nordhaus model no pre-
commitment mechanism exists and so only a Nash equilibrium can be
supported.[1] Hall and Yates (1999) highlight that this would seem to be
logically inconsistent because even before the policy game is played out
the FA is able to credibly pre-commit to central bank independence. Why
then is the FA not able to go one step further and commit to cooperating
with the MA and thus achieve a Pareto superior outcome?[2] A serious
drawback of the Nordhaus model is that it is a one-shot game and so
cannot incorporate reputational equilibria possible in dynamic games. In
repeated games with reputation, the cost of reneging on a pre-
commitment accumulates over time, and with forward-looking
behaviour this can support a credible commitment in the first and each
subsequent period.

In the UK where the Treasury sets both the fiscal and the monetary
policy objectives it clearly makes no sense for the MPC to renege on its
operational task of hitting the symmetric inflation target. Fiscal policy
is constrained by the fact that the MPC is required to ensure that
monetary policy counteracts any inflationary consequences of fiscal
policy that would otherwise cause inflation to deviate from target,

thereby limiting any potential gain to the Government from a profligate fiscal expansion. In addition, the Government could not revoke the independence of the Bank of England and take control of interest rates without suffering a significant loss of reputation that would damage policy credibility.[3]

Other features of the UK framework

As well as having conceptual weaknesses, the Nordhaus model fails to capture several important features of the UK macroeconomic policy framework. In particular:

- the macroeconomic framework ensures a high degree of transparency in fiscal and monetary policy
- enhanced transparency built into the Bank of England Act 1998 and the Code for Fiscal Stability requires the MPC and the Treasury to put greater emphasis on communicating policy stance not only to expert commentators but also the general public. Greater clarity in macroeconomic policy enhances public debate and scrutiny of the mix of monetary and fiscal policy and has helped to establish credibility
- the presence of a Treasury representative at MPC meetings, who speaks but does not vote, ensures that there is an exchange of information between the Treasury and the Bank of England which helps in the coordination of policy
- fiscal policy is constrained by the inflation target because the Treasury must take into account the likely response of the MPC to different fiscal policy settings. Thus when setting the fiscal stance, the Treasury is effectively setting the policy mix. In the past when the Chancellor was in control of monetary policy, it was by no means clear to the public or to commentators whether the same thought experiment and debate was taking place in the Treasury. Even if it was, the fact that such a debate is now more transparent has enhanced the credibility of macroeconomic policy
- the Government sets the MPC's operational target and the fiscal rules ensuring that they are mutually consistent with its desired policy mix. Unlike the ECB or the Bank of Japan, the MPC does not define its own price stability objective.

The MPC's remit is set out annually by the Chancellor and has kept the UK inflation target at 2.5% for RPIX inflation and has suggested that goal stability is important for building credibility. While the remit sets the target it does not specify how aggressive the MPC should be in bringing inflation back to target once it deviates from it. Whatever policy action the MPC decides upon will have implications for the volatility of output – a more aggressive policy that aims to bring inflation quickly back to target is likely to result in higher output volatility, other things being equal.

The remit is deliberately incomplete for very sensible reasons: (a) it is impossible to write a complete state-contingent contract for the MPC; (b) it is not possible to monitor the MPC's actions perfectly, partly because of uncertainties over the true model of the economy and the difficulty of identifying shocks.

How, then, does the MPC ensure that its actions are not out of line with the Government's preference over output volatility and inflation volatility?[4] Using a small macro model calibrated to UK data, Bean (1998) plots an efficient policy frontier for the UK (a Taylor curve) and finds it to be close to rectangular. Therefore, a wide range of relative weights on output volatility vis à vis inflation volatility generates a very similar point on the policy frontier.[5] As long as the preferences of the Government are not extreme (not putting too much relative weight on either output volatility or inflation volatility) the MPC should be able to choose a policy that puts it close to the Government's output volatility–inflation volatility choice on the efficient policy frontier.

The role of the Treasury representative on the MPC

In a system where fiscal and monetary objectives are set by the Chancellor, it is important that the MPC is kept well informed about the Chancellor's thinking on how fiscal policy will operate. The two fiscal rules provide a good medium-term guide but the MPC's focus on the evolution of the economy over the two years ahead gives it a particular interest in how fiscal measures will influence the economy over this period.

At the monthly MPC meetings, it is the job of the Treasury representative, who has a voice but no vote, to ensure that the MPC is aware of any information about Government policy and fiscal developments that might be relevant for hitting the inflation target. In practice this is mostly done at official level between the Bank and the Treasury to ensure the pre-MPC briefings are accurate and up to date. Before each Budget and Pre-Budget Report a Treasury team led by the Treasury representative briefs the MPC on the latest economic forecast and fiscal projections.[6] The purpose of this exercise is to allow the MPC to come to a better judgement about the net contribution to demand that will result from the Government's fiscal decisions.

In general the MPC has decided to use the Government's projections for nominal spending in its own Inflation Report forecasts. It will also have generated revenue forecasts based on effective tax rates derived from the Government's revenue projections. At each Budget a judgement is made about the likely spending outturn for that particular year which may show a deviation from the allocation due to over- or underspends.

This is a fairly complex process and in a year where there is a spending review additional judgements have to be made. The Treasury representative's job, with the support of other Treasury officials, is to explain all this to the MPC. The MPC takes account of the latest fiscal measures when making its decisions and the discussion on these issues is recorded in the minutes. In this way the independent monetary authority contributes to better fiscal policy as well as improving monetary policy.

The Treasury representative also explains how the Government intends to respond to shocks (for example, the outbreak of Foot and Mouth disease) which have implications for the fiscal position. It is also important to realise that the MPC makes its forecasts on the basis of the most up-to-date fiscal projections. For instance, it will have incorporated the latest Budget projections as it sees fit in its latest Inflation Report. These projections are then updated to reflect subsequent outturn data for the public finances. Hence when it comes to the next PBR the 'news' for the MPC will be the difference between the Treasury's latest projections and those made by the MPC in its latest Inflation Report.

This is why the Treasury puts a lot of emphasis on comparing the projected fiscal balances with those contained in its most recent publications. Budget projections are compared with those from the last PBR and the last Budget. These give an estimate of the 'news' to the MPC in the fiscal announcements, subject of course to the amount of the 'automatic' updates undertaken by the MPC. For these reasons it is important that the Treasury has a representative, not just an observer, on the MPC. The clear principle is 'a voice but no vote'. Should the Government decide to change the inflation target the Treasury representative would be able to explain to the MPC the basis for the decision.

The representative also reports back to the Chancellor on how well the Committee is functioning, keeping him informed about the key issues and problems facing the UK economy as seen by the MPC. The Bank itself has taken an excellent approach to evaluation by asking Don Kohn, the Director of Monetary Affairs at the Board of Governors, US Federal Reserve System, to report on how well the MPC was working. His thorough report (Kohn 2000) to the non-executive directors of the Bank was published in October 2000 and has been discussed by the Treasury Select Committee.

The policy mix

How monetary and fiscal policy is coordinated is likely to have an impact on the policy mix. Simple textbook economics implies that tighter fiscal policy, by reducing domestic demand, means that a given inflation target can be achieved with lower interest rates. However, if there is a credible and permanent fiscal tightening through higher taxes then rational agents may impute that the net present value of future taxes will be lower and will therefore reduce their own private savings today. Depending on the strength of this effect, aggregate demand may not fall much and theoretically could even increase following a credible fiscal tightening.

There may also be wealth effects if long-term interest rates fall as people become more confident about the sustainability of the long-term fiscal position. The fall in long rates boosts wealth, which in turn boosts demand. The fiscal tightenings in Ireland and Denmark in the 1980s are often cited as examples of this effect. These uncertainties over the relationship between fiscal policy and aggregate demand suggest that the impact on the exchange rate of a fiscal tightening may be ambiguous and difficult to predict.[7]

In the UK over the last four years there has been a fiscal tightening in structural terms of 4.5 per cent of GDP. However, over this period, sterling's nominal exchange rate against the euro has risen by 16 per cent while the structural fiscal tightening in the UK has exceeded that in the euro-area by 3 percentage points on OECD estimates.

What is important for coordination is to have clarity of fiscal plans so that the MPC's task of hitting the Government's inflation target is made easier. The UK fiscal plans have been set by the Government in a medium-term framework and the MPC is aware of the need to incorporate these plans as part of the picture when assessing the future path of interest rates needed to meet the inflation target. Of course in any year, public spending may not turn out at the planned level and revenues may not turn out as expected. But the MPC has a well informed view about how the Government will react to such shocks. Successive Budgets have also established the practice of trying to move back towards the path laid out in the previous Budget. All of this means that the Government's fiscal reaction function is better known to the MPC, just as the MPC's reaction function is well known to the Government.

Conclusion

The new UK macroeconomic framework has been developed on the principles of credibility, flexibility and democratic legitimacy. Some have argued that there is a price to be paid for having an independent central bank in terms of less coordination between the monetary and fiscal authorities. This chapter has shown how specific UK institutional arrangements have been set up to avoid these possible costs and conflicts. The main conclusion is that the establishment of this kind of independent central bank based on these three principles improves not only monetary policy, but also fiscal policy and the coordination of the two. Without doubt the current arrangements will have to evolve over time. Nevertheless, as will be seen in Chapter 19, a preliminary assessment suggests that the new institutions are a clear improvement on previous policy regimes. The next few years will prove a decisive test.

7
Reforms to Financial Regulation

This chapter sets out the economic rationale for the regulation of financial services, the current scope of financial regulation, how that scope developed, and why it was necessary to bring it all within the ambit of a single regulator – the Financial Services Authority. The chapter also discusses briefly other new elements in the Government's policy towards financial regulation, including the benchmarking of financial services and stakeholder pensions. The chapter reflects the situation as of July 2001.

Introduction

In May 1997, the Government announced that the main regulators of financial services would be consolidated into a single statutory body. This announcement has given rise to one of the longest running and most complex pieces of legislation to be overseen by this government and led to a major change in the regulatory environment faced by the UK financial services sector – which is responsible for an estimated 6 per cent of UK GDP and employs over a million people (British Invisibles 2000). The Financial Services and Markets Act (FSMA) completed its passage into legislation in June 2000. The FSMA will come into force on 1 December 2001.

The consolidation of nine bodies into one has been only one part of the Government's activity in the field of financial regulation. Another major set of financial products – mortgages – is being brought within the ambit of financial regulation. And the traditional forms of regulation have been augmented by the introduction of government-set benchmark standards (for Individual Savings Accounts and mortgages) and a whole new product, or family of products, with tightly defined product criteria (stakeholder pensions).

This chapter is more limited in its ambitions. It begins by setting out an economic rationale for regulation of financial services. It then goes on to summarise the current scope of financial regulation before briefly describing how that scope developed and why and how it was seen as necessary to bring it all within a single regulator – the Financial Services Authority (FSA). The chapter concludes with a few words about the other new elements in the Government's policy towards financial regulation, in the form of a brief section on benchmarking of financial services and on stakeholder pensions.

The economic rationale for financial regulation

Before describing the details of regulation it is important to understand why an entire regulatory framework should have been built up around financial services: what is the rationale for regulation?[1]

Unlike the privatised utilities, monopoly power is not a rationale for regulation in the financial services industry. For banking regulation, externalities are a central issue, while moral hazard is created by some of the regulatory interventions themselves.

Asymmetric information

Ensuring widespread availability of information to consumers is one of the fundamental reasons for having a regime of financial regulation. This is important in a number of areas.

Retail financial products can be extremely complex. Charging structures and levels can be very opaque, as can the other terms of the contract. It can be very hard for consumers to distinguish good value products from poor value products. In this situation a competitive equilibrium will not evolve because price competition cannot occur where prices and features are not clearly identified. Either the market will not develop at all or consumers will end up in a position of disadvantage leading to exploitation by producers. In retail financial services, for example, without regulation there really was no consistent way of comparing the prices of similar products – endowments, personal pensions, and so on. And, even with regulation and mandated disclosure, the vast array of products and pricing structures makes such comparisons difficult to understand.

In this type of world, where the effort required from consumers to distinguish good-value from poor-value products is so high, problems might be rectified by the emergence of a class of informed intermediaries who could advise consumers for a fee. But this solution does not emerge or work by itself. Consumers may find it difficult to distinguish between good and bad intermediaries, while the interests of intermediaries may not be properly aligned with those of their customers. If you do not understand the market, how can you know that your adviser has directed you towards the best product, especially when most financial products take years or even decades before they come to fruition?

These problems lead directly to some of the features of current regulation described below – features which require disclosure of costs and charges and which influence the behaviour of intermediaries. Asymmetric information is generally assumed to be less of a problem where professionals or firms are dealing with one another rather than with an ill-informed general public. Reflecting this, there is a different regime for such interprofessional dealings.

Information problems also matter in banking and insurance. In particular, consumers will not know which firms are financially sound – and it would be inefficient for them to spend much time determining this. Yet the market for deposit taking or insurance requires consumers to have confidence that the long-term contracts entered into will be honoured. In part this can be overcome through publicly sponsored insurance and compensation schemes, and through detailed prudential regulation of the businesses themselves.

Externalities and systemic risk

The classic rationale for banking regulation is systemic risk. Banks play a pivotal role in the payments system. The failure of one bank can lead to the failure of other, sound, banks as a result of loss of confidence and runs on deposits. Potentially, the cost of any one bank's failure is much greater than the cost to that bank's shareholders, for the failure can impact not only on other banks but also, through a general loss of liquidity, on the economy more generally. Since the total costs of failure are much higher than the costs to the individual bank, its own managers and shareholders will not commit the socially optimal level of resources to ensuring its success. In short, the failure of a significant bank can create major wide-ranging problems so that there are substantial potential gains to be had from reducing the probability of failure. An indication of the scale of problem that can arise is that the costs to three Scandinavian governments of recapitalising their banking systems following bank failures in the late 1980s and early 1990s ranged from 4 per cent to 8 per cent of GDP. They took this action to avoid the potentially greater cost of losing substantial parts of their banking systems.

The information asymmetries already referred to can themselves lead to this type of systemic collapse. Individual consumers do not have the information to know which banks are safe and so they react in an individually rational, but collectively irrational, fashion in withdrawing deposits.

Moral hazard and deposit insurance

Deposit insurance can help to reduce the cost of systemic failure, but this in itself creates another problem – moral hazard. Individuals have even less need to inform themselves about the safety of the institutions, while the institutions themselves know that the consequences of failure for their customers are much reduced – and may behave accordingly, taking on more risk. The classic example of this is the US savings and loan industry in the 1980s.

The scope of financial regulation

The economic rationale for regulation is clear enough. This section describes briefly the scope of financial regulation in the UK.

Even before the FSMA was enacted, the FSA was in effect operating as a single financial services regulator. It had formally assumed the responsibility for banking supervision,[2] and in the other regulatory areas it had taken over the staff previously employed by the separate regulatory bodies. For the time being, the FSA supplies regulatory services back to the boards or commissions of those bodies, which retain their formal responsibility until the FSMA comes into force. The FSA has already moved all staff into a single building and has introduced a single management and organisational structure.

Regulated financial services firms can be broadly split into two categories. Those that carry on investment business are subject both to prudential regulation and conduct of business regulation. The rest are subject only to prudential regulation. The latter are mainly banks, building societies, friendly societies, credit unions and general insurance companies, although many such firms also carry on investment business and so are subject to conduct of business regulation as well.

The FSA supervises about 600 banks as a result of their deposit-taking activities. No one may accept deposits from the public, as part of a deposit-taking business, without authorisation from the FSA. In its role as banking supervisor the FSA is concerned with the safety and soundness of banks, 'with the aim of strengthening, but not ensuring, the protection of depositors'.[3] A bank has to meet a number of regulatory criteria: it has to satisfy the FSA that its business is conducted in a prudent manner with adequate capital, that it has adequate liquidity, that it has adequate systems and controls, that its directors, managers and controllers are fit and proper and that the business is carried on with integrity and skill. In the event of any threat to depositors the FSA can take away a bank's authorisation or can restrict its scope by requiring it to operate in a certain way or to limit its operations. The FSA supervises banks through information from statistical returns, through specially commissioned reports and through visits and formal interviews. The FSA explains that:

> supervisors must not and do not try to supplant a bank's management in judging the best commercial strategy for a bank to follow. But the supervisors have to be satisfied that the downside is properly covered and the risks of the bank's failure reduced.[4]

Note particularly that the purpose of regulation is not to reduce the probability of bank failure to zero. The costs, both in terms of resources and in terms of impact on behaviour, of eliminating risk entirely would be enormous. Thus the purpose of banking regulation is to reduce the risk of failure, just as one would derive from the underlying economic rationale.

Until the FSMA is implemented the FSA is in effect regulating about 70 building societies on behalf of the Building Societies Commission, 270 friendly societies on behalf of the Friendly Societies Commission and 650 credit unions on behalf of the Registry of Friendly Societies. Although the detail of the way they are supervised differs from that of bank supervision, the broad principles are similar, even though in these cases it is hard to argue that systemic issues are important. Here, the central issue is one of acting to increase the safety of deposits, because consumers do not have the information to judge financial soundness for themselves.

Similarly, the FSA is regulating the 850 insurance companies that remain the formal responsibility of the Treasury until the FSMA is implemented. The long-term nature and uncertainty of many of the companies' future liabilities mean that much of insurance company supervision is concerned with how the liabilities are valued and ensuring that the excess of assets over liabilities is sufficiently large to guard against future uncertainties.[5] Insurance companies doing life and pensions business are also regulated in their conduct of business, but that is the responsibility of the regulatory bodies concerned with investment business, and not of the Treasury.

This section now turns to firms that carry on investment business. Investments are defined to include shares, loan stock, warrants, options, futures, units in collective investment schemes and long-term insurance contracts – but not real property or other tangible items, even if they are used for investment purposes. Investment business includes advising on investments, managing investments, dealing or arranging deals in investments, or offering custody of investments. Any firm carrying on investment business must be authorised (or belong to one of a few categories of institution which are exempt).

Until the FSMA is implemented the formal responsibility for regulation of the 6000-odd investment businesses is conducted by three self-regulating organisations (SROs). Each of the SROs is overseen by the FSA and makes its own rules within the framework laid down by the Financial Services Act 1986. As in the other sectors of financial services, the FSA is already acting as regulator on behalf of the SROs. The three SROs are the Investment Management Regulatory Organisation (IMRO), which deals mainly with fund management firms; the Personal Investment Authority (PIA), which deals with providers of retail financial services (including life assurance companies and independent financial advisers), and the Securities and Futures Authority (SFA), which covers securities and derivatives firms. The activities currently exercised by the FSA on behalf of the SROs include:

- checking whether firms are fit and proper to conduct investment business
- monitoring the adequacy of firms' financial resources and their internal systems and controls
- overseeing firms' dealings with investors, to ensure, for example, that information provided to investors is clear and not misleading and that advice given is suitable
- making arrangements for handling investors' complaints
- dealing with those who have broken the rules; for example, by censuring or fining them, requiring them to compensate investors harmed by bad advice or, in the worst cases, removing their authorisation.

There is a special regime for members of certain professions (for example, solicitors or accountants) who carry on a limited amount of investment business in addition to their professional activities, with regulation for both activities conducted by their professional bodies. Around 15 000 firms are currently authorised in this way but, as explained later, this will change once the FSMA is implemented.

Firms may be authorised for investment business not only through membership of an SRO or a recognised professional body (RPB) but also by being an 'appointed representative' of an authorised firm. In such cases, the authorised firm is responsible for the actions of its appointed representative. This status was originally designed for self-employed life and pensions salesmen, but is also used, for example, by firms that tie themselves to a single life office. There are some 10 000 appointed representatives.

A feature of the current regulatory regime is 'polarisation'. Anyone advising on or selling packaged products (such as life and pensions policies and unit trusts) has either to represent a single corporate group or be an independent intermediary. In the former case the adviser can deal only in the products of that group; in the latter, he must scan the whole market in order to find the best product for the investor. The original purpose of polarisation was to help ensure that the status of any adviser or salesman was clear to the consumer. However, regulators have since introduced a range of measures to provide consumers with information on products and on the advisers through whom they deal. Because of this and because polarisation distorts competition, its future is currently under review.

The regulatory regime contains little in the way of explicit product regulation. The main exception is for collective investment schemes (for example, unit trusts), where the FSA is responsible for making detailed rules and for authorising schemes in accordance with those rules. New government forays in the direction of product regulation are considered in the final part of this chapter.

Compensation schemes providing payments to private investors who lose money through the failure of a regulated firm are integral to regulation and provide important back-up to the rest of the regime. Currently each sector of the financial services industry has its own separate compensation scheme. The costs of each scheme are met by levies on firms in the relevant sector. There are limits on the amounts that can be paid to each investor and these limits vary from scheme to scheme. Even if the investor's loss is less than the limit of the relevant scheme he may have to bear a proportion of the loss, the proportion varying from scheme to scheme. The purpose of this co-insurance is to guard against the moral hazard that can be a consequence of compensation arrangements.

Investment exchanges are required to be recognised and supervised by the FSA. A recognised investment exchange (RIE) is responsible, among other things, for ensuring that business on the exchange is conducted 'in an orderly manner and so as to afford proper protection to investors'.[6] There are seven UK RIEs, including the London Stock Exchange (LSE) and the London International Financial Futures and Options Exchange (better known as LIFFE). The FSA also recognises and supervises the clearing houses which organise the settlement of transactions on RIEs.

Finally, one cannot leave even the briefest of descriptions of the scope of financial regulation without mentioning one body that will not be brought under the FSA umbrella – the Occupational Pensions Regulatory Authority (OPRA). Occupational pensions are trust-based arrangements that are put in place by employers for the benefit of employees. About half of employees are members of an occupational pension scheme. OPRA started work in 1997 and is responsible for seeing that trustees and employers do not act in ways that could put at risk the security of the schemes and the benefits for members. The schemes themselves are subject to minimum funding requirements (overseen by each scheme's actuary).

History and reasons for change

That is the current scope of regulation. But how did financial services get to where it was in 1997? In the early 1980s the UK financial services industry was very different from what it is today and there was much less regulation. Although starting to change, the industry was much more compartmentalised than today. Historically, banks just provided banking services, insurers just provided insurance, and so on. As a result, the regulatory regime had evolved in a piecemeal fashion, with no consistency between the requirements for different sectors. Insurance companies had been subject to statutory prudential regulation for over a hundred years, whereas statutory prudential regulation of banks dated only from the Banking Act 1979, even though the Bank of England had wielded considerable informal supervisory power for many years. Many other sectors of the financial services industry had no prudential requirements, formal or otherwise. In the area of securities and investments, regulation was mainly through the Prevention of Fraud (Investments) Act 1958, whose name reflected its limited aims and whose scope was correspondingly limited. There was very little regulation of conduct of business and, in general, the lay investor was given little useful information. The only significant area of product regulation was of unit trusts and had originally been introduced in the 1930s in response to particular problems.

A trigger for change was the 1981 failure of investment management firm Norton Warburg, which resulted in the loss of millions of pounds of investors' money. The Government appointed Professor L.C.B. Gower, an expert in company law, to review the protection needed for investors in securities and the controls needed for investment managers, investment consultants and dealers in securities. Gower was scathing about the then regime. He summarised its perceived defects as:

> complication, uncertainty, irrationality, failure to treat like alike, inflexibility, excessive control in some areas and too little (or none) in others, the creation of an elite and a fringe, lax enforcement, delays, over-concentration on honesty rather than competence, undue diversity of regulations, and failure to achieve a proper balance between Governmental regulation and self-regulation. (Gower 1982, p. 137)

Although Gower's remit was fairly narrow, his recommendations were wider, also covering life and pensions policies that were used as investment vehicles and everyone who sold or advised on such investments. He recommended not a fully statutory regime but one in which firms would be regulated by self-regulatory agencies. The self-regulatory agencies would make their own rules within a statutory framework and would be subject to statutory oversight. Gower felt that self-regulatory agencies would be much more flexible and responsive to change than statutory bodies. He recommended also that there should be differential levels of regulation for wholesale and retail investment business. His overall view was that any extension to financial services regulation

> should not be greater than is needed adequately to protect investors and this, emphatically, does *not* mean that it should seek to achieve the impossible task of protecting fools from their own folly. All it should do is to try to prevent people being made fools of. (Gower 1984, p. 6)

Gower's recommendations formed the basis of the current system, which was implemented by the Financial Services Act and which came into being in 1988. Initially there were five SROs overseen by the Securities and Investments Board (SIB), but some of the five later merged to produce the three mentioned above (PIA, IMRO and SFA). The SIB was initially overseen by the Department of Trade and Industry but this responsibility subsequently moved to the Treasury. The system set up by the Financial Services Act took a while to settle down but it undoubtedly had many successes: it weeded out many of the bad apples and bad practices; it introduced requirements on training and competence; through these and other measures it improved the general quality of advice; polarisation helped to focus attention on the merits of genuinely independent advice; disclosure requirements acted as an incentive for firms to reduce their charges and gave potential investors understandable information about what they are buying; investors benefited from the various compensation schemes and complaints mechanisms; the degree of practitioner involvement in the regulatory regime helped its flexibility; and the differential levels of regulation for wholesale and retail business proved justified.

Nevertheless, a number of deficiencies in the regime became clear. The regime was frequently criticised for being too legalistic and bureaucratic, despite efforts by regulators to improve their approach. The division between the SIB and the SROs (and RPBs) came to be seen as inefficient, confusing for investors and lacking accountability and a clear allocation of responsibilities. Part of the inefficiency arose because distinctions between different types of financial institution had become increasingly blurred. An increasing number of firms were providing a wide range of financial services, whereas previously they would have concentrated on just one. As a result, many firms were being regulated by a variety of different bodies, thereby increasing the cost and reducing the effectiveness of regulation. An illustration of this is that before the creation of the FSA over 800 financial services firms had more than one regulator and at least another 1000 firms were members of groups that were subject to more than one regulator. Difficulties arose when issues cut across the boundaries of different regulatory bodies and some problems therefore took too long to resolve. There were also accusations that some of the regulatory bodies paid too much attention to the views of their member firms and not enough to investors. Despite the improvements brought about by the regime, there were instances of extensive mis-selling, most notably of personal pensions – although this does date from the earlier years of the regime. There were also some high-profile failed prosecutions.

The regime established by the Financial Services Act accounted for only part of the statutory underpinning of financial regulation in the

UK. There were separate Acts governing insurance, banking, building societies, friendly societies, and credit unions. There was little consistency between these six Acts.

When the present government came to power in May 1997 one of its first acts was to announce that it would devise an improved and simplified system. The draft Bill giving effect to the Government's ideas was published in July 1998, by which stage the SIB had already been renamed as the FSA and had taken over responsibility for bank supervision from the Bank of England. As in the system established by the Financial Services Act, the FSMA's general approach is to give the FSA a series of enabling powers, so that it can act as it considers appropriate within that framework, for example by making rules.

A single regulator

The most important change to the regulatory system was the merger of nine regulatory bodies into one statutory body. When announcing the intention to create a single regulatory body, the Chancellor identified a number of advantages. He believed that having a single regulator would deliver more effective and more efficient supervision, thereby reducing compliance costs, giving both firms and customers better value for money and hence improving the competitiveness of UK financial services. It would also increase the confidence of both large and small investors in the regulatory regime and would reduce confusion amongst private investors. Finally, as the financial services industry increasingly cuts across geographical boundaries, the UK financial services industry needed a regulator that could deliver the most effective supervision in the world.

The main driver behind having a single regulator is the blurring of financial boundaries, mentioned above. This blurring of boundaries is partly due to mergers and acquisitions between firms in different financial sectors, partly to existing financial services firms moving into new areas, and partly to new entrants to financial services who have chosen to offer a wide range of financial products.[7] However, the desirability of having regulatory oversight of the whole of a financial conglomerate does not automatically imply a need for a single regulator. An alternative would be for each 'specialist' regulatory body to be responsible for its own aspects of the conglomerate's activities and for one of those bodies to act as 'lead' regulator. The lead regulator would coordinate the conglomerate's regulation and would take an overall view on matters such as capital adequacy, the quality of senior management and the high-level systems and controls. This is in fact the system that UK regulators have used until now. Such a system is certainly workable but the expectation is that a single regulator will be more efficient.

In reporting on the Government's proposals the International Monetary Fund (IMF) has commented that the 'creation of a unified supervisory authority [is] an appropriate response to the uneven quality of supervision and consumer protection across various financial sectors and to the increasing importance of large financial institutions operating across traditional lines of business' (IMF 1999a).

Objectives

Apart from the creation of the single regulator, one of the most important changes is that the FSMA sets the FSA explicit statutory objectives and requires it to report annually on its achievements against them. There are four objectives, plus seven principles to which the FSA must have regard. With some simplification of their detailed wording, the objectives are:

- *Market confidence*: to maintain confidence in the UK financial system.
- *Public awareness*: to promote public understanding of UK financial services, including promoting awareness of the benefits and risks of different kinds of investment and providing appropriate information and advice.
- *Protection of consumers*: to secure appropriate protection for consumers, having regard to the differing degrees of risk involved in different kinds of transaction, the differing degrees of experience and expertise of different types of consumer, the needs of consumers for advice and accurate information and the general principle that consumers should take responsibility for their decisions.
- *Reduction of financial crime*: to reduce the extent to which regulated businesses can be used for financial crime, with particular regard to the desirability of regulated persons being aware of the risk, taking appropriate measures and devoting adequate resources to preventing, detecting and monitoring financial crime.

These explicit objectives are very broadly drawn, but are at the centre of FSA regulation. Note the wording of the consumer protection objective. It is not absolute, it depends on consumers' characteristics and it explicitly lays down the principle that consumers must take at least some responsibility for their own decisions. This is backed up by an entirely new public awareness objective that is trying to attack at its root the problem of asymmetric information described earlier.

When carrying out its duties the FSA will be required to have regard to the following (again simplifying the detailed wording):

- the need to use its resources in the most efficient and economic way
- the responsibilities of those who manage the affairs of authorised firms
- the principle that any burdens or restrictions imposed by the FSA should be proportionate to the expected resulting benefits
- the desirability of facilitating innovation
- the international character of financial services and the desirability of maintaining the UK's competitive position
- the need to minimise the adverse effects on competition
- the desirability of facilitating competition between those who are subject to FSA regulation.

The Bill originally had just a single competition requirement, namely that the FSA should have regard to the principle of not impeding or distorting competition unnecessarily. In his interim report on the UK banking sector (Cruickshank 1999), Don Cruickshank recommended that the FSA should instead be given an explicit objective to minimise the anti-competitive effects of its actions. Such a change would have obliged the FSA to place much greater emphasis on competition. The FSA argued that an explicit objective to promote competition would often run counter to its other four objectives and that it would be difficult for the FSA to balance conflicting objectives. For example, in relation to the soundness of banks, a conflict could arise between promoting market confidence and promoting competition. On the other hand, as we have seen, many of the rationales for financial regulation stem from market failures that stifle genuine competition and in some areas promoting consumer protection and promoting competition can be seen as two sides of the same coin. In response to Cruickshank's recommendation, the Government decided to strengthen the competition requirements but not to introduce an explicit competition objective. The responsibility for deciding whether a particular rule or practice is anti-competitive will lie with the Competition Commission, which can also decide that the rules or practices are nevertheless justified.

Other changes in the Financial Services and Markets Act

Much of the FSMA is concerned with establishing the single regulator with a single set of powers, bringing together and harmonising the provisions of the various predecessor Acts for different sectors of the financial services industry. The Government made it clear that it wanted to keep the good features of the existing regime and would not make major changes unless there were good reasons for doing so. However, the FSMA contains certain other significant changes to the regime, some of which are set out briefly below.

- *Flexible rule-making powers, subject to consultation and cost-benefit analysis.* The FSMA gives the FSA wide and flexible powers to make rules and issue guidance, thereby enabling it to respond to market developments. The FSA will continue to be able to tailor its approach to different types of business, recognising for example the difference between wholesale markets and business done by members of the public. A corollary of these wide rule-making powers is an obligation to consult. As part of each consultation the FSA will typically have to publish an analysis of the costs and benefits of the proposals. The cost-benefit analyses will focus on the economic costs and benefits of the proposals. The FSA would usually not go ahead unless the latter outweighed the former. However, there might sometimes be factors, such as equity or the furtherance of an important social objective, which would justify a course of action where the analysed benefits were outweighed by the costs. In each consultation the FSA will also have to state why the proposals are compatible with its objectives and 'have regard to' principles. These explicit requirements, particularly on cost-benefit analysis, are a new feature of the regulatory scene.
- *Powers to change the scope of regulation.* To improve the regime's ability to respond to changing circumstances, the FSMA empowers the Treasury to change, through secondary legislation, the scope of what is regulated. The Treasury is already making use of this power. It announced in January 2000 that it would introduce a statutory instrument to give the FSA responsibility for regulating most residential mortgages. All mortgage lenders will have to be authorised by the FSA and to be specifically permitted to provide mortgage loans. The FSA will regulate mortgage advertising and all mortgage lending will have to include clear disclosure of the main features of the loan.

- *Civil fines for market abuse.* Abuse of financial markets can take forms such as misuse of inside information, giving misleading impressions about the demand for a particular investment, or attempts to manipulate prices. Such abuse distorts the efficient operation of the markets, causes losses to market participants and, in the longer term, can lead to a reduction in investment and higher transaction costs, thereby damaging the economy as a whole by increasing the cost of raising capital. In order to guard against this, the FSA will be able to impose unlimited civil fines and order offenders to make restitution and to give up any profit arising from the abuse – even if the offenders are not regulated by the FSA. The civil fines will complement, not replace, the existing criminal sanctions. The first draft of this part of the FSMA attracted some criticism that its provisions on market abuse ran counter to the European Convention on Human Rights. The Government made changes to its original proposals in order to deal with these concerns.

- *Independent appeals tribunal.* Firms will be able to refer FSA decisions to a tribunal which will be part of the Lord Chancellor's Department and wholly independent of the FSA. The tribunal will be able to substitute its own ruling for the original decision, rather than just refer the case back.

- *Single ombudsman and compensation schemes.* Historically there has been a multiplicity of separate ombudsman schemes and compensation schemes in the financial services industry. Some of the ombudsman schemes are not even compulsory for firms in the relevant sector. The FSMA replaces the existing schemes by a single ombudsman scheme and a single compensation scheme, each of which will be compulsory for all regulated firms. This will reduce the scope for investor confusion about the roles and responsibilities of different schemes.

- *Professional firms.* Responsibility for regulating the investment business of professional firms will move from the RPBs to the FSA. However, the FSA will only regulate professional firms who provide so-called 'mainstream' investment services and not those whose only investment business is incidental to their professional business. As a result, it is estimated that only around 2000 professional firms will be subject to FSA regulation.

- *Regulation of employees and controllers.* The regulatory framework focuses primarily on firms (and sole traders). However, regulators also need to have some direct influence over individuals with positions of responsibility in the firms. SROs' rules extend regulation to such employees. The FSMA gives the FSA similar powers in relation to all types of firm. It also harmonises the existing provisions regarding controllers of firms, such as major shareholders and shadow directors.

- *Listing authority*. The LSE has traditionally been responsible for setting the requirements which have to be met by issuers of securities on the UK primary markets and for policing compliance with them. However, when the LSE decided to demutualise, it was considered inappropriate for the LSE to continue to be the listing authority. The FSMA therefore makes the FSA the listing authority. In fact the transfer of responsibility took place in May 2000, ahead of the FSMA's enactment. The FSMA also enhances the listing authority's ability to enforce the listing rules by giving it the power to fine companies and their directors for breaches of them.

- *Other changes*. Other areas of change in the FSMA include: giving the FSA extensive intervention and authorisation powers over the Lloyd's insurance market; introduction of a single cohesive approach to financial promotion, partly prompted by difficulties in applying the present regime to the promotion of financial products via the internet; extending to all sectors of financial services the arrangements for Treasury scrutiny of competition issues following a report by the Director General of Fair Trading; additional powers for the FSA in relation to insolvency and winding up of companies; and formalising the arrangements for whistle-blowing by auditors and actuaries.

Many of the details of the new regime are still taking shape. In addition one can expect developments in the coming years, particularly as technological developments render observation and analysis of actual transactions much easier, and as a more comprehensive and consistent 'risk based' approach to supervision is introduced. Indeed, precisely these types of innovation are made much more likely by the existence of a single relatively well resourced regulatory body. Exactly the extent to which the shift to a single statutory regulator will affect the effectiveness and efficiency of the regime remains to be seen, but the reasons for making the move look well enough founded to suggest that a positive outcome is likely.

Product standards

The Government has also been active in promoting and changing financial regulation in ways other than through the creation of the FSA. In contrast to the relatively hands-off approach of previous administrations it has, in three areas especially, been directly involved in setting product standards. In addition the Chancellor, in his 1999 Budget Speech, specifically gave the FSA the task of looking into the construction and publication of comparative information or 'league tables' on the features of retail financial products.

Because this is a new direction for regulation, and because it may well form a pattern on which future governments build, in this section we look in a little more detail at the setting of product standards for Individual Savings Accounts, mortgages and stakeholder pensions.

CAT standards

From April 1999 Personal Equity Plans (PEPs) and Tax Exempt Special Savings Accounts (TESSAs) were replaced by a new tax-advantaged savings scheme, the Individual Savings Account (ISA), which allows holdings of cash and of equities within the same account. In itself this was but a small development. But the launch of the ISA was accompanied by a very significant regulatory development – the CAT standard. Products that meet a government-determined set of criteria on charges, access and terms can advertise themselves as meeting the CAT standard. For example, the CAT standards for a stocks and shares ISA include that total charges must be no more than 1 per cent of asset value each year, that the minimum investment must be no more than £500 as a lump sum or £50 per month and that units and shares must be single priced. Product providers are, however, free to market ISAs which do not meet the CAT standards. Indeed, at the time of writing, only a minority of ISAs are advertised as meeting the CAT standards.

The purpose of CAT standards is perhaps best expressed in the Treasury's consultation document of May 1998:

> Benchmarked ISAs should always offer savers a reasonable deal. The deal may not be the very best on the market, but savers using products which meet – or better – the standard should not get ripped off. (HM Treasury 1998g)

The same document stresses that the CAT products are likely to be particularly suitable for 'inexperienced savers' and 'people new to saving, who may not have a great deal to put away'.

In January 2000 the Government announced its intention to extend the CAT concept to mortgages. The CAT standards were published in April 2000 and could be used by lenders straight away. Amongst other requirements, CAT standard mortgages must have no arrangement or redemption fees, no separate charge for mortgage indemnity guarantee insurance and an interest rate that is no more than 2 per cent above the Bank of England base rate and that responds to falls in base rate with a lag of no more than a month. As with CAT ISAs, lenders are free to market mortgages that do not meet the CAT standards.

Stakeholder Pensions

Stakeholder pensions (SHPs) clearly form one of the central elements of the Government's pension policy. They are intended to be a form of money-purchase pension scheme, available to all. In that sense, in their underlying structure, they are not dramatically different from personal pensions (PPs) which are just individual money purchase schemes and which have, of course, been available since 1988.[8]

The actual difference between PPs and SHPs is twofold. SHPs are effectively group schemes, run either by a board of trustees or by an FSA-authorised scheme manager. In that sense they look more like occupational money-purchase schemes. Second, and more importantly, they have to meet strict criteria regarding charges, access and terms. The only allowable charge is an annual one of no more than 1 per cent of the fund under management. This has to cover all costs associated with recruiting members, including the provision of information and explanatory material, and all the continuing costs of running the scheme. Schemes can, however, charge an extra fee for the provision of individual financial advice. Schemes have to accept any contribution of at least £20 at these charges.[9]

Stakeholder pensions are explicitly aimed at individuals earning £9000 a year and above. In designing these schemes it was the view of the government that the available personal pensions were not offering good value, especially to those with low to middle earnings, or broadly £9000 to £18 000 a year.[10] The level and structure of charges payable on most PPs was one reason for this concern. The other was the complexity of the system. In the Green Paper (DSS 1998) the observation was made that:

> Individuals can find personal pensions difficult to understand and nearly impossible to compare. Many are put off by the prospect of seeking financial advice; those who do can find it difficult to get impartial and cost effective advice.

This issue of complexity and other problems faced by consumers is stressed repeatedly in the Green Paper, recognising explicitly the very problems of the market failure driven by asymmetric information discussed earlier. For example, the paper also says:

> most personal pensions are difficult products for people to understand. People find it hard to know whether a pension offers them a good deal and are unable to make easy comparisons ... individuals have limited power in the pension market. Personal pensions are complex. Individual consumers have no real power to negotiate with pension providers. Shopping around effectively is difficult. When they join, they have no influence on the terms of their contract and no power to press for improvements after they have joined. (DSS 1998, p. 51)

As with CAT standard ISAs, stakeholder pensions should provide consumers with a product that is a reasonable deal – not necessarily the best on the market but one which, because it meets the standards set by government, is intended to be good enough for most of the target audience.

Will product standards solve consumers' problems?

The Government's proposals for stakeholder benchmarks and CAT standards for ISAs and mortgages are drawn together by two basic concerns: to make saving easier and more available for lower income individuals, and to give them confidence in receiving at least a reasonable product standard without going through the full advice process. This suggests the Government felt that even the new regulatory regime might not achieve this by itself. The specific problems identified were:

- lack of consumer understanding; difficulty in shopping around, and so on
- ineffective competition; product terms that caused detriment to many of those taking out the products
- difficulty in identifying a good or at least a reasonable deal.

These are very much the same problems that were discussed earlier and which form the basic economic rationale for regulation. This leads to a number of questions about the role of these government imposed standards relative to the conduct of business and other process regulation of the FSA.

The concerns expressed are founded in reality. Product charges are often higher than would be readily affordable by many lower income consumers, the structure of those charges penalises people who, for example, stop contributing to a personal pension or an endowment policy in the early years of the contract and a high proportion of people do have poor persistency in these products. Consumers express lack of confidence in choosing products and it is the large portion of the population on low or fluctuating incomes who have most difficulty. There are two questions: Why does this apparently sub-optimal outcome persist in the face of the raft of regulation currently in place? And can the situation be improved by the government proposals?

One simple answer to the first question is that much of the current regulatory approach is based on regulating the process of giving individual advice. Providing advice on a one-to-one basis is not likely to be cheap – it requires that a considerable amount of time be devoted to each sale by a reasonably well remunerated professional. The costs of providing that advice are unlikely to be any less for a low income consumer with low potential savings than for someone willing and able to save more. Proportionally, therefore, the costs involved in saving will be relatively high for low earners. This need not be seen as a failure of current regulatory practice; it is just an inevitable aspect of a regime based on regulating the process of sale and advice.

Nevertheless, in one sense this problem is partly alleviated by the usual form of remuneration – commission. Commission is usually a percentage of the amount invested, regardless of the size of the amount. Thus in pounds and pence the use of commission rather than fees benefits those investing small amounts. However, the use of commission does create obvious incentive problems and it also means that those who do buy a policy end up in effect paying for the advice given to those who do not buy.

Second, it is very hard indeed for people, or their advisers, to have any realistic idea of how long they are likely to be able to contribute to a pension or other long-term savings product. This is a particular problem with pensions because of the complexity of the environment within which they operate. So with front-loaded costs – a feature of many products – people will suffer detriment if they do not contribute for the full term.

Third, while the current disclosure regime has some beneficial effect, there almost certainly remains a lack of clear understanding among consumers about the costs involved with the product they are purchasing and in particular about the costs of early stopping of contributions.

The current regime is not set up to deal with any of this directly. One should also stress that many of the problems relating to personal pensions arise directly from the complexity of the environment within which they operate, rather than from any features of the products or the regulatory regime that one could reasonably blame.

But the question remains as to whether such new tools can work. There is evidence that significant problems remain in the savings markets and reasons for believing that the current approach might need to be augmented. But can CAT standards and standards for stakeholder pensions work to address the problems identified?

It is impossible to give definitive answers at this stage. One can, however, point to the possible advantages and problems. Especially for CAT standards in isolation the real problem is one of consumer information and understanding. The products are available but if people do not understand what they are and why they are there then they will have little impact. This is particularly likely to be a problem where products are sold through advisers and where the CAT standard does not leave enough room to pay the adviser commission – so effectively ensuring that such products are unlikely to be promoted by advisers. There is also the risk that the uninformed consumer may interpret the standard as a guarantee of future performance.

This problem is likely to be less severe for stakeholder pensions because they will be branded as an entirely new product specifically intended to be made available through employers and not through the traditional personal advice based route. They are also specifically designed, through their features and especially through the structure of their charges, to address many of the problems mentioned above. However, they are to be plunged into the complex maelstrom that is the current pension environment and people will still be left to make complex choices. The intended advantage of the stakeholder design is that if people make that particular choice then they ought not to go far wrong. Persuading people of that is going to be a difficult task, and it will be an especially hard task for government, and for the regulator, to determine how to go about this. Without the government or the regulator 'selling' the virtues of stakeholder pensions they may very well fail to take off. But judging the appropriate level of public commitment, especially given the embarrassments suffered following the launch of personal pensions, will be difficult.

Conclusions

The Government has launched a genuinely new regulatory regime for financial products. The bringing together of nine existing regulatory bodies into one has itself been a major task with a clear justification given the increasingly diverse nature of the activities of financial institutions. The opportunities for savings from bringing a single regime and a single regulator to bear on such large and diverse institutions are potentially substantial. There are also potential gains from economies of scale and opportunities for regulators of different types of firms to learn from one another.

But the changes have not been limited to the form of regulation. The powers of the FSA are different to those of its predecessor bodies, incorporating for example, a civil fines regime, a single ombudsman and compensation scheme and considerable flexibility over rule making. The scope of the regime will also be extended to cover professional firms and the Lloyd's insurance market. The Treasury will also maintain the ability to change the scope of regulation further without resorting to primary legislation. All of this, though, comes with extremely important new responsibilities to consult widely with the regulated industry and to publish consultation documents when rule changes are proposed. Importantly, the FSA also has to publish analyses of the costs and benefits of any proposed rule changes.

Finally, the Government has also added to the regulatory arsenal by introducing a degree of product regulation – voluntary in the case of CAT standards for ISAs and mortgages and compulsory in the case of stakeholder pensions. These standards will act as back up to the rest of the regulatory regime, helping government to pursue its wider agenda of increasing the amount of savings done by lower earners and leading to the creation of what might be regarded as 'safe haven' products.

8
An Overview of the New Fiscal Policy Framework

This chapter provides an overview of the new framework for fiscal policy, including the features of the Code for Fiscal Stability.

Introduction

Fiscal policy and the control and planning of the public finances more generally has undergone a period of rapid change. Whereas previously, the framework within which fiscal policy decisions were being made was often vague, decisions are now taken within a tightly defined framework, built around a set of commonsense principles of fiscal management. A diagrammatic representation of the new fiscal policy framework is set out in Figure 8.1.

The new framework operates on a number of different levels. At the highest level, the 1998 Finance Act provides legal underpinning for the Code for Fiscal Stability. The Act requires the Government to lay before Parliament a Code for Fiscal Stability; allows governments to issue an amended Code (but only with the approval of the House of Commons); and specifies the minimum provisions that the Code must contain.

The next level represents the Code for Fiscal Stability itself. The Code elaborates on the requirements of the Act, setting out, for example, the information which must be included in the published fiscal policy reports. However, the Code leaves some issues open, giving rise to a third level to the framework. Notably, for reasons explained later in the chapter, the choice of fiscal rules and objectives is left to the government of the day, though the rules and objectives chosen must be stated explicitly and be consistent with the set of key fiscal principles enshrined in the Act.

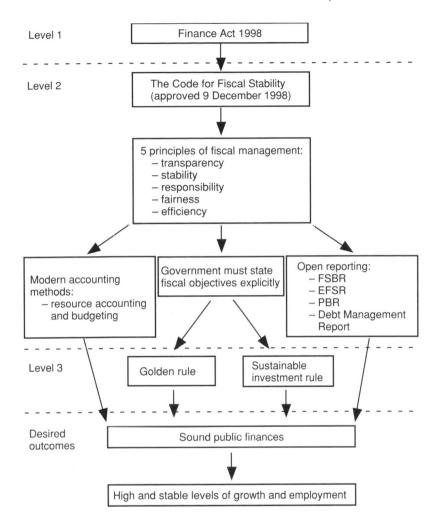

Figure 8.1   The new fiscal framework

The remainder of this chapter discusses the framework, the Code and its key components.

The objectives of fiscal policy

In 1997, the Government was faced with a large structural fiscal deficit, low net investment, rising public debt and falling public sector net worth. This situation had come about in part as a result of a lack of clear and transparent fiscal objectives, together with fiscal reporting that did not permit full and effective public and parliamentary scrutiny. The Government therefore took steps to implement a new framework for fiscal policy – one that complements the Government's significant reforms to the monetary policy framework.

The objectives for fiscal policy set by the Government under the new regime are based on an assessment of what fiscal policy can realistically achieve over both the short and longer term, and how this relates to the Government's wider policy goals and functions. The core functions of government include the provision of high quality public goods and services, and financial and other assistance to those most in need. In providing and financing these activities, the Government must ensure that its actions are consistent with the maintenance of economic stability, both in the short term and beyond. Stability promotes the long-term investment and planning necessary for sustaining high levels of growth and employment.

Given the central importance of economic stability, the key objectives of the Government's fiscal policy are:

- over the medium term, ensuring sound public finances and that spending and taxation impact fairly both within and across generations. In practice this requires that:

  - the Government meets its key tax and spending priorities while avoiding an unsustainable and damaging rise in the burden of public debt
  - those generations who benefit from public spending also meet, as far as possible, the costs of the services they consume

- over the short term, supporting monetary policy by:

  - allowing the automatic stabilisers to play their role in smoothing the path of the economy in the face of variations in demand
  - where prudent and sensible, providing further support to monetary policy through changes in the fiscal stance. For example, it is likely to be more appropriate to change the fiscal stance in this context if the economy is projected to be some way from trend.

The medium and shorter-term objectives are linked. For example, the scope for, and likely success of, using fiscal policy to support monetary policy during a downswing in the economic cycle is likely to depend on the soundness of the medium-term fiscal position. Loosening fiscal policy when the underlying structural fiscal position was poor could damage consumer and business confidence, thus having the opposite effect to that intended.

The framework for fiscal policy

The new framework for fiscal policy has been designed carefully to deliver the fiscal policy objectives discussed in the section above. Central to the framework are five principles of fiscal management:

- *transparency* in the setting of fiscal policy objectives, the implementation of fiscal policy and in the publication of the public accounts
- *stability* in the fiscal policy-making process and in the way fiscal policy impacts on the economy
- *responsibility* in the management of the public finances
- *fairness*, including between generations
- *efficiency* in the design and implementation of fiscal policy and in managing both sides of the public sector balance sheet.

These principles were enshrined in the Finance Act 1998 and in the Code for Fiscal Stability, approved by the House of Commons in December 1998. The Code explains how these principles are to be reflected in the formulation and implementation of fiscal policy in practice. For example, consistent with the principle of transparency, the Code sets out explicit requirements for the setting and explaining of fiscal policy objectives and for reporting developments in the public finances; for example, the requirement on the Government to publish the *Economic and Fiscal Strategy Report* and a list of the minimum information it must contain.

The Government has specified two key fiscal rules that accord with these principles. These are:

- *the golden rule*: over the economic cycle, the Government will borrow only to invest and not to fund current spending
- *the sustainable investment rule*: public sector net debt as a proportion of GDP will be held over the economic cycle at a stable and prudent level.

The fiscal rules – the rationale for which is discussed in more detail in Chapter 9 – provide benchmarks against which the performance of fiscal policy can be judged. The Government will meet the golden rule if on average over a complete economic cycle the current budget is in balance or surplus. The Government also believes that, other things being equal, a modest reduction in net public sector debt to below 40 per cent of GDP over the economic cycle is desirable.

Rationale for the Code

As explained in earlier chapters, the need for policy credibility and transparency, and the advantages, are well recognised, particularly in the context of monetary policy. Credibility and transparency are, however, just as important when it comes to setting fiscal policy. It is in this context that the Government saw a role for the Code for Fiscal Stability.

The Code sets out clearly the Government's commitment to a commonsense and honest approach to managing the public finances in the long-term interests of Britain. It is motivated by three key considerations:

- a stable economic environment is vital if growth and employment are to prosper
- the conduct of fiscal policy is a critical influence on economic stability
- the framework for fiscal policy inherited by the Government had failed to deliver a stable economic environment. Indeed, fiscal policy had been an important source of instability in the economy.

The Code for Fiscal Stability is designed to address past weaknesses in the fiscal policy framework. In particular, it strengthens the openness, transparency and accountability of fiscal policy, features that also characterise the framework for monetary policy following the introduction of the 1998 Bank of England Act. It improves the quality of information given to the public, the lack of which in the past was an important factor underlying policy mistakes.

The Code draws together and makes clear the framework within which fiscal policy will operate. It acts to demonstrate the Government's commitment to this framework, putting its reputation firmly and squarely on the line. In doing so, the Code represents an attempt to ensure that fiscal policy is time consistent, that is, that the optimal policy for the Government remains the same over time, so that short-term expediency does not take precedence over long-term planning.

The Code provides a valuable discipline on fiscal policy, and helped to rebuild trust in economic policy more generally. This approach is not unprecedented. Both New Zealand and Australia have used similar vehicles, backed by legislation, to enhance the credibility of their fiscal policies. And the IMF has published a Code of Good Practices on Fiscal Transparency (IMF 1998a) to provide a benchmark for worldwide comparison (see Box 8.1).

Box 8.1   The IMF Code of Good Practices on Fiscal Transparency

As discussed, the Code for Fiscal Stability underpins fiscal discipline and has helped to re-establish fiscal policy credibility in the UK. In a similar way, and on the recommendation of the Chancellor, the IMF has been at the forefront in improving fiscal practices at an international level by developing the Code of Good Practices on Fiscal Transparency. This code promotes the role of transparency in achieving economic stability and growth.

The IMF fiscal code covers four key areas of transparency:

- clarity of roles and responsibilities, reflecting the importance of establishing clear boundaries between the Government's fiscal, monetary and public corporation activities
- public availability of information, to promote the timely and comprehensive reporting of fiscal information
- open budget preparation, execution and reporting, to encourage the appropriate levels of coverage, accessibility and integrity of fiscal information with particular emphasis on harmonising with international accounting and statistical standards
- independent assurances of integrity, to enhance fiscal credibility through external audit, statistical independence and independent scrutiny.

For each of these areas it sets out a number of 'good practices' against which actual practices can be compared.

The UK lines up well against the IMF fiscal code and the Government has published a summary comparison which shows it meets all the criteria. In addition, the IMF has released an experimental transparency report noting that the UK 'has achieved a very high level of fiscal transparency' (IMF 1999c). The IMF assessment also draws particular attention to reforms in the UK's policy making process and the 'strong framework for fiscal management [that] is provided by the Code for Fiscal Stability'. This reflects the consistency between the principles of fiscal management – the first of which is transparency – and the IMF fiscal code.

An explanation of the Code

This section discusses the key provisions contained in the Code for Fiscal Stability. A summary of the key provisions is set out in Box 8.2.

Box 8.2   Key provisions of the Code for Fiscal Stability

Under the Code, the Government undertakes a number of commitments. It will:

- conduct fiscal and debt management policy in accordance with a set of specific principles
- state explicitly its fiscal policy objectives and operating rules, and justify any changes to them
- operate debt management policy to achieve a specific primary objective
- disclose, and quantify where possible, all decisions and circumstances which may have a material impact on the economic and fiscal outlook
- ensure that best-practice accounting methods are used to construct the public accounts
- publish a *Pre-Budget Report* to encourage debate on the proposals under consideration for the Budget
- publish a *Financial Statement and Budget Report* to discuss the key Budget decisions and the short-term economic and fiscal outlook
- publish an *Economic and Fiscal Strategy Report* outlining the Government's long-term goals, strategy for the future, and how it is progressing in meeting its fiscal policy objectives
- publish a specific range of information from its economic and fiscal projections, including estimates of the cyclically adjusted fiscal position
- invite the National Audit Office to audit changes in the key assumptions and conventions underpinning the fiscal projections
- produce a *Debt and Reserves Management Report* outlining the Government's debt management plans
- refer all reports issued under the Code to the House of Commons Treasury Select Committee
- ensure that the public have full access to the reports issued under the Code.

The principles of fiscal management

At the heart of the Code lie the five fiscal principles described earlier; that is, transparency, stability, responsibility, fairness and efficiency.

Transparent government is a fundamental part of a democracy. It ensures that Parliament and the wider public can scrutinise the

Government's economic and fiscal plans. It is likely to encourage governments to give more weight to the longer-term consequences of their decisions, leading to more sustainable fiscal policy. It also encourages people and businesses to plan for the long term, rather than basing decisions only on what makes sense in the short term, so that resources are allocated efficiently. Given these advantages, the Government believes that transparency should be the rule rather than the exception, and the Code has been drafted accordingly.

There are certain situations where complete transparency may have undesirable effects. For example, if the Government decided to sell an asset, it would not make sense to disclose in advance the sum it expected to receive for the asset. Disclosure could compromise negotiations, reducing the return to the taxpayer. Similarly, the Code should not intrude on legitimate privacy. Accordingly, the Code provides for less than full disclosure but only where this would be in the public interest. The situations where full disclosure is not to be required are set out in the Code.

The principle of stability reflects explicitly the Government's central economic objective of achieving high and stable levels of growth and employment. The principle means that governments should, so far as possible, operate policy with a reasonable degree of predictability and in a way that supports stability and long-term growth in the economy.

Responsible and prudent management of public assets, liabilities and fiscal risks is also fundamental to managing the public finances in the long-term interests of Britain. The principle of responsibility means that governments should plan and operate policy so as to ensure the longer-term sustainability and viability of public services, while avoiding either an ever-increasing tax burden or excessive levels of public debt.

The Government is committed to the principle of fairness, both between and within generations. When making fiscal and debt management policy decisions it is important that governments take into account the financial effect on future generations. It would be unfair to make future generations meet the cost of policies that primarily benefit the current generation. Similarly, the current generation should not be expected to pay unduly for policies that will only benefit future generations. Fairness within broad groups of the current generation is also important. The Code requires that fairness is taken into account when policy decisions are made.

Last, but not least, is the principle of efficiency. This principle means that governments should not waste resources themselves, nor should governments cause resources to be wasted elsewhere in the economy.

Productivity in the public sector clearly has a major influence on productivity in the economy as a whole. Value for money in use of scarce resources is of prime importance if Britain is to achieve its economic and social goals.

The setting of fiscal and debt management objectives

The principle of transparency demands that governments are open about their fiscal and debt management objectives and the rules that govern how policy will seek to achieve them. The Code requires governments to specify and explain their fiscal objectives and rules and that they are formulated and implemented in accordance with the principles of fiscal management. Any departures from these objectives and rules must also be fully explained and justified.

The fiscal rules described earlier – the golden rule and the sustainable investment rule – were first set out in the July 1997 *Financial Statement and Budget Report* and are discussed in detail in Chapter 9. An alternative approach would have been to embed the Government's two fiscal rules in the Code. However, this would be unduly restrictive. The ongoing process of strengthening the fiscal framework might, in time, require that the fiscal rules themselves are modified. For example, once conceptual and data problems are tackled, it is possible that balance sheet considerations might play a more substantial role in the fiscal framework. Moreover, it is for the elected Government of the day to choose and announce its fiscal policy objectives and rules, provided these are consistent with the fiscal principles laid out in the Code.

The Code requires debt management policy to minimise – over the long term – the costs of meeting the Government's financing needs. At the same time, policy is required to take account of risk and of the need to avoid, so far as possible, conflict with monetary policy. This objective, which is discussed in more detail in Chapter 15, has been embedded in the Code as there is little reason for this objective to change.

Accounting practice

High-quality information provides the basis for good policy making. The Government has introduced a new system of accounting for central government – Resource Accounting and Budgeting (RAB) – which improves on the previous cash-based arrangements (see Chapter 13 for more detail on RAB). The Code places this development firmly within the new framework for managing the public finances. The use of accruals-based accounting and budgeting recognises that the economic implications of capital expenditure are not the same as those of current expenditure, and also records expenditure as it is incurred rather than when cash is paid.

It is worth noting, however, that cash measures remain relevant – for example, in determining the Government's financing needs. Moreover, the tax forecast continues to be based largely on cash measures. This is because for some types of tax, such as income tax, cash and accruals-based measures give very similar results. And for others, such as corporate taxation, accruals-based concepts are difficult to apply.

The Code also requires the Government ensure that accounts are to be prepared for the whole public sector. To the extent reasonably practicable, the Code also records the aspiration that these accounts be consolidated. This will make it easier to assess the overall state of the financial affairs of the public sector as a whole.

Fiscal reporting

The Pre-Budget Report

It is essential that governments draw upon the skills and experience of people and businesses across the economy when forming policy decisions. The Budgetary process has for too long been shrouded in secrecy. This is why the Government first published a *Pre-Budget Report* (PBR) in November 1997 in order to stimulate a national debate about the major economic issues facing Britain.

The Code ensures that the PBR will continue to be a regular feature of the Budget process. Other than prior to the first Budget of a new Parliament, the Treasury is obliged to publish a PBR each year outlining, so far as reasonably practicable, any significant policy proposals under consideration for introduction in the Budget.

The Code recognises that consultation may not be possible in some areas, in particular where consultation would carry a significant risk of forestalling activity by current or prospective taxpayers, or significant temporary distortions in taxpayer and market behaviour, including disruption to financial markets. The Code also requires the PBR to present an up-to-date assessment of the economic and fiscal outlook, so that the debate is well founded. The PBR is to be published at least three months prior to the Budget, thus allowing adequate time for consultation.

The Financial Statement and Budget Report

Under the Code, the *Financial Statement and Budget Report* (FSBR) is the main vehicle for describing the Government's short-term economic and fiscal projections and the detailed policy announcements contained in the Budget. The FSBR is also the vehicle for explaining the policy measures taken to get the economic and fiscal strategy back on track if the longer term goals look like they might not be achieved.

The Economic and Fiscal Strategy Report

The Government believes that a forward-looking, long-term and strategic approach to policy will make Britain well placed to meet the challenges of the twenty-first century. The Code provides for a separate report to ensure that this occurs.

Under the *Economic and Fiscal Strategy Report* (EFSR), the Government is required to set out its long-term economic and fiscal strategy, including any objectives for the key fiscal aggregates. Importantly, it requires the Government to explain how the strategy and objectives relate to the principles of fiscal management and the Government's European commitments, in particular, the terms of the Stability and Growth Pact. It also requires governments to assess recent outcomes and the short-term forecasts contained in the *Financial Statement and Budget Report* against the longer-term strategy.

Two further innovations are worth noting. First, the Code requires the EFSR to present an analysis of the impact of the economic cycle on the key fiscal aggregates, including estimates of the cyclically adjusted fiscal position. This ensures that effects of the cycle are not ignored when policy decisions are made. Second, in keeping with the long-term focus of the report, illustrative projections are presented – based on a range of plausible assumptions – for a period not less than ten years ahead. While the level of uncertainty is inevitably greater the further out the projections go, the long-term projections nonetheless help to shed light on the intergenerational impact and sustainability of fiscal policy. They also encourage debate about the longer-term issues and challenges that Britain will face in the future.

The economic and fiscal projections

In the past, the Government has faced only limited obligation as to which elements of the economic and fiscal projections should be published. Schedule 5 of the Industry Act 1975 sets out a limited selection of economic variables for which forecasts are required. Consistent with the principle of transparency, the Code encompasses the requirements of this part of the Industry Act, and goes further, in particular in relation to information on the public finances.

The PBR and the FSBR – both of which must include an economic and fiscal projection – are required to disclose certain specific information as a minimum. This information includes the key assumptions underlying the projections and information on the outlook for key economic and fiscal aggregates.

Transparency implies that the Government's economic and fiscal projections represent a fair and honest assessment of the outlook. Accordingly, the Code requires that the projections incorporate, so far as reasonably practicable, all Government decisions and all other circumstances that may have a material impact on the economic and fiscal outlook.

If these decisions and circumstances can be quantified with reasonable accuracy prior to the day the projections are finalised, the Code requires that the impact be built into the projections. If an accurate estimate of the impact is not possible, the Code requires that the decision or circumstance be listed as an explicit fiscal risk. As noted earlier, a decision or circumstance might not be disclosed, if this would be contrary to the public interest, under the terms of paragraph 4(a) and (b) of the Code.

The role of the National Audit Office

Starting with the July 1997 Budget, the Government invited the National Audit Office (NAO) to audit key assumptions and conventions underpinning the fiscal projections. The aim is to ensure that the forecasts are consistent with the principles of transparency and responsibility.

The involvement of the NAO has been an important factor helping to build confidence in the basis for government fiscal projections. In keeping with this new approach, it is appropriate that the NAO should have a formal role under the Code. The Code requires the Treasury to invite the NAO to audit any changes to the key assumptions and conventions underlying projections of the public finances and to ensure that any advice received is published. Since Budget 2000, the NAO has been asked to carry out a rolling review of key assumptions before each *Pre-Budget Report* and Budget to ensure those it audited three years previously remain reasonable and cautious.

The conduct of debt management and the *Debt and Reserves Management Report*

Just as the Code obliges the Government to report on its handling of fiscal policy, so it obliges the Government to report on its debt management operations. This innovation allows Parliament and the public to scrutinise the conduct of debt management policy. It also allows market participants to plan their investment strategies with greater certainty.

The Code requires the publication of a *Debt and Reserves Management Report* each year. The report sets remits for its agents and discusses the overall debt portfolio. It also provides a forecast of net funding through National Savings, the overall size of the gilts issuance programme for the coming year and the planned maturity structure and the proportions of index-linked and conventional gilts. An outline of the planned gilt auction calendar is also included.

Referral to Select Committee

The Treasury Select Committee of the House of Commons has a very important role to play in scrutinising the conduct of fiscal and debt management policy. It is already customary for Treasury Ministers and officials to appear before the Committee and answer questions on fiscal policy when requested. The Government believes that it is helpful to emphasise the importance it attaches to the Committee's scrutiny role by stating explicitly, and hence formally, in the Code that the Treasury refer to the Committee all reports produced under the Code.

The distribution of reports

The public also have a fundamental interest in fiscal policy and a key role to play in scrutinising policy. It is important that the public has ready access to the reports that the Code requires the Government to produce. The Code thus requires the Treasury to ensure that a notice is published explaining where copies of the report can be viewed or purchased. The Treasury is also required to make copies of the report available for a period not less than six months following publication and to make all reports freely available on the Treasury's internet website.

APPENDIX: THE CODE FOR FISCAL STABILITY AND SUPPORTING LEGISLATION

This appendix reproduces the Code for Fiscal Stability, as approved by Parliament on 9 December 1998, and the relevant sections of the 1998 Finance Act.

The Code for Fiscal Stability

Purpose of the Code

1. The purpose of the Code is to improve the conduct of fiscal policy by specifying the principles that shall guide the formulation and imple-

mentation of fiscal policy and by strengthening the reporting requirements incumbent on the Government.

2. In this Code, except where the contrary is stated, fiscal policy includes debt management policy.

Principles of Fiscal Management

3. The Government shall conduct its fiscal policy in accordance with the following principles:

   a. **transparency** in the setting of fiscal policy objectives, the implementation of fiscal policy and in the publication of the public accounts;
   b. **stability** in the fiscal policy making process and in the way fiscal policy impacts on the economy;
   c. **responsibility** in the management of the public finances;
   d. **fairness**, including between generations; and
   e. **efficiency** in the design and implementation of fiscal policy and in managing both sides of the public sector balance sheet.

4. The principle of **transparency** means that the Government shall publish sufficient information to allow the public to scrutinise the conduct of fiscal policy and the state of the public finances, and shall not withhold information except where publication of that information would:

   a. substantially harm:

      i. the national security, defence or international relations of the United Kingdom;
      ii. the investigation, prosecution, or prevention of crime, or the conduct of civil proceedings;
      iii. the right to privacy;
      iv. the right of other parties to undertake confidential communications with the Government;
      v. the ability of the Government to undertake commercial activities; or

   b. harm the integrity of the decision-making and policy advice processes in Government.

5. The principle of **stability** means that, so far as reasonably practicable, the Government shall operate fiscal policy in a way that is predictable and consistent with the central economic objective of high and stable levels of growth and employment.

6. The principle of **responsibility** means that the Government shall operate fiscal policy in a prudent way, and manage public assets, liabilities and fiscal risks with a view to ensuring that the fiscal position is sustainable over the long term.

7. The principle of **fairness** means that, so far as reasonably practicable, the Government shall seek to operate fiscal policy in a way that takes into account the financial effects on future generations, as well as its distributional impact on the current population.

8. The principle of **efficiency** means that the Government shall seek to ensure that it uses resources in ways that give value for money, that public assets are put to the best possible use and that surplus assets are disposed of. The Government shall also have regard to economic efficiency and compliance costs when forming taxation policy.

Fiscal and Debt Management Objectives and Operation of Fiscal Policy

9. Subject to paragraph 12, the Government shall state and explain its fiscal policy objectives and the rules by which it intends to operate fiscal policy over the life of the Parliament. These objectives and operating rules shall accord with the principles stated in paragraph 3, and shall be restated in each Budget.

10. The Government may change its fiscal policy objectives and operating rules, provided that:

    a. any new fiscal policy objectives and operating rules also accord with the principles stated in paragraph 3; and
    b. the reasons for departing from the previous objectives and operating rules are stated.

11. The Government may depart from its fiscal objectives and operating rules temporarily, provided that it specifies:

    a. the reasons for departing from the previous fiscal policy objectives and operating rules;

    b. the approach and period of time that the Government intends to take to return to the previous fiscal policy objectives and operating rules; and

    c. the fiscal policy objectives and operating rules that shall apply over this period.

12. The primary objective of debt management policy shall be to minimise, over the long term, the costs of meeting the Government's financing needs whilst:

    a. taking account of risk; and

    b. seeking, so far as possible, to avoid conflict with monetary policy.

Accounting Practice

13. The Government shall ensure that accounts are to be produced for the whole public sector. Where reasonably practicable, these accounts also shall be produced on a consolidated basis.

14. The Government shall, as soon as reasonably practicable, adopt a Resource Accounting and Budgeting approach for planning and accounting for the costs of resources consumed by Government, based on Generally Accepted Accounting Practice in the United Kingdom, adapted as necessary for the public sector.

The Pre-Budget Report

15. If, as is usual, there is only one Budget in a financial year, the Treasury shall publish a Pre-Budget Report (PBR) at least three months prior to it, unless this is the first Budget of the Parliament, in which case a PBR shall not be required. In addition, if there is more than one Budget in any financial year, only one PBR shall be required.

16. The PBR shall be consultative in nature, and shall include, so far as reasonably practicable, proposals for any significant changes in fiscal policy under consideration for introduction in the Budget. However, the PBR shall not be taken as an indication of all tax policy areas where the Government may choose to act. In particular, consultation may not be possible in areas which:

a. carry the risk of significant forestalling activity by existing or prospective taxpayers; or
b. could lead to significant temporary distortions in taxpayer and market behaviour, including disruption in financial markets.

17. The PBR shall also include, either in the main document, or in a subsidiary document:

a. an Economic and Fiscal Projection (as defined in paragraphs 20–25); and
b. an analysis of the impact of the economic cycle on the key fiscal aggregates, including estimates of the cyclically-adjusted position, so as to shed light on progress against the fiscal objectives stated under paragraphs 9–11.

The Financial Statement and Budget Report

18. The Treasury shall publish a Financial Statement and Budget Report (FSBR) at the time of the Budget. The FSBR shall provide, at a minimum:

a. an Economic and Fiscal Projection (as defined in paragraphs 20–25);
b. an explanation of significant fiscal policy measures introduced in the Budget; and
c. an explanation, where necessary, of how these policy measures restore the path of the public finances to a position consistent with:

i.   the fiscal policy objectives and operating rules specified in paragraphs 9–11; and
ii. the Government's European commitments, in particular the terms of the Stability and Growth Pact.

The Economic and Fiscal Strategy Report

19. The Treasury shall publish an Economic and Fiscal Strategy Report (EFSR), usually at the time of the Budget. But if there is more than one Budget in any financial year, only one EFSR shall be required.

Within the context of the specified principles of fiscal management, the EFSR shall:

a. set out the Government's long-term economic and fiscal strategy, including any long-term objectives for the key fiscal aggregates;

b. assess both recent outcomes and the short-term economic and fiscal outlook contained in the Financial Statement and Budget Report against this longer-term strategy;

c. assess whether the short-term outlook and long-term strategy is consistent with the Government's European commitments, in particular, the terms of the Stability and Growth Pact;

d. present illustrative projections of the outlook for the key fiscal aggregates for a period not less than 10 years into the future, based on a range of plausible assumptions, so as to shed light on the inter-generational impact and sustainability of fiscal policy; and

e. present an analysis of the impact of the economic cycle on the key fiscal aggregates, including estimates of the cyclically-adjusted position.

Economic and Fiscal Projections

20. Where a report published under this Code contains an Economic and Fiscal Projection, that report shall contain, as a minimum:

a. the key assumptions, forecasts and conventions underpinning the projection;

b. projections of:

   i. GDP and its components;

   ii. retail prices (including any measure of prices that is the formal inflation target of the Government); and

   iii. the current account position of the balance of payments.

c. upon the implementation of Resource Accounting and Budgeting, an operating statement, reflecting the Government's projected current revenue and current expenses for each financial year;

d. a statement of cash flows, reflecting projected cash flows for each financial year;

e. a statement outlining proceeds received from the sale of public assets;

f. any other such statements as are necessary to reflect fairly the projected financial performance of the Government; and

g. an analysis of the risks surrounding the economic and fiscal outlook, including Government decisions and other circumstances that have still to be quantified with certainty, other material contingent liabilities and an indication of past forecast errors for aggregates noted in paragraph 20(b) and for Public Sector Net Borrowing.

21. The financial statements issued under paragraph 20 shall include projections of key fiscal aggregates, including: current spending and current revenue, the Surplus on Current Budget, Public Sector Net Borrowing, the Public Sector Net Cash Requirement, the General Government Financial Deficit, General Government Gross Debt, Public Sector Net Debt and a measure of net wealth. Where possible, the statements shall provide a breakdown of expenditure and revenue by sector and economic and/or functional category.

22. The financial statements shall also include any other such indicator as is required to judge achievement against the Government's fiscal policy objectives and rules and against the Government's European commitments, in particular the Stability and Growth Pact.

23. Every economic and fiscal projection contained in a report published under this Code shall be based, so far as reasonably practicable, on all Government decisions and all other circumstances that may have a material impact on the fiscal outlook:

a. where the fiscal impact of these decisions and circumstances can be quantified with reasonable accuracy by the day the projections are finalised, the impact should be included in the published projections.

b. where the fiscal impact of these decisions and circumstances cannot be quantified with reasonable accuracy by the day the projections are finalised, these impacts should be noted as specific fiscal risks.

24. The projection horizon is to be a period of not less than two full financial years following the date of publication. For each of the statements, comparative figures for the key fiscal aggregates covering the previous two financial years are to be published.

25. The Treasury shall also provide an explanation of all significant accounting policies, including any changes from previous practice.

Role of the National Audit Office

26. The Treasury shall invite the National Audit Office (NAO) to audit any changes to the key assumptions and conventions underlying the Fiscal Projections. The Comptroller and Auditor General shall ensure that any advice is communicated to the Treasury and laid before Parliament.

Conduct of Debt Management and the Debt and Reserves Management Report

27. The Government shall report annually on the structure of its borrowing and the cost of the government debt, giving sufficient information to allow the public to scrutinise the conduct of its debt management policy. The overall debt portfolio used to finance past fiscal deficits will be presented in the Debt and Reserves Management Report, to be issued within each financial year. The Government's agents for implementing debt management policy, the Debt Management Office and National Savings, shall publish more detailed information in their own annual reports and accounts.
28. The Government shall set remits for its agents in the annual Debt and Reserves Management Report. This report will include:

    a. a forecast of the net funding through National Savings;
    b. the overall size of the gilts issuance programme for the coming financial year;
    c. the planned debt maturity structure and the proportions of index-linked and conventional gilts; and
    d. the gilt auction calendar.

29. The remits shall be subject to revision or confirmation as the Government publishes more subsequent fiscal projections.

Referral to Select Committee

30. The Treasury shall refer to the House of Commons Treasury Select Committee every report published as a requirement of the Code.

Disclosure of Other Information

31. The Treasury shall publish, from time to time, other information that it determines would better enable the public to scrutinise fiscal policy and the state of the public finances.

Publication and Inspection of Reports

32. The Treasury shall, in respect of every report published as a requirement of the Code, arrange for the publication of a notice indicating:

    a. where copies of the report are available for inspection free of charge; and
    b. where copies of the report are available for purchase.

33. The Treasury shall make available copies of each report for inspection or purchase for at least 6 months following publication. Copies of all reports shall also be made available on the Treasury's internet website.

1998 Finance Act – Sections pertaining to the Code for Fiscal Stability

Part VI, Miscellaneous and Supplemental

Fiscal stability

155 (1) It shall be the duty of the Treasury to prepare and lay before Parliament a code for the application of the key principles to the formulation and implementation of:

   (a) fiscal policy, and
   (b) policy for the management of the National Debt.

   (2) The key principles are transparency, stability, responsibility, fairness and efficiency.
   (3) The code prepared under this section must set out, in particular

(a) the Treasury's understanding of what each of the key principles involves inn relation to fiscal policy and policy for the management of the National Debt;

(b) the provision appearing to the Treasury to be necessary for the purposes of so much of section 156 below as refers to the code; and

(c) the methods and principles of accounting to be applied in the preparation of accounts, forecasts and other documents used for the purposes of the formulation and implementation of the policies mentioned in subsection (1) above.

(4) Where any code has been laid before Parliament under subsection (1) above, the Treasury may from time to time modify that code; but if they do so, they shall lay the modified code before Parliament.

(5) A code (including a modified code) that has been laid before Parliament under this section shall not come into force until it has been approved by a resolution of the House of Commons.

(6) It shall be the duty of the Treasury to publish, in such manner as they think fit, any code which has been laid before Parliament and approved by the House of Commons under this section.

(7) The first code to be laid before Parliament under this section shall be so laid before 31st December 1998.

156 (1) It shall be the duty of the Treasury, for each financial year, to prepare and lay before Parliament the following documents, that is to say:

(a) a Financial Statement and Budget Report;

(b) an Economic and Fiscal Strategy Report; and

(c) a Debt and Reserves Management Report.

(2) The preparation and laying before Parliament of the Financial Statement and Budget Report for any financial year shall be preceded, in such cases and by such period as may be set out in the code for fiscal stability, by the preparation by the Treasury of a document to be known as the Pre-Budget Report.

(3) The Treasury shall lay before Parliament any Pre-Budget Report prepared by them under subsection (2) above.

(4) The contents of the documents which the Treasury are required to prepare and lay before Parliament under this section, and

the occasions on which those documents are to be so laid, must conform to ant provision about those matters made by the code for fiscal stability.

(5) It shall be the duty of the Comptroller and Auditor General to examine and report to the House of Commons on such of the conventions and assumptions underlying the preparation by the Treasury of the documents prepared by them under this section as, in accordance with the code for fiscal stability, are submitted to him by the Treasury for his examination.

(6) A report by the Comptroller and Auditor General under subsection (5) above must be made at the same time as, or as soon as reason practicable after, the laying before Parliament of the documents to which it is referable.

(7) It shall be the duty of the Treasury to secure the publication in the manner required by the code for fiscal stability of any document which they have laid before Parliament under this section.

(8) In this section 'the code for fiscal stability' means the code for the time being in force under section 155 above.

(9) The first financial year for which the documents mentioned in subsection (1) above are required to be prepared and laid before Parliament is the year beginning with 1st April 1999.

157 (1) The Comptroller and Auditor General:

   (a) shall have a right of access, at all reasonable times, to all such relevant Government documents as he may reasonably require for the purpose of carrying out any examination under section 156(5) above; and

   (b) shall be entitled to require from any person holding or accountable for any relevant Government documents any assistance, information or explanation which he reasonably thinks necessary for that purpose.

   (2) In this section 'relevant Government documents' means documents in the custody or under the control of the Government department primarily responsible for the adoption or formulation of the convention or assumption in question.

9
Understanding the Fiscal Rules

This chapter looks in detail at the rationale for fiscal rules and, in particular, at the specification of the golden rule and the sustainable investment rule. The chapter explains how clear rules, and firm implementation of them, can deliver sound public finances and, in doing so, assist greatly in restoring the credibility of fiscal policy.

Introduction

As discussed in Chapter 8, the Code for Fiscal Stability, put on a statutory footing by the 1998 Finance Act, requires the Government to state explicitly its fiscal rules and objectives and issue regular reports to show how it is meeting them. The rules chosen by the Government – first set out in its 1997 election manifesto and subsequently confirmed in subsequent Budgets – are:

- the *golden rule*: over the economic cycle, the Government will borrow only to invest and not to fund current spending
- the *sustainable investment rule*: over the economic cycle, public debt as a proportion of GDP will be held at a stable and prudent level.

This chapter considers the rationale for fiscal rules and, in particular, the specification of the golden rule and the sustainable investment rule. A number of practical issues concerning their implementation are also discussed.

Rules – rationale and considerations

Many countries have adopted rules (or targets) to guide their respective fiscal policies. This section explains the key reasons why the Government believes that a rules-based approach is also right for the UK and the broad factors that were considered by the Government when choosing its fiscal rules. A more specific rationale for each rule is discussed in subsequent sections.

Lessons from macroeconomic policy experience

Chapter 1 explained how the UK's past growth performance has been poor compared with other industrial countries. Growth has also been highly volatile. The failure to provide a platform of stability has proved costly for investment and long-term growth. Indeed, the 'boom and bust' experience wasted resources and led to significant economic and social costs.

Macroeconomic policy, if set correctly, should be a stabilising force. But the powerful influence of government borrowing and interest rates on the economy can be destabilising, if not managed effectively. The evidence suggests that fiscal and monetary policies over the last two full cycles had failed to provide the requisite stability.

In the past, the failure of policy to be sufficiently forward-looking and transparent led to fiscal policy being loosened at the wrong moment – increasing the volatility of policy as attempts were made to 'catch up' and destabilising the economy in the process. Moreover, monetary and fiscal policy failed to work together effectively at certain critical periods, notably in the boom of the late 1980s. This exacerbated the task of returning the economy to a stable long-term growth path.

Chapter 1 explained the important lessons for fiscal policy that can be learnt from the past. A key lesson was that policy makers should be *open and transparent* by setting stable fiscal rules and explaining clearly fiscal policy decisions.

Rebuilding credibility in fiscal policy

Economic theory sheds light on the UK's past experience and strengthens the rationale for stating explicit fiscal rules. Much of the relevant literature focuses on monetary policy (see Chapter 6); however, the same principles can be applied to fiscal policy. In particular, the benefits of establishing a sound and stable fiscal framework will be maximised if the framework is credible – that is, if households and firms believe firmly that the Government will deliver its commitments.

If the policy framework lacks credibility, households and firms will continue to base their decisions on previous experience. So savings and investment decisions will continue to anticipate a return to high inflation and poor fiscal management. The benefits of a new framework will, therefore, be delayed until the Government is able to establish a convincing track record of favourable policy outcomes.

A number of approaches have been taken by policy makers to try to bridge the 'credibility gap' that often occurs when a new framework is first put in place. One approach is to strengthen the force of the Government's commitment by giving the framework legislative backing. This was the approach followed by the Government in reforming monetary policy. A similar, though not identical, approach has been adopted for fiscal policy. Handing over fiscal policy decisions to an independent committee of experts is not a desirable option. Making decisions about taxation and public spending is part of the essence of a democratically elected Government, requiring economic and social judgements that only the Government can make.

As explained in Chapter 8, a different approach has been used to obtain the same properties of transparency, openness and accountability. The Code for Fiscal Stability draws together and makes clear the framework in which fiscal policy operates. In particular, the Code requires the Government to state explicitly its fiscal rules and objectives and to report regularly on how it is achieving them. Through this open and transparent framework, the Government has been able to bridge the credibility gap that developed after years of poor fiscal management.

Firm fiscal rules also remove the tendency for fiscal policy to deviate from sound economic principles to provide short-term gains to certain interest groups. Indeed, as Keech (1985) suggests, even if a fiscal rule is not 'optimal' in a perfect world, it may well be the best economic response in a situation where the unconstrained political process produces outcomes that are even less desirable.

Retaining sensible levels of flexibility

Rules, by their very nature, are intended to impose restrictions on behaviour. Fiscal rules must ensure that the public finances are managed prudently and maintained within sensible boundaries so that Government meets its spending commitments without jeopardising economic stability or running up an unfair bill for future generations.

It is important, however, that the chosen rules allow sufficient flexibility to react sensibly to economic developments – the right balance needs to be struck between a rigid mechanical approach and an approach based on unfettered discretion. In particular, there must be scope to accommodate the impact of the economic cycle and room to act in the event of exceptional economic shocks.

As discussed in more detail in Chapter 11, fiscal policy can help to stabilise the economy through the operation of the 'automatic stabilisers'. As the economy strengthens, incomes tend to rise, resulting in higher income and corporation tax receipts and lower social security spending. The budget balance will therefore tend to rise when growth is strong and fall when growth is relatively weak. These movements support monetary policy by dampening economic cycles without putting at risk the long-term sustainability of fiscal policy. It is vital that the chosen rules do not override this inbuilt capacity to respond to changing economic circumstances.

The chosen fiscal rules must also allow for sensible discretionary adjustments to fiscal policy. For example, in the first years of the Govenment's term fiscal policy was tightened to support monetary policy and restore the structural integrity of the public finances. In addition, the rules must incorporate a measure of flexibility to accommodate exceptional shocks, not associated with the usual economic cycle. The Code for Fiscal Stability permits the Government to deviate from its fiscal rules in exceptional circumstances (such as wars or natural disasters) but requires the reason for this change to be explained in public.

Finally, on a more practical note, if the rules were to require the budget to be balanced every year, the Government would need to change its spending plans or tax rates on a regular basis. The administrative cost of such a system – both to the Government and taxpayers – makes it highly impractical.

Encompassing the public sector

A further consideration is that the chosen rules should apply to the whole *public sector* – central and local government (together referred to as general government) *and* public corporations. The liabilities of public corporations could fall ultimately on the taxpayer, so it is appropriate that the Government's fiscal rules extend beyond the general government sector. Moreover, if the rules were applied to just some government activities (general government, for example), this could lead to perverse incentives to reclassify spending in an attempt to get around the fiscal rules.

Consistency with European commitments

In formulating its fiscal rules, the Government was also mindful of its commitments under the Stability and Growth Pact, described in detail in Chapter 18.

The Stability and Growth Pact aims to deliver sound public finances in support of European monetary stability. Under the Stability and Growth Pact, member states are committed politically to the medium-term budgetary objective of keeping the budget balance (defined in terms of the general government financial balance) close to balance or in surplus. In EMU, member states can ultimately be fined if they run persistent deficits exceeding the reference value of 3 per cent of GDP (subject to certain caveats). The Maastricht Treaty also emphasises the importance of public debt (defined in terms of gross general government debt) falling or being below 60 per cent of GDP in determining if member states should be fined.

The aim of the Government's fiscal policy – sound public finances – is commensurate with the Stability and Growth Pact, and the Government's fiscal rules are designed to deliver outcomes that are consistent with the Pact.

The golden rule

This section focuses on the rationale for the golden rule; that is, *over the economic cycle, the Government will borrow only to invest and not to fund current spending.*

The section explains why balancing current receipts and current spending over the economic cycle is an integral part of a sound approach to managing the public finances.

Features of the rule

Current spending (and revenue) and capital spending

One of the key features of the golden rule is that it draws a distinction between current spending (and revenue) and capital spending. It follows naturally that the definitions of current and capital spending are important to the application of the rule.

The basic principle is clear. Spending that produces benefits that are consumed in the same year as the spending occurs is classed as current spending. By contrast, spending that produces a stream of services over time (in excess of one year) is classed as capital spending. In practice, spending is spread across a range of items, some of which are clearly current – such as the payment of public sector salaries – and some of which are clearly capital – such as the purchase of engineering machinery. There are, however, some grey areas in between (discussed later in this section).

The economic cycle

A further key feature of the golden rule, as the Government has adopted it, is that it is defined 'over the economic cycle'. This characteristic is shared with the sustainable investment rule.

At a stylised level, the economic cycle can be thought as fluctuations in the economy around the trend level of output, alternating between periods of above-trend and below-trend activity. As noted earlier, these fluctuations have an impact on the public finances. The golden rule is evaluated in a way that abstracts from the impact on the public finances of the normal cyclical variations in the economy. This means that the inbuilt capacity of fiscal policy to respond to changing economic circumstances is not compromised.

The theory and rationale

Avoiding discrimination against capital spending

The previous fiscal policy regime concentrated on various targets, usually expressed in terms of what is now called the public sector net cash requirement. This regime made no formal distinction between capital and current spending.

A significant shortcoming of this approach was that it created a bias against capital spending. Current and capital spending could be offset against each other, making capital projects where returns appear only in the future – an easy target when it became necessary to tighten the overall fiscal policy stance. The bias against capital has contributed to a considerable under-investment in public assets (HM Treasury 2000d) (see Figure 9.1).

The golden rule draws a distinction between current and capital spending and therefore is designed to remove the bias against capital spending. It recognises that both current and capital spending have important roles to play in the provision of public services and that decisions on all spending – whether current or capital – must be considered on a value for money basis. Departments can no longer take the easy route of maintaining current payments at the expense of worthwhile investment.

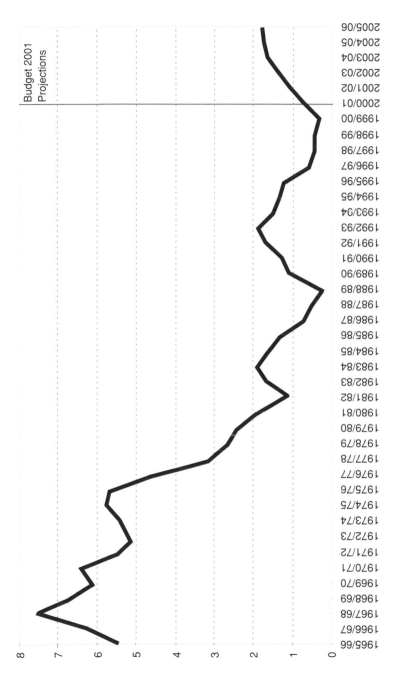

Figure 9.1 Public sector net investment (per cent of GDP)

Fairness between generations

In adopting the golden rule the Government has also given consideration to fairness, and in particular, fairness between generations. Indeed, fairness is one of the five key principles of fiscal policy outlined in the Code for Fiscal Stability to which the chosen fiscal rules have to relate.

Government decisions on spending and revenue may have important implications across generations. For example, large investments such as roads produce benefits over the investment's effective life, which may be in excess of 40 years. It is only fair that those generations who benefit from this spending are those that also meet the cost.

It is not practical, of course, to match the timing of the streams of costs and benefits for each and every spending proposal. But, in aggregate, the Government takes the view that current spending, which mainly provides benefits to existing taxpayers, should be paid for by the current generation of taxpayers. Similarly, because capital spending produces a stream of services over time, it is fair that this form of spending is financed initially through borrowing. This behaviour should ensure that, to the extent practicable, each generation pays for the benefits of the public services that it consumes.

The Government continues to try to develop ways to improve its analysis of long-term sustainability and intergenerational equity. In particular, the Treasury and the Bank of England, assisted by the National Institute for Economic and Social Research, have produced a first set of generational accounts for the UK. These accounts estimate each generation's net tax and benefit position over their respective remaining lifetimes compared with those of a newborn. The Institute published the findings of their study on 4 December 1998 (Cardarelli et al. 1998).

The Treasury has also developed a set of illustrative long-term fiscal projections as required by the Code for Fiscal Stability. These projections, which were first published in the *Economic and Fiscal Strategy Report* in Budget 99, provide additional information on the sustainability of the Government's financial plans over a period of not less than ten years.

Turning theory into policy

What the figures show

Figure 9.2 illustrates how the UK has performed in meeting the golden rule.

As the Figure shows, the golden rule has not been met since the early 1970s. Indeed, in each of the last two full economic cycles to 1997,

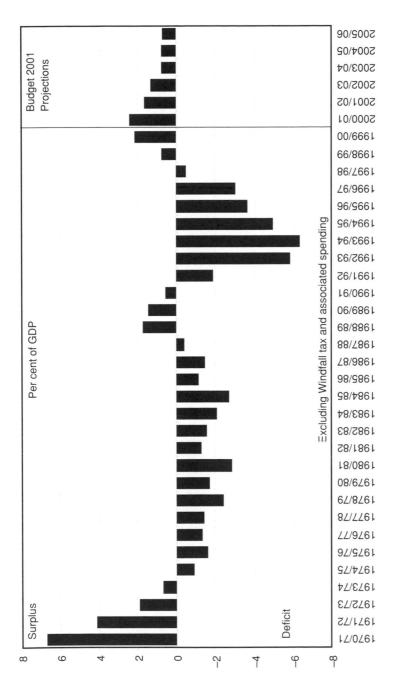

Figure 9.2 Surplus on current budget (per cent of GDP)

current spending consistently exceeded current revenue, by an amount averaging over 1½ per cent of GDP. Consequently, governments over this period were borrowing to finance current spending as well as borrowing for investment. The result of this can be seen in Figure 9.3, which shows a significant fall in public sector net wealth as a proportion of GDP.[1]

The Government has taken firm action to put the public finances back on a sustainable long-term basis. As a result, the projections contained in Budget 2001 indicate that the Government will meet the golden rule over the current economic cycle (as shown in Figure 9.2). Public sector net wealth is expected to remain broadly stable as a proportion of GDP (as shown in Figure 9.3), halting its continuous fall over the last decade.

Implementing the golden rule

The factors discussed above explain why the Government has chosen the golden rule. However, in order to implement the rule in practice, a number of issues have had to be considered.

Defining the economic cycle   As noted earlier, the fiscal rules are defined over the economic cycle. Consequently, the measurement of the economic cycle has a key influence on any assessment against the rules. However, defining the cycle is not trivial. In particular, determining when the economy is on trend requires careful assessment of economic indicators and a view on past and expected future growth rates.

The Treasury's assessment, based on analysis of labour market statistics and indicators of capacity utilisation, is that the economy was on trend, on average, over the first half of 1997. This coincides with the implementation of the new Government's framework, and is a suitable time from which to begin assessing performance against the fiscal rules.

In Budget 2001 the Government indicated its provisional judgement that the economy may have completed a full, albeit short and shallow, economic cycle between the first half of 1997 and mid-1999 when the current cycle is assumed to begin.

The symmetry, or asymmetry, of economic cycles is also of importance in implementing the fiscal rules. For example, it is likely to be more difficult to achieve current balance over a cycle involving a relatively longer period of below trend output. Thus one of the reasons why the Government has built a margin for uncertainty into its fiscal plans is to allow for the possibility of an asymmetric cycle.

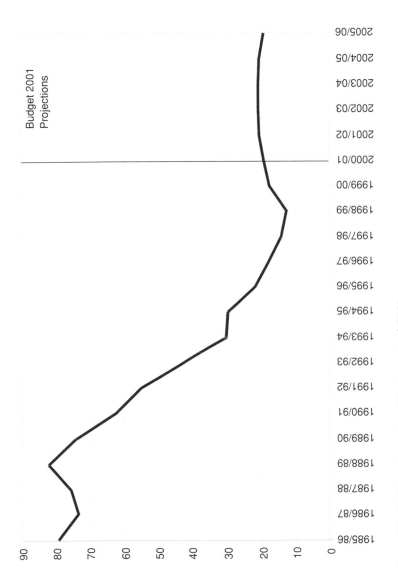

Figure 9.3 Public sector net wealth (per cent of GDP)

Defining current and capital spending   As suggested earlier, although the basic principles underlying the distinction between current and capital spending are clear, there are nonetheless some grey areas in between.

For the purpose of the fiscal rules, the Government considers the best measure of capital currently available is that used in the national accounts (ONS 1998). This definition, which is based on international standards and used by the majority of developed countries, comprises:

- the purchase, net of sales, of fixed assets which are themselves used repeatedly or continuously in production processes for more than one year (for example, buying a lorry or machine)
- the purchase, net of sales, of natural assets over which ownership may be enforced and transferred
- or taking steps to increase the value of natural assets realised by the productive activity of economic entities.

Box 9.1   Policies on the budget deficit – an international comparison

Many countries around the world have sought to achieve specific budget targets using a variety of definitions of the budget deficit.

- Some follow the broad approach used in the UK. In Germany, legislation commits the Government to seek the achievement of a version of the golden rule in every year, except in circumstances of a significant 'macroeconomic disequilibrium'. New Zealand's Fiscal Responsibility Act institutionalises a version of the golden rule by requiring the current budget to be in balance or surplus over a 'reasonable' period of time.
- Some countries, however, focus on the overall budget deficit, including both current and capital spending (a concept similar to the UK's definition of net borrowing). For example, in order to comply with the Maastricht reference values, EU member states have to ensure their budget deficits – defined in terms of the general government financial deficit – remain below 3 per cent of GDP. Moreover, in order to allow the automatic stabilisers to work while avoiding the risk of fines under the excessive deficits procedure of the Stability and Growth Pact, many member states participating in the single European currency focus on a budgetary position that is close to balance when the economy is on trend.
- In the US, the Balanced Budget Act of 1997 was introduced to move the budget into surplus by 2002. Similarly, Australia's medium-term objective is to balance its overall budget (net of policy lending and equity transactions) over the economic cycle.

The key feature of this definition is that it equates capital spending with future benefits. The definition excludes some items of spending which have some, but not all, of the characteristics of investment. A prominent example is spending on education. Although education gives rise to a stream of benefits over time, the capital value of education and its depreciation rate is not something which can be estimated easily or reliably.

The sustainable investment rule

[I]n general there is no debt or deficit neutrality. The level of debt and deficits matters, and is a legitimate subject of public debate. (Buiter 1985)

This section focuses on the rationale for the sustainable investment rule: *over the economic cycle, public debt as a proportion of GDP will be held at a stable and prudent level.*

It explains why holding public debt at a stable and prudent level is an integral part of a sound approach to managing the public finances. It also outlines why the Government believes that, other things being equal, reducing net public debt to below 40 per cent of GDP is desirable to meet this rule with confidence.

Public debt concepts

Net debt versus gross debt

Public debt figures can be quoted gross or net. *Gross* figures capture the total amount of the Government's financial liabilities – they take no account of offsetting financial assets. These figures are readily available and widely publicised, thus making them useful for international comparisons. The Maastricht public debt criterion is based on a gross measure of public debt.

Net figures subtract a measure of liquid financial assets from the measure of gross debt. Because net debt provides a fairer reflection of a government's immediate solvency, the net concept is usually preferred to the gross concept where figures are available. The net debt measure is that preferred by the Government.

The level of debt versus the debt to income ratio

Equally, figures on the public debt can be either pounds sterling or as a proportion of GDP. The distinction between these two measures is important because of the impact of inflation and real growth in the economy. It is possible for the level of debt to rise in *cash terms*, but fall when expressed as a *proportion of GDP*.

As discussed later in this section, concerns about high cash levels of public debt often reflect their implication for spending on debt servicing and the tax rates that are required to fund this. However, as the economy grows, the tax base also becomes larger, so the amount of tax collected increases even if tax rates are unchanged. A government can, therefore, finance higher levels of public debt in cash terms without increasing the effective tax burden. For example, in 1865, gross public debt was approximately £0.8 billion, just 0.2 per cent of the current level (£381.1 billion in 2000–01). However, when expressed in relation to the size of the economy, in 1865 the public debt was around twice as large as it is today.[2]

It makes more sense to refer to public debt in relation to national income (GDP) and, therefore, the Government's sustainable investment rule is specified on this basis.

Public sector debt versus general government debt

As noted earlier, the Government believes that its fiscal rules should apply across the whole public sector. This is because the burden of repaying the debt of public corporations could fall ultimately on the taxpayer. Therefore the sustainable investment rule applies to the *public sector* measure of debt.

Public debt versus external debt

A final point to note is the distinction between *public debt* – owed by the Government – and *external debt* – owed by all British residents in all sectors of the economy (government and private sector) to overseas residents. This distinction is sometimes confused. This chapter focuses on the Government's policy on the public debt, most of which is held by British residents (either directly or via investment funds). However, deficits and debt in the private sector can contribute to deficits on the current account and thus higher levels of external debt.

The theory and rationale

This section sets out the reasons why governments issue debt and why too much debt can have a detrimental impact on growth and employment.

Why do governments issue debt?

Governments issue debt (that is, borrow) for much the same reason as individuals – to allow them to smooth expenditure in the face of fluctuations in income. If borrowing was prohibited, in order to smooth consumption the Government would need either to maintain a stock of net liquid financial assets or tax rates would need to rise or fall each year to finance the spending plans. In the latter case, as already noted, the administrative costs would be prohibitive. But more fundamentally, frequent tax rate changes also run counter to the theory underlying the concept of tax smoothing. If there is a 'deadweight cost'[3] incurred when raising taxation, a cost that increases as the tax rate rises, cost minimisation implies that the tax rate should be constant over the economic cycle, rather than varying from year to year.

The smoothing of spending occurs over various time horizons. Individuals typically smooth their spending over their entire lifetime, borrowing earlier in their adult life, building up net assets over their main working years, and running down their assets after retiring from the workforce. Any remaining assets usually transfer to the individual's descendants after death.

The Government's motives to borrow reflect considerations related to fairness between generations and factors related to the economic cycle. Borrowing allows the government to spread the upfront costs associated with capital projects across generations, so that the costs and benefits are matched more fairly. Each generation pays only for the capital that it consumes.

In exceptional historical circumstances associated mainly with war, public debt has risen sharply and has been reduced only gradually over many years (see Figure 9.5). Funds borrowed during wars paid for the extraordinary spending required on Britain's defence. This benefited both current and future generations, and thus it was fair that the cost was spread over time.

As noted earlier, the golden rule is applied *over the economic cycle*. This means that the current budget is allowed to move into surplus when the economy is above trend and into deficit when the economy is below trend, thus helping to stabilise the economy. However, current spending and revenue must be matched over the economic cycle. Therefore, public debt will tend to fall as a proportion of GDP during periods of strong growth, and rise as a proportion of GDP during periods of weaker growth.

Even in the absence of major catastrophes such as war, most countries have positive levels of net public debt. In part, this may reflect an explicit recognition of the intergenerational factors associated with investment spending. However, in many cases this is also symptomatic of poor control of public spending. Borrowing continually to fund consumption merely pushes the cost onto future generations.

Why might an upper limit on public debt be desirable?

As noted above, the golden rule allows governments to borrow for the purpose of investment. But if left unconstrained, it is conceivable that borrowing could reach levels that are 'too high', notwithstanding the specific merits of the underlying investment. This possibility motivates the Government's sustainable investment rule.

It is also important to note that many of the benefits derived from public investment are social, rather than financial. This stands in contrast to most investment in the private sector. Because such public investment is not self-financing, the repayment of the associated debt requires, all other things being equal, either future reductions in other public services or higher taxes. This needs to be taken into account when producing long-term projections of the public finances.

The sustainability of fiscal policy   Much of the discussion in academic literature is focused on issues related to either the *solvency* or *sustainability* of fiscal policy.

The concept of *solvency* is straightforward. A government's fiscal policy is said to meet the test of solvency if the present discounted value of future expected primary balances[4] is equal or greater than the outstanding stock of public debt; that is, if:

$$PB + \frac{PB_{t+1}}{\left(1+d\right)} + \frac{PB_{t+2}}{\left(1+d\right)^2} + \ldots + \frac{PB_{t+\infty}}{\left(1+d\right)^{\infty}} \geq \text{Debt}$$

where PB is the primary balance, d is the discount rate, and Debt is the debt stock.

The concept of *sustainability* involves analysing the conditions required to stabilise public debt at a given proportion of GDP. On this basis, a fiscal policy is usually defined as sustainable if, given reasonable assumptions, the government can maintain its current policies indefinitely while continuing to meet its debt obligations. It is possible to calculate the primary balance (as a proportion of GDP) required to stabilise the net public debt ratio at a given target level using the following formula:

$$\frac{PB}{GDP} = \left(r - g\right) \times \left(\frac{\text{Debt target}}{GDP}\right)$$

where r is the real interest rate, g is the real economic growth rate, and PB is the primary balance.

Figure 9.4 illustrates these calculations for three possible targets for the public debt ratio. The chart relates the surplus on the primary balance to the size of the gap between the real interest rate and the real growth rate.

As long as the real interest rate is less than or equal to the real growth rate, the government does not need to achieve a primary surplus to stabilise the debt ratio. However, if the real interest rate exceeds the real growth rate (that is, the gap is positive) – as it has in the UK for most of the last two decades – a primary surplus is required to prevent the debt ratio from rising (assuming, of course, that the starting debt ratio is greater than zero). The extent of that surplus is dependent on the size of the interest rate–growth gap and the target public debt to GDP ratio.

The risks that are faced by a country with high levels of public debt are readily apparent. Consider the case of a country seeking to stabilise net public debt at 80 per cent of GDP. If the Government can borrow at real interest rates of 3 per cent and the country's real economic growth rate is 2 per cent (that is, the gap is 1 percentage point) a primary surplus of 0.8 per cent of GDP is needed in order to stabilise successfully the public debt ratio at the target level. But if an economic shock leads to a rise in world real interest rates, raising the Government's real borrowing rate to, say, 4.5 per cent (and the gap to 2.5 percentage points), a primary surplus of 2 per cent of GDP is now required (more still if, as is likely, higher real interest rates lead to lower levels of growth). If prolonged, such a substantial change in the fiscal position would necessitate significant cuts in public spending or large increases in tax rates. Without such change, the public debt ratio would rise beyond the target level. Indeed, in the absence of corrective action, the public debt would climb from 80 per cent of GDP to over 100 per cent of GDP inside ten years.

This experience can be contrasted with that of a lower debt country eg one trying to stabilise public debt at around 40 per cent of GDP. Such a country would need only to boost its primary surplus from 0.4 per cent of GDP to 1.0 per cent of GDP if faced by an identical shock. This represents a much less traumatic adjustment. Moreover, if corrective action was not taken immediately – perhaps reflecting priorities for public spending – the public debt ratio would rise by a more modest 11 percentage points of GDP over a ten-year period.

As discussed further below, if anything these figures probably understate the risks, as countries with very high levels of public debt may

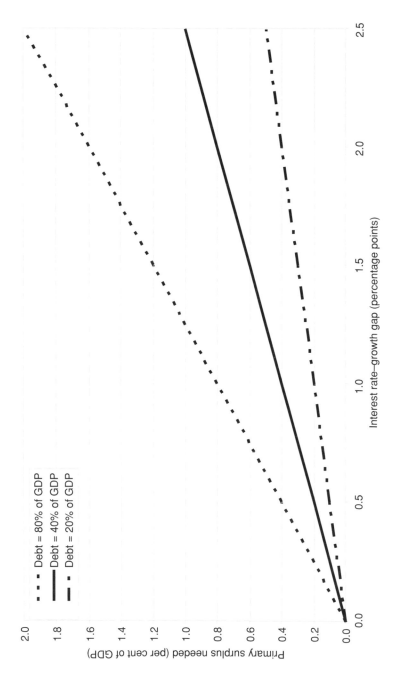

Figure 9.4 Primary budget surplus required to stabilise the public debt ratio (per cent of GDP)

fàce less favourable combinations of interest rates and economic growth than those with lower levels of public debt.

These figures show that a seemingly sustainable fiscal policy can quickly become unsustainable. The costs of fiscal policy becoming unsustainable are likely to be high. The corrective action needed to avert a fiscal crisis or the debt servicing obligations created by the rising debt might threaten the economic and political stability of the economy. Therefore, a more disciplined fiscal policy approach is required.

A prudent fiscal policy can be defined as one that is likely to be sustainable even in the event of adverse shocks. Thus, a prudent fiscal policy is likely to lead governments to select a lower level of public debt.

Other effects of public debt   As discussed above, high levels of public debt make the economy vulnerable to the need for large adjustments in fiscal policy due to changes in the debt servicing burden. But there are also a number of other ways in which high debt levels might have a negative impact on economic growth, thus reducing the consumption possibilities of all generations. High levels of public debt:

- *reduce the Government's ability to use fiscal policy to cushion major shocks*: if the debt level is not maintained at low levels during favourable economic times, there will be reduced scope for supporting monetary policy and cushioning the economy when faced with unfavourable shocks. Indeed, it is conceivable that high levels of public debt could lead to perverse short-run responses to changes in the fiscal stance (for example, a tightening of the fiscal stance could have an expansionary impact on the economy as concerns about long-term fiscal sustainability diminish)
- *lead to a risk premium in interest rates*: high public debt levels increase the risk that the Government might seek to relieve the debt burden by non-conventional means, either by allowing inflation to rise, or in the extreme, by defaulting. As a result, lenders will demand a risk premium when lending to the Government. Higher interest rates will dampen or 'crowd out' interest-rate-sensitive components of aggregate demand, in particular spending by businesses on investment goods, lowering living standards throughout the economy
- *lead to a low level of Government services per unit of tax collected, lower levels of economic welfare and higher levels of structural unemployment*: high debt levels imply high levels of debt servicing – resources that would otherwise be available for spending on programmes or to be

distributed as tax cuts. For example, reducing public debt by 20 percentage points could free resources equivalent to around 1.4 percentage points of GDP. For a given level of spending, a higher level of taxes needs to be collected in order to finance the interest payments on the debt, and because taxation (other than on a lump-sum basis) is distortionary, this has a detrimental impact on economic welfare. To the extent that higher taxes on labour are necessary, high debt can also contribute to high structural unemployment.

Is there an optimal level of public debt?   Even if fiscal policy is sustainable, the public debt ratio may not be at an optimal level. As suggested earlier, some level of public debt is justified. At the same time, however, high levels of public debt make the economy vulnerable to the need for large adjustments in fiscal policy and are likely to have negative consequences for long-term growth and employment. This suggests that there may be a middle ground – a level of debt that represents an *optimal* trade-off between the need to undertake public investment (and funding this in an equitable way) and the economic costs associated with higher levels of public debt.

A small number of academic studies have tried to identify the optimal public debt ratio using empirical means. Three approaches have been attempted:

- *Inferring the optimal debt ratio by observing debt/equity ratios prevailing in the private sector.* The assumption implicit in this approach is that whatever the optimal debt ratio may be, the private sector has solved this to its own satisfaction. Thus given the Government's estimated assets, one could argue that the optimal debt ratio for the UK may lie somewhere in the range of 30–50 per cent of GDP (based on private sector gearing ratios of between 40/60 and 60/40). However, given the differing risk characteristics of activities in the public sector, the use of private sector benchmarks is questionable, and even more so when applied at an aggregate level.
- *Inferring the optimal debt ratio from tests of 'dynamic efficiency'.* This approach stems from economic theory and involves analysing differentials between investment and profit levels, or alternatively, economic growth rates and interest rates. One US study based on this approach by Zee (1988) suggested that the optimal public debt level is less than around 20 per cent of GDP, although the results are conditional on the parameters and assumptions made in the model.

- *The estimation of the optimal public debt ratio using statistical techniques.* One study by Smyth and Hsing (1995), using US data, suggested that economic growth was maximised when public debt levels are around 50 per cent of GDP. Robson and Scarth (1997) argue for a target of 20 per cent of GDP in the Canadian context. However, another US study (Asilis 1994) suggested that the costs of being away from the optimal level are quite small – public debt levels need to rise substantially before serious damage to the economy will occur. And more generally, it is important to note that the public debt that maximises growth need not correspond to that which maximises welfare.

The methods and assumptions underpinning each of these approaches are open to a good measure of criticism. And the range of results obtained illustrate the difficulty encountered in arriving at a precise answer.

Turning theory into policy

What the figures show – an historical comparison

The longest run of data available for the Government's indebtedness is that for the *national debt*. This represents the gross liabilities of the National Loans Fund, and includes most of central government's borrowing.[5] Figure 9.5 illustrates movements in national debt as a proportion of GDP since 1855.

Debt stood above 100 per cent of GDP at the beginning of the period (reflecting the financing of earlier wars) but fell almost continuously during the second half of the nineteenth century and the beginning of the twentieth century. By 1914 public debt had declined to around 26 per cent of GDP. The onset of World War I saw an extremely sharp rise in the level of debt which was sustained through the Great Depression. By 1933, the public debt had reached 183 per cent of GDP. Thereafter, economic recovery saw a large but short-lived reduction in the debt ratio before the onset the World War II led to a further very sharp increase. National debt peaked at just over 252 per cent of GDP in 1946.

Since World War II, public debt as a proportion of GDP has been characterised largely by a steady decline, reflecting growth in nominal GDP (the inflation component in particular). However, little reduction occurred over the last two decades and as a result of the rise during the 1990s, the debt ratio prevailing when the present Government took office remained slightly higher than that prevailing prior to World War I. (See Box 9.2 for international comparisons.)

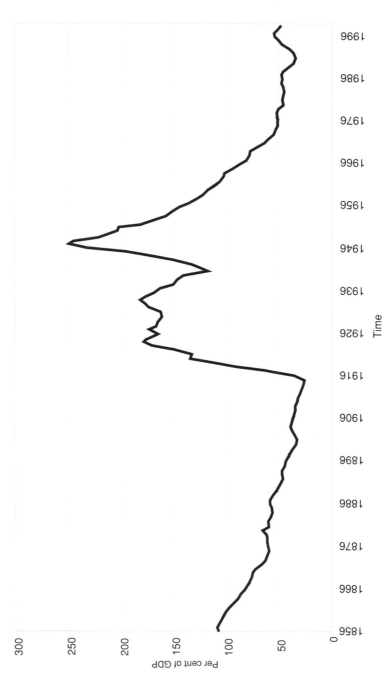

Figure 9.5   Public debt in the UK (National debt, per cent of GDP)

Box 9.2   Public debt – an international comparison

The chart below compares the level of public debt prevailing recently in the UK with that in the other members of the G7 and a selection of other developed countries. In this chart public debt is measured using general government net financial liabilities as a proportion of GDP.

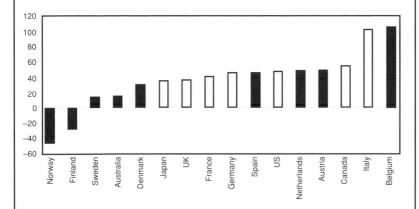

Figure 9.6   General government financial liabilities (per cent of GDP, 2000)

On this basis, the chart shows that the level of public debt in the UK is towards the lower end when compared against other members of the G7 (the unshaded bars) but very much in the middle of the pack once a broader range of countries is considered. Italy and Belgium both have public debt levels in excess of 100 per cent of GDP. In contrast, the general government sectors of Norway and Finland each have net financial assets.

The Government's policy on public debt

Neither theory nor empirical evidence provide a definitive guide for policymakers. This is reflected in comments made in the *Manual on Fiscal Transparency*, released by the IMF:

> judgements about excessive debt, and particularly excessive debt-to-GDP ratios, are hard to make ... assessments of fiscal sustainability have to be made on a country-specific basis, relying on particular knowledge about the implications of, and market reactions to, the government's past and future fiscal policies. (IMF 1998b)

Thus judgements on the desirable public debt ratio for any one country are contingent on the size and frequency of the economic shocks to which that country has been exposed and the worthwhile investment opportunities that are available to the government. Care needs to be taken, therefore, when extrapolating empirical evidence and overseas policies in an attempt to learn lessons in the British context. Nonetheless, the Government's policy is consistent with the emphasis on debt reduction seen recently in many industrial countries (see Box 9.3).

In producing the fiscal plans set out in Budget 2001 (and in earlier *Economic and Fiscal Strategy Reports*), the Government has weighed up the need to:

- invest in the reform and modernisation of the public sector that is necessary to deliver the public services Britain needs
- fund that investment in a way that does not impose an unfair burden on current or future generations
- maintain public debt at levels which do not expose the Government to risk and that are unlikely to have a substantive negative impact on long-term growth and employment.

After considering the various arguments carefully, the Government concluded that, other things equal, a reduction in net public debt – to below 40 per cent of GDP – is consistent with a balanced and responsible approach to fiscal management. At the same time, this reduction is consistent with a doubling in net public sector investment to meet the Government's key spending priorities.

This conclusion was reflected in the projections outlined in Budget 2001. As Figure 9.7 shows, net public debt is planned to fall well below 40 per cent of GDP. This plan will also ensure that the gross general government debt remains comfortably below 60 per cent of GDP (the Treaty reference level), thus allowing Britain to meet its European commitment.

Conclusion

Since taking office the Government has reformed economic policy in the UK within a more open and transparent framework. The reforms have been aimed at rebuilding confidence in economic management.

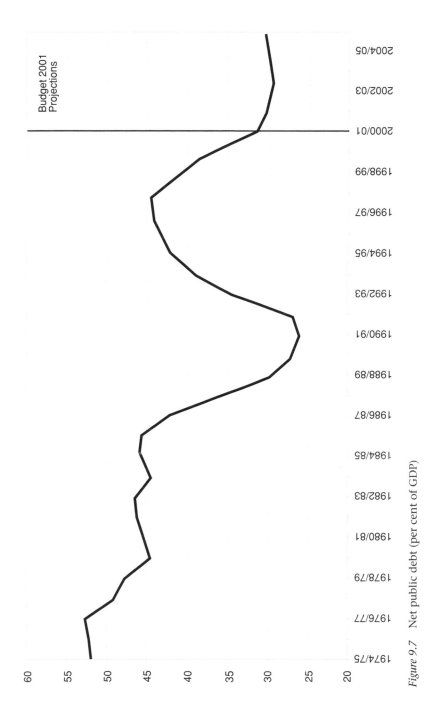

Figure 9.7 Net public debt (per cent of GDP)

Box 9.3   Policies on public debt – an international comparison

As the chart below shows, many industrial countries saw rising levels of public debt during the 1980s and early 1990s.

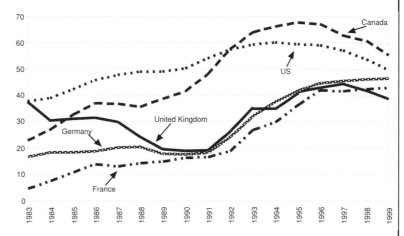

Figure 9.8   General government net financial liabilities (per cent of GDP)

Because of the potentially harmful effects of high debt, many governments have taken action to stabilise or reduce public debt as a proportion of GDP.

- In Europe, the Maastricht reference level is for member states to maintain their public debt ratios (defined in gross general government terms) at no more than 60 per cent of GDP. Some European countries have set more ambitious objectives.
- Debt reduction is also on the agenda in North America. Canada has implemented a Debt Reduction Plan so that, for the first time in 20 years, net public debt has started to fall significantly when expressed as a proportion of GDP.
- Australia has reduced the central government component of general government debt to below 10 per cent of GDP, compared with the 1995/96 level of 20 per cent.

The fiscal rules play a key role in these reforms. Parliament and the public are being informed explicitly about the direction of fiscal policy and the underlying economic objectives. Meeting these fiscal rules will demonstrate the Government's commitment to sound public finances.

This chapter concludes that clear rules, and firm implementation of them, will deliver sound public finances and, in doing so, assist greatly in restoring the credibility of fiscal policy.

With respect to the golden rule:

- when coupled with the sustainable investment rule, it will ensure that the public finances remain on a sustainable long-term basis
- it addresses past fiscal failings by removing the bias against capital spending while remaining within a sound fiscal framework
- it provides a workable approximation to the principle of achieving fairness between generations.

With respect to the sustainable investment rule:

- it is desirable to focus on a net measure of public debt covering the whole public sector and expressed as a proportion of GDP
- within bounds, public debt can act to facilitate public investment and intergenerational equity. However, high levels of public debt reduce a government's ability to buffer the economy against major shocks. High levels of debt may also impose other costs, such as higher interest rates and efficiency losses due to the higher tax rates needed to service the debt or reduced spending on priorities
- current levels of public debt in the UK are not high by historical or international standards. However, a modest reduction in net public debt – to below 40 per cent of GDP – is consistent with a balanced and responsible approach to fiscal management.

10
Analysing UK Fiscal Policy

This chapter provides a guide to analysing fiscal policy under the new framework. It discusses the key fiscal aggregates and how fiscal policy is set in practice, using Budget 2001 to illustrate the points made.

Introduction

As described in previous chapters, the Government has taken significant steps to strengthen the framework for fiscal policy. Fiscal policy is now directed firmly towards maintaining sound public finances over the medium term, based on strict rules. It also supports monetary policy over the economic cycle. This approach, together with the new monetary policy framework, provides the platform of stability necessary for achieving the Government's central economic goal of high and sustainable levels of growth and employment.

High-quality external scrutiny of the conduct of fiscal policy plays a key role in ensuring that the benefits of the new framework are delivered fully. This chapter aims to help understanding by providing a guide to analysing fiscal policy under the new framework.

It is important to understand the role each fiscal aggregate plays in analysis of policy. Using an inappropriate aggregate can result in misleading conclusions. For example, while the public sector net cash requirement is a good measure of the public sector's financing needs, it is not the best measure of the impact of fiscal policy on the economy or the long-term sustainability of fiscal policy.

Subsequent sections discuss the key fiscal policy aggregates, how fiscal policy operates within the new framework and how careful assessment of the key aggregates – combined with more detailed analysis – can help form an accurate picture of developments in the public finances and their impact on the economy both over the short and the long term. Budget 2001 is used to illustrate the points made.

The key fiscal aggregates

Two important features of the new fiscal policy framework are a high level of transparency in fiscal reporting combined with greater emphasis on fiscal aggregates with economic meaning. This contrasts with the previous framework in which the public sector net cash requirement (formerly the PSBR) was the primary focus of policy decision making, notwithstanding the fact that it is an inadequate measure of the economic impact or sustainability of fiscal policy.

A further major shortcoming of the various public sector net cash requirement targets adopted was that they failed to prevent a bias against capital spending. Current and capital spending could be offset against each other, making capital projects – where the benefits appear only in the future – an easy target when it became necessary to tighten the fiscal stance. This bias contributed to considerable under-investment in the public capital stock.

Under the new framework a variety of fiscal aggregates are now reported regularly by the Government, some of which take on particular importance. Each fiscal aggregate is usually reported in both nominal terms and as a proportion of GDP, the latter providing a better indicator of trends since it allows for the impact of inflation and real growth in the economy. In addition, many of the indicators are also reported in cyclically adjusted terms; that is, they are adjusted for the estimated impact of the economic cycle so that the underlying or structural trend can be seen more easily. The impact of the cycle on the public finances is discussed in detail in Chapter 11.

Each of these aggregates has a role to play in analysis of policy. Understanding the differences between fiscal aggregates is essential to form an accurate picture of developments in the public finances and their impact on the economy. It is important to use the right aggregate – or combination of aggregates – for the task at hand. Table 10.1 provides a brief guide to the appropriate indicators that are used.

Using the key fiscal aggregates

Analysing progress against the medium-term fiscal policy objectives

Ensuring that the public finances remain sound is the primary objective of fiscal policy. In this respect public sector net debt is a key indicator under the Government's new framework. It is the measure of debt against which the sustainable investment rule is assessed. The golden rule also plays a major role in keeping borrowing levels consistent with a prudent net debt ratio because the current budget is a major driver of public sector net borrowing (PSNB). But there are several other fiscal indicators that also have a role to play in assessing the long-term sustainability of the public finances.

- *Net debt versus gross debt*: public debt figures can be defined either in gross or net terms. Gross figures capture the total amount of the Government's financial liabilities whereas net figures subtract from this figure the value of liquid financial assets. Net debt is used in the Government's framework since it provides a fairer reflection of the Government's immediate solvency. The Maastricht measure of debt, which is comparable across EU member states, is based on gross general government debt.
- *Primary balance*: PSNB excluding net debt interest payments. It represents the fiscal position excluding the impact of past deficits. It is possible to calculate the primary balance required to stabilise the ratio of net debt to GDP over the long term at different levels. A large primary balance is required if debt is high or if the interest rate is well above the growth rate.[1]
- *Public sector net worth*: measures the Government's net asset position; that is, the difference between the total assets, including non-financial assets (such as roads), and liabilities. It represents the approximate stock counterpart to the current balance, and links appropriately with the golden rule. Changes in net worth provide an indication of the extent to which the net assets of the public sector are changing. However, many Government assets and liabilities are difficult to measure accurately. The estimates of tangible assets, for example, are dependent on broad assumptions which may not be appropriate in every case. This is why public sector net debt continues to play an important role in the fiscal policy framework. However, the Office for National Statistics (ONS) is currently in the process of improving the quality of balance sheets. These developments may allow net worth to play a greater role in the fiscal framework in the future.
- *Prospective net worth*: provides a forward-looking measure of the Government's net asset position. It represents current net worth plus the discounted value of all future spending and receipts that the Government will face as a result of its current policies. In

practice, many of these future cash flows are particularly difficult to measure. However, it can be argued that including estimates of some of the more 'lumpy' items – such as unfunded pension liabilities – may provide useful information on the wider sustainability of the Government's fiscal position.

- *Long-term fiscal projections*: published with the *Economic and Fiscal Strategy Report* (EFSR) each year in accordance with the Code for Fiscal Stability, also help to assess the sustainability of the public finances. They examine the effects of demography and other influences on long-term spending and taxation. The first set of long-term projections, published in the 1999 EFSR, suggested that the UK's future public finances are on a broadly sustainable path.

A further medium-term objective is to ensure that, as far as possible, those generations who benefit from public spending also meet the costs of the services they consume. This is part of the rationale behind the golden rule, whereby the Government is committed, over the economic cycle, to borrow only to invest and not to fund current spending. The key indicator of progress against this rule is the average current budget over the economic cycle. The current budget represents the difference between current receipts and current expenditure including depreciation. The golden rule is met when the average current budget over the economic cycle is in balance or surplus.

Generational accounts can also provide an indication of the fairness of policy across generations. They provide a means, on the basis of maintaining current policies, of comparing the net burden of taxation and transfer payments on present generations with that faced by future generations. The Treasury has supported a study by the National Institute for Economic and Social Research to produce and publish the first set of generational accounts for the UK.

Analysing the short-term fiscal policy stance

While the primary objective of fiscal policy is to ensure the medium-term sustainability of the public finances and fairness between generations, fiscal policy can also play a short-term role in supporting monetary policy. It is for this reason that the two fiscal rules are set over the economic cycle – it allows PSNB to vary between years, in keeping with the cyclical position of the economy.

The impact of fiscal policy on the economy is very complex, especially in the short term. It depends on the composition of spending and taxation as well as on the balance between them. Some changes in the Budget will have mainly a short-term impact on aggregate demand;

others may have an impact on both aggregate demand and aggregate supply. Inflation can have an impact too, though with monetary policy set firmly to achieve price stability, this is not a particularly significant issue in the UK. How the economy responds to fiscal policy also depends on businesses and individuals' expectations – whether fiscal policy developments have been anticipated or not and how people expect fiscal policy to develop in the future.

However, as a first approximation, and in the absence of a significant compositional shift in taxation and spending in the Budget, the key indicator for assessing the overall fiscal impact is the change in public sector net borrowing. PSNB differs from the surplus on the current budget because it includes net investment. Government investment spending will have an impact on economic activity and so should be included when assessing the economic impact of fiscal policy.

The overall fiscal impact is therefore made up of changes in:

- that part of PSNB resulting from cyclical movements in the economy; that is, through the operation of the automatic stabilisers
- that part of PSNB resulting from changes in the fiscal stance (which is equivalent to changes in cyclically adjusted or structural PSNB).

The fiscal stance can change as a result of:

- discretionary Budget measures: for example, a decision at Budget time to reduce tax rates will have the effect, other things equal, of increasing cyclically adjusted PSNB. Similarly, a decision to raise Government expenditure will increase cyclically adjusted PSNB. The opposite would occur following an increase in tax rates or a reduction in public spending.
- non-discretionary factors: for example, a rise in the price of oil will, other things equal, reduce cyclically adjusted PSNB, through an increase in North Sea tax receipts. Other developments that can result in unplanned changes in cyclically adjusted PSNB include changes in spending habits. For example, a reduction in demand for tobacco will reduce the tax take for given increases in GDP.

Information about these non-discretionary factors will be available to the Government when making Budget decisions. A key policy issue is whether to accommodate their expected effects or whether to augment or offset their impact through Budget measures. In this way, the Government can determine the expected or desired fiscal stance.

The future is uncertain so, as events unfold, the actual fiscal stance that evolves may differ from that expected at the time of the Budget. For example, an intended tightening of the fiscal stance may be transformed into an unexpected loosening due to an unanticipated decline in revenue that is unrelated to the economic cycle (for example, due to a fall in the effective rate of VAT). Factors like this need to be taken into account when analysing the evolution of the fiscal stance (see Box 10.1).

Box 10.1   Key elements in determining the projected fiscal stance

Discretionary Budget measures to change the fiscal stance
+
effects of all non-discretionary factors which have altered,
or which are expected to alter, the fiscal stance
=
the change in the fiscal stance
+
the effect of the automatic stabilisers stemming
from the cyclical position of the economy relative to trend
=
the change in the overall fiscal impact (measured as a first order
approximation by the total change in the PSNB)

The absolute fiscal stance is given by the change in cyclically adjusted PSNB during the period covered by the Budget projections. However, it is also appropriate to analyse the change in the fiscal stance between Budgets. This analysis reveals the extent to which the fiscal stance is tightening or loosening relative to the previous Budget projections. It is possible, for example, for the fiscal stance to be tightened in relative terms, while continuing to loosen in absolute terms.

The Budget projections of cyclically adjusted PSNB indicate the extent to which the Government is planning to undertake a discretionary tightening or loosening of the fiscal stance. This tightening or loosening may come about due to one or both of:

- a discretionary Budget measure to achieve the desired change in the fiscal stance
- a Budget decision to accommodate or offset the impact of non-discretionary factors that are expected to affect the fiscal stance.

In a cyclical downturn, provided that there was no threat to the sustainability of the fiscal position, policy would be set to accommodate an increase in PSNB. This will allow the automatic stabilisers to support monetary policy in the 'below trend' phase of the cycle with a positive overall fiscal impact on demand. It would generally be inappropriate in such circumstances to offset the automatic stabilisers by tightening the structural fiscal position to prevent a rise in borrowing, since this could be destabilising for the economy and act against the interests of monetary policy.

Box 10.2 gives some examples of how changes in the public finances can be interpreted using these concepts.

Box 10.2   Explaining changes in the public finances – some examples

Scenario 1: Budget economic projections show the economy moving below trend. Budget projects unchanged cyclically adjusted PSNB over coming year but actual PSNB is projected to rise.

- Fiscal policy is acting to support monetary policy by allowing the automatic stabilisers to play their role. The overall fiscal impact on demand is positive in the short-term. However, the fiscal stance remains unchanged.

Scenario 2: Budget economic projections show the economy moving well below trend. Budget projects a rise in cyclically adjusted PSNB over coming year due exclusively to a Budget decision to reduce tax rates or increase spending. Actual PSNB is forecast to rise over and above the increase in cyclically adjusted PSNB.

- Fiscal policy is acting to support monetary policy by allowing the automatic stabilisers to play their role as the economy goes below trend. Fiscal policy provides additional support by supplementing the operation of the automatic stabilisers with a discretionary loosening in the fiscal stance. This leads to a positive overall impact on demand in excess of that provided by the automatic stabilisers.

Scenario 3: Budget economic projections show the economy remaining on trend. However fiscal projections show an increase in the effective tax rate over the coming year, leading to a reduction in cyclically adjusted PSNB. Government takes Budget decisions to lower revenue from other sources or raise spending to offset this, thus leaving cyclically adjusted PSNB unchanged over the coming year.

- This is an example of a projected non-discretionary tightening of the fiscal stance. To offset this tightening, discretionary Budget measures are taken so as to leave the fiscal stance unchanged.

How fiscal policy decisions are made in the Budget

The Budget presents a definitive statement of the Government's desired fiscal settings given the information it has to hand.

At each Budget, two key issues are considered before decisions are made about any changes to the aggregate fiscal policy settings:

- what outcomes for the key fiscal aggregates are required to ensure that, over the economic cycle, the Government meets its fiscal rules and thus its broader medium-term fiscal objectives
- what path for the key fiscal aggregates best ensures that, over the economic cycle, fiscal policy supports monetary policy in dampening fluctuations in the economy to help stabilise activity.

Establishing a path for the key aggregates consistent with meeting the fiscal rules

The Government is committed to meeting its fiscal rules. But projections of the public finances necessarily involve a significant element of uncertainty and the Government needs to take this into account in setting policy. For example, public revenue and spending projections depend heavily on economic growth and on assumptions made about the position of the economy in relation to its long-term trend. Deviations from what is assumed carry significant consequences for the fiscal balances. In addition, projections of particular tax revenues and spending are subject to specific risks and uncertainties.

Accordingly, in setting fiscal policy, the Government takes a deliberately cautious approach. This has to balance the costs of potentially underachieving the fiscal rules against those associated with running an unduly restrictive fiscal policy stance. It also recognises that some adjustment of the fiscal stance is possible within the cycle, if actual outturns and updated projections suggest the Government is no longer likely to meet its objectives.

This prudent approach is implemented, among other things, by adopting a cautious assumption about the economy's trend growth rate. The Government's economic policies are designed to raise this growth rate beyond the level assumed for fiscal policy purposes. For the purposes of fiscal planning, however, it would not be prudent to take credit for any success of these policies until firm evidence emerges. This approach ensures the risks of costly policy reversals are minimised.

Dealing with pipeline measures

When forming a view on the desired fiscal stance, the Government takes into account all pipeline measures. These are measures announced in previous Budgets, yet to come into effect, but which nevertheless will have an impact on the fiscal position. Pipeline measures are included in the baseline projections and are therefore included when decisions are made over the policy action required to bring those projections into line with desired outcomes. The fiscal indicators published in the EFSR, the FSBR and the *Pre-Budget Report* (PBR) all include the full effects of these pipeline measures.

An example of such a pipeline measure is the decision in the March 1998 Budget to introduce the Working Families Tax Credit (WFTC) as part of the Government's package of measures to make work pay. While the announcement of this policy was made in March 1998, the WFTC did not come into effect until October 1999. Accordingly, its effect on the fiscal position did not begin until then, with the full effect not coming in until 2000–01. The numbers presented in the Budget 99 projections included the full effects of the introduction of the WFTC.

Arriving at the Budget decision

At Budget time a judgement is reached about the appropriate fiscal stance given the need to meet the fiscal rules. This judgement also takes into account the need to ensure, insofar as possible, that the overall fiscal impact supports monetary policy through the economic cycle. The Government then implements discretionary Budget measures to the extent that they are necessary to deliver the appropriate fiscal stance, taking into account the impact of non-discretionary factors which change the baseline fiscal projections (including pipeline measures).

Keeping the Monetary Policy Committee informed

One of the objectives of fiscal policy is to support the operation of monetary policy, so it is essential, to ensure proper coordination of fiscal and monetary policy, that the Monetary Policy Committee (MPC) is fully informed of the Government's approach to fiscal policy. The Treasury representative on the MPC (who speaks at the meetings but does not have a vote) provides an important conduit through which this communication takes place.

In accordance with the overall policy of transparency, the MPC minutes always make clear when the Committee has been briefed about fiscal developments in advance of information becoming publicly available.

The role of the *Pre-Budget Report*

Under the Code for Fiscal Stability, the Government is committed to publishing a *Pre-Budget Report* at least three months prior to the Budget. One of the roles of the PBR is to increase transparency, which it does in two key ways. First, it provides an opportunity for the Government to consult the public on specific policy initiatives under consideration for the forthcoming Budget. Second, it presents an update on the outlook for the economy and the public finances, taking into account economic and other developments since the Budget.

It is important to note that the public finance projections contained in the PBR present an interim forecast update. The PBR projections do not necessarily represent the outcome the Government is seeking. They have a quite different status to the projections contained in the EFSR and FSBR at Budget time. The figures presented are preliminary and the projections are subject to change in the period before the Budget. Forecast errors can be large, even in the near term. A further assessment is made at Budget time before decisions are taken to ensure the fiscal rules are met.

The status of the PBR projections carries implications for the way in which deviations from the Budget projections are interpreted. For example:

- If tax revenue appears likely to turn out lower than expected as a result of an unexpected fall in the effective tax rate, other things equal, the surplus on the current budget will be forecast to be smaller than that expected in the Budget (equivalently PSNB and public sector net debt will be forecast to be higher). If the PBR forecast is confirmed ahead of the subsequent Budget, decisions will be taken to ensure that the Government continues to meet its fiscal objectives. This may result, for example, in changes in taxation policy to offset the unexpected loss of revenue. Alternatively, no change (or limited change) may be necessary if changes in revenue are matched by an equivalent and offsetting unexpected change in spending.
- If expenditure on Annually Managed Expenditure (AME) appears likely to turn out lower than projected at the time of the Budget, the forecast 'savings' will be reflected in a higher AME margin, rather than in a higher surplus on the current budget (or lower PSNB). On the other hand, if expenditure on AME items appears likely to be higher than expected in the Budget, the AME margin

will be drawn down. Any additional projected spending necessary beyond that allowed for by the AME margin will be reflected in a reduction in the surplus on the current budget and higher PSNB. If the PBR projections are validated ahead of the subsequent Budget, decisions will be taken at that time to ensure that fiscal policy settings remain consistent with the Government's rules and objectives.

- Limited variation is expected in expenditure on Departmental Expenditure Limits (DEL) given the enforcement of strict multi-year plans. In the first instance, unexpected pressures on DEL are expected to be resolved by reprioritising DEL expenditure. One exception is that any underspend in one year can be carried over to subsequent years.

Analysing the impact and performance of fiscal policy – an example

This section illustrates in practical terms how the fiscal indicators discussed above can be used to form an impression of the state of the public finances and their impact on the economy.

Table 10.1 shows how the fiscal position can be analysed. The analysis uses the indicators and approach discussed above and is organised around five key themes: fairness and prudence, sustainability, economic impact, financing and meeting European commitments.

Fairness and prudence

The position on the current budget has improved markedly since 1996–97 when there was a deficit of 3 per cent of GDP, to stand at a surplus of 2.4 per cent of GDP in 2000–01.

The 3 per cent deficit inherited by the Government, which had been preceded by even bigger deficits, meant that there had previously been borrowing over the cycle to finance current spending as well as borrowing for investment. As well as being imprudent, this meant that future generations were being required to pay for services consumed by the previous generation of taxpayers. Fiscal policy is now operating in a more prudent manner and one that is fairer between generations – the Government is no longer borrowing to finance current spending, which means that, as far as possible, those taxpayers who benefit from current spending also bear its costs.

Simply looking at the surplus on the current budget can be misleading when trying to assess the underlying position. The cyclically adjusted

Table 10.1 Using the key fiscal aggregates

Issue under examination	Appropriate Fiscal Measure									Other Information		
	Surplus on current budget over the cycle	Public sector net debt	PSNB	Cyclically adjusted PSNB	Net Worth	Primary balance	General government financial deficit	General government gross debt	Central government net cash requirement	Generational accounts	Long-term fiscal projections	Composition of spending and revenue
Medium-term fiscal policy objectives:												
Ensuring fiscal policy is prudent, i.e. consistent with sustainability	●	●			●	●				●	●	
Fairness of fiscal policy across generations	●									●		
Short-term fiscal policy objectives:												
Fiscal stance				●								●
Overall fiscal impact			●									●
Other objectives:												
Consistency with European commitments							●	●				
Government's financing requirement									●			

Table 10.2 Summary of Budget 2001[1]

	Outturn 1999–00	Estimate 2000–01	Per cent of GDP		Projections 2003–04	2004–05	2005–06
			2001–02	2002–03			
Fairness and prudence							
Surplus on current budget	2.1	2.4	1.7	1.4	0.8	0.8	0.8
Average surplus since 1999–2000	2.1	2.3	2.1	1.9	1.7	1.5	1.4
Cyclically adjusted surplus on current budget	1.9	2.1	1.4	1.1	0.6	0.7	0.7
Long-term sustainability							
Public sector net debt[2]	36.8	31.8	30.3	29.6	29.7	29.9	30.0
Net worth[2]	17.4	18.8	21.3	21.6	21.4	21.0	20.4
Primary balance	4.2	4.0	2.5	1.7	0.8	0.7	0.6
Economic impact							
Net investment[2]	0.4	0.8	1.1	1.5	1.7	1.8	1.8
Public sector net borrowing (PSNB)	–1.8	–1.7	–0.6	0.1	0.9	1.0	1.0
Cyclically adjusted PSNB	–1.6	–1.4	–0.3	0.3	1.1	1.1	1.1
Financing							
Central government net cash requirement[2]	–1.0	–3.5	0.0	0.5	1.5	1.4	1.4
European commitments							
Maastricht deficit[3]	–1.7	–1.7	–0.5	0.1	0.9	0.9	1.0
Maastricht debt ratio[4]	43.7	40.6	37.6	36.1	35.7	35.6	35.6
Memo: Output gap	0.2	0.6	0.5	0.3	0.2	0.1	0.0

Notes:
1 Excluding windfall tax receipts and associated spending.
2 Including windfall tax receipts and associated spending.
3 General government net borrowing on an ESA95 basis. The Maastricht definition includes the windfall tax and associated spending.
4 General government gross debt.

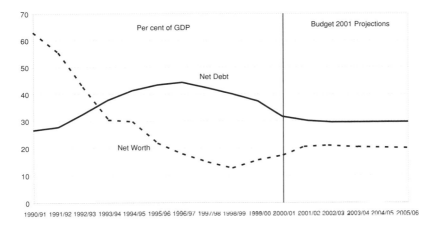

Figure 10.1   Public sector net debt and net worth

surplus on the current budget presented in Table 10.2 demonstrates that the improvement in the position of the current balance has been structural, rather than merely a result of cyclical developments.

The golden rule not only tries to ensure fairness between generations, but also contributes to a prudent approach to the public finances. Current spending and revenue are the most significant drivers of trends in PSNB. Hence, achieving the golden rule plays a major part in keeping borrowing to levels consistent with a prudent and sustainable net debt ratio. In this way, the golden rule and the sustainable investment rule work together to deliver sound public finances.

Through a full economic cycle the economy will move above and below its trend growth path. It is therefore to be expected that the actual current budget surplus will vary between years. For this reason the golden rule is set over the cycle, not for each year. The key indicator to judge whether the Government is on track to meet the golden rule is the average surplus on the current budget over the whole cycle. On the basis of the Budget 2001 numbers, the Government was on track to meet the golden rule over this cycle.

Sustainability

Substantial progress has been made in reducing the public sector net debt ratio since 1996–97. The Budget 2001 fiscal projections (set out in Table 10.2) show net debt falling to around 30 per cent of GDP in 2001–02 and remaining broadly constant at this level for the remainder of the projection period. The projections for net worth also pointed to a sustainable fiscal position. Having fallen from over 70 per cent of GDP in 1990–91 to under 14 per cent in 1998–99, mainly as a result of large deficits on the current budget, a steady recovery from then on was projected to around 21 per cent of GDP by 2004–05 (see Figure 10.1).

The primary balance has swung from a deficit of ½ per cent of GDP in 1996–97 to an estimated surplus of 4 per cent of GDP in 2000–01. Although the surplus is projected to decline to ½ per cent of GDP in 2005–06 it remains positive throughout the projection period.

Illustrative long-term fiscal projections, discussed in detail in Chapter 14, also help to assess the long-term sustainability of the public finances by projecting the key fiscal aggregates over a longer time period. The latest set of long-term projections, published in Budget 2001, showed that over the next 30 years the UK's public finances are broadly sustainable.

Economic impact

PSNB fell from 3.6 per cent of GDP in 1996–97 to –1.8 per cent of GDP by 2000–01, that is, a net repayment. Some of the fall in PSNB since 1996–97 can be attributed to a strengthening economy. However, there was a signicant fall in cyclically adjusted PSNB. From a deficit of 3 per cent of GDP in 1996–97, cyclically adjusted PSNB in Budget 2001 is estimated to have moved into balance in 1998–99 and to a surplus of around 1½ per cent of GDP in 1999–2000 and 2000–01. Modest deficits are projected from 2002–03 onwards, as the share of public sector net investment to GDP rises.

The support for monetary policy continues to come through the operation of the automatic stabilisers as shown by the projected modest increase in PSNB over this period.

Table 10.2 shows the ratio of net investment to GDP is projected to more than double to 1¾ per cent of GDP by 2003–04. The rapid growth of net investment results in a declining surplus this year and modest overall deficits over the remainder of the forecast period.

Financing

As noted previously, the public sector net cash requirement (formerly known as the PSBR) represents the public sector's short-term net cash financing requirement. This net cash measure no longer plays a significant role in the fiscal policy framework as it is not the best measure of the sustainability or economic impact of fiscal policy. However, it is

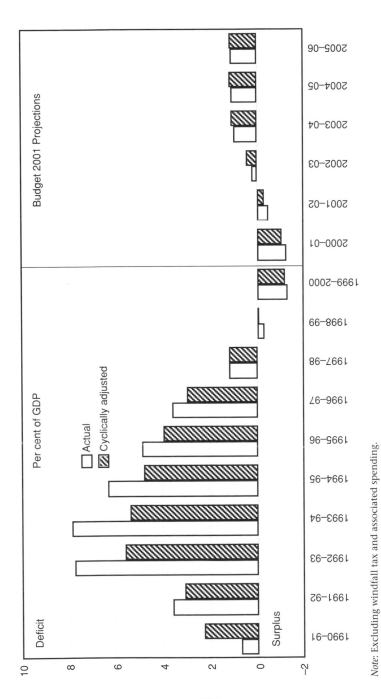

Note: Excluding windfall tax and associated spending.

Figure 10.2 Public sector net borrowing – actual and cyclically adjusted

still used to calculate the Government's gross debt issuance, since debt management operations necessarily involve cash financing.

The Government finances its net cash requirement plus maturing debt and any net finance required for the foreign exchange reserves though the issuance of debt, which includes gilts sales, National Savings products, Treasury Bills and other short-term cash management instruments. The central government net cash requirement was a repayment of 1 per cent of GDP in 1999–2000. The repayment in 2000–01 was 3.8 per cent of GDP, largely reflecting receipts from the auction of radio spectrum licences. The net cash requirement moves into deficit from 2002–03 onwards, reflecting the profile of PSNB.

Based on projections in Budget 2001, the Government aims to issue debt in 2001–02 to meet a gross financing requirement of £20.4 billion, which is based on a forecast for the central government net cash requirement of £0.3 billion, plus gilt redemptions of £16.7 billion, £1.0 billion in gilt buy-backs, £1.3 billion pre-financing of foreign exchange debt and £1.1 billion of accrued uplift on maturing index-linked debt.

The £1 billion purchase of gilts through secondary market buy-backs and the £1.3 billion pre-financing of foreign currency debt due in 2003 both help to increase the financing requirement and this will help to address liquidity problems in the gilts market. Gross gilt sales are planned to be £13.5 billion in 2001–02. Additionally, the pre-financing of foreign currency debt provides better value for money for the taxpayer than continued foreign exchange borrowing.

European commitments

The Stability and Growth Pact, agreed in Amsterdam in 1997, strengthens and clarifies the excessive deficits procedure outlined in Article 104 of the Treaty. Key requirements of the Stability and Growth Pact, discussed in more detail in Chapter 18, are:

- a medium-term budgetary objective of close to balance or surplus
- that excessive deficits should be avoided. In particular, if the deficit (defined as general government financial deficit, the 'Maastricht deficit') exceeds 3 per cent of GDP member states may be fined, although as an 'Out' the UK cannot be fined.

The Treaty also provides a reference value for general government gross debt of 60 per cent of GDP. The Budget 2001 projections are consistent with these Treaty requirements and are in line with the Stability and Growth Pact. Gross debt is projected to fall to 37.6 per cent in 2001–02 and then to nearly 35 per cent by the end of the forecast period, well below the reference value. Consistent with the Government's fiscal rules, the general government financial balance moves into a small deficit in the medium term reflecting the impact of increased investment in priority public services announced in the 2000 Spending Review. It remains well within the 3 per cent reference value.

The cautious case

The Government takes a deliberately cautious approach in setting fiscal policy to ensure it meets its fiscal objectives. Projections of the public finances necessarily involve a significant element of uncertainty and are therefore based on deliberately cautious assumptions audited by the National Audit Office. Ex ante, these projections include a small surplus on the current budget to provide a safety margin over that which would strictly be necessary to meet the golden rule.

The Government publishes an additional projection based on a more cautious case in which trend output is assumed to be 1 percentage point lower than in the main projection. This scenario models the implications of assuming that a greater proportion of the projected surplus on the current budget results from the cyclical strength of the economy. Figure 10.3 shows that even under the more cautious case the Government would still remain on track to meet the fiscal rules.

Conclusion

The new fiscal policy framework, with its emphasis on transparency, means that there is a wide range of relevant fiscal policy information reported in the Budget and supporting documents. Understanding which pieces of information are appropriate for each purpose is crucial to forming an accurate impression of developments in the public finances, both in terms of the short-term impact of fiscal policy on the economy and the soundness of fiscal policy settings over the medium term.

Each PBR provides the Government's latest projections for both the economy and the public finances. As outlined earlier, these do not necessarily represent the Government's view of desired outcomes. While the PBR projections are used as a basis for policy planning in the lead up to the Budget, it is the Budget itself in which any desired changes to fiscal policy will be undertaken.

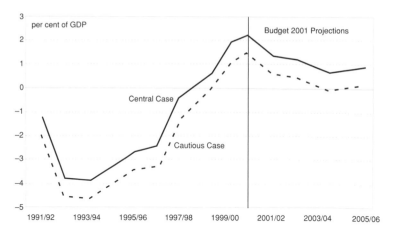

Note: Cautious case assumes trend output 1 per cent lower in relation to actual output than in the central case.

Figure 10.3   Meeting the golden rule – cautious assumptions

APPENDIX: THE FISCAL ARITHMETIC

This appendix describes how each of the key fiscal indicators is defined. It also provides a brief explanation of the cyclical adjustment methodology used by the Treasury and the arithmetic underlying the relationship between the public sector primary balance and the net debt ratio.

Abbreviations

CB   surplus on current budget
CACB   cyclically adjusted current budget
CR   current revenue
CE   current expenditure
D   depreciation
PSNW   public sector net worth
ND   public sector net debt
GD   public sector gross debt
PSNB   public sector net borrowing
CAPSNB   cyclically adjusted PSNB
PSNCR   public sector net cash requirement
PSNI   public sector net investment
PSPB   public sector primary balance

GDP   gross domestic product
GDPT   trend gross domestic product
OG   output gap
t time period (1 year)

Flow measures

$$CB_t = CR_t - CE_t - D_t$$

$$PSNB_t = - CB_t + PSNI_t$$

$$PSNCR_t = PSNB_t + \text{financial transactions}_t{}^2$$

$$PSPB_t = - PSNB_t + \text{net debt interest payments}_t$$

Stock measures

$$PSNW_t = PSNW_{t-1} + CB_t + \text{net asset revaluation}_t$$

$$ND_t = ND_{t-1} + PSNCR_t + \text{balancing item}_t{}^3$$

$$GD_t = GD_{t-1} + \text{new debt issued}_t - \text{debt redeemed}_t$$

Each aggregate above can be expressed as a proportion of GDP (and it is often more sensible to do so, as it abstracts from the impact of inflation and real growth in the economy).

Cyclical adjustment

In addition, each of the flow balances can be adjusted to illustrate the underlying or structural position (which excludes the impact of the economic cycle).[4] For example, the Treasury calculates the cyclically adjusted current budget as a percentage of GDP as:

$$CACB_t = CB_t - 0.4 * OG_t - 0.3 * OG_{t-1}$$

whereas cyclically adjusted PSNB equals:

$$CAPSNB_t = PSNB_t + 0.4 * OG_t + 0.3 * OG_{t-1}$$

where:

$$OG_t = ((GDP_t - GDPT_t)/GDPT_t) * 100$$

It should be noted that the coefficients of 0.4 and 0.3 shown above will become 0.5 and 0.2 due to the corporation tax instalment regime announced in the March 1998 Budget.

The public sector primary balance and the net debt ratio

It is possible to calculate the public sector primary balance (as a proportion of GDP) required to stabilise the net public debt ratio at a given target level using the following formula:

$$\frac{\text{PSPB}}{\text{GDP}} = \left(r - g\right) \times \left(\frac{\text{ND target}}{\text{GDP}}\right)$$

where r is the real interest rate, and g is the real economic growth rate.

Table 10.A1 shows the PSPB (as a per cent of GDP) required to stabilise the net public debt ratio at 40 per cent under different rates of growth and different real interest rates. It shows that, all else remaining equal, a higher primary balance is required when growth is lower and when interest rates are higher.

Table 10.A1   Public sector primary balance required to stabilise net public debt at 40 per cent of GDP

Growth rate (g)	2.5%	2.0%	2.5%	2.0%
Interest rate (r)	2.5%	2.5%	4.0%	4.0%
Difference ($r - g$)	0.0%	0.5%	1.5%	2.0%
PSPB required (as % GDP)	0.0%	0.2%	0.6%	0.8%

11
The Public Finances and the Economic Cycle

This chapter describes how the Treasury measures the level of trend output, the output gap, and the economic cycle. The chapter shows how estimates of the output gap can be used to estimate the responsiveness of the main components of tax revenues and public expenditure, and consequently the fiscal aggregates, to the economic cycle.

Introduction

The economic cycle has important short-term effects on the public finances. These effects need to be taken into account when assessing the underlying (structural) position of the public finances. As set out in Chapter 1, experience has shown that serious mistakes can occur if purely cyclical improvements in the public finances are treated as if they represented structural improvements, or if a structural deterioration is interpreted as a cyclical effect. This is why the Code for Fiscal Stability requires the Government to publish estimates of the cyclically adjusted fiscal position.

How the cycle impacts on the public finances is liable to change over time, for a number of reasons. New data observations may change our view about where the economy is relative to trend. Policy changes may affect how quickly different effects feed through. And developments in techniques for estimating the effects of the cycle may also lead to different views.

This assessment of the effects of the cycle on the public finances focuses on the Government's fiscal aggregates and takes account of the implications of the move to the new European System of Accounts (ESA 95). The key aggregates are the surplus on current budget, which is used to judge performance against the golden rule; net borrowing, which on a cyclically adjusted basis provides an indication of the overall fiscal stance; and the ratio of public sector net debt to GDP, which is used to judge performance against the sustainable investment rule.

This chapter is divided in two parts:

- The first section describes in detail how the Treasury measures the economic cycle. It focuses on measuring the level of trend output, and the output gap, with particular reference to determining on-trend points.
- The second section uses these estimates of the output gap to estimate the responsiveness of the main components of tax revenues and public expenditure, and consequently the fiscal aggregates, to the economic cycle.

The appendix to this chapter sets out the estimation results in detail.

Potential output and the output gap

This section considers the concept of potential output (also referred to as trend output) and describes how the Treasury derives estimates of potential output and the output gap.

Potential output and inflation

The output gap

The path of output has a trend and a cyclical component. The trend is a function of continual advances in technology and production techniques as well as demographic changes. In the long term the economy tends to grow consistently. But over shorter periods, cyclical movements mean that the economy may at any given point in time be operating either above or below this long-term trend.

The output gap is the difference between the actual level of output and its potential level, usually expressed as a percentage of the level of potential output. When actual output is above potential output, there is a positive output gap; when actual output is below potential output, the output gap is negative.

Government expenditure and revenue are both highly cyclical, with expenditure falling and revenue rising in an economic upswing. Hence the public finances will be stronger when the economy is operating above trend, and weaker when the economy is below trend. This makes estimating the output gap extremely important. If the economy is operating close to trend, then this suggests that the public finances should be broadly in balance to be sustainable. But if the economy is operating above trend, then in the absence of any change in fiscal policy the public finances must be expected to deteriorate as output subsequently returns to trend.

The output–inflation trade-off

We can use our estimate of the output gap as an indicator of the risk of inflation: inflation tends to rise when output is above potential (that is, a positive output gap), and fall when output is below potential (a negative output gap). Therefore, a short-run trade-off (usually known as a Phillips Curve relationship) is said to exist between output and inflation.

In line with the consensus among economists, we assume that a positive output gap can typically only be sustained while inflation is higher than expected. It is this 'surprise' element that brings forward the extra employment and output, as real wages are temporarily reduced by the unexpectedly higher inflation.

Once inflation expectations adjust, output returns to its potential level, but at a higher rate of inflation. Hence in the long run, there is no trade off and periods of excess demand serve only to ratchet up the inflation rate (in technical terms, the long-run Phillips Curve is vertical).[1]

Unfortunately, the relationship between the output gap and inflation is not simple. The inflation rate is dependent on a number of other temporary factors, such as movements in the real exchange rate. Even abstracting from such short-term influences, it is possible that the trade-off may be asymmetric and non-linear. And there may be 'speed limits' on how fast a negative output gap can be closed without putting upward pressure on inflation, for instance, due to supply bottlenecks.

However, the implication of this underlying view of the economy is that we must assume actual output cannot be sustained above the level of potential output without eventually generating ever-increasing levels of inflation. Hence even if there are no immediate signs of inflation, in assessing the sustainability of the public finances we must assume that output will return to trend.

Asymmetry and non-linearities in the trade-off

There is some evidence that excess demand conditions are more inflationary than excess supply conditions are disinflationary; i.e. inflation may rise by more when output is above potential than it falls when output is below potential (see Turner 1995, Debelle and Laxton 1996). This might happen, for instance, if people resist any downward pressure on the rate at which their earnings grow. In the context of reducing inflation, this means an unfavourable trade-off: the lost output needed to bring about a given fall in inflation is greater than the temporary increase in the output that can be achieved while generating a similar rise in inflation. This asymmetry makes it important to prevent inflationary booms: any increase in inflation today may require a larger future loss of output in order to get inflation back down.

Speed limits

A 'speed limit' arises if an increase in inflation can be attributed to rapid or uneven output growth, despite output being below potential. This could be because plant capacity takes time to plan and install, or because wages might be responsive to the change in unemployment, not just the level. For example, rapid growth in the manufacturing sector in 1994 and the service sector in 1995 and 1996 caused the economy to run into bottlenecks, leading to higher inflation, even though the output gap was probably still negative.

Estimating potential output over the past

Trend extraction methodology

Neither the level nor the growth of trend output is directly observable. A variety of methods can be used to estimate trend output over the past, including statistical techniques, economic models of productive potential, or econometric models of the economy. The approach used currently in the Treasury is to estimate the trend rate of growth between comparable points in the cycle. While the Treasury believes its approach is the most appropriate for the analysis of the public finances, it regularly monitors and keeps abreast of the other techniques. A summary of the different approaches employed is summarised in Box 11.1.

Cyclical peaks are easy to identify, and hence are commonly used for estimating trend growth. However, peak-to-peak comparisons can yield misleading results if cycles are of different intensity. The Treasury's approach, therefore, is to use survey data to identify points when the economy is believed to have been on trend. In contrast to statistical techniques, this approach brings to bear a wide variety of economic information. It also allows for changes in the trend growth rate over time, though changes are restricted to occur at on-trend points.

Box 11.1   Trend extraction methods

There are four basic methods commonly used to determine the trend rate of growth from historical data.

One approach is to apply univariate statistical filters such as the Hodrick Prescott (HP) filter. The HP filter estimates a trend path minimising the difference between the trend path and actual GDP outturns subject to a smoothness constraint. The greater the degree of smoothness imposed, the closer the trend path will be to a linear trend. Theoretically, the chosen smoothness constraint should reflect the relative variance of demand to supply shocks hitting the economy. The main reasons for using the HP filter are relative simplicity and limited resource and data requirements.

A limitation of the HP filter is that it requires the user to set the smoothness constraint, i.e. the user must already be able to identify demand and supply shocks hitting the economy. In practice, most studies use the value set in early work by Hodrick and Prescott, though there is no guarantee that this produces valid results. One important limitation concerns the ability of the filter to account adequately for variations in output at the end-point of the sample, where estimates of trend output are most needed by policy makers.

An alternative approach is to use a multivariate statistical filter, of which the Kalman filter is one technique. It supplements the statistical approach by bringing to bear additional information based on known economic relationships that are useful for estimating the cyclical position of the economy; for example, the Phillips curve relationship or movements in import penetration. This approach adds a degree of complexity to the HP filter and has increased data and resource requirements. However, it can generate more accurate estimates of trend output with the 'end-point' problem reduced.

A further intuitive approach is to estimate trend output using structural methods, typically within a production function or growth accounting framework. It allows a decomposition of long term growth into growth in labour and capital inputs, and technological progress. While a more comprehensive analysis of the factors influencing economic growth is possible using this approach, it is more complex – assumptions need to be made about the form of the production function, for example – requires more resources, and is heavily dependent on the availability and quality of the relevant data. Obtaining good capital stock data is a particularly significant constraint. In addition, failure to cyclically adjust the components means that the aggregate estimates of trend output using this approach often tend to be pro-cyclical: trend output rises in response to higher investment spending and greater labour force participation, even though these may be cyclical effects.

The Treasury looks at a variety of different measures of trend output, including those derived using the methods outlined above. However, the approach preferred is to use a wide range of cyclical indicators – typically those which are not themselves trended, such as the results of various business surveys, the level of unemployment and vacancies, wage inflation – to inform a judgement of the dates at which the economy is on trend. For completed cycles, the estimate of trend output is simply a linear interpolation between on-trend points. Thus this approach imposes a linear trend growth path which may vary between successive cycles, but which is assumed constant within each cycle. This approach is highly transparent. Estimates of the output gap formed on this basis are also less subject to revision in the face of new GDP data than other approaches.

The CBI survey and other indicators

On-trend points can be identified by looking at a range of indicators. For manufacturing, time series are available from the Confederation of British Industry (CBI) Industrial Trends Survey, which has a long and established track record. The Survey includes questions on capacity utilisation (see Figure 11.1) and the perceived constraints imposed by plant capacity and the availability of skilled labour. For the service sector, sources include the British Chambers of Commerce Survey (available only since 1989) and the CBI Distributive Trades Survey. There are a range of other indicators – unemployment, vacancies, average earnings – which also relate to the degree of slack in the labour market.

The response to survey questions can, however, be affected by subjective bias. For instance, the answers will be difficult to interpret if firms' perceptions about the normal rate of capacity utilisation vary with the economic cycle or over time. And while survey evidence offers a broad guide to pressures on capacity in particular sectors, no single survey question has the breadth to measure capacity utilisation across the whole economy. In practice, different sectors or regions of the economy are likely to be subject to different pressures, especially in the short run. It is unfortunate that the surveys of the service sector only go back as far as the late 1980s.

Estimating the trend across full cycles and half cycles

In practice, the inferred trend growth rate can be sensitive to the precise dating of on-trend points. For example, the economy passed rapidly from its peak in mid-1979 to a deep trough in early 1980, and the choice

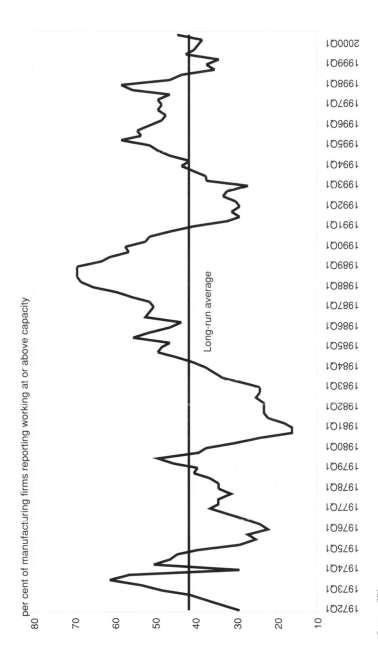

per cent of manufacturing firms reporting working at or above capacity

Long-run average

Source: CBI.

Figure 11.1   CBI survey of capacity utilisation in manufacturing

of on-trend point between these dates affects estimated trend growth over this period. In the 1970s and early 1980s, a smoother and more robust trend line can be obtained by interpolating across full cycles – that is, across three on-trend points – avoiding the need to identify explicitly every on-trend point.

Cycles in the late 1980s and early 1990s were longer and could be measured by a broader range of survey indicators. As a result, it is possible to estimate trend growth across the half cycle – that is, between each cyclical mid-point – with a greater degree of certainty.

Historical estimates of potential output and the output gap

Figure 11.2 shows the Treasury's estimate of trend output together with the actual level of output.

The Treasury's trend output series is derived by obtaining estimates of trend output for the non-oil component of GDP using the approach discussed above. The oil component of GDP is added to the estimate of trend non-oil GDP to give an estimate of total trend output. Table 11.1 shows historical growth in trend output (both including and excluding oil) between points when the economy is thought to have been on its trend growth path. The first two periods considered represent full economic cycles. The last two periods represent each half of the cycle which ended in the first half of 1997.

Table 11.1   Historical growth in trend output

Date of on-trend point	Non-oil GDP (per cent per annum)	Total GDP (per cent per annum)
1972Q4 to 1978Q1[1]	1½	1½
1978Q1 to 1986Q2[1]	1¾	2
1986Q2 to 1990Q4/1991Q1[2]	2¾	2½
1990Q4/1991Q1 to 1997Q1/1997Q2[2]	2¼	2¼

Notes:
[1]   Full cycle.
[2]   Half cycle.

Over the past 30 years or so, growth in trend output (including oil) is estimated to have ranged between 1½ per cent (during the period 1972Q4 to 1978Q1) to 2½ per cent (during the period from 1986Q2 to 1990Q4/1991Q1).

Due to short-term cyclical variations in economic activity, the economy may at any given point in time be operating either above or

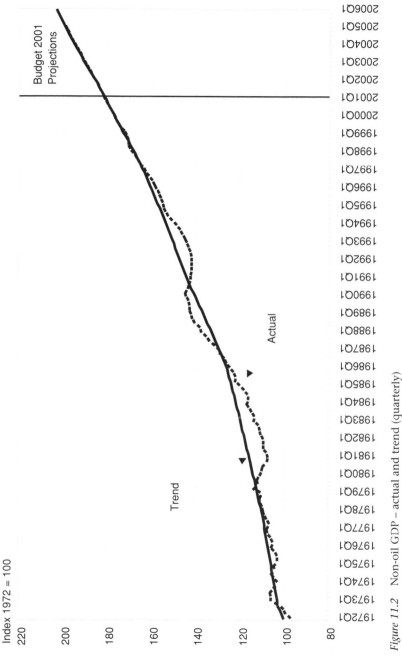

Index 1972 = 100

Budget 2001 Projections

Trend

Actual

Figure 11.2 Non-oil GDP – actual and trend (quarterly)

below its long-term trend. Figure 11.2 shows that in sharp contrast to the experience of the past 20 years, the Government's new approach to monetary and fiscal policy is helping to deliver a period of economic stability. The Budget 2001 projections (HM Treasury 2001) showed the economy remaining close to the estimated trend growth path over coming years.

Future prospects for trend growth

Trend growth varies over time and predicting its future path is not straightforward. The factors that influence trend economic growth over the medium term can be grouped under two headings: those that determine growth in trend employment, and those that determine trend growth in output per employee; that is, trend labour productivity.

The outlook for employment

The outlook for employment over the next few years is dependent upon many factors. Some of these factors reflect demographic trends, such as population growth and changes to the population structure. Other factors are influenced deliberately by Government policy.

The projections for future employment growth are based on projections of:

- the increase in the population of working age
- the future proportion of the working age population in employment, often known as the employment rate.

The Government Actuary's Department project that the working-age population (defined as men aged 16–64 and women aged 16–59) will grow by an average 0.5 per cent per annum until 2005. This rate is somewhat faster than the average during the 1990s but slightly lower than in the 1980s. These variations reflect differences in past birth rates: the baby boom of the early 1960s contributed to the rapid increase in working age population in the 1980s, and the low number of births in the late 1970s has resulted in slower growth over the past ten years.

As highlighted in Figure 11.3, average growth in the population of working age masks significant changes in the population structure. As discussed below, the composition of the working-age population can also affect employment levels as employment rates among the age groups are not the same.

Figure 11.3 shows employment rates are the highest for persons aged 25–49. Most other age categories typically have much lower employment

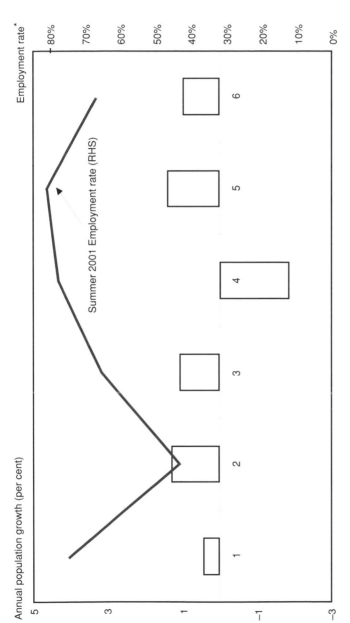

Annual population growth (per cent)

Employment rate*

Summer 2001 Employment rate (RHS)

* Employment as a proportion of working-age population group.

Sources: Labour Force Survey (employment rate); Government Actuary's Department (population changes).

Figure 11.3   Average population growth until 2005 and the current employment rate

rates. In the case of younger age categories, the lower employment rate reflects the greater numbers undertaking further and higher education and training before seeking employment. Lower employment rates for those aged 55 or older reflect early retirement. In part this reflects a choice by some people to retire early on an occupational pension. But others may have been forced into earlier retirement due to the damaging effects of past instability, where the downturns of the 1980s and early 1990s resulted in their becoming unemployed, losing vital skills, and being unable to rejoin the workforce later when economic conditions improved.

The figure also shows that the employment rates of growing segments of the working age population, such as the 55–59 age group, are lower than those which are projected to fall, such as the 25–34 age group. Such developments, in isolation, would suggest that employment may grow less rapidly than the working age population in the period ahead. However, demographic effects on the employment rate are small relative to the effects of the economic cycle. Looking forward, trends in labour market activity, coupled with steady growth, would more than offset the demographic effects and support a higher employment rate over the medium term.

Policies to increase stability are likely to raise the employment rate by avoiding the damaging effects of instability on the labour market. These are backed by the Government's employment policies which include tax and benefit reforms to make work pay and tackle the unemployment and poverty traps. Initiatives targeted at reducing unemployment, such as the New Deal, will ensure the unemployed and economically inactive are more likely to find work by reconnecting them to the labour market, and helping them to compete effectively for the jobs that a dynamic labour market creates.

While the macroeconomic framework and the employment programmes implemented by the Government are relatively new, early indications suggest that they are delivering results. Employment has increased by over 1 million since spring 1997;[2] there are now more people in work than ever before. By July 2001 over 490 000 people had found work through the New Deal programmes.

Compared to the earlier 1990s, the most striking development in recent years has been the sharp increase in the employment rate. Allowing for employment responding to output with some lag, this is estimated to have risen by 0.5 per cent a year on a trend basis between 1997 and 2000. With the labour market inactivity rate having only edged down over this period, the employment rate trend corresponds to a fall in the NAIRU of similar magnitude. Thus over the past three years the NAIRU might have fallen by around 1½ percentage points, to around 5½ per cent, broadly in line with the fall in the actual unemployment rate.

Making modest allowance for the positive impact from labour market policies, the employment rate is projected to rise by 0.1 per cent per annum, on average, over the next few years. When combined with the 0.5 per cent per annum increase in the working-age population, employment is projected to increase by an average 0.6 per cent per annum until 2005.

The outlook for labour productivity

Figure 11.4 shows labour productivity growth rates during the period 1980–2000.

Over the past 20 years, average labour productivity growth (defined in terms of GDP per employee) has been slightly below 2 per cent per annum. There have been periods where labour productivity growth rates have been higher, and periods when it has been lower. Much of the variation can be explained by cyclical effects.

A number of factors are likely to have a bearing on the outlook for average labour productivity. Factors that could lead to faster labour productivity growth include:

- greater macroeconomic stability making it easier for people, businesses and government to plan ahead with more clarity. Business investment has increased from 11 per cent of GDP to 14 per cent of GDP in the 5 years to 2000
- the trend to a more educated workforce
- greater diffusion of technology stemming from recent investment, including the rapid increase in Information and Communications Technology (ICT) usage
- the possibility that the Government's microeconomic policies may deliver results sooner than expected.

On the other hand, factors that could lead to slower productivity growth include:

- if the employment rate grows faster than projected. Labour productivity growth tends to be depressed by increases in the employment rate as the newly employed typically have lower productivity than those already employed. Total output rises because

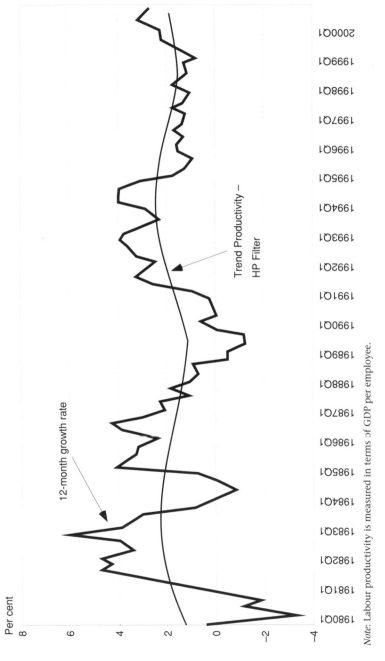

Note: Labour productivity is measured in terms of GDP per employee.

Figure 11.4 Annual and smoothed labour productivity rates

216

the newly employed would otherwise have been unproductive; however, average labour productivity may be depressed by more than assumed
- the possibility of diminished scope for productivity 'catch-up' as the productivity gap with leading countries narrows.

While this may act to depress future labour productivity growth, it is unclear to what extent. The UK's productivity gap against its main competitors remains large. Organisation for Economic Cooperation and Development (OECD) estimates for labour productivity in 1999 indicate that the UK was 45 per cent behind the US, 11 per cent behind Germany and 18 per cent behind France in terms of GDP per worker. The recent improvement in productivity growth in the US may also indicate that recent years have seen increased room for catch-up.

While a good case can be made for higher labour productivity growth in the years to come, lessons from recent economic history suggest that a more cautious assumption would be prudent. It is too early to assume any break from past trends. Therefore the underlying rate of productivity growth over the period ahead is assumed to be 2 per cent, as estimated for the pre-1997 cycle. In this sense the Government's neutral estimate of trend growth is subject to upside risk. The Government is determined to take a prudent approach by erring on the side of caution when uncertainties exist.

Overall conclusion

Based on a careful and balanced assessment of the evidence, over the period ahead:

- employment growth is projected to contribute 0.6 per cent per annum to trend growth, due to both growth in the working age population and an increase in the employment rate
- productivity growth is projected to contribute 1.9 per cent per annum to trend growth. This reflects an underlying trend labour productivity rate of 2.0 per cent, moderated slightly by the impact of changes in the employment rate.

It is reasonable to conclude, therefore, that a neutral estimate of the UK's annual trend growth rate over the coming period is 2½ per cent. Table 11.2 decomposes trend growth over the 1990s and sets out the prospects for the coming years.

Table 11.2 Contributions to annual trend growth

	Estimated trend rates of growth[1] (per cent per annum)				
	Trend labour productivity[2] Underlying[5] Actual		Trend employment rate[3]	Population of working age[4]	Trend output
	(1)	(2)	(3)	(4)	(5)
1990Q4 to 1997H1	2.0[6]	2.1	−0.2	0.3	2¼
1997H1 to mid-1999	1.9	1.6	0.5	0.5	2½
Forecast[7]	2.0	1.9	0.1	0.5	2½

Notes:
1 Treasury analysis based on judgement that 1990Q4, 1997H1 and mid-1999 were on-trend points of the output cycle, and allowing for employment lagging output in order to estimate trend growth rates for employment and labour productivity.
   Figures independently rounded. Columns (2) + (3) +(4) = (5).
2 Output per workforce job.
3 Ratio of workforce jobs to working age household population.
4 UK household basis.
5 Adjusted for effect of changes in employment rate, i.e. assuming the employment rate had remained constant. Column (1) − column (2) = (1-a).column(3), where a is the ratio of new to average worker productivity levels. The figuring is consistent with this ratio being of the order of 50 per cent, consistent with LFS data on relative entry wages.
6 Estimated from regression of productivity growth on employment rate growth and output gap over complete output cycle from 1986Q2 to 1997H1.
7 Neutral case assumptions underlying the mid-point of the GDP growth ranges from 2001Q1.

Public finances and the cycle

As discussed in the previous section, the economic cycle has an important short-term impact on the public finances. These effects need to be taken into account when assessing the underlying or 'structural' position of the public finances.

This is why the Code for Fiscal Stability requires governments to provide analyses of the impact of the economic cycle on the key fiscal aggregates, and to publish estimates of the cyclically adjusted fiscal position. It is also why the Government's two strict fiscal rules are defined over the economic cycle.

The automatic stabilisers

Fiscal policy can help to stabilise the economy through the operation of the 'automatic stabilisers'. For example, other things equal, lower unemployment when the economy is above its trend level means temporarily lower social security spending, higher income tax receipts and higher National Insurance contributions. Higher company profits generate higher corporation tax receipts, and higher spending by consumers yields higher VAT receipts and excise duties.

This implies that Government borrowing will tend to fall when output is above trend, and rise when output is relatively low. Rising government borrowing represents a net increase in domestic demand, so this automatic fiscal effect will tend to moderate economic downturns. Conversely, falling government borrowing helps to dampen economic booms. Over most economic cycles, the effects of these automatic stabilisers will come close to balancing out.

Setting the fiscal rules over the economic cycle means that the automatic stabilisers can continue to dampen economic cycles without endangering the long-term sustainability of the public finances. While their effect may be less visible than, say, changing interest rates, taking action to suppress the automatic stabilisers is likely to significantly increase fluctuations in output.

Allowing the automatic stabilisers to operate, however, must not jeopardise the underlying fiscal position. Experience has shown that serious policy mistakes can occur if purely cyclical improvements in the public finances are treated as if they represented structural improvements, or if a structural deterioration is thought to be merely a cyclical effect (see HM Treasury 1997b). When assessing fiscal prospects, it is essential to adjust fiscal indicators for the effects of the economic cycle.

Adjusting for the effects of the economic cycle

Methodology

A Treasury Occasional Paper published in 1995 – 'Public Finances and the Cycle' – set out in detail the methodology used for deriving ready reckoners for cyclical adjustment (HM Treasury 1995a). In brief, spending and revenue totals are regressed against estimates of contemporaneous and lagged output gaps. The resulting estimates indicate the responsiveness of the public finances to an average cycle.

The Treasury regularly monitors its estimates of the cyclicality of the public finances, as new data is released and series are revised. The current re-estimation uses for the first time data on the basis of the new ESA 95, and the Government's new fiscal aggregates.

The new 'ready reckoners'

The Treasury's latest ready-reckoners for calculating cyclically adjusted estimates of key fiscal indicators – the surplus on current budget and public sector net borrowing – are calculated using estimates of the cyclicality of total managed expenditure (TME), public sector current expenditure (PSCE), and public sector current receipts (PSCR). These are set out in Table 11.3.

Table 11.3   Treasury 'ready reckoners' for estimating cyclically adjusted (CA) fiscal indicators[1]

CA net borrowing	=	net borrowing	+	0.40 OG[2]	+	0.30 lagged OG
CA current budget	=	current budget	–	0.40 OG	–	0.30 lagged OG
CA TME	=	TME	+	0.40 OG	+	0.10 lagged OG
CA PSCE	=	PSCE	+	0.40 OG	+	0.10 lagged OG
CA PSCR	=	PSCR			–	0.20 lagged OG

Notes:
[1] All measures in this table are ratios to money GDP. Cyclically adjusted public sector net cash requirement can be calculated using the same parameters as for cyclically adjusted net borrowing.
[2] OG is the output gap, defined to be positive when output is above trend.

Further information is provided in the Appendix to this chapter.

Re-estimation suggests a small reduction in cyclicality and shorter lag

The latest re-estimation suggests a very small reduction in the estimated effect of the cycle on tax receipts from that set out in the 1995 Occasional Paper. Overall, a 1 per cent increase in output relative to trend is estimated after two years to:

- reduce the ratios of Total Managed Expenditure and Public Sector Current Expenditure to GDP by about half a percentage point
- increase the ratio of Public Sector Current Receipts to GDP by just under a quarter of a percentage point
- and so increase the ratio of surplus on current budget to GDP – the focus of the Government's golden rule – by just under three-quarters of a percentage point
- reduce the ratio of public sector net borrowing to GDP – the Government's preferred measure for assessing fiscal stance – by just under three-quarters of a percentage point.[3]

In terms of timing, the updated ready reckoners suggest that the first-year effects of higher output relative to trend are:

- a fall in the total spending/GDP ratio, due to the increase in GDP
- current spending behaves in a similar way to total expenditure since public investment does not vary automatically with the cycle
- no change in the ratio of receipts to GDP – although receipts will, of course, rise in cash terms.

The effects of higher output in the second year are:

- expenditure/GDP ratios fall further due to falls in cyclical social security payments (mainly reflecting fewer unemployed) and debt interest payments
- additional tax receipts, which come some time after the increase in output, increase the ratio of current receipts to GDP.

The re-estimation also suggests that a greater proportion of the overall effect comes in the first year. In terms of the effect on net borrowing of a 1 per cent increase in output relative to trend:

- in the first year, the new estimates suggest a fall in net borrowing of 0.4 per cent of GDP, up from 0.25 per cent
- in the second year, the new estimates suggest a further fall in net borrowing of 0.3 per cent of GDP, down from 0.5 per cent
- so overall, the new estimates imply that a 1 per cent increase in output relative to trend would reduce borrowing by 0.7 per cent of GDP after two years.

Reforms to the corporation tax system involving the abolition of payable tax credits on dividends and advance corporation tax (ACT) and the introduction of quarterly instalment corporation tax payments for large companies are increasing the timeliness of receipts to changes in economic activity. By 2003–04, when the adjustment to the new system is complete, a 1 per cent increase in the output gap would be expected to increase the current budget surplus by 0.5 per cent of GDP in the same year, and by a further 0.2 per cent of GDP a year later.

These estimates are approximate and simplified representations of the true dynamic impact of the output gap on the public finances – for instance, we would not always expect the full effect to come through within two years. And they are subject to margins of error since estimates of the output gap are uncertain and are based upon a stylised cycle: in practice, every cycle is different and so will be the effect on the public finances. Nevertheless, other estimates of the cyclicality of the UK's public finances, for example those produced by the IMF, OECD and European Commission and based on slightly different methodologies, yield similar although not identical results (see Giorno et al. 1995, Buti et al. 1997, Van den Noord 2000, Bouthevillain et al. 2001).

Estimates of cyclically adjusted fiscal indicators

The Treasury's estimates of the output gap and cyclically adjusted deficits were published for the first time in the July 1997 *Financial Statement and Budget Report* (HM Treasury 1997a) and have been published subsequently in other budgetary documents and papers.[4]

Figures 11.5 and 11.6 present historical series and projections from the March 2001 Budget for the key fiscal flow indicators – the surplus on current budget and public sector net borrowing – in actual and cyclically adjusted terms, together with the projections of Budget 2001, excluding the effects of windfall tax receipts and associated spending.

Historical estimates

As the figures show, for much of the early 1980s both the current and the overall budget were in deficit. However, when the severity of the recession is taken into account, cyclically adjusted estimates show net borrowing remaining reasonably close to balance, and in structural surplus on the current budget.[5]

As output moved significantly above trend in the late 1980s, the current and total budgets moved into surplus. However the cyclically adjusted figures were in deficit, suggesting that the overall surplus was due to the effect of the cycle. As fiscal policy was relaxed in the light of the emerging surpluses, the cyclically adjusted fiscal position deteriorated markedly. And large deficits were recorded when the economy moved into recession in the early 1990s.

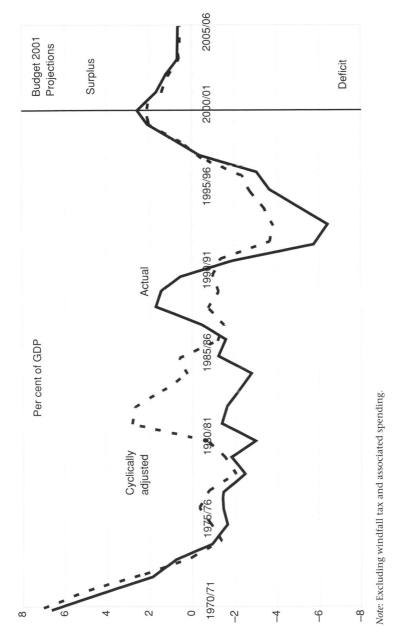

Note: Excluding windfall tax and associated spending.

Figure 11.5 Surplus on current budget – actual and cyclically adjusted

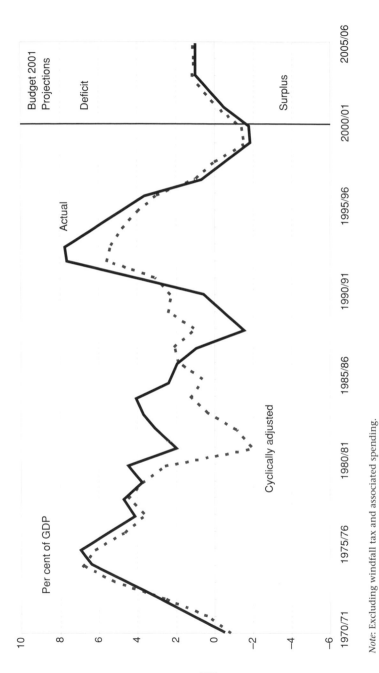

Note: Excluding windfall tax and associated spending.

Figure 11.6 Public sector net borrowing – actual and cyclically adjusted

APPENDIX: ECONOMETRIC RESULTS

OP = *Occasional Paper (1995)*
New = *Updated estimates (March 1999)*

Table 11.A1(a)   General government expenditure (GGE) (excluding privatisation proceeds) and the cycle

Output Gap	E/Y	Constant	GGE(X) (−1)	GGE(X) −(2)	Gap	T66	T75	R^2	Standard Error
OP	GGE excl.	25.6 (5.21)	0.66 (3.40)	−0.34 (−2.09)	−0.40 (−4.98)	0.56 (2.87)	−0.71 (−2.92)	0.8	1.41
New	private proceeds	28.68 (6.46)	0.68 (4.23)	−0.42 (−3.23)	−0.38 (−3.74)	0.48 (3.42)	−0.61 (−3.67)	0.8	1.16

Note:
Estimation period OP 1966–67 to 1992–93, estimation period new 1966–67 to 1997–98.
T-statistics in brackets.
E/Y = ratio of GGE excluding privatisation proceeds to whole economy GDP.
Gap = output gap as per cent of GDP.
T66 = time trend beginning in 1966–67; T75 = time trend beginning in 1975–76.
Long-run effects of the output gap are −0.59 for OP and −0.51 for the new estimation.

Table 11.A1(b)   Total managed expenditure (TME) and the cycle

Output Gap	E/Y	Constant	TME (−1)	TME (−2)	Gap	T66	T75	R^2	Standard Error
New	TME	23.72 (6.05)	0.83 (5.12)	−0.42 (−3.28)	−0.34 (−3.36)	0.45 (3.38)	−0.61 (−3.76)	0.9	1.1

Note:
Estimation period new 1966–67 to 1997–98.
T-statistics in brackets.
E/Y = ratio of TME excluding privatisation proceeds to whole economy GDP.
Gap = output gap as per cent of GDP.
T66 = time trend beginning in 1966–67; T75 time trend beginning in 1975–76.
Long-run effect of the output gap is −0.58.

Table 11.A1(c)   Public sector current expenditure (PSCE) and the cycle

Output Gap	E/Y	Constant	PSCE(X) (−1)	PSCE(X) (−2)	Gap	T66	T80	R^2	Standard Error
New	PSCE	15.43 (5.70)	0.94 (5.69)	−0.45 (−3.06)	−0.24 (−2.90)	0.34 (3.96)	−0.38 (−3.64)	0.9	0.9

Note:
Estimation period new 1966–67 to 1997–98.
T-statistics in brackets.
E/Y = ratio of PSCE excluding privatisation proceeds to whole economy GDP.
Gap = output gap as per cent of GDP.
T66 = time trend beginning in 1966–67; T80 = time trend beginning in 1980–81.
Long-run effect of the output gap is −0.47.

Table 11.A2   Cyclical social security and the cycle

Output Gap	E/Y	Constant	Gap (−1)	Time	R^2	Standard Error
OP	Cyclical social	−0.11 (−0.27)	−0.12 (3.87)	0.08 (4.35)	0.6	0.27
New	security	1.08 (6.83)	−0.08 (−3.54)	0.05 (4.03)	0.5	0.3

Note:
Estimation period OP 1978–79 to 1992–93, estimation period new 1978–79 to 1997–98.
T-statistics in brackets.
E/Y = ratio of cyclical social security (GB only) to whole economy GDP.
Gap = output gap as per cent of GDP.
Time = time trend beginning in 1978–79.

Table 11.A3   Debt interest and the cycle

Output Gap	E/Y	Constant	GGDIP (−1)	GGDIP (−2)	Gap	T66	T75	R^2	Standard Error
OP	GG debt	0.24 (0.60)	1.07 (4.67)	−0.14 (−0.55)	−0.02 (−1.18)	0.02 (1.18)	−0.04 (−1.31)	0.9	0.22
New	interest payments	0.67 (2.21)	1.18 (6.49)	−0.35 (−2.04)	−0.02 (−1.34)	0.02 (0.77)	−0.03 (−1.04)	0.9	0.21

Note:
Estimation period OP 1966–67 to 1992–93, estimation period new 1966–67 to 1997–98.
T-statistics in brackets.
E/Y = ratio of general government gross debt interest payments to GDP.
Gap = output gap as per cent of GDP.
T66 = time trend beginning in 1966–67; T75 = time trend beginning in 1975–76.
GGDIP = general government debt interest payments

Table 11.A4(a) Aggregate tax burden and the cycle: Occasional Paper results

Eqn	T/Y	Constant	Gap	Gap (–1)	GDPT	Time	R^2	Standard Error
1	Income	–82.9	–0.17	0.17	7.37	–	0.89	0.35
		(–9.50)	(–4.40)	(3.80)	(10.44)			
2	Corporation	2.09	–	0.21	–	0.03	0.76	0.32
		(9.77)		(6.93)		(2.76)		
3	VAT	5.65	0.05	–	–	–	0.41	0.15
		(154.4)	(3.57)					
4	Excise Motor	1.19	–	–	–	0.06	0.72	0.23
		(7.66)				(7.32)		
5	Excise Other	6.25	–	–	–	–0.15	0.94	0.23
		(42.12)				(–18.91)		
	Sum (1–5)	–67.8	–0.12	0.38	7.37	–		
6	Aggregate	–83.8	–	0.29	8.63	–	0.91	0.44
		(–7.67)		(6.87)	(9.79)			

Table 11.A4(b) Aggregate tax burden and the cycle: new results

Eqn	T/Y	Constant	Gap	Gap (–1)	GDPT	R^2	Standard Error
1	Income	–72.25	–0.18	0.20	6.15	0.87	0.39
		(–11.14)	(–4.21)	(4.54)	(12.44)		
2	Corporation	–26.64	–	0.17	2.25	0.84	0.27
		(–6.07)		(9.19)	(6.74)		
3	VAT	5.58	0.03	–	–	0.1	0.22
		(105.51)	(1.83)				
4	Excise Motor	55.64	–	–	–3.97	0.88	0.13
		(8.87)			(–8.44)		
5	Excise Other	92.16	–	–	–6.77	0.93	0.29
		(19.05)			(–18.38)		
	Sum (1–5)	54.49	–0.15	0.37	–2.34		
6	Aggregate	–104.49	–	0.23	9.74	0.88	0.7
		(–3.57)		(2.39)	(4.37)		

Note:
Estimation period 1971–72 to 1992–93 for OP results and 1971–72 to 1997–98 for new results, except for VAT (1975–76 to 1992–93 for OP results and 1975–76 to 1997–98 for new results).
T-statistics in brackets.
T/Y = ratio of tax revenue (adjusted for discretionary changes) to non-oil GDP.
Gap = output gap as per cent of GDP.
GDPT = trend GDP (in logs).
Time = time trend beginning in 1971–72.
Excise motor regression also includes ratio of stocks of petrol to diesel vehicles, estimated coefficient was –0.05 with t-statistic of –11.64.
The error term on the new aggregate equation is modelled as an AR(2) process to avoid serial correlation.

Table 11.A5(a)   Tax bases and the cycle: Occasional Paper results

Eqn	Base	Constant	Gap	Gap (−1)	Gap(−2)	Time	R^2	Standard Error
1	Income	71.0	−0.54	0.74	–	0.08	0.47	1.54
		(68.80)	(3.08)	(3.84)		(1.57)		
2	Corporation	8.98	0.61	–	–	−0.08	0.55	1.42
		(9.57)	(5.04)			(1.74)		
3	VAT	30.2	0.15	−0.14	–	–	0.24	0.47
		(268.9)	(2.63)	(2.28)				
4	Excise Motor	1.43	–	–	–	0.01	0.45	0.19
		(8.58)				(1.59)		
5	Excise Other	8.17	−0.05	–	−0.06	−0.08	0.94	0.15
		(80.49)	(4.05)		(4.04)	(14.94)		

Note:
1Estimation period 1971–72 to 1992–93, except for VAT (1975–76 to 1992–93).
T-statistics in brackets.
Base = tax base.
Gap = output gap as per cent of GDP.
Time = time trend beginning in 1971–72.

Table 11.A5(b)   Tax bases and the cycle: new results

Eqn	Base	Constant	Gap	Gap (−1)	Gap (−2)	Time	R^2	Standard Error
1	Income	71.38	−0.61	0.66	–	0.02	0.18	2.07
		(83.92)	(−2.63)	(2.85)		(0.46)		
2	Corporation	9.18	0.51	–	–	0.04	0.65	1.08
		(20.71)	(6.83)			(1.61)		
3	VAT	33.95	−0.10	0.07	–	–	−0.09	2.56
		(55.26)	(−0.34)	(0.23)				
4	Excise Motor	2.01	–	–	–	−0.00	−0.02	0.27
		(18.94)				(−0.68)		
5	Excise Other	7.50	−0.04	–	−0.05	−0.09	0.96	0.15
		(125.39)	(−3.47)		(−4.33)	(−24.35)		

Note:
Estimation period 1971–72 to 1997–98, except for VAT (1975–76 to 1997–98).
T-statistics in brackets.
Base = tax base.
Gap = output gap in per cent GDP.
Time = time trend beginning in 1971–72.

Table 11.A6(a)   Receipts and the tax base: Occasional Paper results

Eqn	T/Y	Constant	Base	Base (–1)	Gap	Gap (–1)	Time	R^2	Standard Error
1	Income	–0.43	0.09	–	–0.15	0.16	0.12	0.91	0.31
		(–0.13)	(1.88)		(–3.40)	(3.16)	(10.5)		
2	Corporation	0.88	–	0.13	–	0.12	0.05	0.8	0.29
		(1.60)		(2.35)		(2.45)	(3.87)		
3	VAT	1.09	0.15	–	–	–	–	0.11	0.19
		(0.43)	(1.78)						
4	Excise Motor	1.12	0.61	–	–	–	–	0.12	0.35
		(1.86)	(2.00)						
5	Excise Other	–7.42	1.64	–	–	0.13	–	0.83	0.4
		(–6.78)	(10.06)			(2.99)			

Note:
Estimation period 1971–72 to 1992–93, except for VAT (1975–76 to 1992–93).
T-statistics in brackets.
T/Y = ratio of tax revenue (adjusted for discretionary changes) to non-oil GDP.
Base = tax base.
Gap = output gap as per cent of GDP.
Time = time trend beginning in 1971–72.

Table 11.A6(b)   Receipts and the tax base: new results

Eqn	T/Y	Constant	Base	Base (–1)	Gap	Gap (–1)	Time	R^2	Standard Error
1	Income	–1.41	0.11	–	–0.12	0.14	0.12	0.9	0.27
		(–0.74)	(4.25)		(–3.66)	(4.07)	(18.13)		
2	Corporation	1.69	–	0.07	–	0.14	0.04	0.8	0.27
		(3.50)		(1.36)		(4.15)	(5.48)		
3	VAT	3.21	0.07	–	–	–	–	0.5	0.17
		(6.41)	(4.66)						
4	Excise Motor	1.12	0.61	–	–	–	–	0.2	0.33
		(2.32)	(2.48)						
5	Excise Other	–5.93	1.46	–	–	0.11	–	0.9	0.36
		(–9.48)	(14.78)			(4.30)			

Note:
Estimation period 1971–72 to 1997–98, except for VAT (1975–76 to 1997–98).
T-statistics in brackets.
T/Y = ratio of tax revenue (adjusted for discretionary changes) to non-oil GDP.
Base = tax base.
Gap = output gap as per cent of GDP.
Time = time trend beginning in 1971–72.

12
Planning and Controlling Public Spending

This chapter explains how the Government has learned the lessons of previous public expenditure control systems in allocating resources and achieving good value public services.

Introduction

The control of public spending raises some of the most complex problems which any government has to face. In the UK and much of the developed world, spending pressures grew relatively unchecked for much of the post-war period until the early 1970s. In the UK expenditure grew from 38.1 per cent of GDP in 1964 to 49.5 per cent in 1975. After diminishing somewhat it returned to over 48 per cent during the early 1980s, largely due to the increase of social security payments linked to rising unemployment. Severe macroeconomic instability due to unsustainable deficits and debts led to a period in which governments sought mechanisms to restrain expenditure to sustainable levels. In many cases the need to limit spending highlighted inefficiencies in public spending control systems and the political economy of controlling public spending.

The principal problem was how to apply an overall resource constraint while channelling resources to agreed priorities – since this implied reducing resources available to some ministers and departments. This problem then exacerbated a number of others.

The first was that of annual bargaining over resources. While the UK (and many other countries) had since the 1960s a notional multi-annual expenditure allocation, in practice outer year limits were meaningless as departments renegotiated spending allocations each year, as the government changed its spending plans according to economic conditions. In addition to the short-term thinking encouraged by annual renegotiations, considerable inefficiency was introduced through wasteful end-of-year surges in spending. A second general problem was the extent to which historically spending control has focused on resources allocated to departments or programmes (inputs) rather than the outcomes of the spending.

The reforms in public spending control instituted since 1997 should be seen as a response to these problems, which build upon attempts over the past decade to reconcile expenditure control with allocation of resources according to priorities and the need to focus on the provision of quality public services within a controlled and affordable growth path.

The fiscal framework explained in Chapters 8 and 9 provides a clear basis for deciding on the affordability of total expenditure. This chapter highlights a number of key problems, and then explains in detail how the reforms introduced improved the incentives to deliver better value for money from the resources available.

Previous problems in the expenditure framework

From the mid 1970s to the mid 1990s the expenditure framework was in a process of continual evolution. A key characteristic was that during most of this period some control total for aggregate spending would be targeted. In the mid 1990s this total was known as the Control Total and covered 85 per cent of Central Government spending, but excluded cyclical social security and government debt interest payments. Each year spending plans would be set for three years ahead, but the process was essentially one of annual bargaining through the Public Expenditure Survey (PES). The system tended to be incremental, with the previous year's expenditure serving as the basis for negotiations in the next year. From the early 1990s a number of fundamental expenditure reviews were carried out to inform the negotiations. In practice, however, the allocation of spending still tended to be top-down.

Under the previous arrangements, a key problem was the short effective planning horizon created for departments by the annual spending negotiation, and a weakening of incentives for value for money through the effective annual renegotiation of spending allocations. Careful thought about programmes that might not bear fruit for some time was not encouraged by a system in which everything could potentially be reopened each year. The indicative three-year-ahead plans, included with the PES, were treated with scepticism and could not be used reliably by either the Treasury or departments.

Compounding this culture of uncertainty and short-termism was the annuality rule, ensuring that departments were unable to carry forward more than a small proportion of resources from one financial year to another. Underspends had to be surrendered to the Exchequer. This led to a 'use it or lose it' mentality and poor-value-for-money spending at the year-end. Departments and agencies could not be sure that the resources would not otherwise be lost in next year's spending round. This had been recognised as a problem since 1983 when a limited carry-over of capital spending – End-Year-Flexibility (EYF) – was introduced. In the early 1990s this was extended to other areas including EYF for running costs, defence costs and much NHS expenditure. Nevertheless, these reforms were piecemeal and were unsuccessful in convincing officials that departments would not be penalised for carrying forward underspends. Poor value for money from some spending at the year-end was inevitable in these circumstances.

A sharp decline over time in net investment spending by the public sector has exposed the *bias against capital spending* inherent in the old system. The spending control framework did not effectively distinguish between capital and current spending. At times when there was pressure to reduce spending, investment spending was quick to suffer in negotiations as a lack of investment in the maintenance and enhancement of infrastructure might not feed through into the dilapidation of schools, hospitals, roads and housing until long after the decision not to fund.

The old framework did little to encourage the good management of assets. A strategy for improving asset management was difficult to devise with the poor and imprecise information available to departments and Ministers about quantity, value and condition of public assets. Cash budgets provided no incentive to count the full economic cost of retaining assets over time. Institutionally the system had a tendency to put disproportionate resources into the detailed study and critique of individual investment decisions, but missed the overall picture on asset investment and disposal. Departments had little incentive to dispose of underused assets, as the normal assumption was that the resources would be retained by the centre and not by the department.

Prior to the mid 1990s the evolution away from the control of inputs (a standard feature of budgetary systems the world over until recently) was relatively slow. Little was done to encourage an evidence-based approach, matching the outcomes of various policy options with their input cost, on a systematic basis. This could lead to an emphasis on some elements of spending that had little to do with what they achieved, and encouraged a political debate around public spending which focused on winners and losers in input terms rather than holding the Government to account for its achievements against its objectives. The planning of spending under the old system was performed entirely on a *departmental basis*. Despite widespread acceptance that many policy issues required a coordinated response from public agencies, the planning system encouraged departments to maximise their own resources without regard for the impact of their programmes on common objectives across Government, or the work of other agencies. This led to resource decisions designed to fit existing Government organisational units rather than the underlying nature of problems.

The principles of the new control framework

The new approach attempts to challenge the behavioural and systemic effects of the old system through a series of interlinked reforms. The principles behind the reforms can be summarised as follows:

- government should be open and transparent about its objectives, and clearly relate the inputs it makes to the outputs and outcomes it is seeking to achieve
- the level of future planned spending should be governed by a fiscal framework
- the horizon for public spending planning should be longer term, and departments given the flexibility and certainty needed to tackle issues in a far-sighted way
- decision makers should have the financial information they need to make spending choices based on their full economic cost, and the budgeting system should reflect this
- the bias against capital spending should be corrected, and the incentives for asset management improved
- issues should be approached from the perspective of the real-world agents involved, rather than the current administrative structure, cutting across departmental boundaries where necessary.

The fiscal framework is described in Chapters 8 and 9 while the importance of changes to the budgeting and accounting framework are discussed in Chapter 13. The remainder of this chapter explains the way in which the Government has applied the other principles in devising its new system of planning and control. It is important to note briefly the integration of the fiscal and spending frameworks.

Integration of the fiscal and spending frameworks

The spending framework is firmly embedded in the fiscal framework. For given tax rates the fiscal rules determine the overall spending envelope and the breakdown between current and capital spending. Departmental allocations are determined by economic assessment of outcomes and value for money and not an arbitrary target for spending as a proportion of GDP. The introduction of standard accounting principles ensures that control of aggregate spending, and particularly the capital current distinction will be mirrored at departmental level. The frameworks thus represent an integrated and coherent approach to public spending.

Moreover, the credibility of the fiscal framework reinforces the credibility of medium term spending allocations and thus promotes better use of resources at departmental level while the golden rule controls spending without imposing a bias against investment. The spending framework and the evidence based spending reviews make it easier (from a political economy point of view) to control expenditure pressures and so maintain the fiscal framework.

Focusing on the outcomes of spending

The new Public Service Agreements (PSAs) have focused the process of planning public spending on the outcomes of Government activity, rather than on the crude inputs into it. First introduced after the 1998 Comprehensive Spending Review, the PSAs were developed and refined in the 2000 Spending Review, and were central to collective ministerial discussions in the review. Each main department and cross-departmental programme has a PSA setting out its aim and objectives for the three years ahead, and below them, specific, quantified and measurable performance targets against which progress can be judged.

PSAs are agreed with departments alongside new spending plans. The process of agreeing objectives and targets highlights links between departments' activities, allowing Government to develop increasingly complementary policies in overlapping areas. Agreements make the goals of each main programme clear, so that public sector managers know what they are working towards. They make responsibility for delivery explicit. The Government's plans are now much more transparent to Parliament and public since taxpayers can see what they are getting for the money and can hold Government to account for the outcomes. Performance against the targets is reported annually in Departmental Annual Reports. This public reporting provides a strong incentive to deliver the commitments contained in the PSAs, and the Cabinet Committee on Public Services and Public Expenditure (PSX), supported by the Treasury, rigorously monitors departmental performance, assessing progress against agreed milestones.

There are important benefits to be gained from the transparency, staff motivation and clarity of objectives brought in through the PSA initiative. It is recognised, however, that the system is still young, and will probably need to develop further in the future. Two important sources for good practice in performance measurement and management are the private sector and the local government sector. Private sector expertise is being tapped through the Public Services Productivity Panel chaired by the Chief Secretary. This body is made up of 20 change management practitioners with a mixture of private and public sector experience. They have been conducting studies and working with departments, aimed at improving the systems in place to deliver key PSA targets. National objectives need to be met at a local level. Local PSAs link national targets to local services. Local PSAs were a radical departure from traditional ways of working, so they were piloted with 20 authorities. They were well received and over the next two years will be extended to 150 upper-tier local authorities. Successful local authorities will secure significant financial rewards and extra flexibility in delivering central priorities.

The focus of outcomes and value for money also implies the adoption of performance measurement techniques common in the private sector, and, where it can improve outcomes, private sector involvement in the form of Private Finance Initiatives (PFI) and Public–Private Partnerships (PPP). These provide greater flexibility to the public sector in service delivery.

Planning for the long term

Within the overall spending totals set to meet the fiscal rules, the Government now lays down firm limits for departments' spending (Departmental Expenditure Limits, or DEL) that guarantee their level of funding for three years ahead rather than just one. This gives public services the stability to plan their operations on a sensible timescale without the fear that resources may be cut back the following year. By the same token, departments cannot now look to an annual survey to bid up their funds. Thus the credibility of medium-term plans has been enhanced at both central and departmental level. All capital and most running cost expenditure (including wages) is included in DEL.

Within the longer planning horizon provided by DEL, it has been possible to remove unnecessary lower level controls on spending, operating instead through overall limits and performance targets rather than on micro-management through a detailed system of approvals. Departments now have the flexibility inside overall limits to reprioritise expenditure to meet their objectives most efficiently. Management focus can turn to delivery of high quality services within a known resource total.

The new framework means an end to annual budgets and a move to firm three-year plans. An End-Year Flexibility (EYF) system has been set up to avoid wasteful spending at the end of the financial year by enabling departments to carry over 100 per cent of unspent resources into the following financial year.

Some expenditure cannot reasonably be subject to firm, multi-year limits. These are demand-led items that are budgeted as Annually Managed Expenditure (AME). AME includes social security benefits, local authority self-financed expenditure, payments under the Common Agricultural Policy, debt interest, and net payments to EU institutions. Controlling this more volatile spending outside three-year totals means sensible long-term planning is not disrupted by short-term demand-led fluctuations. The close integration of the tax and benefit system also provides a strong rationale for consideration of AME in the annual budget cycle. However, AME is subject to tough scrutiny as part of the Budget process. Policy measures which would have the effect of increasing spending on elements of AME are not taken unless the effects of these decisions can be accommodated prudently within the fiscal rules and can be financed by a fair and efficient tax system that promotes incentives to work, save and invest.

Together, DEL plus AME make up Total Managed Expenditure (TME). Although this total is carefully scrutinised, it does not have the same role as the control totals in previous frameworks. The separate control of capital and current DEL enables the Government to integrate its spending and fiscal frameworks. It is interesting to note that that while under previous spending regimes, an arbitrary target of reducing government spending to below 40 per cent of GDP was often pursued but not achieved, the current system has achieved this objective without having targeted it explicitly.

Correcting the bias against capital spending and improving the incentives for asset management

The history of the last 30 years suggests that special treatment is needed for capital spending to protect investment for the future from being cut back to fund short-term current pressures. A combination of the fiscal rules and Resource Accounting and Budgeting now require distinct control arrangements for capital and current spending, reflecting their different lifespans and economic effects. Each department is therefore set distinct capital and current DEL budgets. The capital budget is ringfenced, but departments are free to transfer current spending to longer-term capital projects. In addition, almost £5 billion has been set aside for a Capital Modernisation Fund, allocated on a challenge basis to innovative new projects, helping to unlock ideas from within services about where new investment can be allocated to new ways of delivering services.

A central reform to the allocation and monitoring of capital is the linking of new investment to the state and management of the £500 billion public asset base. Departmental Investment Strategies (DISs), negotiated as part of the 2000 Spending Review and published subsequently, ensure that decisions on new investment are taken within a long-term strategic context and are informed by the condition and use of the existing asset base. They also set out the appraisal, management and evaluation mechanisms that ensure capital projects deliver value for money.

This is part of a concerted approach to improve the quality as well as the quantity of public investment. Alongside the introduction of DISs, commercial accounting techniques are being introduced in departments (explained in more detail in Chapter 13) which will bring important incentive effects to bear on asset management behaviour. Under the cash accounting system operated by the UK until recently, assets were treated as a free good once bought. The true cost of delivering objectives was therefore understated. Departments and agencies had no economic incentive to dispose of underutilised assets despite the opportunity costs of retaining them.

Resource budgeting, introduced in the 2000 Spending Review, corrects these problems by making departments aware of those true costs (in particular, depreciation and cost of capital). In addition, all large, novel and contentious projects are put through a rigorous process of scrutiny by the new Office of Government Commerce. Finally a comprehensive list of government assets and their value has been published. The National Asset Register will be updated regularly, with full details of progress on asset management.

Tackling issues which cross departmental boundaries

The way in which spending surveys were conducted led to an excessive emphasis on delivering policy and services through embedded administrative units, rather than thinking laterally across organisational boundaries in areas where a common approach might be more efficient and effective. Tackling problems like drugs, crime and social exclusion requires better coordination and teamwork across a wide range of departments and agencies. In the 2000 Spending Review, the Government conducted 15 cross-cutting reviews to address these difficult policy areas. For the 2002 Spending Review the cross-cutting reviews have been reduced to seven focused areas:

- *Children at risk*: this review will establish the key outcome targets for children's services and identify the main obstacles to meeting those targets
- *Public sector labour market*: a study of recruitment and retention across the public services
- *Improving the public space*: this review will build on the Prime Minister's work on 'liveability', to improve local quality of life
- *Small business support*: a review to assess government services for small business, including information, advice, financial support
- *Science and research*: a review of funding of the UK science base, to ensure that it delivers maximum long-term benefits to the economy and quality of life
- *Health inequalities*: this study will analyse the impact on health of poverty, employment, education, crime, transport, fuel poverty and related factors
- *Role of the voluntary sector in providing services*: a review to analyse the current contribution of the voluntary sector in service delivery, and possibilities for improving the range and quality of services offered by the voluntary sector.

The Review has introduced new and better mechanisms for coordinating effort in many of these areas. Departments will now manage joint budgets where that makes sense. In Chapter 25 of the Public Service Agreement (PSA) White Paper (Cm 4808, July 2000) the Government identified 26 targets in departmental PSAs that had a strong link to the outcomes of the 15 cross-departmental studies. These complement the 21 targets agreed in the Sure Start, Criminal Justice System, Action Against Illegal Drugs, and Welfare to Work reviews, which became separate PSAs. There is therefore now a strong steer to departments to work together on issues which affect more than one of them.

13
Resource Accounting and Budgeting

Following the successful introduction of Resource Accounting and Budgeting (RAB), the Government now plans, controls and accounts for public expenditure on a resource rather than a cash basis, bringing government into line with the practices of much of the rest of the economy. This chapter looks at the benefits of RAB, its implementation, and how RAB supports the new public expenditure and fiscal framework.

Introduction

From Gladstone's public finance reforms of the mid-1860s until the full introduction of Resource Accounting and Budgeting (RAB) in 2001–02, public spending was, by and large, controlled, planned and accounted for on a cash basis. Cash payments and receipts were scored in the year they were made or received, regardless of when resources were used up. There was no measure of the cost of using capital assets over time through depreciation or capital charging.

RAB involves producing the equivalent of the main financial statements from commercial accounts, in particular a balance sheet and the equivalent of a profit and loss statement. Expenditure scores on an accruals basis. RAB therefore ensures that the full economic costs of government activity are measured properly both by including non-cash costs and by matching costs to the correct time period. The main non-cash costs are depreciation, which measures the consumption of assets, a cost of capital charge, reflecting the extent to which there is an opportunity cost in holding assets, and accounting based provisions which record a binding obligation for future expenditure. As a result, RAB provides a better basis for allocating and managing resources and better incentives for the public sector to manage those resources properly.

Under RAB, the information contained in the financial statements forms the basis of: how the Government plans public expenditure through the three-year budgeting process; how Parliament provides the legal authority for departmental spending through the supply procedure; and how the government accounts to Parliament for the expenditure it has authorised through the production of departmental resource accounts.

Subsequent sections in this chapter look in more detail at the benefits of the move to a resource based system of public spending control, including how it supports the other fiscal, public spending and service delivery reforms introduced by the government, and gives more detail on how resource accounts, Estimates and budgets are structured.

The benefits of RAB

As well as providing better information for those charged with allocating, managing and scrutinising public spending by measuring the full economic consequences of government activity, RAB also brings major improvements in the treatment of capital spending. Cash planning for capital, by scoring the cost in full in the year of acquisition, but not depreciating or recognising the opportunity cost in future years, puts in place an initial bias against the acquisition of capital and provides no incentive to manage capital once it is purchased. Under RAB, the cost and consumption of capital is spread over its useful life.

Macro and micro benefits of RAB

Overall, RAB offers benefits at both the micro and the macro level. At the macro level it delivers:

- a clearer view of the real costs of providing individual services, which takes account of the full costs of holding assets
- a more accurate figure for the cost of depreciation in central government
- a more transparent split of capital and current spending, (including a clearer presentation of the investment of public corporations and other public bodies)
- a better measure of the total value of central government assets, building on what has already been achieved through the National Asset Register.

At the micro level, resource budgeting offers:

- better incentives to manage assets and dispose of those no longer needed, and better incentives in planning investment, as this affects the cost of capital charge
- better information for managing cash
- new incentives to manage working capital (debtors, creditors and stocks)
- a clearer distinction between loans and grants.

RAB, the fiscal framework and the expenditure control framework

RAB is fully consistent with and supports the new public expenditure framework developed by the Government. The new public expenditure system is based on firm three-year spending limits underpinned by a spending envelope based on strict fiscal rules, a clear separation of capital and current expenditure with an end to the historic discrimination against investment, and the setting of outcome and output targets against which departments must report their performance.

Under RAB, expenditure continues to be split between firm three-year Departmental Expenditure Limits (DEL) and expenditure which cannot be subject to multi-year limits, known as Annually Managed Expenditure (AME). Capital investment and current spending continue to be managed separately, with the treatment of capital in budgeting improved by the move to RAB. Three-year targets for delivery – known as Public Service Agreements (PSAs) – supported by Service Delivery Agreements (SDAs) are agreed alongside spending allocations, with departments setting out clearly and publicly what they will deliver in return. RAB supports this not just by providing a better measure of the costs of meeting these targets, but through a formal requirement in resource accounts to report on resource allocation by departments' high level objectives which underpin the PSAs (this part of the accounts is known as Schedule 5).

The benefits of RAB can be seen in the production of Departmental Investment Strategies (DISs). As part of the new planning process, departments prepare DISs setting out how they will get the best value from their spending review capital allocations. DISs contain analyses of the existing state of the capital stock, alongside plans for future investment and asset disposal. As a result of RAB, DISs contain financial information about the cost of depreciation and the opportunity cost of capital (through the levying of a cost of capital charge). Resource accounts also provide information for the National Asset Register, the first version of which was published by the Government in 1997. The 2001 version contains valuation information on the assets.

The Government announced in the Code for Fiscal Stability in 1998 its intention to produce, if possible, Whole of Government Accounts (WGA), using the newly available RAB information. As a set of consolidated financial statements covering the whole public sector, they would be a further step in underpinning the new fiscal framework. Using RAB information, the aim would be to produce audited and published WGA from 2005–06.

Figure 13.1 sets out the linkages between the fiscal framework, the spending control framework and RAB.

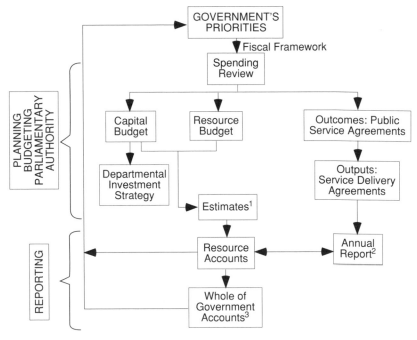

[1] From 2002, the Estimates, together with the Public Service and Service Delivery Agreements, will be included in a Departmental Plan published in the spring.

[2] From 2002, departments will prepare an annual report published in the autumn which will report on the achievement of the targets in the Public Service & Service Delivery Agreements and include a copy of the previous year's Resource Accounts.

[3] Central Government Accounts to be published from 2003–04, with the aim of moving to publication of full Whole of Government Accounts from 2005–06.

Figure 13.1   Linkages between the fiscal framework, the spending control framework and RAB

The implementation of RAB

The successful conversion to Resource Accounting and Budgeting represented one of the most significant reforms in public finance for more than a century. The project was launched in 1993 by the previous government, with all-party support. This was followed by a White Paper in 1995 (Cm 2929).

The move to RAB presented a significant challenge for departments. This was particularly true of departments with large asset bases, such as the Ministry of Defence, where the department was required to draw up a balance sheet covering some £80–90 billion of assets from scratch. Consequently, departments were required to improve their systems, processes, and provision of qualified financial staff to enable them to operate the more sophisticated financial framework introduced by RAB.

The trigger point strategy

Moreover, given the role played by Parliament in authorising expenditure and scrutinising how public money is spent, the Treasury sought from an early stage to win Parliament's support for the modernisation of the public finances brought about by RAB. The Treasury gave an early undertaking to the relevant parliamentary committees – the Public Accounts, Treasury and Procedure Committees – that the cash based system of accounts and Estimates would not be discontinued until Parliament was satisfied that departments were ready to implement and operate the new resource based system.

To reassure Parliament that implementation was proceeding on track and that any emerging problems were dealt with as they arose, the Government identified four 'trigger' points along the route to implementation. These were:

- Trigger Point 1 (April to December 1998) was an assessment of departmental systems and their readiness to produce resource accounts
- Trigger Point 2 (April to June 1999) was an assessment of the departments' opening balance sheets for 1999–2000
- Trigger Point 3 (autumn 1999) was an audit of departments' first set of dry run resource accounts for 1998–99
- Trigger Point 4 (April 2000) was the presentation to Parliamentary select committees of a set of shadow resource Estimates for 2000–01.

Outside the trigger point framework, the government continued to develop resource budgeting as the means for the administrative control of public expenditure. The 2000 Spending Review, which set firm allocations for departments for the years 2001–02 to 2003–04, was the first public expenditure survey to be conducted on a resource basis.

In August 2000, based on their assessment of departmental performance at the various trigger points, the Committees approved the Treasury's request to switch off the cash based system of accounting and Estimates from 2001–02, in line with the original project timetable. Accordingly, the Government then brought into force the Government Resources and Accounts Act 2000, which provides the statutory basis for resource-based supply.

Resource accounts

Resource accounts are the main financial reports of departments. They are designed to meet the primary aims of financial reporting by central government and to underpin the Government's planning, monitoring and management of public expenditure.

Accounting policies and practices

Departmental resource accounts are audited by the National Audit Office (NAO) in line with the *Resource Accounting Manual* (RAM). The RAM is approved by the Financial Reporting Advisory Board (FRAB), an independent body including representatives from the Treasury, the NAO, departments, agencies and the private sector. The policies presented in the RAM are based on UK Generally Accepted Accounting Practice (UK GAAP) which govern the accounting and disclosure requirements in the rest of the economy. Where appropriate, the FRAB considers adaptations of GAAP to take account of the public sector context.

Accounts are presented to Parliament by the Treasury each year.

The structure of the accounts

Departmental resource accounts comprise five schedules, plus notes. The first Schedule reflects Parliamentary control, comparing outturn – the actual expenditure and income – with the resource Voted by Parliament in the Estimate, including the cash requirement Voted. Schedules 2, 3 and 4 correspond broadly to the main financial statements of the private sector and other parts of the public sector where accruals accounts are already in place. Schedule 5 shows resource inputs grouped by the overall departmental objectives as set out in the Spending Review White Paper on Public Service Agreements.

The five schedules are:

- Schedule 1: Summary of resource outturn
- Schedule 2: Operating Cost Statement and Statement of Recognised Gains and Losses
- Schedule 3: Balance Sheet
- Schedule 4: Cash Flow Statement
- Schedule 5: Statement of Resources by Departmental Objectives

Resource estimates

Estimates are the process by which Parliament votes resources to departments for their expenditure on an annual basis. The limits voted by Parliament in Estimates are legally binding; any overshoot requires authorisation in a supplementary Estimate, or, if at year-end, by way of what is known as an Excess Vote.

The structure of resource Estimates take account of control requirements, a clear presentation of departments' expenditure and the responsibilities of the Accounting Officer, who is normally the Permanent Secretary of the department. Under resource Estimates, departments' requests for authorisation of expenditure are termed 'Requests for Resources' (RfRs). Parliament, in approving an Estimate, imposes a strict limit on departmental resource consumption known as the net resource requirement. Several larger departments will have more than one RfR and hence more than one net resource requirement.

Irrespective of the number of RfRs, Parliament votes a single net cash requirement in respect of each requirement. This represents the actual level of cash needed to fund the resource consumption and capital investment authorised in the Estimate. The reconciliation between the net resource requirement and the net cash requirement is set out on the face of each Estimate. Like the net resource requirement, the net cash requirement is a legally binding ceiling, overshoots of which are only valid with prior or retrospective approval by Parliament. This, combined with the cash management scheme introduced by departments, means there is no question of RAB leading to a loss of control of the Government's cash position.

Each resource Estimate also contains a forecast cash flow statement for the department concerned, as well as a forecast Operating Cost Statement. Included in the other notes is a reconciliation with the resource budget outturn, which sets out the linkages between what

Parliament Votes to departments and the administrative budgetary measures of DEL and AME which are set and forecast respectively during spending reviews.

Resource budgeting

As noted previously, under resource budgeting, the separation of current and capital spending continues. Current expenditure has now been re-named resource expenditure so as better to reflect the fact that what is being measured is the consumption of resources in any one year.

The resource budgeting framework

So, under resource budgeting, each department has:

- A resource budget, representing the spending plans for a department's programme measured in resource terms to reflect the full cost of its activities. It includes the departmental administration and programme expenditure on an accruals basis, together with capital charges. Capital charges, which reflect the opportunity cost of the public sector holding assets, are normally levied at 6 per cent. The resource budget continues to separate expenditure into three-year expenditure limits (DEL) and expenditure that is controlled annually (AME).
- A capital budget, which identifies the department's new capital expenditure net of asset sales within its programme. The capital budget also includes net lending and credit approvals to local authorities. The capital budget is also divided into DEL and AME, although there is relatively little capital expenditure which is managed annually.

Another important feature of resource budgeting is its application in full to public sector bodies sponsored by departments, which fall outside the boundary of departmental accounts. These bodies are normally classified as non-departmental public bodies, such as various museums and galleries, and public corporations and trading funds, such as the Meteorological Office and English Partnerships. Under cash, these bodies affected the budget usually only in terms of the loans made and grants paid to them by departments. Under RAB, the budget scores the full resource consumption and capital investment by sponsored bodies. This expenditure is normally controlled in DEL, except in the case of a small number of genuinely self-financing public corporations which are managed annually in AME. This category includes, for example, Consignia and British Nuclear Fuels Ltd.

Stage 1 resource budgeting

As the essence of RAB is measuring the full costs of economic activity by government, it is right in principle that non-cash costs – such as depreciation, a cost of capital charge and accounting based provisions to meet future commitments – are counted and controlled alongside cash based programme expenditure. This will not happen fully until 2003–04. This is because, in order to minimise the risks associated with transferring from a cash- to a resource-based system of expenditure planning, Ministers decided to introduce resource budgeting in two stages.

In Stage 1, which runs throughout the years covered by the 2000 Spending Review – 2001–02 to 2003–04 – these costs will score as part of AME. The Government has decided to move these costs into DEL in the 2002 Spending Review, which will set spending plans for 2003–04 to 2005–06.

This means that the benefits of resource budgeting, particularly at a micro level, will not be fully realised until Stage 2, as departments will not benefit in terms of programme expenditure from astute management of capital, nor will they suffer from poor decision making or management. However, the improved flow of information on these assets is in itself a spur to better management. In preparing plans for capital investment over the spending review period, departments are required to calculate the non-cash consequences (depreciation and cost of capital charge) of their asset acquisition and disposal strategies. These numbers appear in DISs and outturn against them is reported on in departments' annual reports. As a result of the move to resource budgeting, the Government expects to see real benefits for the management of public resources, particularly after its full implementation in 2003–04.

In-year control

Just as Parliamentary Estimates and accounts move to a RAB basis from 2001–02, so too does the Treasury's system for the administrative control of public expenditure. Monthly departmental returns on expenditure outturn are now submitted on a resource basis, and the calculation of departments' entitlement to End-Year Flexibility, the scheme that allows for a carry-forward of underspends, is also carried out on the basis of resource budgeting outturn information.

RAB and the fiscal rules

The move to RAB does not affect the measurement of the Government's performance against the fiscal rules. Total Managed Expenditure, Public Sector Current Expenditure and Public Sector Net Investment will continue to be measured on a basis consistent with the internationally recognised national accounts and thus fully consistent with measurement of the fiscal rules. The fiscal rules already incorporate some resource concepts such as the inclusion of depreciation in measuring adherence to the golden rule. The budgeting items of cost of capital charge and provisions do not feed through into the fiscal aggregates but are removed through accounting adjustments. The Government is committed to producing, for the first time, consolidated accounts for the entire public sector. The Whole Government Accounts (WGA) project, which will be compiled in accordance with GAAP, is scheduled for the financial year 2005–06. The WGA will further improve the quality of information available for fiscal policy makers by bringing together the better information in RAB into a single financial statement for government.

14
Assessing Long-Term Sustainability

Achieving long-term fiscal sustainability is of key importance to every British person. It not only affects the welfare of future generations but also the future well-being of each existing generation. For this reason the assessment of the long-term effects of current policy settings needs to be a central part of the fiscal framework.

Introduction

The management of the public finances typically focuses on a short-term horizon. This reflects the numerous important spending and taxation decisions that arise for Government on an regular basis. However, it is also important to examine the implications of longer-term factors. This is particularly important for achieving intergenerational equity – one of the principles of fiscal management set out in the Code for Fiscal Stability.

As with all OECD countries, over the next 30 years, the structure of Britain's population and the nature of the services they will require is likely to undergo substantial change. Decisions made now will therefore have significant implications for the future state of the Government finances.

The issue, however, is not entirely about demography. Other potential developments may also have significant effects on long-term sustainability. For example, the advancement of medical technology will have unclear implications for the cost of providing health services. Similarly, nuclear decommissioning will impact on the public finances in the future.

This chapter sets out some of the long-term issues facing the UK and examines how to measure the impact of these issues on the public finances. It also discusses the evidence from the examinations of long-term sustainability that have already been undertaken for the UK.

Sustainability issues

The focus on long-term sustainability has largely been driven by demographic trends. The ageing of the population, and consequent shrinking proportion of people of working age, will affect both the demand for services as well as the capacity for the Government to provide services. As a result, a number of countries, along with international organisations such at the OECD, have undertaken studies to examine the implications of the ageing of the population.

Figures 14.1(a) and (b) clearly show the changing nature of the UK population. By 2036 around one in four people in the UK will be aged over 65, compared to around one in seven in 2000.

Despite this stark change the UK is well placed compared to other EU and OECD countries. The total old-age dependency ratio (defined as the number of people aged 65 and over as a percentage of the number of people aged between 20 and 64) is expected to rise gradually from around 26 per cent in 2000 to 47 per cent by 2036, and fall marginally thereafter. In contrast, the old-age dependency ratio is expected to be around 53 per cent in Germany and 64 per cent in Japan by 2050. The EU average is projected to be slightly above 53 per cent by 2050. This does not, however, mean that the Government does not have to be aware of, or plan for, issues affecting the long-term sustainability of the public finances.

One effect of the ageing of the population is that it reduces the relative size of the working-age population. This can have flow on effects in the labour market and potentially reduce the productive capacity of the economy. The relationship between labour market and growth also flows through into the public finances. As growth slows so does the expansion of the tax base resulting in lower revenue collections for Government.

The relative reduction in the population of working age can be offset by increased participation and productivity. Increasing labour force participation by around 5 percentage points would offset the reduction in labour supply due to ageing. This decline can also be offset by reducing unemployment and raising productivity levels. For this reason the Government has implemented a number of programmes aimed at increasing labour market participation and generating productivity improvements. These programmes focus both on moving people into the labour force and moving people from the labour force into employment.

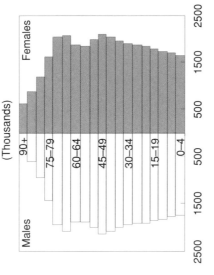

(Thousands)

Source: HM Treasury (2000c)

Figure 14.1(a)   UK population by age and sex, 2000

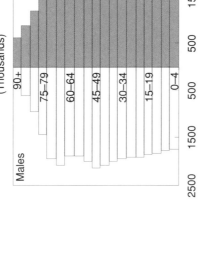

(Thousands)

Source: HM Treasury (2000c)

Figure 14.1(b)   UK population by age and sex, 2036

The projected demographic trends may also have an impact on Government spending. In particular, there are two main areas of interest: health and social security.

The cost of providing *health* expenditure, and particularly hospital and community health services, is directly related to the age of the population. At present, the average annual cost of providing health care to each person aged over 65 is over three and a half times the average for the remainder of the population. However, it is highly uncertain what effect the ageing of the population will have on the cost of providing health services. On the one hand, it has been argued that as the number of older people in the population rises there will be increased demand for health care. In the 1999 *Economic and Fiscal Strategy Report* (EFSR), the Government estimated that on the basis of the existing distribution of health costs across age groups, real health spending would have to grow by two-thirds of a per cent each year, independent of current policies to improve speed and quality of treatment (HM Treasury 1999a).

On the other hand, it has been argued that longer life will translate to a longer healthy life. This means that the age at which the bulk of health care needs arises will move outwards with the effect of substantially reducing the pressure on health services. For example, should health costs by age move outwards by five years (in other words healthy life increases by five years) this would reduce the potential health care cost of ageing by around one-third by 2036.

Adding to the uncertainty about the cost of health care services is the effect of technological advancements. These developments can result in new treatments or more efficient practices that reduce the cost of medical procedures. However, as noted by Lee and Skinner (1999) this can also result in surgery being deemed appropriate for a greater proportion of patients. This increase in medical activity may well drive an increase in total costs despite the reduction in costs per procedure. There are also some developments which will clearly reduce the cost of medical treatment, particularly those which work to prevent the need for costly surgical procedures.

The effect of an ageing population on the demand for health services is therefore unclear. However, it is clear that this is an area which the Government must continue to evaluate with a view to providing an appropriate level of health services to the public while at the same time ensuring that the public finances remain sustainable.

Social security, and particularly age-related pension, costs also have long-term implications for the public finances. As the proportion of retired persons increases this will increase the number of people claiming benefits and, *ceteris paribus*, the share of spending that is required to provide social security services. The importance of the issue is considerably reduced in the UK by the fact that most social security benefits are indexed by prices rather than wages. This means that the real value of the social security benefits is maintained over time, however, the cost per person as a share of GDP will decline over time. The net effect of this is dependent on the growth rates of the number of people claiming pensions and the real rate of GDP growth. However, as discussed below, the relatively small ageing effect and strong rate of real economic growth means that total social security payments are expected to decline as a share of GDP over time.

This situation is unique to the UK. In a 1996 working paper the OECD showed that only the UK is expected to have public sector pension contributions exceeding payments by 2050. For most other OECD countries a large gap is expected to develop. Furthermore, the OECD projects that total pensions payments in the UK will peak in 2035 at just over 5 per cent of GDP compared with peak payments of around 18 per cent and 22 per cent of GDP in Germany and Italy respectively (OECD 1996).

Much of this trend is related to the continuation of social security benefit increases being linked to prices. The Government Actuary has estimated that the total cost of social security benefits would double by 2050 if benefit expenditure was increased in line with earnings (Government Actuary's Department 1995). For this reason it is important to continue to monitor developments in social security benefits for their impact on long-term sustainability.

Spending in a number of other areas will also be affected by long-term factors. In many cases these factors are difficult to predict or are not expected to have a significant impact on the public finances. For this reason they are not discussed here. However, in looking at the long term it must be kept in mind that it is not possible to compile a comprehensive list of risks and Governments should remain vigilant in being prepared for longer-term pressures in unexpected areas.

Long-term fiscal projections

The UK Government is required by the Code for Fiscal Stability to publish illustrative long-term projections of the public finances for a period of at least ten years. Consistent with this requirement, the first set of long-term projections for a period of 30 years was published in the 1999 EFSR. This section summarises the main findings and conclusions from the set of illustrative projections in the 2001 EFSR, presented in the 2001 Budget.

The purpose of long-term fiscal projections is to extend the framework traditionally used to project public spending and revenue over the medium term; that is, to examine the information available and to estimate the direction of spending. This can be done in several ways depending on how much information is available and the intended purpose of the output. The idea is generally to show from the Government's perspective whether the current taxation and spending policies can be sustained over time.

The Government published sets of long-term projections in the 1999, 2000 and 2001 EFSRs. The approach taken in these reports was to examine the resources available to fund current spending while meeting the Government's fiscal rules over the long term. This was done by projecting forward taxation and transfer payments (mainly social security payments, current grants and debt interest payments) with the difference between them representing the available resources for current consumption spending; for example, spending on health and education. Investment is projected forward at a constant share of GDP consistent with the sustainable investment rule.

As with all fiscal projections, the outcomes are largely determined by the underlying assumptions. In this regard the choice of *economic parameters* is important. In order to produce a cautious set of projections, the baseline presented in the 2001 EFSR used a long-term rate of economic growth which is lower than the Government's neutral projections of trend economic growth (see Table 14.1).

Table 14.1   Long-term economic assumptions

	Average annual real growth (per cent)	
	2006–07 to 2010–11	*2011–12 to 2030–31*
Productivity	2.00	1.75
Labour force	0.25	0.00
GDP	2.25	1.75
Inflation	2.50	2.50

Source: HM Treasury (2001).

The *taxation* system is subject to a number of effects in both the short and long term. For example, patterns of income and spending are changing constantly, giving rise to considerable uncertainty about taxation bases. As a result, the projections presented in the EFSR do not try to project variations in the tax base; rather, the approach used is to project total current receipts as a constant share of GDP without making assumptions about the source of that revenue. This provides a simple but workable assumption about the long-term resources available to meet the Government's spending programmes.

The assumptions about *spending* relate to the growth in transfer payments. The largest transfer is social security spending where projections of spending have been developed in consultation with the Department of Work and Pensions and the Government Actuary's Department. The projections represent a plausible outcome based on the interaction of the current social security system with demographic, economic and other factors. They cannot be interpreted as reflecting the direction of future policy.

Debt interest payments were calculated based on an assumed average interest rate and the path for the debt stock. In the baseline projection, investment is assumed to continue at its 2005–06 share of GDP until 2030–31. For simplicity, other transfers were also projected forward at a constant share of GDP.

The *baseline long-term fiscal projections* are set out in Figure 14.2. These illustrative projections show that, given the assumptions for transfer payments, current public consumption can grow at an average real rate of over 2½ per cent each year for the next 30 years and still remain consistent with the fiscal rules.

The main reason for the declining trend for transfers is the projection path for social security benefits. As the majority of benefits are indexed by prices, they remain constant in terms of purchasing power and fall as a share of GDP over time. Falling debt interest payments as a share of GDP also contribute to the decline.

These results are very similar to the ones presented in the 1999 and 2000 EFSRs. In addition to the baseline case, alternative scenarios have also been presented. For example, the long-term fiscal projections presented in the 2000 EFSR (which are based on nearly identical assumptions and the same methodology as in the 2001 EFSR) also examined the potential effect of the Government's policies aimed at raising the labour market participation rate and thereby, *ceteris paribus*, employment and the rate of economic growth. As the tax base is assumed to grow in line with the economy, then higher growth will further reduce the relative share of revenue that is spent on social security payments (reflecting the greater difference between prices and wages growth). This is partly offset by rises in other transfer payments which are assumed to grow more in line with the economy. As a result, total transfers will fall as a share of GDP but continue to rise in real terms.

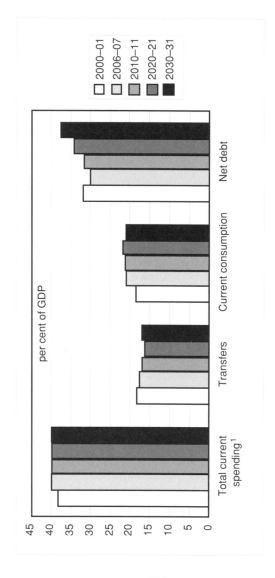

Note: [1] Total current spending equals current receipts from 2006–07 onwards.
Source: HM Treasury (2001).

Figure 14.2   Baseline projections

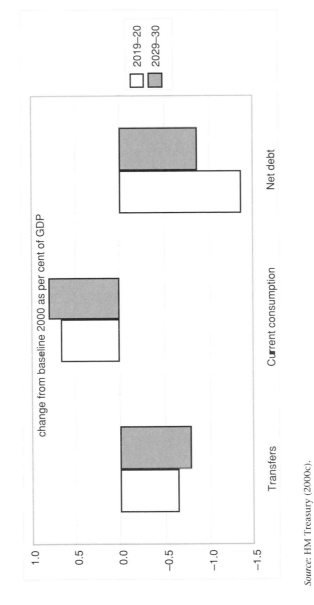

Source: HM Treasury (2000c).

Figure 14.3 Effects of higher labour market participation rate

This allows for a faster rate of growth for current consumption consistent with meeting the golden rule. The outcome is shown in Figure 14.3 which shows the effects in 2019–20 and 2029–30 of a gradual increase of the participation rate across all age groups by 4 percentage points above the baseline scenario between 2010 and 2020.

Given the assumptions made, the key result of higher growth is therefore greater resources to spend on current consumption, or in other words, meeting the Government's priorities in health, education, defence and other spending. The 2000 alternative scenario highlights the importance of the Government's programme of reforms aimed at delivering higher productivity growth and improved labour market participation.

It is important to recognise that these scenarios do not illustrate the effect of spending pressures on health or education; rather, they show the amount of funds available to the Government to meet demand in these areas. While some analysis of the effect of ageing on health and education services was reported in the EFSR, continued analysis of the pressures on each spending portfolio will therefore be required to ensure that the costs of demographic or other long term effects do not result in unsustainable public finances. A similar examination of taxation trends is also essential.

Generational accounts

The development of generational accounting also reflects the importance of assessing long-term fiscal balances. These accounts seek to answer the question of how large a fiscal burden do current policy settings imply for future generations. They also attempt to identify what adjustment to policies would be required to ensure that future generations face the same fiscal burden as the current generation.

Generational accounts have now been produced for a number of countries. In the UK, the National Institute for Economic and Social Research (NIESR) produced a set of generational accounts for the UK in November 1998. This section examines the usefulness of these accounts and examines some of the key NIESR findings. The specification of these accounts are set out in Cardarelli et al. (2000).

Generational accounts are defined as the present value difference between the taxes an individual pays to the government and the net benefits he derives from the government over his remaining life. These accounts are calculated by age groups and summed to show the total amount that the current generation is contributing towards the cost of providing government services. Where the current generation is receiving net benefits from the government sector, this implies that the bill for those services is being passed on to future generations. The size of any generational imbalance is most evident in comparing the generational accounts of current and future newborns. These two groups both face a full lifetime of taxes and benefits and hence where the future newborns have a higher generational account then this infers that future generations will have to meet the cost of spending by the current generation.

As with long-term projections, generational accounts are based on a series of assumptions about future spending and taxation. For taxes and transfer payments, as well as spending on health and education, the accounts impute a value to particular generations. However, for other spending on goods and services the accounts do not assign the benefits to any particular generation. This reflects the difficulty in doing so. Therefore, the accounts 'do not show the full net benefit or burden that any generation receives from government policy as a whole' but do identify 'which generations will pay for the government spending not included in the accounts'.

NIESR's key finding from its generational accounts is that 'compared with other leading industrial countries like the US, Japan and Germany, the imbalance in UK generational policy is ... quite modest; ie there is not a major intergenerational problem'. However, despite the fiscal rectitude, such as through indexing pension benefits by prices, there is still some generational imbalance.

As with long-term projections, the outcomes derived from generational accounts models are dependent on the assumptions used. For example, raising productivity growth by a quarter of a percentage point each year in the NIESR model would entirely eliminate the imbalance. The success of the Government's programme of encouraging labour market participation and raising productivity could potentially have the effect of ensuring that future UK generations are unlikely to be faced with a higher tax burden as a result of spending by past and present generations.

Other long-term studies

The issues underlying long-term sustainability are the result of micro-economic policy decisions. Ultimately, the total amount spent on health or education will always be a decision for the government. However, it remains important to understand the factors that may affect these decisions to examine whether the current levels of service can be sustained in the future.

To this end a number of international organisations have undertaken cross-country studies that consider the effect of ageing on specific aspects of spending. These studies generally support the broader fiscal analysis undertaken above.

A key study in this regard was undertaken by the OECD in 1996. This study found that pension payments in the UK were expected to rise very marginally from 2005 to 2035 but then fall back to below the 1995 levels from around 2040 onwards. The OECD also highlighted the fact that the total pension cost for the UK was currently among the lowest in the 20 countries studied. It also showed that indexing pensions by wages could effectively double the cost of providing pensions by 2045. As a result, the provision of pensions was not expected to significantly affect the UK's primary balance in the long run. On the European level, the Economic Policy Committee's Working Group on the implications of ageing populations conducted a similar study in 2000 (Economic Policy Committee 2000). Its findings support the OECD's general conclusions. In a 'current policy' scenario, for example, pension expenditure as a percentage of GDP in the UK is projected to gradually fall from 5.1 per cent in 2000 to 3.9 per cent by 2050. In contrast, most other countries are projected to experience a more or less marked increase in pension expenditure as a percentage of GDP over the coming decades. Sensitivity analysis shows that these results are relatively robust to changes in the underlying assumptions, for example regarding demographic development, labour market performance and productivity growth rates.

The OECD also examined the effect of ageing on health care costs. For the UK they suggested that if health care costs grow at the same rate per person then total health care costs will remain broadly constant at around 6 to 7 per cent of GDP[1] over the 35 years of the study. However, if health costs grew by an additional 1 per cent per person each year, then total costs could rise to around 8½ to 9½ per cent of GDP – an increase of approximately 50 per cent. This emphasises the importance of government decision making in setting the total provision of health services at an affordable level not just at present but also for the future.

Policy implications

The general conclusion from the various studies is that the UK does not have a significant long-term problem as a result of the ageing of the population. However, aside from demographic uncertainty, there are a number of expenditures which the Government will face in the future for which the cost is uncertain – such as nuclear decommissioning. In addition, there are uncertainties about the demand for, and cost of providing, public services over time. This considerable uncertainty means that the government must continue to be prepared for an unexpected outcome which could be either a significant improvement or deterioration of the public finances.

There are three key areas where policies should be formed with a view to long-term sustainability. At the macroeconomic level, economic growth is a key to sustainable long-term public finances. It not only means that individuals are better off but also that the government receives sufficient tax revenue to fund an appropriate level of spending. The benefits of higher growth (as a result of higher labour market participation rates) were shown in Figure 14.3. For this reason, the Government has already announced programmes to raise productivity and labour market participation, and hence increase trend economic growth.

At a more microeconomic level, the Government must also develop policies to counteract any potential pressures in health and social security. Here the Government has already started to develop policies that take the ageing of the population into account and minimise the risk of the public finances becoming unsustainable. The future increase in the retirement age for women from 60 to 65 will play a key role in reducing long-term spending pressures. In addition, the Government has announced:

- policies to deliver welfare reform and service modernisation
- assistance for people to provide for retirement incomes for themselves through the State Second Pension (S2P) and stakeholder pensions
- reforms, such as Public Service Agreements and the Public Service Productivity Panel, aimed at raising productivity throughout the public services and ensuring resources are used to their best effect.

The cumulative effect of these programmes will assist in ensuring that the Government is well prepared should the long-term fiscal position turn out worse than projected.

Conclusions

The ageing of the population presents a challenge for almost all industrial countries. As the relative size of the workforce declines and that of aged dependents grows, it will place pressure on the public finances. The UK, however, is in a stronger position than most. The ageing of population is expected to be considerably less marked than in countries such as the US, Japan, France and Germany. Nonetheless, the average age of the population is still expected to rise significantly over the next 30 years.

In the light of these, and other, developments, the long-term sustainability of the UK's public finances has been examined by the Government and external organisations. The approaches taken have varied from producing aggregate long-term projections to generational accounts to more specific studies of key spending areas. Despite the different approaches and assumptions, the overall conclusion of all these studies is that the UK is not facing significant long-term sustainability problems.

The uncertainty surrounding these projections, however, means that the Government cannot be complacent. Rather it must ensure that its spending and taxation policies are developed with one eye on the potential risks that may eventuate over time. In this regard, the Government has already put in place some measures designed to control the risks of unsustainable demand for social security and health spending. In fact, to a large extent it is because of these measures that the studies of long-term sustainability show the UK in such a positive light.

15
The Public Sector Balance Sheet

This chapter discusses how the public sector balance sheet is produced and presented in the UK at present and how it could better match the needs of fiscal policy makers.

Introduction

The rationale underlying the changes to the fiscal policy framework outlined in previous chapters have led policy makers to place greater emphasis on resource use and stocks, and less emphasis on cash and flows. Naturally, this has raised the profile of the public sector balance sheet as a potential analytical tool.

This chapter sets out:

- the balance sheet data presently available
- how the balance sheet might fit into the fiscal policy framework, highlighting issues of how the balance sheet is measured and what should be included
- how the balance sheet approach could be developed in the coming years to meet more fully the needs of fiscal policy makers.

What is the balance sheet?

In simple terms, a balance sheet is a record of all assets and liabilities held by an entity. Assets (for example, loans, accounts receivable, buildings) represent benefits of past actions that will be realised in a future period, whereas liabilities represent the costs from past actions (for example, debt, accounts payable) that will arise in a future period. As such the balance sheet indicates whether past actions will result in net future costs or benefits.

All companies are required to produce balance sheets as part of their financial reports. They provide valuable information to investors about the financial strength of companies by indicating their capacity to meet their liabilities by selling assets. The valuation of companies by financial markets takes account of this information.

Governments also accumulate assets and liabilities. For this reason, the Office for National Statistics (ONS) compiles balance sheets for the public sector. The ONS is currently improving the quality of the balance sheets data by replacing a number of assumed asset values with hard values being determined as part of the move to Resource Accounting and Budgeting (RAB – see Chapter 13). Once RAB has been fully introduced balance sheets will also become a more familiar part of the Government's financial accounts.

It is important, however, to recognise that public sector balance sheets cannot be interpreted in exactly the same way as those in the private sector. For example, a company with a negative balance sheet indicates technically insolvency. However, it may be appropriate for the Government to hold a negative balance sheet at a particular period of time reflecting the fact that it has social, as well as financial, objectives. The financing of assets at lower levels of government may also make it appropriate for the central government to hold negative assets over a longer period of time if lower levels of government have strong positive balances. Careful interpretation of public sector balance sheets is therefore required before users and advisers can reach conclusions about the sustainability of the public finances.

The different balance sheet measures are discussed in later sections of this chapter. However, at this stage it should be noted that the bottom line measure (total assets less liabilities) is known by several different names – net wealth, net worth, net asset position and balance sheet position to name a few. For the purposes of this chapter the bottom line measure will be referred to as net worth. This title is also consistent with that used in the 1995 European System of Accounts (ESA 95).

The public sector balance sheet

As set out in Chapter 9, fiscal policy in the UK is assessed looking at the whole of the public sector – that is, central government, local government and public corporations. This is because it would be the taxpayer who would ultimately have to meet the cost if a public corporation had difficulty meeting its debts. Accordingly, the ONS publishes national and sectoral, including public sector, balance sheets for the UK.[1]

As shown in Table 15.1, the public sector was estimated to hold total assets of £699.3 billion, while having total liabilities of £540.1 billion. The balance between these, public sector net worth, was £159.2 billion.

Table 15.1 Public sector balance sheet, end 1999

Assets	(£bn)	Liabilities	(£bn)
Non-financial assets	503.3	Currency and deposits	74.7
Tangible assets	498.7	Securities other than shares	341.9
Residential buildings	83.0	Loans	98.2
Agricultural assets	3.7		
Commerical, industrial and		Other	25.3
other buildings	145.4		
Civil engineering works	231.9		
Plant and machinery	26.4		
Vehicles, including ships etc	6.3		
Stock and work in progess	2.0		
Intangible assets[1]	4.6		
Financial assets	196.0		
Currency and deposits	29.5		
Securities other than shares	19.8		
Loans	82.6		
Other	64.1		
Total assets	699.3	Total liabilities	540.1
Total net worth			159.2

Note: [1] Includes computer software, mineral exploration and artistic originals.

Source: ONS (2000).

This positive public sector net worth indicates that as a result of past policy settings the Government has built up a strong financial position. It means that the future benefits arising from past government activity will exceed the future costs of that activity. It is important, however, that this result is interpreted carefully given this measure of the balance sheet does not include all public sector assets and liabilities. For example, some heritage assets are not able to be valued for balance sheet purposes. Similarly, unfunded pension liabilities are not presently recorded.

Figure 15.1 shows recent trends in public sector tangible assets, net financial wealth and total net worth. Total net worth was relatively stable through the early 1980s; however, it has fallen considerably since 1988. This reflects two main factors:

- increasing net financial liabilities due to the deterioration in the public finances as the economy went into recession in the early 1990s
- declining total non-financial assets, reflecting both falling land prices and the effect of privatisation whereby public corporations' tangible assets were transferred to the private sector.

The latter of these trends in part reflects the fact that over the last 20 to 30 years the character of the UK public sector has changed considerably. Many large utilities, including British Telecom, British Gas and the water and electricity companies, have been privatised and transferred to the private sector. Health reforms have seen hospitals, now owned by National Health Service Trusts, transferred to the public corporations sector.

As shown in Figure 15.2, these changes have altered the structure of net worth held by each level of government. Central government net worth fell sharply as borrowing increased in early 1990s, despite the offsetting effect of high inflation eroding the real value of government debt. Net worth of public non-financial corporations fell steadily between 1980 and 1990 largely reflecting the privatisation programme. However, since 1990 their net worth has been relatively stable.

The net worth of local authorities has also declined during the 1990s, although the extent of this decline has been somewhat smaller than for other levels of government. This reflects the fact that while local authorities account for around one quarter of total public spending, they are financed primarily by grants from the central government sector and do not borrow significantly on their own account. This means that there is no offsetting liability for much of the asset accumulation undertaken by the local government sector. In contrast, the central government sector undertakes borrowing on behalf of both local authorities and public corporations, and this explains the negative net worth for this sector for much of the 1980s and then since 1992.

The public sector balance sheet also provides useful information on the composition of the public sector's assets and liabilities. As presently defined, the main tangible assets held by the public sector are: civil engineering works (including roads); commercial, industrial and other

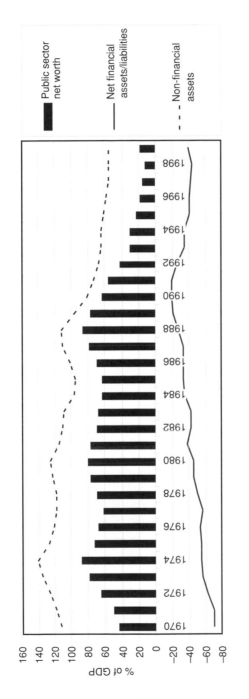

Source: HM Treasury (internal).

Figure 15.1 Public sector net worth

267

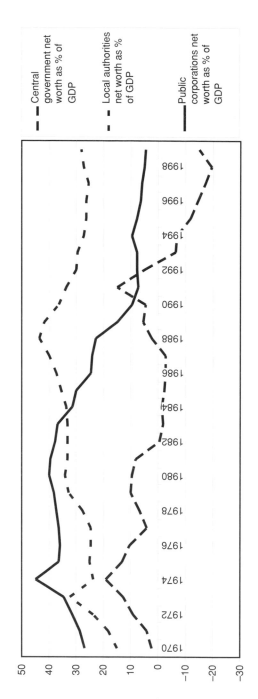

Central government net worth as % of GDP

Local authorities net worth as % of GDP

Public corporations net worth as % of GDP

Note: Break of series in 1991 (see ONS 2000, p. 264).
Source: HM Treasury (internal), ONS (2000).

Figure 15.2 Net worth by level of government

268

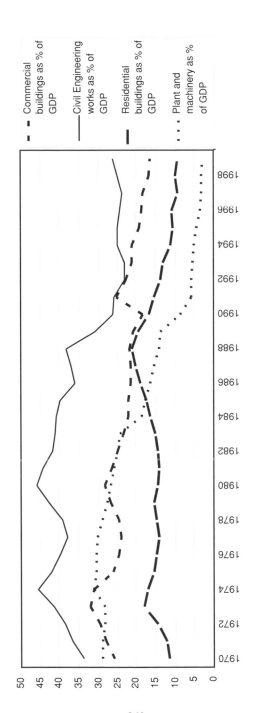

Figure 15.3 Public sector net worth by type of (tangible) asset

Note: Break of series in 1991 (see ONS 2000, p. 264).
Source: HM Treasury (internal), ONS (2000).

buildings; and residential buildings. The main financial liabilities are government securities and National Savings.[2]

Figure 15.3 shows how holdings of tangible assets have varied over time. It is evident that there has been a steady decline in public sector holdings of both commercial, industrial and other buildings as well as plant and equipment. This reflects the effects of privatisation and reduced government involvement in these types of activities. The movements in residential buildings tend to follow house price trends (suggesting this is primarily a valuation effect). Civil engineering works declined sharply at the end of the 1980s, reflecting falling land prices and privatisation of water utilities and electricity.

Balance sheets and fiscal policy

For many years, fiscal policy in the UK focused on questions of sustainability, with the primary indicators being public sector borrowing and debt. This rather narrow approach does not recognise that fiscal policy has many different facets, acting upon the economy through both macroeconomic and microeconomic channels.

Even in the purely macroeconomic context, there is no single ideal measure of the fiscal stance which can capture all the mechanisms in play. At various times, we might look for indicators of:

- fiscal sustainability: would present tax and spending policies mean that public borrowing remains under control?
- the impact on the economy: changes in both the balance between tax and spending and the disposition of public sector assets and liabilities will have effects on the wider economy
- the intergenerational impact of fiscal policy: how will the net burden of tax and transfers borne by the current generation compare with that borne by future generations?

There are a variety of indicators with which to examine these questions and no single indicator is appropriate for answering all the variants of these questions. For example, different indicators are needed to examine questions of long-term sustainability and short-term economic impact. As a result a number of different fiscal indicators are widely used by economists.

The balance sheet does not provide a magical measure that answers all the needs of economists and decision makers; rather, it increases the number of measures available for considering these issues. What use is made of the balance sheet therefore depends on how useful these measures are in answering the above questions. In other words, the balance sheet increases the size of the economist's toolbox; however, careful use of fiscal indicators will still be required to ensure the correct assessment is made.

In assessing fiscal policy there are roles for both stock and flow measures. Stock measures provide a snapshot of the net future effects of past budget decisions. Flow measures show how this position will change over time. In this light stock measures can be thought of as giving a picture of the strength of the current fiscal position while flow measures show how this position is changing. Naturally, projections of both stocks and flows can provide information on the future impact of current decisions.

At present the main stock indicator used to assess the public finances is net debt. Net debt is the difference between gross debt and liquid financial assets. As such it is a partial indicator of the Government's financial position. The most comparable balance sheet measure to net debt is that of net financial assets. This indicator differs from net debt in two main ways. First, it includes all financial assets; and second, it records both assets and liabilities at market values. In doing this it provides a wider measure of sustainability and one which indicates whether the existing stock of financial assets will cover the stock of financial liabilities at the present point in time.

The value of the net financial assets measure is dependent on how it is used. The wider coverage is generally considered to provide a better basis for looking at longer-term sustainability. By contrast, if the idea is to examine the ability of the public sector to meet its liabilities at the present time then it may only be able to call on its short-term or liquid liabilities. Furthermore, if the Government does not intend repurchasing its debt then the actual cost, and hence the best value for sustainability purposes, is the face or nominal value. As such both net debt and net financial assets provide useful information in assessing sustainability.

The net worth measure builds on both these financial indicators, and can be defined as net financial assets plus non-financial assets. As such it provides complete coverage of all the Government's assets and liabilities. In making an assessment of the sustainability of the public finances, net worth therefore provides a more comprehensive approach than either net debt or net financial assets and indicates to what extent borrowing is being used to finance the accumulation of assets or spending on current consumption. In addition, it also allows analysts to look which particular assets and liabilities are changing over time.

Even when taking just the rather narrow criterion of sustainability, the net worth measure can provide a richer indication than the more usual borrowing and debt figures, because its takes account of changes in government assets as well as liabilities. One example of how balance sheet data can show a different picture to conventional debt measures is evident in that the decline in the net public debt ratio for much of the 1980s was not matched by a decline in the measured ratio of public sector assets to GDP, with public sector net worth (including tangible assets) fluctuating between 60 per cent and 80 per cent of GDP. These relative movements are shown in Figure 15.4.

Some countries already make formal use of balance sheet data in their fiscal policy. For instance, New Zealand's Fiscal Responsibility Act includes an objective for net worth. To date, balance sheets have not played a large part in the UK fiscal policy framework. Nonetheless, the UK fiscal framework, and in particular the golden rule, is in fact closely aligned with net worth. If a government borrows only to finance investment, then any new debt will be matched by an increase in government assets, leaving net worth broadly unchanged (as long as both net worth and the current balance are measured using consistent definitions of capital spending and of depreciation). Therefore, in principle, the main influence on public sector net worth should be the balance on the public sector's current budget – the difference between current receipts and expenditure. A surplus on current budget means that a government is financing current spending from current receipts and is adding to net worth, rather than by borrowing which would increase government liabilities and reduce net worth. The current budget is not affected by government borrowing to finance *investment* and there should be little or no effect on net worth, as the addition to the stock of public sector assets offsets the extra liability.

Meeting the golden rule should therefore prevent further large falls in the level of public sector net worth (although not necessarily in the ratio of net worth to GDP) arising from Government policy decisions. The sustainable investment rule places a constraint on the amount of investment that may be financed by borrowing, preventing an escalation of public debt that might cause difficulties (even if it was backed by a similar build-up of public sector assets).

In addition to movements in the current budget, changes in the valuation of assets or liabilities can also increase or decrease net worth. These changes will need to be interpreted carefully as they may not

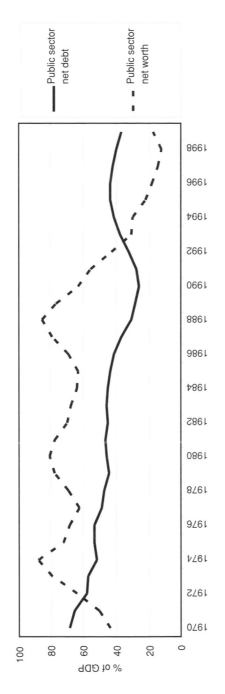

Source: HM Treasury (internal).

Figure 15.4 Net worth versus net debt

273

necessarily reflect the sustainability of current fiscal settings. For example, a change in the value of an asset that is unlikely to be sold does not affect the position of the Government. However, in other cases fiscal policy may need to adjust to offset these valuation effects such as where the revaluation reflects an increased cost of production. In these cases the increased asset value may flow through to the current budget in the form of higher depreciation and ultimately a higher cash cost in replacing the asset in the future. As such these movements have a real effect on the sustainability of the public finances. Box 15.1 examines further the factors that affect the balance sheet.

Improving the quality of balance sheet data

The usefulness of balance sheets in fiscal policy is also dependent on the quality of the asset valuations on which it is based. Difficulties in valuing non-financial assets can therefore undermine the value of balance sheet information.

Box 15.1   What affects the balance sheet?

Many changes in net worth reflect net acquisitions of tangible and financial assets. However, changes in the price of existing assets and liabilities can also have a significant effect on measured net worth. Table 15.2 compares the changes in public sector net worth (PSNW) over the last ten years with the public sector current balance, which measures the extent to which the public sector borrows to finance current spending. We would expect the current balance to account for a significant part of changes in net worth, if both were measured consistently (for example, including an allowance in the current balance for the effect of asset price changes).

The figuring does not, however, include estimates of the other factors discussed in the main text (for example, gilt prices and privatisations) because such calculations would require fairly extreme approximations.

Table 15.2   Public sector net worth and the current balance

(£bn)	1987	1988	1989	1990	1991	1992	1993	1994	1995	1996	1997	1998	1999
Change in PSNW	69	68	–6	–41	–27	–67	–64	8	–46	–20	–22	–10	53
Current budget	–2	8	8	3	–11	–36	–41	–34	–26	–23	–4	7	19
Other	71	60	–14	–45	–16	–31	–23	42	–20	3	–18	–17	34

Source: ONS (2000).

There are particular difficulties in valuing assets for which there is no market. For example, the value of roads and bridges must be determined from other information such as construction costs or the alternative use of the resources. Heritage and other assets that only provide social returns are also hard to value. Given these difficulties, the changes in the balance sheet must be interpreted carefully to determine their relevance for fiscal policy. A Treasury discussion paper (HM Treasury 1997d), published in December 1997, discussed these issues further and examined the assets and liabilities that make up the public sector balance sheet.

A key component of improving the quality of balance sheet data is the introduction of resource accounting and budgeting. This accruals framework will require each government department to value their assets and liabilities and construct balance sheets. This will build on the National Asset Register, published in 1997, that listed but did not value all government assets.

The ONS are also looking at ways to improve the quality of balance sheet information. In particular, they are currently reviewing the data and methodology used to determine public sector net worth. A major part of this project was to incorporate information from the introduction of RAB. This has allowed the ONS to move away from model-based estimates to use hard valuations provided by Government departments. These developments are reported in the ONS *Economic Trends* (West 1998, West and Clifton-Fearnside 1999). The outcomes are still preliminary but considered to be a significant improvement on the past data.

The Government is also looking at how to improve the quality of data beyond the central government sector. The UK's fiscal framework is defined for the public sector, incorporating central government, local government and public corporations. However, the introduction of RAB will only provide reliable data for most of the central government sector. If the balance sheet is to have a greater role in UK fiscal policy, it is necessary to improve the quality of local authority and public corporation balance sheets. Some progress is being made by the ONS in this area. The Treasury is also examining this issue as part of its Whole of Government Accounts project, particularly in the context of the need for common methodology and valuation techniques. However, it is unlikely that quality data for Central Government will be available until at least 2004, and possibly later for local government data. This suggests that full use of balance sheets will not occur for some time.

Future developments

To date, most of the work in improving the use of balance sheets in fiscal policy has focused on improving the data. However, to ensure that the measure of net worth used for fiscal policy is the most relevant for that purpose, the scope and coverage of the balance sheet also need to be considered.

One potential development that has been suggested is the use of forward-looking balance sheets which provide a measure of prospective net worth. The rationale behind this approach is that the unique nature of government means that its ability to raise revenue and its potential liabilities go beyond the standard balance sheet definitions. The most commonly used example is the Government's ability to levy taxes in the future. Proponents of prospective net worth argue that this 'right to tax' and other 'future assets' are as important as the value of other assets and should therefore be included in assessing the sustainability of the Government's fiscal position.

An example is unfunded pension schemes, which could potentially impose a large burden on future generations in some developed countries.[3] Although the UK faces much less of a potential problem than some other G7 countries, there is still a relevant argument that omitting this sort of information means that the balance sheet can only give a partial view of net worth. It seems likely that the combined effect of unfunded public service pensions together with state pension schemes could still look large in relation to the present level of net worth and the annual balance on the current budget.

An approach for including a measure of unfunded pension liabilities might be to focus on pension rights already accrued on a 'past service' basis, reflecting years of service and contributions already provided. This would typically be seen as an entitlement already earned, although the final liability will depend on factors such as length of employment, final salary and life expectancy. There are established actuarial techniques for valuing the extent of such pension liabilities already incurred: deriving a figure that represents, in effect, the extent of additional funding that would be needed to match these 'past service' liabilities if they had been funded.

In reality, however, to obtain a present value of all future cash flows is extremely difficult. The ability of the Government to amend these flows, for example by increasing or reducing tax rates, adds to the complexity. It has also been argued that the value of balance sheets is to indicate to what extent the Government may need to change tax collections in the future and so to include these flows in the assessment will detract from the usefulness of the measure.

Ultimately the choice of net worth or prospective net worth as a fiscal indicator comes down to how they will be used in the policy making process and how they will affect policy decisions. If net worth is used mainly as an *indicator* of fiscal policy, there might be relatively little advantage from using a comprehensive measure of net worth over and above simply looking at reported net worth relative to a view of how it should be heading over time, taking into account known influences on the longer-term prospect. However, if net worth were treated as an *objective* or a *target* of fiscal policy, then there would be greater force in the argument that a hybrid measure does not reflect consistently all aspects of a policy change – an intertemporal version of the well known temptation to switch between items that are on and off the balance sheet.

In part, this question probably comes down to one of whether the more detailed calculations are tractable in such a way that would provide a good foundation for fiscal policy. There would be a trade-off between the gain from including all possible information in the balance sheet and the loss of precision and clarity that might come from all the extra components. The argument may also be affected by the extent to which we might or might not be able to identify an optimal level for comprehensive net worth, or indeed for the narrower measures of net worth.

On balance the difficulties outlined above suggest it is not practicable, and possibly not desirable, to attempt to measure the value of all future cash flows. However, a strong case can be put for including at least some of the more 'lumpy' items such as unfunded pensions liabilities. Many of these items have similar characteristics to other assets in that they accrue over time and will have an impact on future public finances. As with all stock variables the potentially large size of these liabilities for the UK will need to be carefully explained as the associated cash flows are spread over a number of years and may only add a small amount to annual financing costs.

Regardless of which approach is used, the close link between the public sector balance sheet and the current balance means that the same definition should in principle be used for both the stock and the flow. The same conceptual problems affect both, and the difficulty of deciding what to include in the balance sheet is not avoided by focusing only on the current balance. So although the discussion in this chapter is framed in terms of balance sheets, the implication of choosing a very wide measure of net worth would be that the current balance should also include changes in discounted future spending and receipts.

Conclusion

The discussion above highlights how some of the influences on the balance sheet differ from those that affect the current budget. Some of these reflect the different bases for the two, and in particular the backward-looking nature of conventional balance sheets. Others, however, reflect aspects of the balance sheet valuation that would not be desirable in a fiscal policy indicator – for instance, we would not want significant changes in public sector net worth due to changes in long-term interest rates or to privatisation.

This does not mean to say that the balance sheet must be measured in such a way that it only changes in line with the public sector's surplus on current account. Looking at the balance sheet requires policy makers to address questions such as what should be the ultimate aim of fiscal policy and how to take account of changes in relative asset prices in setting fiscal policy.

The potential importance of balance sheets for fiscal policy, and the practical difficulties, are not new. Some Treasury thinking on fiscal policy, including balance sheets, in the mid-1980s was set out in Odling-Smee and Riley (1985). The authors stressed the importance of looking at both public sector assets and liabilities. However, they argued against Buiter's (1985) comprehensive net worth measure; for example, because of the difficulties of including a value for the right to tax future incomes, which might well not change over time anyway. Nevertheless, in their conclusions they argued that:

> In the medium to long term, the path for government debt should generally be set so that the net worth of the public sector, appropriately defined, is unchanged. Debt will therefore alter in line with other assets and liabilities such as the capital stock of the public sector, the present value of North Sea revenues and unfunded state pension liabilities. There are considerable difficulties with such a policy because of problems with defining and measuring the appropriate concept of public sector capital stock and other assets and liabilities. Nevertheless the analytical framework is helpful. (Odling-Smee and Riley 1985)

The principal fiscal policy requirement for the balance sheet is to provide a reliable guide to the balance between public sector assets and liabilities, that relates well and in a systematic way to the other fiscal indicators, and that moves in line with known influences on the public finances. The new fiscal framework outlined in earlier chapters now fits comfortably with balance sheet information. The concept of public sector net worth relates very closely to the golden rule and the public sector's surplus on current budget, so it is highly desirable that the current budget and the balance sheet should be measured in as consistent a way as possible.

Publishing and monitoring balance sheet data are only the first stages of bringing balance sheets into the fiscal framework. Building on the already significant improvements in the quality of balance sheet data and developing a better understanding of how to interpret public sector balance sheet data are essential if balance sheets are to have a greater role in the fiscal framework.

As well as pursuing these improvements, the next stage will be to consider how balance sheets might best fit into the fiscal framework in the future. What changes to the present definitions could provide more appropriate fiscal indicators? How far could, or should, we make progress towards the forward-looking, comprehensive net worth measures? What can be said about the desirable, or prudent, or optimal levels of public sector net worth?

16
Debt Management: Theory and Practice

This chapter looks at government debt management objectives and policy in the UK. The aim is to provide a brief assessment of the main theoretical motivations for debt management, and compare them with debt management policy. The conclusion is that current research has provided some useful insights into debt management policy. However, it does not yet offer strong guidance as to the composition of the optimal portfolio. Further research is needed, particularly with respect to the nature of the risks faced by the government.

Introduction

The primary objective of UK debt management policy is 'to minimise cost over the long term, taking account of risk, whilst ensuring consistency with the objectives of monetary policy' (HM Treasury 2000a). However, defining what makes up the 'optimal' portfolio to meet this objective is a difficult problem – there is little consensus as to the optimal debt portfolio. Looking at the literature suggests several different motivations for debt management:

- minimising cost
- minimising risk
- improving the allocation of risk in the economy
- helping to reinforce the credibility of fiscal and monetary policy.

This chapter reviews some of the arguments and considers the practical implications for debt management. It then offers some suggestions for future research to improve debt management policy.

Minimising cost

The trade-off between cost and risk

An obvious motivation for debt management is to minimise the cost of debt servicing – the lower the cost of debt servicing, the lower the burden of taxation. However, it is important to distinguish between the different means by which cost savings can be achieved; in particular, if the cost of different types of debt reflects a fair payment for risk, then the cheapest forms of funding may expose the taxpayer to too much risk.

The cost of different types of debt will depend on the term structure of interest rates. This depends on expectations as to future interest rates (so that if short-term rates are expected to rise in the future, then long-term rates will be higher than short-term rates) and investors' preferences for risk. Sources of risk include uncertainty over the future path of interest rates (both real and nominal), and also default or credit risk.

Economic theory suggests that the riskiness of an asset depends on the degree to which the return on the asset varies with fluctuations in investors' incomes. Assets which help to reduce the riskiness of an investor's portfolio will be highly valued – in particular an asset which has a high payoff when investors' incomes are unexpectedly low helps to insure the portfolio and will be highly valued, whereas an asset which has the same payoff when investors' incomes are unexpectedly high will be less valuable, because it tends to add to income volatility. The more valued an asset, the lower the return the borrower needs to pay in order to induce investors to hold that asset. This means the cheapest form of debt will be the security that offers a high return when incomes are unexpectedly low, because it offers investors the greatest degree of insurance. However, this is also the most risky form of debt for the borrower, because it tends to magnify their own income shocks. If taxpayers and investors face similar shocks to incomes, then taxpayers will then have to pay out a higher return on government debt when their own incomes are unexpectedly low; that is, the cheapest forms of debt are also the riskiest forms of debt for the taxpayer.

Why should the government avoid risk?

At first glance it does not seem obvious that the government should avoid risk. For example, Tobin argued that the government should act as if it were risk neutral, and choose the cheapest form of debt: 'If anyone is in the position to be his own insurer, it is the Secretary of the Treasury' (Tobin 1963, p. 192). However, the optimal taxation literature argues that more risky forms of financing can impose costs, if they increase the variation in taxes. Because the welfare losses from taxation increase more than linearly with changes in taxes, the total loss from raising taxes in one period and then lowering them in the next period will be higher than if taxes were the same over both periods (for a given amount of taxation over the two periods). In order to minimise the cost of taxation, the government should try to smooth away variations in taxes as much as possible. For example, the government should try to smooth taxes over the business cycle, running deficits in bad times and surpluses in good times.

If markets are complete (so that investors can insure against any possible event) and efficient (so that there are no arbitrage opportunities), the difference in returns between different types of bonds represents a fair payment for risk; all debt portfolios will be fairly priced. Under these circumstances cost becomes irrelevant, because (on a risk-adjusted basis) all portfolios have the same 'cost'. Instead, the government should focus on risk minimisation. Ideally, debt costs should *fall* when incomes are low or when other financing needs are high, and *rise* when incomes are high or when other financing needs are low.

A role for cost minimisation

In reality, markets are not perfect. Because of this, the government will not necessarily face a simple trade-off between risk and return. Market opportunities may arise which enable the government to lower the cost of debt-servicing without incurring greater risk, due to the following factors:

- asymmetric information
- missing markets for some securities
- segmented markets
- imperfections in the bond market.

Asymmetric information

Because the government sets monetary and fiscal policy, it has a significant advantage over the market in predicting the path of interest rates. Theoretically, this could be used to lower the cost of debt-servicing. Monetary policy authorities are likely to have a better idea of the path of the short-term interest rates, if not longer-term rates. However, this could also work against the government – if it became clear that the government's actions were motivated by forthcoming policy changes, then rational investors would begin to anticipate this; for example, the sale of significant quantities of short-term debt could be interpreted as a signal of imminent monetary policy tightening. If this were the case, investors would demand a higher return before they were willing to buy more short-term debt. As a result, this policy may not lead to lower costs in the long run. In fact, many governments have moved to separate debt management and monetary policy, to avoid the perception that the debt managers have access to confidential information and also to avoid confusion over the direction of monetary policy.

In the absence of superior information, it seems unlikely that governments should be able to 'beat the market' on a consistent basis. However, one exception might be where the government has yet to earn credibility for a low-inflation policy. In this case, long-term rates may be too high, reflecting market expectations of high inflation in the future. If, in the government's opinion, market expectations did not fully reflect its commitment to low inflation, it should be able to lower its debt-servicing costs by selling inflation-linked bonds and/or short-term bonds. This would have the added advantage of reinforcing its commitment to low inflation. The role of government debt in improving the credibility of monetary policy is discussed below (pp. 293–5). However, one caveat is that policy makers are not always the best judge of their commitment to particular policies – markets may be in a better position to make an unbiased judgement of future policy developments.

Missing markets

If the private sector does not provide some types of securities, there may be an opportunity for the government to lower debt servicing costs by providing the missing security. This can improve welfare if it improves the allocation of risk. For example, by creating a market for risk-free debt, governments may assist risk sharing within the economy. Relatively risk-averse investors could hold the risk-free asset, while less risk-averse investors could 'short' the risk-free asset. However, this has implications for the overall trade-off between risk and return. For example, the price of other, more risky assets, may need to fall in order to induce investors to hold them. This means that in theory, some people could be worse off when the government issues a risk-free asset (Peled 1985).

However, if investors value the risk-free asset, then they will be willing to pay a premium for the bond. This could potentially be redistributed to the potential 'losers'. For example, in Gale (1990), government debt improves welfare by allowing risk sharing between generations. Suppose each generation lives for two periods. When they are young, investors invest in a risky asset which has an uncertain return when they are old. In the absence of government debt, the old generation bear all the risk. By issuing government debt, the government can reduce some of that risk since investors can now invest in a safe asset with a guaranteed return. The government pays off the debt by taxing the young – hence debt transfers risk from the old to the young. However, in order to ensure that there is an overall welfare gain, investors must be willing to accept a negative return on government debt – that is, they must pay the government for the right to hold the bond. The government then redistributes the surplus as a transfer. This ensures that nobody is made worse off by the introduction of the bond. While this example may appear somewhat unrealistic, it does highlight the fact that governments need to be aware of the potential risks associated with risky debt; ideally, the premium paid by investors would be sufficiently large to offset the costs to taxpayers of any additional risk.

Segmented markets

If government debt helps some investors to insure against risks that are peculiar to them (or idiosyncratic risk), then this is less likely to have adverse implications for the overall riskiness of the government portfolio, since the risks associated with such securities should be independent of shocks to taxpayer incomes. One argument is that some investors may have 'preferred habitats' – they may have a preference for a particular type of bond because it matches a particular liability – for example, pension funds may prefer index-linked bonds because they offer annuities which are indexed to the rate of inflation. If the government is the only source of such bonds, then it can earn a monopoly profit from their sale. However, there must also be an imperfection somewhere in financial markets that prevents private markets from selling into these markets; otherwise, in efficient financial markets, all idiosyncratic risk can be arbitraged away.

Imperfect financial markets

Because of market imperfections, financial markets may not always price assets 'fairly'. Factors such as search costs, transaction costs and imperfect information may drive a wedge between buyers' true valuations and the price they are willing to pay. For example, there may be transaction costs associated with private sector securities – investors must ensure the company is creditworthy, and they may also incur monitoring costs in assessing the financial health of their debtors. Government debt, on the other hand, is likely to be relatively free of these costs; since governments have the right to tax both current and future generations, they are much less likely to default. This drives a wedge between the return on government debt (with low or zero monitoring costs) and corporate debt. Therefore, issuing government debt lowers debt servicing costs and improves welfare by reducing wasteful monitoring costs. Government debt may also be more liquid than other forms of debt; because governments can draw upon future endowments through the right to tax future generations, government bonds can always be liquidated, whereas private equities cannot (Holmstrom and Tirole 1998). These sorts of market imperfections suggest that government debt may earn a premium for reasons unrelated to the risk-return trade-off.

However, even the market for government debt is unlikely to be completely efficient. Uncertainty over the true price of debt will be increased by volatility, illiquidity, and thin markets. In turn, this reduces the price that investors are willing to pay (that is, increases the return) for government debt. By reducing these inefficiencies or imperfections, governments can reduce debt servicing costs without increasing risk, because these types of imperfections are not related to risk.

Since the 1980s, most countries have introduced reforms aimed at improving the liquidity and efficiency of the market for government debt. These policies include the establishment of a system of primary dealers, who have an obligation to promote a liquid secondary market; the use of auctions to sell debt rather than placement through banks; the issue of benchmark bonds, that is, large fungible bond issues with the same coupon and maturity date; the establishment of 'repo' markets (allowing for the sale and repurchase of bonds); and the introduction of 'strips' (where a bond is separated into its individual cashflows).

A key step is to try to reduce general uncertainty in the market by ensuring issuance policy is predictable and transparent. Clearly a major influence is the conduct of monetary and fiscal policy, which may lie beyond the remit of the debt manager; however, the debt manager can also reduce uncertainty through keeping the market informed of issues affecting supply; for example, many countries adopt a regular auction programme, and pre-announce quantities for sale before each auction.

Liquid secondary markets may help to reduce borrowing costs by increasing demand, and by reducing transaction costs and risks. Investors are likely to prefer government securities with easily observable prices and which can be easily traded. This may reflect the existence of search costs, or trading externalities, which make it costly to price less standard debt instruments. Individual dealers may also prefer highly liquid securities, since it reduces their exposure to market risk in taking on unhedged positions in individual securities. Benchmark bonds, because they are a standardised instrument in large supply, may therefore command a liquidity premium over other securities. For the UK, anecdotal evidence suggests that the benchmark premium is often around 3–4 basis points, and sometimes higher.

There is also a substantial literature on the potential impact on revenue from different auction mechanisms. The recent move by the US to adopt a uniform price mechanism for auctioning all its bonds is motivated by the theory that uniform-price auctions may help to encourage greater participation and improve revenue by reducing the 'winner's curse'.[1] However, this is still an issue of debate among academics and practitioners – uniform-price auctions could also reduce revenue, for example, by increasing the risk of collusion. The UK uses a multi-price auction format for conventional gilts, but has chosen to adopt a uniform price format for auctions of index-linked bonds, because of the different nature of the risks involved to the bidder for each type of security. In particular, given the lack of liquidity in the index-linked market, and the absence of a 'hedge' through a futures market, bidders for index-linked gilts may potentially face greater risks from the winner's curse.

The advantage of implementing cost minimisation policies at the 'microeconomic' level is that they are largely independent of the type of bond sold – hence they should allow reductions in cost without having adverse implications for risk. However, a concern for liquidity may place some constraints on the types of bond sold. New or novel instruments may be quite costly to introduce to the market. This may narrow the range of instruments available. In turn, this might limit the degree to which government debt can offer insurance against particular risks, either to the government or to bondholders.

Cost minimisation in practice

The Treasury has generally avoided taking views on interest rates, as it does not have an intrinsic advantage over the market in assessing the future path of interest rates. In addition, because it is a large issuer, it is unlikely that it could enter and exit the market without affecting prices. Hence the Treasury does not try to actively trade to 'beat the market'. Instead, the Treasury primarily looks for cost savings that can be achieved through the underlying structure of the market for government debt.

In order to enhance predictability and transparency, the Treasury publishes an annual remit for the Debt Management Office covering issuance policy (amount, maturity, and timing of auctions). Because it is not a rigid calendar, the Debt Management Office retains some discretion over the amount and type of bond to be sold at each auction following consultations with market makers and investors; however there is a quarterly pre-commitment to stocks. The Treasury also retains the right to issue on 'tap' for market management reasons. Variations to the auction programme may be justified in light of market conditions or unexpected events (for example, to avoid clashes with the timing of Budget announcements). The Treasury tries to ensure that any such variations are clearly explained and understood by the market. It also tries to signal in advance through the remit how its issuance policy might change in the light of new information; for example, changing fiscal forecasts. This is to avoid the perception that such discretionary actions might be undertaken for more opportunistic reasons.

Issuance policy is focused on supporting benchmark issues, because of the perceived cost advantages. The Treasury generally concentrates issuance policy on building up benchmarks in three areas – the 5-, 10-, and either the 25- or 30-year maturities. While issuance has been fairly evenly spread over these maturities, there has been a slight bias towards the short and long end – although it is difficult to establish conclusively the existence of 'preferred habitats', anecdotal evidence suggests a willingness to pay a premium at both the short end (from banks) and at the long end (from pension funds).

The market for index-linked gilts tends to be less liquid than that of conventional gilts. Turnover is lower than in the conventional market, with fewer traders (for the year to March 2001, total turnover in the conventional gilts market was over 30 times that of the index-linked market). This may reflect the fact that index-linked gilts tend to be bought by end-investors who hold them for liability matching reasons, rather than as an actively traded financial instrument. There is a question as to whether the relative illiquidity of index-linked gilts has a significant cost. Up to now, index-linked gilts have tended to be a cheaper form of financing than conventional gilts. This could reflect the willingness of investors to pay a premium to avoid inflation risk, or it could simply be a result of forecast error – investors underestimated the government's commitment to low inflation. With the government now committed to low and stable inflation, the inflation risk premium attached to conventional gilts should fall, which may reduce the cost advantage of index-linked gilts in the future.

Taking account of risk

The optimal taxation approach

Optimal taxation theory suggests that the government should use debt management to try to reduce unexpected variations in taxes. However, calculating the optimal taxation policy can be quite difficult. One way to simplify the problem is to assume that the loss function from taxation is quadratic, so that the expected loss is proportional to the square of the tax rate (Barro 1979). Then the optimal policy for the government is to set the tax rate so that it remains the same over all future periods, given expected future developments in income and spending (hence the term 'tax smoothing'). This means the government would expect to run a deficit when spending requirements were expected to be high, and surpluses when spending requirements were relatively low. However, as unanticipated shocks hit the economy, the tax rate would need to change in order to ensure that the government continued to meet its intertemporal budget constraint; this means the tax rate would actually fluctuate randomly over time.

If, however, the return to debt could be made dependent on such shocks (or state contingent), then theoretically the government could smooth out its spending commitments through the changing return on debt, rather than by changing the tax rate. In Lucas and Stokey (1983) the government can issue debt instruments of any maturity, contingent on the outcome for government spending. Because markets are complete, it can issue a full set of instruments to 'insure' against any possible shock. This means that whatever the shock to government spending in future periods, the government will always be able to meet its intertemporal budget constraint. If state-contingent debt were available, then debt (and taxes) need not change very much at all in response to fiscal shocks – debt management could provide full fiscal insurance.

This also implies that the riskiness of debt can be defined by the impact it has on the government's intertemporal budget constraint. Low-risk securities hedge against unexpected fluctuations in the government's intertemporal budget constraint (which would otherwise lead to changes in taxes); high-risk securities add to the variation in the government's intertemporal budget constraint.

In practice, although governments have access to a range of different securities with different risk characteristics, most governments do not issue state-contingent debt. Making the return on debt contingent on government spending outcomes would create a strong incentive for the government to consistently overspend – it is unlikely that any government would be able to find a buyer for such bonds at a sensible price. This still does not explain why governments could not issue securities whose returns were linked to output or consumption. However, new and novel debt instruments may, at least initially, be relatively costly to introduce because of illiquidity. In addition, there might be considerable data problems involved in ensuring that any index used in such a bond would be acceptable to all investors, easily measured and not subject to revision.

Using conventional securities

Since governments do not issue state-contingent debt, a number of papers have looked at whether the optimal fiscal policy could be supported by conventional debt instruments. Bohn (1990) assumes a quadratic loss function for taxes and derives the optimal debt policy in the presence of uncertainty in the rate of return on different debt instruments. The optimal tax policy is to stabilise taxes across all possible states of nature. This means that the optimal debt policy should be structured to minimise against sources of uncertainty in taxes (unforeseen changes in spending and output), and hence minimise the variation in tax rates.

The precise structure depends on the composition of shocks that hit the economy. However, aggregate supply shocks lead to a negative correlation between prices and (real) output. This leads to a positive correlation between the return on nominal debt (as measured by the holding period return) and tax revenues (as inflation rises, the cost of nominal debt falls, offsetting the impact of falling tax revenues), and can reduce overall budgetary volatility. Aggregate demand shocks on the other hand lead to a positive correlation between prices and output. In this case, nominal debt adds to the overall variation in finances, because the cost of nominal debt rises when output and tax revenues decline. These effects are increased as the maturity of the debt lengthens; persistent changes in the price level will have a greater effect if the debt portfolio is composed mostly of long-term nominal debt than if it were composed of short-term nominal debt.

This line of reasoning can also be extended to foreign-currency debt. Because the return to foreign-currency debt is affected by unexpected variations in the real exchange rate, its return (in domestic currency) is more volatile than domestic debt. For this reason, the UK has tended to avoid issuing substantial amounts of foreign-currency debt, except to the extent that it is used to hedge foreign-currency reserves. However, if the real exchange rate tended to appreciate when output fell, (so that the domestic cost of debt also fell) and depreciate when output was unexpectedly high, then foreign-currency debt could potentially be used to hedge against shocks to output and tax revenue.

Debt maturity can also partly compensate for the absence of contingent debt. In general, a change in interest rates will affect the intertemporal budget constraint, because it changes the price at which new debt is issued. If interest rates rise, taxes may also need to increase in order to meet the intertemporal budget constraint (the exact amount will depend on the exact pattern of surpluses relative to debt repayments, since a change in the real interest rate also affects the net present value of surpluses). In this case, long maturities provide some insurance against real interest rate changes – in the extreme, issuing index-linked perpetuals insulates the government entirely against random interest rate changes (Barro 1998).

However, if real interest rates are correlated with changes in output and government spending, then shorter maturities could also potentially provide a degree of insurance, depending on what sort of relationship holds. Issuing short-term debt effectively indexes the cost of debt-servicing to the interest rate. Conversely, long-term debt leads to a negative correlation between real interest rates and debt servicing costs, in the sense that if real interest rates rise, then the holding-period return on long-term debt falls. This means that if increases in real interest rates are associated with *higher* output (and higher tax revenues), then short-term debt is a better hedge than long-term debt – here long-term debt potentially worsens the intertemporal budget constraint. Alternatively, if higher real interest rates are associated with weaker output and higher government spending, then long-term debt is a better hedge, since the holding-period return on long-term debt and government financing needs will be positively correlated.

This means that the optimal debt structure will depend on the interaction between changes in inflation and changes in government spending and revenue, and will vary from country to country, depending on the structure of the tax system, the nature of the government's spending commitments and the different types of shocks the economy is subject to. But this also suggests that it is difficult to pick any particular type of debt as being more or less risky than another, since this will depend on assumptions as to what sort of shock is most likely to occur – and shocks are inherently unpredictable.

Empirical results

Empirical studies have so far yielded mixed results. Missale (1997a) looks at the optimal portfolio mix for a range of OECD countries over the period 1985–97. For most countries, nominal debt performs a useful hedging role, and index-linked debt is less important. However, the results are period-specific – in the UK, the optimal portfolio is composed largely of index-linked debt for the period from 1991 onwards. This reflects the impact of unexpectedly low inflation and output, and unexpectedly high levels of government spending. Missale also considers whether there is a role for short- and long-term nominal debt; for most countries he considers, long-term debt comprises only a relatively small proportion of the optimal portfolio. Interestingly, his work helps to justify the lack of issuance of foreign currency debt in the UK – not only is foreign currency debt more variable in real terms than other forms of debt (because of the volatility of the real exchange rate), but because the real exchange rate tends to appreciate when output and spending are unexpected high (and so the return on foreign debt tends to fall), it exacerbates overall budgetary volatility.

Dale, Mongiardino and Quah (1997) look for the portfolio which hedges against variations in the net present value of the primary deficit (that is, deficit smoothing). This is a slightly different problem from tax smoothing, but it is clearly related. However, they also find that the optimal portfolio for the UK is composed of index-linked debt, although they do not find conclusive evidence for or against particular maturities of debt.

Alternative definitions of risk

The definition of risk offered by the optimal taxation literature varies considerably from more traditional measures of risk. For example, in a recent review of debt management policy, the National Debt Management Agency of Ireland identified two different types of risk: market risk (fluctuations in the market value of the government's portfolio), and also short-run fluctuations in (nominal) debt servicing costs. These had conflicting implications for the debt portfolio – although short-term debt helped to stabilise the market value of the portfolio, it also led to much greater fluctuations in annual debt servicing costs. Although they acknowledged that the variation in the market value of the portfolio was a more 'economic' way of thinking about the cost of debt servicing, concerns over fluctuations in debt servicing costs had led them to target a longer maturity for their debt portfolio (Nars 1997).

These concerns may be sensible given the constraints faced by policy makers. If, as is the case in Belgium and Ireland, there is a budgetary limit on the amount that can be spent on debt servicing costs, then debt managers will be highly motivated to avoid overstepping that limit (remembering that their own forecasts are likely to be a major factor in setting the limit). The more predictable that debt servicing costs are, the easier the debt manager's task.

In contrast, the optimal taxation literature focuses on the contribution of changes in the market value of the debt portfolio to the overall variation in government finances. This has potentially quite different implications for the optimal portfolio. Although some forms of debt may imply relatively large fluctuations in debt servicing costs and/or holding period returns, they could potentially lead to a lower variation in the government's financing costs overall.

One reason for the divergence may lie in accounting conventions – for most countries, changes in the value of the market portfolio of the debt are not reflected in measures of the government's financial balance, and therefore tend to be ignored when taking policy decisions.[2] Instead, governments are more likely to target variables such as the fiscal deficit and levels of debt, which at least have the virtue of being relatively easy to measure. This may be reinforced by concerns over creditworthiness, if investors and credit-rating agencies take the deficit measure as the relevant measure of fiscal sustainability. This bias will be reinforced by fiscal rules (such as the Maastricht criteria) which focus on deficit or debt measures.

Implications for debt management

Overall, evidence for the UK highlights the potential insurance value of index-linked debt, but is less illuminating on what might be the optimal maturity mix. However one problem is that the results seem very sensitive to the period chosen. The experience of the 1990s has been very different from the 1980s, which is not surprising, given the substantial fall in inflation and the impact of structural reform on the economy. As a result, it is not clear whether debt managers could rely strongly on the empirical results from these models. The incidence of any particular type of shock is difficult to predict. Historical covariances can change over time, particularly if the economy is subject to structural change and/or policy changes. This makes it difficult to pin down the optimal risk-minimising portfolio. For example, as the UK moves into a period of price stability, the insurance value of index-linked debt is likely to fall. As Missale (1997b) concludes after looking at evidence for the UK and for Italy, 'choosing debt instruments to minimise budget risk appears to be quite a difficult task' (p. 86).

Another caveat is that for most empirical studies of tax-smoothing, the optimal share of particular bonds is often many times in excess of GDP. For example, Bohn (1990) finds that for the US over the period 1954–87, the best outcome would have been to hold substantial quantities of index-linked bonds as an asset, and issue around 2680 per cent of GDP in nominal bonds. This is because the calculations are made using quarterly data. Over a three-month period, the variance of inflation is very small relative to output, so that any hedging instrument must be held in very large quantities to provide a sufficient hedge against output fluctuations and spending shocks. One strategy is to calculate the optimal share constraining the share of debt issued in any one instrument to be non-negative. However, if debt levels are low, and governments are reluctant to hold large quantities of assets, the ability of debt management to hedge against macroeconomic shocks to the government's finances may be limited.

Another problem is that if there are only a limited number of possible types of debt, then it may be difficult to design portfolios that can offer the optimal degree of insurance against all of the shocks, all of the time. By their nature, shocks are unpredictable – even though demand shocks have dominated in the past, this may not be true in the future (particularly given the move to more predictable and stable macroeconomic policies). In the face of uncertainty, a diverse portfolio may be a more attractive strategy than issuing only one kind of debt.

Time consistency and government debt

Is debt management the best means of ensuring time consistency?

Another aspect of debt management which has been emphasised in the academic literature is that of time consistency and whether the government can improve policy outcomes through particular debt structures. The issue of public debt creates the potential for time inconsistency of fiscal and monetary policy – once investors have committed to holding a certain amount of government debt, the government has an incentive to reduce its costs by reneging on its promise to pay back the investor, either through inflation, unexpected changes in interest rates, explicit taxation, or outright default. This is called the time-(in)consistency problem (because incentives do not remain consistent over time). However the maturity and composition of debt could potentially help to enforce time-consistent behaviour. For example, the government could reduce the incentive to inflate by issuing either foreign-currency debt or index-linked domestic debt – in either case, it cannot inflate away its debt obligations. Alternatively, it could issue short-term nominal debt or floating-rate debt.

However, while such strategies may reduce the incentive to inflate, they can also increase the probability of default, because the government will find it more costly to service the debt in times of financial stress. For example, short-term debt increases the frequency of refinancing. If refinancing coincides with an adverse fiscal shock, this increases the burden of debt servicing. In turn, this increases the risk of default, and hence further increases the cost of debt servicing. In an extreme situation, it could lead to a self-fulfilling 'confidence crisis' where the loss of investor confidence increases the burden of debt servicing to such an extent that the government is forced to default (fulfilling investor expectations), even if initially it was fiscally solvent.

To see how this might happen, suppose the cost of debt-servicing were to increase suddenly due to an adverse interest-rate shock. This increases the probability that the government might prefer to default on its debt-servicing repayments rather than increase taxes. If investors expect default, they may refuse to roll over the debt, forcing the government to repay its debt immediately. This would increase substantially the potential tax burden, which could then lead to default. This might occur even if the government was previously financially solvent – the problem is triggered by investors' refusal to roll over the debt. In contrast, issuing long-term debt limits the costs faced by government, by reducing the amount of new debt that needs to be financed at any one time – if all debt were composed of perpetuals then a confidence crisis would be much less likely because the debt would never be rolled over.[3]

Time-consistency issues may be more important when debt levels are high. At low levels of debt the incentive to inflate is likely to be relatively small, and time consistency issues are likely to be less important. Missale and Blanchard (1994) argue that countries have tended to use short-maturity debt to enhance credibility when debt levels are high, but that this is likely to be less important at low levels of debt. Hence, those countries with high levels of debt tend to have shorter average maturity structures.

This suggests that for countries with relatively low levels of debt, the use of debt management to enforce time-consistent behaviour is not very relevant. At low levels of debt, the level of long-term nominal debt seems unlikely to be the dominant factor in determining a country's predilection for inflation (although the argument may have had greater relevance for the UK in the past). The UK, like many other countries, has now moved to resolve the time-consistency problem for inflation by giving operational autonomy over interest rates to the Bank of England. Such institutional solutions may be more sustainable than those based on debt management.

Conclusions

What does the literature tell us?

Overall, it appears that the literature is some distance from being able to determine the optimal portfolio. However, a number of conclusions can be drawn from it:

- the first step towards lower financing costs is likely to be a liquid and efficient secondary market for government debt. In addition, the government may be able to reduce the cost of financing through its choice of institutional design for the market
- if markets are efficient, there will be a trade-off between cost and risk. The most attractive debt instruments for investors are likely to be those which provide the greatest insurance against bad outcomes (such as unexpectedly low incomes). To the extent that investors and the government face similar risks, this means that the cheapest debt instruments are likely to be the most risky for the government
- the optimal taxation literature makes a strong case for the objective of minimising budgetary risk (that is, insuring against unexpected fluctuations in government revenue and expenditure). However, further work is needed before it could be used to provide a practical basis for debt management. In particular, given uncertainty over the nature of future shocks, and also practical constraints on the size of government financial asset holdings, there does not yet appear to be a consensus on the optimal risk-minimising portfolio.

On this basis, UK debt management policy appears to be consistent with a number of aspects of the literature:

- issuance policy is consistently focused on transparency and pre-dictability. The Government avoids active trading or trying to 'beat the market'

- although the Government's objective is that of cost minimisation, this is primarily focused at the microeconomic level: for example, concentration on benchmarks, the recent introduction of repo and strips markets, and the choice of auction format
- the portfolio is reasonably diversified, with a relatively high proportion of index-linked debt and also long-term nominal debt. As a result, the debt portfolio provides some insurance against a range of possible shocks. Foreign-currency debt forms only a minimal proportion of the portfolio, and is used to hedge the government's foreign-currency reserves
- because the level of debt is relatively low (both historically and internationally), and the average maturity of the debt portfolio is relatively long, this considerably reduces the risk of possible 'confidence crises'. In addition, issuance policy tends to result in a relatively smooth redemption profile, which reduces the degree of exposure at any point in time to unpleasant shocks.

Improving debt management policy

Looking at the literature also raises questions as to what might be the optimal structure of the portfolio. At the very least, current debt management policy appears to avoid the worst possible outcomes: because the portfolio is relatively diversified, it does not seem unduly risky, and, because the UK market seems reasonably efficient, the debt portfolio has probably not been too costly (government debt is likely to have been fairly priced). This does not mean that there might not be risk-minimising and/or cost-minimising opportunities which could be exploited further – the current portfolio would equate to the 'optimal' portfolio only by chance and could be some distance away. As yet, the literature does not provide us with sufficient guidance as to the best way to move forward – there is no consensus as to what determines the optimal portfolio. However, it does highlight some areas where additional work would be useful:

The most appropriate measurement of risk

Practitioners tend to focus on variations in the debt portfolio alone. To the extent that they try to hedge against risk, they will tend to focus on risks relating to the portfolio itself. In particular, they have tended to concentrate on minimising unexpected variations in debt servicing costs (often ignoring changes in the market value of the portfolio), and also refinancing risk. This is at odds with the academic literature, which looks for the debt structure which helps to minimise unexpected changes in taxes, and tends to ignore refinancing risk. This may reflect different assumptions as to the government's objectives. As a result, they tend to give very different results as to the appropriate risk-minimising portfolio – reconciling the two would help to narrow the gap between theory and practice.

What is the impact of shocks to the economy on the government's finances?

We know theoretically how demand and supply shocks should affect the economy, at least in a very broad sense. But it would be useful to know in more detail how different types of shocks were likely to affect interest costs for different portfolios, and how these were correlated with changes in taxes and spending. In turn, this would allow an assessment of how the costs of different portfolios fluctuated with particular shocks, and hence an assessment of the riskiness of different portfolios.

Can we improve our knowledge of the microeconomics of the bond market?

For example, is it possible to quantify the gains from liquidity and the provision of benchmark bonds? Is it possible to improve the liquidity of the market for index-linked gilts or is illiquidity an intrinsic attribute of such bonds? Are there other insurance possibilities which would be valued sufficiently by the market to offset any increase in risk? Ideally for any debt security we should be able to form an assessment of the potential benefits from lower debt servicing costs, against the potential increase in risk to the government's finances.

How large are the transaction costs involved in changing the portfolio?

Because governments are not small traders on the market, they may be concerned about the impact of financing large quantities of debt at any one time. Selling and buying back debt involves transaction costs, which may not be insignificant. In contrast, most of the literature assumes a perfectly competitive (world) market where governments are able to sell and buy back debt at the prevailing market price. If the costs of changing the portfolio composition (other than through new issuance to replace maturing debt) are prohibitively large, the current structure of the portfolio is, to a large extent, historically determined. However, if these transaction costs are small, then the government has potentially much greater flexibility in determining the shape of the portfolio. This is likely to be relevant in weighing up the costs and benefits of moving to alternative debt portfolios.

Exploring these areas should help to create a better understanding of the costs and benefits of different portfolio structures, such as a higher proportion of index-linked debt; or whether there are any benefits to targeting a particular duration for the portfolio. In turn, this should help to improve our understanding of what might constitute an 'optimal' portfolio.

17
Reforming the International Financial Architecture

This chapter discusses the UK's role in reforming the international financial architecture to help deliver international stability.

Introduction

In their October 1998 Declaration G7 Finance Ministers (Group of Seven 1998) pledged to create an international financial architecture for the new global economy. Over the past three years, the international community has taken rapid and decisive action to put in place new long term disciplines to promote greater stability and to ensure that economies at all stages of development are able to participate fully in the global economy and share in the benefits of rising global prosperity. New international rules have been designed to help deliver stronger national economic and financial systems and an international environment in which financial markets function more effectively. When crises do occur, measures are being put in place to ensure they are managed efficiently and that the public and private sectors both play a part in restoring stability. Taken together, these reforms should reduce volatility and the risk of future economic crises, helping to deliver international financial stability and sustainable world growth.

The UK has played a leading role in initiating, developing and building consensus for this ambitious programme of reform. Through its work in international fora, including the G7, the IMF and the World Bank, the Government is seeing many of the structural changes introduced domestically, and described in earlier chapters, replicated in codes of conduct and examples of best practice for the international arena.

Since the 1998 G7 Declaration, substantial progress has been made across the range of difficult issues this work encompasses, and a large number of important measures have already been agreed. This chapter, after considering the changes in the global economy which have created the need for these reforms, sets out the action being undertaken to:

- promote crisis prevention and containment through reliable surveillance and information sharing
- put in place mechanisms for more orderly and rapid crisis resolution which recognise that the way we resolve crises today will have significant implications for the behaviour of the public and private sectors in the future
- strengthen international cooperation in the financial sector to respond to the challenges posed by global capital market integration and the huge increase in global private capital flows
- strengthen the system of global economic governance to reflect the new reality of the international financial system.

The need for action

The emerging market financial crisis of recent years first took hold in Thailand when the country's exchange rate peg to the US dollar became unsustainable in July 1997. Following the subsequent devaluation of the Thai baht, contagion spread swiftly throughout the region. Currencies which had previously been actively managed by the authorities were freely floated, as huge and rapid capital outflows made intervention unsustainable. By February 1998 equity markets in the Asian crisis countries – Thailand, Indonesia, Malaysia, the Philippines and South Korea – had declined by between 53 and 76 per cent, while exchange rates had fallen by between 40 and 72 per cent on the previous year. GDP contracted sharply, by between 7 and 16 per cent in 1998.

The Asian crisis countries experienced a massive turnaround of capital flows. Inflows of around US$100 billion in 1996 turned to outflows of around US$75 billion in 1998. Net foreign bank lending fell by US$70 billion within two years. The other side of this huge capital account adjustment was a turnaround in current account and trade positions. The IMF estimate that the combined trade positions of these five countries moved from an annualised deficit of roughly US$40 billion –

some 4 per cent of GDP – to a surplus of over US$80 billion in the first half of 1998 – some 12 per cent of GDP.

Difficulties in emerging markets outside Asia soon followed. In August 1998, Russia defaulted on its debt, and lost control of the rouble's external value. Brazil came next, being forced to negotiate an international rescue package in November 1998 as finance to emerging markets dried up and capital fled the country. Though financial pressures in Brazil initially abated, growing doubts about the political feasibility of the planned fiscal adjustment, threats of default by state governments, and fears that monetary policy was insufficiently tight to stem the tide of continued capital outflows, forced the Brazilian government to abandon its crawling-peg exchange rate in January 1999.

The most obvious channel through which these events in emerging markets were transmitted to the rest of the world was through trade adjustments. As the Asian economies fell into deep recession, demand for exports from Europe and the US plummeted. Falling exports to Asia accounted for around half of the £2.25 billion widening of the UK trade in goods deficit in the year to the fourth quarter of 1998, while reduced demand from the major oil producing nations also played a significant part. Overall, net trade reduced UK growth by 1¾ percentage points in 1998.

The other direct impact that events in Asia had on the rest of the world was through the exposure of banking systems. Financial sector contagion from Asia and Russia to Latin America throughout 1998 highlighted the interdependence of economies even where direct trade linkages are minimal.

At the root of these crises were a number of structural and institutional weaknesses, common to many of the affected countries, as well as deficiencies in the architecture and governance of the international financial system. These included:

- poorly regulated and supervised financial systems, through which large amounts of domestic and international credit had been channelled
- the perception that private sector borrowing was backed by implicit or explicit government guarantees and a perception of zero currency risk
- over-investment in economically unsound projects as a result of directed lending practices and close relationships between governments banks and businesses

- a serious lack of transparency in economic and financial policy making
- poor lending decisions and inadequate risk assessment by western banks.

Ultimately, these financial crises highlighted the ways in which the new global economy has changed the environment for domestic policy making. They demonstrated clearly the need for national governments, which are dependent for investment funds on the day to day confidence of international investors, to pursue consistent and credible policies that guarantee stability. They have also changed the demands placed on the institutions which support the international financial system.

Crisis prevention

The changing nature of the global economy demands a shift in the focus of global financial governance away from ex post crisis resolution and toward strengthened ex ante procedures for crisis prevention and containment. At this heart of this new approach lies an enhanced mechanism for international economic surveillance based on a framework of internationally agreed codes and standards of policy best practice and embodying a greater degree of openness and transparency.

Enhanced international surveillance

Enhanced international surveillance is a key element of the reforms being introduced to the international financial architecture and is the foundation of international efforts to establish stronger mechanisms for crisis prevention. The UK has been at the forefront of those arguing for a step change in the breadth and depth of international surveillance, centred on the IMF's Article IV process.

The objective of surveillance is to assess whether a country's economic developments and policies are consistent with the achievement of sustainable growth and both domestic and external stability. In this way, surveillance can help to prevent crises, by identifying potential problems and signalling the need for reforms. The recent emerging market crisis has emphasised the need for a transparent, credible, and comprehensive surveillance process, including:

- enhanced disclosure of information including through the publication of IMF Article IV reports. Timely, reliable and comprehensive data are critical to ensure that market participants are

able to make informed lending and investment decisions and accurately price the risks involved
- a more comprehensive and integrated surveillance process, going beyond short-term macroeconomic indicators to look at the financial sector and the capital account in more detail. Events in 1997 and 1998 showed clearly how weaknesses in structural and financial policies can impact on macroeconomic stability
- greater clarity and transparency in policy advice, to ensure credibility and guarantee accountability.

International codes and standards

To govern effectively in an era of ever more rapid financial flows, governments need to introduce new disciplines into economic policy making including: clear long-term policy objectives; well understood procedural rules for monetary and fiscal policy; and an openness that keeps markets properly informed and ensures that objectives and institutions have credibility.

To address the economic problems that have precipitated emerging market crises, the UK has been working with its partners in the G7 and the IMF to develop an internationally agreed framework of codes of conduct and standards of best practice in a range of economic and financial disciplines. These codes and standards are the cornerstone of international efforts to minimise the risk of crisis. They represent the building blocks of an enhanced surveillance process.

The aim of codes and standards is to provide benchmarks against which countries can assess their own performance, and guidelines to assist them in improving their economic and financial policy frameworks. Once adopted, codes and standards can play an important role in strengthening national financial systems and policies and ensuring the stability of the international financial system. They can also provide the information needed to enable market participants to make informed investment decisions and so stimulate more stable capital flows.

Significant progress has been made in developing and agreeing codes and standards in a wide range of economic and financial disciplines. Codes have now been agreed covering fiscal policy transparency, monetary and financial policy transparency, data dissemination, corporate governance and a host of other banking, securities and insurance standards. The UK has been one of the strongest and earliest supporters of this process, particularly the development of codes of good practice on fiscal transparency and on transparency in monetary and financial policies.

Implementation and surveillance of codes and standards

In addition to participating in the development of codes and standards, the UK, together with its G7 partners, has supported a leading role for the IMF in assessing the degree of implementation. The IMF's Article IV process is a unique international asset and the only impartial surveillance mechanism agreed by nearly all of the world's countries.

The UK has argued that IMF assessments of observance need to be comprehensive and cover the range of codes and standards relevant to macroeconomic and financial stability. This does not mean the IMF should seek to build up expertise in all these areas. Rather it should assess compliance in areas of direct operational relevance to the Fund while coordinating and working in partnership with other institutions to monitor observance in their respective areas of expertise.

Consistent with this approach, the IMF has begun producing Reports on the Observance of Standards and Codes (ROSCs) which assess member countries' progress in implementing progressively a range of codes and standards and provide recommendations on how implementation could be further improved. The UK was among the first group of countries for whom such reports were prepared and published in 1999. In addition, the IMF and World Bank have together established a Financial Sector Assessment Programme (FSAP) through which assessments of domestic financial sector vulnerabilities, and observance of certain financial sector codes and standards, are carried out. The UK will be participating in the FSAP in 2002.

For codes and standards to work effectively there must also be transparency about countries' implementation. This way, market participants can have access to the information they need to make prudent lending and investment decisions. The UK has argued that countries should aim for full disclosure of their record in implementing codes and standards including through publication of ROSC reports. In April 2000, the IMFC encouraged member countries to publish ROSC reports produced for them on a voluntary basis. A significant number of countries have already opted to do so.

UK policy, and the changes that have been introduced since May 1997, mean that the UK already meets many of the standards required. Following its 1998 Article IV consultation discussions the IMF concluded that the UK's impressive economic performance in recent years has been underpinned by a revamping and strengthening of the macroeconomic policy framework through a clear medium-term orientation, guided by the key principles of transparency, accountability and credibility.

Market-based approaches

In addition to implementing codes and standards, the UK has argued that countries must seek to establish closer, more secure relationships with their private sector creditors to improve the flow of information, reduce the probability of sudden reversals in capital flows, and prevent payments problems from degenerating into crises. The 1999 G7 Cologne Report (Group of Seven 1999b) called on countries to 'take ex ante steps to strengthen the framework for the market-based, cooperative and orderly resolution of debt payment difficulties'. These steps include:

- the development of mechanisms for more systematic dialogue between national governments and their main private sector creditors. An open and honest dialogue, in which investors can ask questions and governments can explain their policies will make it less likely that today's problems become tomorrow's crises
- greater use of market-based tools aimed at preventing crises and facilitating adjustment to shocks, including the use of innovative financial arrangements such as private sector contingent credit lines and roll-over options in debt instruments
- wider use of collective action clauses in sovereign bond contracts, along with other provisions that facilitate creditor coordination and discourage disruptive legal action by dissident creditors. The UK has taken a leading role in this area by including majority action clauses in its foreign currency debt.

The Government has also supported enhanced dialogue between the international institutions and the private investors responsible for maintaining the stability of the global financial system. The IMF has now taken steps to actively engage the private sector in a dialogue on surveillance issues through the establishment of a Capital Markets Consultative Group (CMCG) which acts as a forum for strengthening cooperation and information exchange between the official sector and capital market participants.

Contingent credit line

For national governments, participation in the international financial system entails new responsibilities to forge regular and lasting contacts with their private investors and to adopt transparent procedures and comply with internationally agreed codes and standards of best practice in policy making. Countries which accept these responsibilities should find that their actions are rewarded by the private sector through more discerning capital flows. But they must also be able to expect strong support from the official sector.

In September 2000, the IMF agreed reforms to ensure that Contingent Credit Lines (CCLs) for member countries with strong economic policies with a precautionary line of defence against future balance of payment problems that might arise from international financial contagion. The UK strongly supported the development of the CCL. Approval of CCL financing provides a mechanism to signal the IMF's confidence in a country's economic policies and in its determination to adjust them as needed should contagion hit. This will create the right incentives for the adoption of strong policies and adherence to internationally recognised standards. In September 2000 the Fund agreed to develop further the CCL to make it more attractive to countries and to ensure that it offers real protection.

Capital flows

Recent events have shown that large short-term capital movements can be destabilising. The sharp reversal of short-term private capital flows out of many emerging markets during the Asian crisis began has played an important part in destabilising exchange rates and stock markets in some emerging markets.

Nonetheless – despite some pressure for limited capital controls to be reintroduced in extreme circumstances – there remains continued international support for free capital movement. The UK supports international efforts to strengthen the open world trading system, with free trade flows and open capital markets, and endorses an orderly and progressive approach to capital account liberalisation. Widespread unilateral reimposition of controls would damage the world economy.

However, while open capital markets can bring huge benefits, the Government acknowledges that those benefits are most likely to be fully realised in countries which have embarked upon properly sequenced economic reform. Sound macroeconomic policy, open and credible institutions and procedures and a healthy financial sector are essential preconditions for orderly capital account liberalisation. Without these important preconditions being in place, countries will remain vulnerable to capital market volatility.

The Government favours an approach to capital account liberalisation which is bold in concept, but cautious in implementation. Bold in concept because open capital markets allow efficient use of capital and the transfer of technology and expertise, and have brought substantial benefits to industrial and developing economies alike in recent decades. But the need for caution in implementation is now clearer, and more important, than ever. This is not an excuse to go slow on reform – rather it makes the case for strengthening banking sectors all the more urgent. Long term flows (for example, foreign direct investment) should be liberalised before short-term ones.

Consequently, in Cologne, the UK and the other G7 countries urged the IMF to continue its work on the appropriate pace and sequencing of capital market liberalisation, and to explore other issues related to the Fund's role in facilitating an orderly approach to liberalisation. Particular attention should be paid to eliminating policy biases in favour of short-term capital flows, particularly in foreign currencies, and to promoting sound debt management policies.

Crisis management

While the changes to the international financial architecture described above aim to reduce the likelihood and severity of crisis, inevitably they will still occur. The Chancellor has argued that, 'Our aim must be crisis prevention where possible, crisis resolution where necessary' (Chancellor of the Exchequer 1999a). But shifting from a world of ad hoc crisis resolution to one of crisis prevention and containment demands that all actors in the system – public and private – must play a part in maintaining stability and orderly crisis resolution

Role for the official sector

The IMF must not only play an integral role in helping to prevent financial crises. It must also be in a strong financial position and be able to respond quickly and effectively in crisis situations. At times of crisis the financial assistance available through the IFIs (as well as various supplementary bilateral arrangements) combined with strong programmes of economic adjustment, is vital to restore confidence to troubled economies.

Nonetheless, it is clear that when international crises strike, it will not in general be either feasible or desirable for the official sector to provide all the financial support necessary to resolve the situation. The international financial community does not have, nor could it have, an unlimited international lender of last resort.

Role of the private sector

There will continue to be an important role for the IMF in resolving financial crises. But the way crises are resolved today may have important implications for the behaviour of the public and private sectors in the future. The UK has therefore strongly supported work by the international community to develop a new framework of partnership for crisis prevention and resolution between private and public sectors which provides the right incentives and ensures that all parties which benefit from the international financial system play their part in maintaining stability.

This emerging framework should:

- provide the finance for orderly adjustment
- recognise that availability of official resources – backed, ultimately, by taxpayers – is limited in relation to the scale of international capital flows
- limit perverse incentives for investors to invest in a country in the anticipation that they will be bailed out by the official sector if a crisis arises
- strengthen market discipline
- help emerging market borrowers insure themselves against volatility and contagion
- avoid undermining the obligation of countries to meet their debts in full and on time
- and, ultimately, to minimise the incidence and intensity of crises.

Over the past three years the international financial community has made considerable progress toward a more orderly and effective approach involving the private sector in crisis management. In their report to the Cologne Summit in June 1999, the G7 Finance Ministers outlined a broad framework of principles for making judgements about the role of the private sector in crisis resolution and highlighted-the range of tools available to promote appropriate private sector involvement in crisis resolution. While recognising that flexibility is important to cope with the diversity of different cases, this framework was designed to promote more orderly crisis resolution by providing a degree of predictability to shape private and public sector expectations of how crises will be handled in the future.

Since the Cologne Summit, some progress has been made toward making the G7 approach operational. The private sector has been involved in the handling of a number of recent crises cases, including those in the Ukraine, Pakistan and Ecuador. And in April 2000, the IMFC agreed an operational approach to involving the private sector in debt restructuring and debt reduction cases. This approach set out the objectives of the official sector and the division of responsibilities between the different actors in the resolution of these types of crises (Chancellor of the Exchequer 2000). In particular, the approach specified that in cases requiring debt restructuring or debt reduction:

- IMF-supported programmes should put strong emphasis on medium-term sustainability and should strike an appropriate balance between the contributions of private and official external creditors
- the responsibility for negotiations with private creditors should rest with debtor countries who should aim for fairness in the treatment of different classes of private creditors. No class of creditors should be considered inherently privileged
- the IMF should review countries' efforts to secure needed contributions from private creditors in the light of these considerations
- when all relevant decisions have been taken, the IMF should set out publicly how and what policy approaches have been adopted.

This represents an important step in the direction of a more consistent and predictable approach to involving the private sector in the management of debt sustainability crises. But in order to guide expectations more effectively the international community must continue to work to establish clearer presumptions concerning private sector involvement in the full range of potential crises.

International cooperation in the financial sector

Globalisation of economic activity not only strengthens the need for internationally applied standards of good practice in domestic policy making, but also requires the international community to work more closely together to respond to its challenges. The Government takes seriously the responsibilities which come with the UK's leading position on the international economic stage, to work constructively with other countries in various fora to this end.

The financial stability forum

The international nature of global finance and the enormous size and growth of global capital flows makes international cooperation on issues relating to the financial sector particularly important. The volume of international capital flows has increased greatly over the past quarter century. Between 1970 and 1996, the volume of real private sector capital flows grew by a factor of eight, cross-border transactions in bonds and equities in almost all G7 countries have risen from less than 10 per cent of GDP in 1980 to over 100 per cent in 1996, and daily turnover in foreign exchange markets now stands at over US$2 trillion. This means that strengthened global financial regulation is essential alongside efforts to raise the standards of national supervisory arrangements around the world.

Countries with major international financial centres, and the international financial institutions, have an important role to play in ensuring there is effective regulation of financial markets globally and effective coordination on matters of common global interest. This is why in 1998 the UK proposed bringing together the IMF, the World Bank and key regulatory authorities in a new committee charged with delivering the global objective of a stable financial system. The G7 accepted this proposal and Hans Tietmeyer, then President of the Bundesbank, prepared detailed recommendations. The resulting Financial Stability Forum (FSF) now comprises finance ministries, regulators and central banks from the G7 and other[1] major financial centres, together with the World Bank, IMF and key international regulatory groupings. Representatives of relevant non-FSF countries and of the private sector are also involved in the Forum's work.

In launching the Forum, the G7 aimed 'to ensure that [participants] can more effectively foster and coordinate their respective responsibilities to promote international financial stability, improve the functioning of markets and reduce systemic risk' (Group of Seven 1999a). Since its first meeting in April 1999, the Forum has met twice a year, in spring and in autumn with objectives to:

- to assess vulnerabilities affecting the international financial system
- to identify and oversee action needed to address these vulnerabilities
- to improve co-ordination and information exchange among the various authorities responsible for financial stability.

Over time, the Forum can enhance its role in assessing vulnerabilities and provide an early warning system for regional and global financial market risk. This will contribute further to shifting the focus of the international financial architecture from crisis resolution towards crisis prevention.

The FSF initially set up three working groups to draw together work being undertaken in various groupings on offshore financial centres, Highly Leveraged Institutions (HLIs) (including hedge funds and other derivative trading bodies) and the management of capital flows. The Forum also established a task force to look at issues related to the implementation of internationally agreed financial sector codes and standards. All three groups submitted detailed reports to the FSF at its March 2000 meeting.

The work of the group on offshore financial centres, to which the UK contributed resources and expertise, has set standards against which these centres can be judged. This has already been successful in encouraging some of the centres to reform their regulatory structures and working practices, strengthening these links in the world financial system.

The working group on HLIs was chaired by the Chairman of the UK Financial Services Authority (FSA), Sir Howard Davies. It set out a package of measures – primarily aimed at HLIs' counter-parties – including improved risk management, enhanced regulatory oversight and recommendations regarding the Basle review of the regulatory treatment of bank capital. It also recommended new disclosure requirements on HLIs, coupled with more meaningful public disclosure by all financial institutions.

The capital flows working group made a number of recommendations designed to foster enhanced public sector risk and liquidity management.

More recently, the FSF has looked at best practice with regard to deposit insurance schemes, the regulatory implications of e-commerce and a range of other international financial issues. It has also held discussions of current vulnerabilities affecting the stability of the world's financial system.

Strengthen the system of global economic governance

The reforms to the international financial architecture outlined above change the responsibilities of the International Financial Institutions, in an attempt to better reflect the current reality in the financial system. With this change in responsibilities there is a need to look at ways to strengthen global dialogue on international financial issues and strengthen governance.

The international financial institutions

The role of the International Financial Institutions (IFIs) in managing the global economy is more important than ever in today's world of open trade and global capital markets. The rapid growth and integration of capital markets brings great opportunities for growth and prosperity but it also brings risks and potential instability. The IFIs have a key role to play in implementing many of the reforms to the international financial architecture outlined elsewhere in this chapter and in ensuring that all countries, including the poorest, are able to participate in and benefit from the global economy. In order to fulfil this role, the IFIs themselves must adapt and reform.

Transparency and accountability

Consistent with the new emphasis on transparency in the public and private sectors, the Government believes that the IFIs must do more to explain their practices and procedures to the public.

The IMF and World Bank have already taken significant steps to increase their institutional transparency and accountability, through wider dissemination of information about their policies and operations, and increasing contacts with outside groups. The World Bank's Independent Inspection Panel provides a transparent mechanism for investigating allegations of non-compliance with its operational procedures. Reforms agreed at the IMF include:

- greater use of Public Information Notices (PINs) for Fund policy discussions
- a presumption toward release of Letters of Intent/Memoranda of Economic and Financial Policies and Policy Framework Papers underpinning Fund-supported programmes
- expanded publication of information on the Funds liquidity position, members' accounts with the Fund, and the Fund's quarterly financial transactions plan
- publication of the Executive Board's work programme
- the issuance of a Chairman's statement capturing the key points of the Board discussion following Board approval or review of members' arrangements
- the liberalisation of access to the Fund's archives
- the voluntary release of Article IV staff reports.

Following a suggestion from the UK Government, the IMF has established an Independent Evaluation Office to look at all aspects of the Fund's work. The office will contribute significantly to the transparency, openness and accountability of the institution. The IMF agreed a structure and mandate for the office in September 2000. Subsequently, in spring 2001, the Executive Board appointed Mr Montek Singh

Ahluwalia as director of the office. He took up his appointment in July 2001. In order to ensure its independence the office will:

- be independent of Fund Management, and operate at arm's-length from the Fund's Executive Board
- be responsible for its own Work Programme, consulting with Executive Directors, Fund Management, and other interested parties from outside the Fund
- provide regular reports on its activities to the IMFC
- publish its work programme, with a strong presumption that reports will also be published promptly.

The establishment of the Independent Education Office is an important step to promote transparency of policies and operations of the IMF with a view to reinforcing public support for their activities and to improve the level of their accountability.

Multilateral Development Bank reform

The overarching objective of the Multilateral Development Banks (MDBs) must be poverty reduction. All discussion of reform must be built on that principle. An increased focus on poverty should underpin all aspects of the MDBs work including programmes of policy reform, investment projects and capacity building. In July 2000, G7 Finance Ministers in their report to the Okinawa Summit, established a number of principles for reform of the Multilateral Development Banks (Group of Seven 2000). The report affirmed that 'accelerating poverty reduction in developing countries must be the core role of the Multilateral Development Banks (MDBs)'.

Cooperation between the IMF and World Bank

The IMF and the World Bank must work effectively together and continue to seek better structures for cooperation. In recent years, the recognition of the link between private capital flows and economic development has required the two institutions to work ever more closely together. Effective cooperation between the IMF and the World Bank will maximise the impact of their policies to reduce poverty, increase growth, and strengthen the stability of the international financial system.

The Chancellor of the Exchequer in his speech to the Commonwealth Finance Ministers' Meeting in September 2000 outlined why the UK places considerable emphasis on this:

> In many countries the interests and activities of the IMF and World Bank are interdependent. They both have vital roles to play in surveillance and lending in emerging market and developing countries alike. Above all the Bretton Woods institutions have a crucial role to play in forging the new consensus that I believe we need. A consensus that recognises that enhanced international cooperation is the key to prosperity. (Chancellor of the Exchequer 2000)

These ideas have been echoed in the commitment made by the President of the World Bank and the Managing Director of the Fund, Horst Kohler, who stated:

> The IMF was established as the World's central monetary institution, charged with the promotion of international monetary cooperation and international trade. The Bank was established to promote post-war reconstruction and the flow of capital to developing countries. As the world economy has grown and changed, so too the roles of the Fund and the Bank have evolved, their joint efforts now covering the spectrum of developing, transition, and industrialised economies. Both institutions, however, share the same broad objective: helping to improve the quality of life and reduce poverty through sustainable and equitable growth. (Kohler and Wolfensohn 2000)

To be most effective, each institution needs to focus on its respective core tasks, while integrating efforts in the many areas where responsibilities overlap. Progress has already been made to develop new models for cooperation, including cooperation on financial sector reform and the establishment of the Financial Sector Assessment Programme (FSAP); increased collaboration in tackling poverty and debt relief, in particular through the development of the Poverty Reduction Strategy Paper (PRSP) framework and in the implementation of the Enhanced Heavily Indebted Poor Countries (HIPC) Initiative.

G20

In their report to the 1999 Cologne Economic Summit, G7 Finance Ministers agreed to establish 'a new mechanism for informal dialogue in the framework of the Bretton Woods institutional system, to broaden the dialogue on key economic and financial policy issues among systemically significant economies and promote cooperation to achieve stable and sustainable world economic growth that benefits all'.

Discussions in the G20 are intended to complement and reinforce the role of the governing bodies of the Bretton Woods institutions, including the IMF, by providing an opportunity for informal sharing of experiences and the development of common views on key economic issues. In its meetings to date, the G20 has addressed issues such as the opportunities and challenges of globalisation and measures to reduce vulnerability to financial crisis, including private sector involvement and the implementation of codes and standards.

Membership of the G20 comprises Argentina, Australia, Brazil, Canada, China, France, Germany, India, Indonesia, Italy, Japan, Korea, Mexico, Russia, Saudi Arabia, South Africa, Turkey, the United Kingdom, the US and the EU Presidency. In addition, meetings of the G20 are attended by the Chairs of the IMF International Monetary and Financial Committee and the World Bank Development Committee as well as by the Managing Director of the IMF and the President of the World Bank.

Conclusion

While globalisation has brought great opportunities to the world economy it has also brought great challenges and risks, which have been shown clearly in the numerous emerging market crises since 1994, triggered by sudden reversals in capital flows and market perceptions of stability and sustainability. It is not possible to return to a world of controlled capital flows. It is thus essential to support free capital movements with sound macroeconomic policies. In a global marketplace with its increased insecurities and volatility, national economic stability is at a premium. No nation can secure high levels of investment, growth and development, without monetary and fiscal stability and mechanisms to ensure the credibility of domestic policies.

Crises in one country or one area can rapidly change perceptions of sustainability in others with potentially devastating consequences. Thus, more than ever, prosperity and stability are indivisible. The international community is working together to reform the international financial system to meet the challenges of the new global economy, and apply lessons of transparency and accountability at an international level.

Increased global competition, ever more rapid technological change and increasing international tensions, mean that not since Bretton Woods has a generation faced so broad a challenge in the global economy, and so profound a responsibility. Reforming the international financial architecture has required enhanced cooperation between national governments, the private sector, and the international financial institutions to deliver the public goods that the new global economy requires to function efficiently and for the benefit of all. The UK has been at the forefront of this unprecedented international reform effort and has played a leading role in developing and implementing these changes. Taken together, they have laid the foundations of a new international financial system fit for the twenty-first century that will enable all countries to participate in the new world economy and share in rising prosperity.

18
The EU Macroeconomic Framework

This chapter provides a summary of the EU macroeconomic policy framework.

Introduction

The previous chapters have examined in some detail the main components of the UK's macroeconomic policy framework. The purpose of this chapter is to summarise the European Union's macroeconomic policy framework.

The chapter provides:

- a brief review of macroeconomic developments in the EU, and an overview of the macroeconomic framework
- a description of the new institutions of EMU and how monetary policy is conducted within EMU by the European Central Bank
- a discussion about how fiscal policy is coordinated within EMU through the Excessive Deficit procedure and the Stability and Growth Pact.

The macroeconomic environment

In the 1990s, growth and employment levels in Europe lagged behind those of its international competitors. In response to the challenge presented by this poor relative performance, the European Union set out a programme of reform which aimed to create a macro environment which would foster sustainable non-inflationary growth and a high level of employment.

The strategy has focused on creating a stability orientated monetary policy, of which Economic and Monetary Union (EMU) is the culmination, and initiating a sustained effort to consolidate public finances. In addition, guidelines have been formulated for a series of structural reforms aimed at modernising markets for goods, capital and labour, with the objective of stimulating employment, competition, fostering innovation and ensuring efficient price-setting.

Progress towards the single currency

The move towards EMU began in 1990 when the recommendations of the Delors Report were adopted. Previous attempts at different forms of a single European currency, such as the ideas contained within the Werner Report of 1970, had been abandoned in the light of the changing economic circumstances of the decade and the collapse of the Bretton Woods system.

The Maastricht Treaty provided the legal framework and timetable for achieving EMU. The process was envisaged in three stages of progressively more coordination of economic and monetary policy within the EU, with the final stage being the irrevocable fixing of exchange rates and the joint use of a single European currency. See Box 18.1 for more details.

In May 1998, following reports from the European Commission and the European Monetary Institute (EMI), the Council of EU Finance Ministers (ECOFIN) recommended to the European Council that 11 member states had fulfilled the necessary conditions for the adoption of a single currency in accordance with Article 121(4) (ex Article 109j) of the Treaty establishing the European Community.

The detailed criteria for assessing the achievement of a high degree of sustainable convergence are given in Article 121(1) (ex Article 109j) of the Treaty:

- the achievement of a high degree of price stability; this will be apparent from having achieved a rate of inflation which is close to that of, at most, the three best performing member states in terms of price stability
- the sustainability of the government financial position; this will be apparent from having achieved a government budgetary position without a deficit that is excessive, as determined in accordance with Article 104(6) (ex Article 104c)
- the observance of the normal fluctuation margins provided for by the exchange rate mechanism of the European Monetary System,

Box 18.1   Progress towards Economic and Monetary Union

The Maastricht Treaty of 1991 provided the legal framework and timetable for achieving EMU.

Three stages to EMU were envisaged, involving progressively more economic cooperation and sharing of fiscal and monetary objectives. The institutional arrangements for the establishment of the European System of Central Banks (ESCB) and the transitional arrangements from Stage I to Stage III were also established in the Treaty.

Stage I   On the basis of the Delors Report, the European Council decided in June 1989 that the first stage of the realisation of Economic and Monetary Union should begin on **1 July 1990** – the date on which, in principle, all restrictions on the movement of capital between member states were abolished.

The Delors report also recommended the establishment of the **European System of Central Banks** which would have the primary objective of maintaining price stability. The ESCB was to be comprised of a new institution – the European Central Bank (ECB), plus the national central banks.

Amendments to the **EC Treaty** were made **in 1991** which provided the legal and institutional basis for EMU. The convergence criteria for member states to enter third stage of EMU were established, and a timetable set out for key decision points to have been reached. **1 January 1999** was set as the latest time for Third Stage of EMU to start, provided the convergence criteria had been met by some member states in the previous year.

Stage II   Started **1 January 1994**. Member states required to 'endeavour to avoid excessive government deficits' (Article 116(4) – ex Article 109e). Member states were to take steps, where appropriate, to ensure the independence of their national central banks (Article 116(5) – ex Article 109e). The multilateral surveillance programme for member states was intensified and included an assessment against reference values for government debt and deficit ratios. Member states are also required to treat their exchange rate policy as a matter of common interest. ECOFIN recommendations following an assessment of member states' economic policies are non-binding in this stage.

The **European Monetary Institute** (EMI) was established. Included in its objectives were to strengthen cooperation between the national central banks, and 'strengthen the coordination of the monetary policies of the Member States, with the aim of ensuring price stability' (Article 117(2) – ex Article 109f). The EMI was also to make preparations for the third stage of EMU by specifying the regulatory, organisational and logistical framework necessary for the European System of Central Banks to perform its tasks in the third stage.

Stage III   Started **1 January 1999. ESCB** takes over full powers of formulating monetary policy for participating member states. EMI liquidated. National currency rates of participating member states are irrevocably fixed in relation to the ECU and the single currency (the euro) launched with 11 members.

for at least two years, without devaluing against the currency of any other member state

• the durability of convergence achieved by the member state and of its participation in the Exchange Rate Mechanism of the European Monetary System being reflected in the long-term interest rate levels.

A Protocol to the Treaty defines these criteria in more detail.[1]

Furthermore, the Treaty requires that the Commission's evaluation includes an examination of the compatibility between the member state's national legislation, including the statutes of its national central bank, and the Treaty articles and Statutes of the ESCB which give the ESCB monetary policy independence.

Thirteen member states were assessed in accordance with the Treaty in May 1998. Sweden and Greece were judged not to have fulfilled the necessary conditions and hence were not eligible to join the single currency in January 1999. The UK and Denmark exercised their opt-outs and were not assessed. UK policy on the single currency is explained in Box 18.2.

Box 18.2   UK policy on membership of the single currency

The Government's position on membership of the single currency was set out by the Chancellor in October 1997, and restated by the Prime Minister in February 1999. The determining factor underpinning any Government decision is whether the economic case for the UK joining is clear and unambiguous. The Government has set out five economic tests that must be met before a decision to join a successful single currency can be taken. The Government believes that, if a decision to recommend joining is taken by Government, it should be put to a vote in Parliament and then to a referendum of the British people.

The challenge of meeting the Maastricht criteria proved to be a catalyst for stability orientated macroeconomic reform in many participating member states. All participating member states recorded rates of Harmonised Index of Consumer Price (HICP) inflation of around 2 per cent or less in January 1998. Long-term interest rates fell to reach an average EU level of 5.5 per cent at the start of 1998, and divergences in long-term bond yields were practically eliminated between most countries. The average EU fiscal deficit also fell in 1997, as did the EU's debt-to-GDP ratio.

The macroeconomic reform process has continued since the launch of EMU. Each participating member state is required to submit an annual Stability Programme, detailing its fiscal position and key macroeconomic developments such as GDP growth, inflation and unemployment. These programmes are reviewed by the ECOFIN Council, to ensure they meet the Stability and Growth Pact conditions. The process of peer review is placing an increasing focus on the need for fiscal discipline over the cycle and on issues such as long-term sustainability. More details are given in later sections.

It is worth comparing some of the key features of the new euro-area to the US and Japanese economies. The euro-area has a very large internal market which, at its launch in January 1999, represented 15 per cent of world GDP, second only to the US which accounted for 20 per cent world GDP. The economic structure of the euro-area is also broadly similar to the US with agriculture representing only around 2 per cent

Table 18.1   Key characteristics of the euro-area as at the start of EMU Stage III

	Euro-Area	US	Japan
Share of world GDP (%)	15.0	20.0	8.0
Sectors of production, % GDP:			
Agriculture	2.4	1.7	2.1
Industry	30.9	26.0	39.2
Services	66.7	72.3	58.7
General government expenditure, % GDP	49.1	34.5	38.6
% world exports (excluding intra-euro-area trade)	15.7	12.6	7.7
Bank deposits, % GDP	83.9	55.3	98.8
Domestic debt securities, % GDP	90.2	164.7	108.5

Source: *ECB Monthly Bulletin*, January 1999.

GDP, services around 67 per cent, compared to 72 per cent in the US, and industry 31 per cent GDP compared to 26 per cent in the US. There are differences in the size of the government sector – being much larger in the euro-area than in the US. This reflects differences between the areas in the provision of social security and public services. (See Table 18.1.)

Sweden and Greece were assessed again by the ECB and the European Commission in 2000 in accordance with Article 122 (ex Article 109k) of the Treaty. Greece was judged to have fulfilled the necessary conditions for the adoption of the single currency, and joined on 1 January 2001.

The current EU policy framework

A central objective of the EU is the achievement of a stability orientated monetary policy which will foster sustainable growth and high employment. It is supported in this aim by a series of processes and guidelines which focus around the Broad Economic Policy Guidelines (BEPGs).

The BEPGs are the key policy document of the European Union, and form the centrepiece to economic coordination in the EU. They are agreed each year by ECOFIN on the basis of Qualified Majority Voting and are confirmed by the European Council, but are non-binding on member states.

The BEPGs consists of two key sets of guidelines. The first section are Community-wide guidelines on stability orientated macroeconomic policies and on product, labour and capital market reform. The second are country-specific guidelines in these areas.

Feeding in to the BEPGs are the output of a number of other processes and guidelines. The *Luxembourg Process* aims to improve the efficiency of labour markets in the EU through the production of an annual set of employment guidelines. The *Cardiff Process* is designed to improve the functioning of EU product and capital markets through better multilateral surveillance and coordination of structural reforms across member states. Its output includes an annual assessment of EU structural and economic reforms. The *Cologne Process* aims to promote strong non-inflationary growth in the EU through the coordination of economic policy; it involves production of an in-depth analysis of macroeconomic developments and prospects which forms the background to macroeconomic dialogue between ECOFIN, the European Commission, the European Central Bank and the social partners.

Monetary policy and EMU

Operation of monetary policy within EMU

The Treaty establishes a new institution for the third stage of EMU – the *European System of Central Banks* (ESCB). This consists of the *European Central Bank* (ECB) and the national central banks of member states.[2]

The Treaty defines the governance arrangements for the ESCB and provides for its *independence* from the Community institutions, governments of member states or any other body. Member states and the Community are also required to respect this principle of independence, and undertake not to seek to influence the members of the decision making bodies of the ECB or the national central banks in the performance of their tasks.[3]

Figure 18.1 gives the organisational structure of the ESCB and the Eurosystem. The ESCB has no legal personality of its own and its operation is governed by the decision making bodies of the ECB – the *Governing Council*, the *Executive Board* and, as long as there are member states outside EMU, *the General Council.*

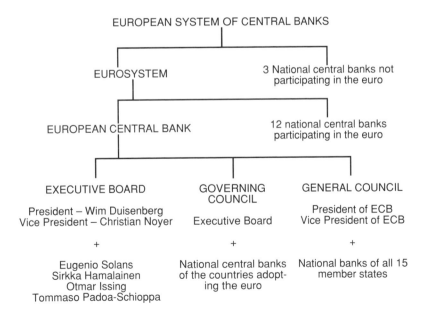

Figure 18.1   Organisational structure of the ESCB

Executive Board

The Executive Board of the ECB consists of six individuals who are appointed by common accord of the Heads of State of member states, on recommendation from ECOFIN, after it has consulted the Governing Council of the ECB and the European Parliament. Their posts are non-renewable, and they are selected on the basis of their recognised standing in the banking and monetary field.[4] Their primary responsibility is in the *operation and implementation* of the Eurosystem's monetary policy.

Governing Council

The Governing Council consists of the six Executive Board members and the Governors of the participating national central banks. The Governing Council is the primary *policy decision making* body of the ECB Each member of the Governing Council has one vote, and decisions are taken on the basis of a simple majority, if a vote is taken. Current practice is for the Governing Council to meet every two weeks in Frankfurt.

General Council

While there are still non-participating member states, a General Council has also been established which consists of all 15 national central bank Governors and the President and Vice President of the Executive Board. This body has taken over some of the functions of the EMI that are still required for member states at the second stage of EMU, and contributes to the ESCB's advisory functions, the collection of statistical information, and the preparations for irrevocably fixing the exchange rates of the currencies of member states with a derogation.

Functions of the ECB

The ECB has been established as the core of the Eurosystem with overall responsibility to ensure that the tasks of the Eurosystem are carried out either by its own activities or those of the participating national central banks. These tasks are defined in the Treaty and the ESCB Statute, and are the following:

- to conduct foreign exchange operations
- to hold and manage the official reserves of the member states
- to promote the smooth operation of payment systems
- to issue banknotes with legal tender status within the euro-area
- to approve the volume of issuance of the euro coins by the member states which have adopted the euro.

In taking its decisions on the way in which the tasks of the ESCB are to be carried out, the ECB follows a principle of *decentralisation*, so that to the furthest extent possible, national central banks handle ESCB operations. In terms of regulatory force, the ECB can issue Regulations, Decisions, Recommendations and Opinions which are addressed to third parties outside the Eurosystem. In addition, the ECB can issue Guidelines and instructions, which are legal instruments that apply to members of the Eurosystem only.

Although the ESCB has been granted a high degree of independence, the Treaty does establish a set of minimum legal reporting requirements to explain how it is carrying out monetary policy for the euro-area.

It must publish quarterly reports on its activities,[5] and it must address an annual report to the European Parliament, ECOFIN, the European Commission and the European Council on its activities in the previous and current year. A presentation must also be made to the Commission and to the European Parliament. The European Parliament is also entitled to hold a general debate on the basis of the ECB's report[6] and request a hearing of the President or other members of the Executive Board at any time.

There is also a formal mechanism built in for developing a relationship between the ECB and ECOFIN. The President of ECOFIN and a member of the European Commission may participate, but without the right to vote, in meetings of the Governing Council of the ECB. The President of the ECB can also be invited to participate in ECOFIN meetings when the Council is discussing matters relating to the objectives and tasks of the ESCB.

These are the minimum reporting requirements laid down in the Treaty. Within this framework the ECB is left with a considerable degree of discretion about how much of its *decision making processes* and activities are made public. To date, short press releases are made available after each fortnightly meeting of the Governing Council. Transcripts of the ECB's press conferences, held after the first Governing Council meeting of each month, are publicly available. Monthly bulletins, in addition to the annual report, are also published by the ECB. In December 2000, the ECB published for the first time its biannual staff macroeconomic projections for the euro-area.

Objectives of monetary policy within EMU

The objectives of monetary policy within Economic and Monetary Union are contained in the Treaty establishing the European Community, as agreed at Maastricht in 1991.

The primary objective of the ESCB is to 'maintain price stability', and subject to that objective, to 'support the general economic policies in the Community with a view to contributing to the achievement of the objectives of the Community'.[7]

By Article 3 of its Statute, the ESCB is also officially mandated to, 'define and implement the monetary policy of the Community'. The Governing Council is mandated with formulating the monetary policy of the Community including, as appropriate, the decisions relating to

---

Box 18.3   Monetary policy in the euro-area

On 13 October 1998, the ECB announced a quantitative definition of 'price stability' and set out a two-pillar approach to monetary policy to achieve this with EMU:

- *a quantitative reference* value for the growth of a *broad money aggregate*
- *a broadly based assessment of the outlook for price developments* and the risks to price stability in the euro-area as a whole.

Price stability
The Governing Council defines price stability as 'a year on year increase in the Harmonised Index of Consumer Prices (HICP) for the Euro area of below 2%'. This definition of price stability is to be 'maintained over the medium term'.

Monetary aggregates
The reference value announced is for *M3* (includes currency in circulation, short-term bank deposits plus financial market securities) *and is for 4.5 per cent growth* (measured on a three-month moving average of the 12-month growth rate).

Any deviations from the reference value would be investigated further to see if the series is giving a signal of inflationary pressures in the euro-area which would help inform monetary policy decisions. The reference value was reviewed in December 2000, and was left at 4.5 per cent.

Outlook for inflation
A wide variety of alternative economic indicators are assessed by the Governing Council, including wage developments, exchange rates, bond prices and the yield curve, fiscal policy indicators, price and cost indices, business and consumer confidence surveys. It also considers the inflation forecasts of independent agencies such as the OECD and produces its own assessment of the future outlook for inflation.

The ECB published staff economic projections for the first time in December 2000.

intermediate monetary objectives, key interest rates and the supply of reserves in the ESCB. In October 1998, the European Central Bank established the strategy that it would follow in carrying out its remit to maintain price stability in the euro-area (see Box 18.3).

Fiscal Policy and EMU

Established within the Treaty, and applicable to all member states, is a process of multilateral surveillance of member states' economic policies and performance. The European Commission and ECOFIN monitor economic developments in each member state to see how they are contributing to the objectives of the EU as a whole, and whether these policies are consistent with the agreed Broad Economic Policy Guidelines – discussed earlier.

In particular, the European Commission and ECOFIN assess the budgetary position of each member state. This is the *excessive deficit procedure* (see below).

The excessive deficit procedure and the multilateral surveillance of the economic policies of all Member States were re-enforced by the *Stability and Growth Pact* (SGP) agreed at Amsterdam in July 1997 (see below).

The excessive deficit procedure

Within the Third Stage of EMU, participating member states are required to 'avoid excessive government deficits' (Article 104 – ex Article 104c). Member states in the second stage (that is, those member states, including the UK, which have not yet adopted the single currency), are only required to 'endeavour' to avoid excessive government deficits (Article 116 (4) (ex 109e(4))).

In either stage, the European Commission has a duty to monitor the development of member states' budgetary positions on the criteria detailed in Article 104(2) of the Treaty (ex Article 104c(2)). This is the excessive deficit procedure and comprises two conditions relating to government deficit and debt ratios.

Deficit

- whether the ratio of the planned or actual government deficit to gross domestic product exceeds a reference value, unless:

  - either the ratio has declined substantially and continuously and reached a level that comes close to the reference value;

    – or, alternatively, the excess over the reference value is only exceptional and temporary and the ratio remains close to the reference value.

Debt

- whether the ratio of government debt to gross domestic product exceeds a reference value, unless the ratio is sufficiently diminishing and approaching the reference value at a satisfactory pace.

The reference value for general government deficit is 3 per cent GDP and for general government gross debt is 60 per cent GDP. If either or both of these criteria are breached, the European Commission will prepare a report, and if it considers that an excessive deficit exists or may occur, may address an opinion to ECOFIN.

The Treaty allows for representations to be made by the member state concerned, and for the European Commission to consider the member state's government investment levels, and its medium term budgetary position. This permits the position in the economic cycle to be taken into account when assessing the budgetary stance of the country concerned.

Where an excessive government deficit is judged to exist, ECOFIN will make recommendations to the member state concerned with a view to bringing the situation to an end within a given period of time. If no effective action has been taken in response to these recommendations, the Council can make its recommendations public.

During the third stage EMU only, further measures can be applied if a member state with an excessive deficit fails to comply with the Council's recommendations. These are:

- a requirement that the member state publish additional information, before issuing bonds and securities
- an invitation to the European Investment Bank to reconsider its lending policy towards the member state
- a requirement that the member state make a non-interest-bearing deposit of an appropriate size with the Community
- the imposition of fines of an appropriate size.

The Stability and Growth Pact

The Stability and Growth Pact (SGP) is based on the objective that sound public finances are a means to strengthen the conditions for price stability and for sustainable growth. The Pact embodies the medium-term objective of 'budgetary positions close to balance or in surplus'. Achieving this will allow member states to deal with normal cyclical fluctuations while keeping the government deficit within the 3 per cent GDP reference value, set out in the excessive deficit procedure of the Treaty (Protocol 20, ex Protocol 5).

The SGP consists of two EC regulations and a political resolution of the European Council. Under Regulation 1466/97 of the SGP, member states participating in the single currency are required to submit *Stability Programmes* and annual updates to the European Commission and ECOFIN. These should detail their adjustment path towards meeting the medium term budgetary objective of the Pact and the expected path of the general government debt ratio. They should also include the assumptions that have been made about the expected economic developments in the country which are relevant to the achievement of the Stability Programme; for example, growth, unemployment and inflation.

ECOFIN will then assess the Stability Programmes and, if it identifies a significant divergence from the medium term budgetary objective, or the adjustment path towards it, can make a recommendation to the member state concerned to take the necessary adjustment measures.

Member states not participating in the single currency are required to submit *Convergence Programmes* and annual updates to the European Commission and ECOFIN. These should detail expected paths for general government deficit and debt ratios, the country's medium-term monetary policy objectives and the relationship of those objectives to price and exchange rate stability. Again, they should include the main assumptions about expected economic developments, and an assessment of the impact of current economic policies on achieving the objectives of the programme.

ECOFIN will assess the Convergence Programmes for progress towards reaching the medium term budgetary objective, and also whether the Programmes facilitate closer coordination of economic policies and are geared to stability. The policies of the member states will also be assessed against whether they are consistent with the Broad Economic Guidelines.

Under Regulation 1467/97 of the Stability and Growth Pact, the definitions in the Excessive Deficit Procedure of the Treaty are clarified and a timetable set out for applying sanctions to member states which fail to take action to correct an excessive deficit as identified under the terms of the Treaty. The level of sanctions is also set out in this regulation (see Box 18.4).

Box 18.4   Sanctions for excessive deficits

Whenever the Council decides to apply sanctions to a member state in breach of the excessive deficit procedure, Regulation 1467/97 states that 'a non-interest bearing deposit shall, as a rule be required' (Article 11).

The first deposit will be a fixed component of 0.2 per cent GDP, plus a variable equal to one tenth of the difference between the deficit as a percentage of GDP and the reference value of 3 per cent.

Each year thereafter, until the situation is corrected, the sanctions will be intensified by one tenth of the difference between the deficit and the reference value, unless the member state has complied with the Council notice.

Any single deposit is restricted to a maximum of 0.5 per cent GDP.

Deposits will normally be converted into fines, if, two years after the decision to require a deposits to be made, the deficit has not been corrected.

However, the sanctions *do not apply to the UK unless it moves to the third stage of EMU* – as set out in the Protocol on Certain Provisions Relating to the United Kingdom of Great Britain and Northern Ireland.

The Eurogroup

The European Council agreed at Luxembourg in December 1997 that Ministers of member states participating in the euro-area could meet informally amongst themselves to discuss issues connected with their shared responsibilities for the single currency. These meetings have become known as the Eurogroup, and now take place regularly before each ECOFIN meeting. They are attended by the euro-area Finance Ministers and by representatives from the ECB and the European Commission.

The Luxembourg conclusions are clear that ECOFIN remains the sole decision making body on economic policy coordination in the EU. However, the Eurogroup provides a useful vehicle for euro-area Ministers to discuss areas of collective interest. It is also acts as a forum for discussions between the fiscal and monetary authorities in the euro-area.

Exchange rate policy within EMU

Lead responsibility for exchange rate policy within EMU rests with the Finance Ministers of ECOFIN. In principle, Article 111 (ex 109) permits the Council to act on a recommendation from the ECB or the European Commission to enter formal arrangements for an international exchange rate system, involving non-EU countries, subject to various conditions.

The Council may still, acting by a qualified majority, 'formulate general orientations for exchange rate policy'. These orientations 'shall be without prejudice to the primary objective of the ESCB to maintain price stability' (Article 111(2) (ex Article 109a)). In the absence of any such general orientations from the ECOFIN Council, Article 105(2) of the Treaty endows the ECB with the power to 'conduct foreign exchange operations consistent with' its primary objective of price stability.

The European Council in December 1997 adopted a resolution which voluntarily restricted the use of its powers to formulate general orientations to 'exceptional circumstances, for example, in the case of a clear misalignment'. The resolution also confirmed that member states believe that 'in general, exchange rates should be seen as the outcome of all other economic policies'.

Conclusions

A number of new procedures and institutions have been set up at an EU level to monitor and coordinate the economic policies of member states as they become more integrated via the single market and the single currency. These procedures and institutions focus on achieving macroeconomic stability, sound public finances and price stability. These are also objectives of the UK Government's economic policy to achieve higher growth, employment and improved standards of living.

19
An Assessment of the New Macroeconomic Policy Framework

This chapter assesses the performance of the new monetary and fiscal policy frameworks in their first four years of existence.

Introduction

Most of the key aspects of the new framework for macroeconomic policy have been in place for approximately four years. Thus it is appropriate that the concluding chapter of this book presents an analysis of how the new regime has performed so far, while recognising that a more complete analysis must await the passage of a longer period of time. This is consistent with the aim of the new framework which is to promote economic stability over the long term, not just over the short term.

The chapter considers:

- the success of the new monetary policy framework in locking in an environment of low and stable inflation
- the success of fiscal policy in locking in sound public finances
- the success of the framework as a whole in maintaining economic stability.

Inflation performance under the new monetary policy framework

This section considers the performance of the new monetary policy framework. As Figure 19.1 shows, the UK's inflation track record has

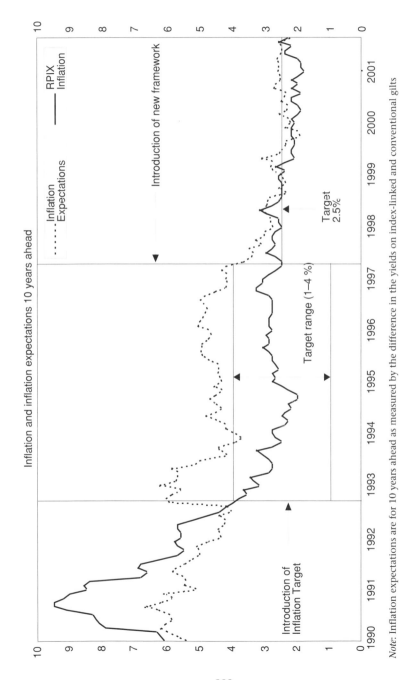

Note: Inflation expectations are for 10 years ahead as measured by the difference in the yields on index-linked and conventional gilts

Figure 19.1   Inflation performance and expectations against target

been very good since the introduction of the new monetary policy framework. Between May 1997 and August 2001, RPIX inflation averaged 2.4 per cent, only slightly below the target. This has been a negligible deviation from target by any reasonable standard of account.

Inflation has not only been low, it has also been stable. Since the introduction of the new framework, inflation has moved in a narrow band, between a low of 1.8 per cent and 3.2 per cent. As a result of this performance, there has been no breach of the thresholds that trigger an open letter from the Governor to the Chancellor.

This performance has of course been helped by disinflationary pressures in the world economy, and inflation was already relatively low under the previous monetary arrangements of a target range for inflation of 1–4 per cent. What is, however, most important is that expectations of inflation ten years ahead, as measured by the difference in yields between index-linked and conventional gilts have now fallen to the target (see Figure 19.1), indicating that the MPC has established credibility and confidence in the framework.

Proactive policy making

The MPC has already established a track record of acting in a proactive manner. There have been a number of examples of the MPC's willingness to act quickly and decisively to maintain price stability.

- Throughout mid and late 1997 the MPC raised interest rates four times to head off mounting inflationary pressure
- Over late 1998 and the first half of 1999 the MPC cut rates aggressively, action that not only lessened the risk of a significant undershoot of the inflation target but has also been widely credited with avoiding a sharp slowdown in activity
- The MPC's decision to raise rates in September 1999 at a time when actual inflation was below target again reflects its proactive approach to monetary policy. This decision was based on its assessment that a rise was necessary to keep inflation on track further ahead, and that an early move could lower the level at which interest rates might otherwise need to be set
- The MPC's decision to cut rates in February 2001 was a precautionary measure in the light of recent developments in the world economy (particularly the slowdown in the US) even though consumer confidence had remained strong and some measures of business confidence had risen in recent months

- The MPC's decision to cut rates pre-emptively in September 2001 (outside its usual schedule of meetings) in response to the effects on confidence and liquidity of the attacks in the US showed that it could react quickly when circumstances required it.

These examples demonstrate that the new monetary policy framework has allowed the authorities to be forward-looking, avoiding the need for large changes in interest rates. Whereas rates peaked at 15 per cent for a year in the last cycle, they reached only 7½ per cent for four months this cycle. The proactive and forward-looking monetary policy has been favourably commented on by international organisations. For example, in its Economic Survey of the UK in a section entitled 'A resolutely proactive posture', the OECD notes that:

> The MPC has thus shown that it is willing to hike rates when current inflation is well below target provided that the forecast will ultimately rise above target, and vice versa ... This contrasts with the more infrequent moves of the Bundesbank or the ECB (in 1999), or of the Federal Reserve in the United States. (OECD 2000)

Figure 19.2 demonstrates the extent to which monetary policy has operated in a more timely fashion since the introduction of the new framework.

Under previous arrangements, the authorities were slow to react to swings in the output gap, allowing the economy to gain (or lose) momentum before tightening or loosening policy. As a result, short-term interest rate movements were more extreme than they otherwise needed to be. In recent years, freed from political considerations, the authorities have acted quickly so that interest rates have approximately matched developments in the output gap. Output has been much less volatile, and interest rates have not had to vary by as much as previously.

This proactive and forward-looking approach has not only helped to smooth activity, but has also been instrumental in keeping inflation low and stable. As Figure 19.3 shows, both output and inflation have been significantly less volatile since the new framework was introduced, compared with previous regimes.

Independent experts

The MPC – bringing together expertise from both within and outside the Bank – has played a major role in the success of the new framework. The

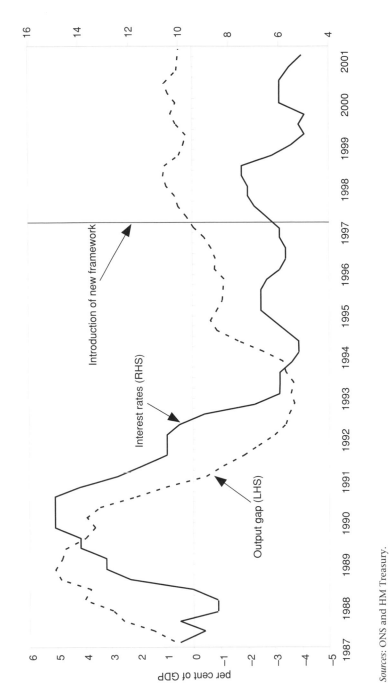

Sources: ONS and HM Treasury.

Figure 19.2   The output gap and interest rates

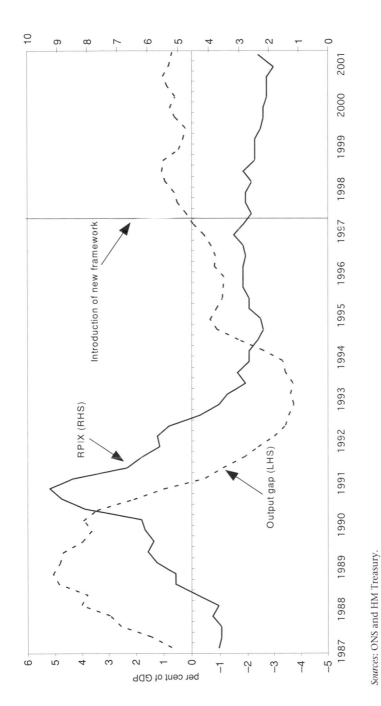

Sources: ONS and HM Treasury.

Figure 19.3   The output gap and inflation

337

quality of the members making up the MPC was recognised by the Treasury Committee which concluded that

> all the MPC members fulfil the criteria of demonstrable professional competence and personal independence. (Treasury Committee 1998)

This quality has been reflected in the wide-ranging and complex debates that have characterised the MPC's deliberations. For example, recently published MPC minutes illustrate that a wide range of economic and financial indicators are considered in reaching their decision. These indicators include the state of the world economy, developments in the monetary aggregates and financial markets, trends in domestic demand, the labour market and growth in earnings, and various measures of inflation and costs in specific parts of the economy. Its decisions are informed further by reports from the Bank's regional agents.

Credibility based on transparency and accountability

One of the key themes of the new monetary policy framework is the need for greater transparency in order to facilitate accountability and build credibility. There is widespread recognition that the framework has delivered on this point. International authorities, such as the IMF and the OECD, have praised the transparency of the UK's monetary policy framework. For example, the IMF noted that:

> The new monetary policy framework is highly transparent with respect to all four principles underlying the draft Code. The frank style and the short time lag in the publication of the MPC minutes provides for an effective transmission of information on the MPC decision-making process. (IMF 1999c)

Accountability and criticism have been instruments for developing the monetary framework. Both the Treasury Committee and the Lords Select Committee have suggested lengthening the terms of appointments and placing confirmation of such appointments on a statutory basis. In addition they have recommended improvements in the procedures for producing the Bank's forecast.

The criticisms and divergences of opinion are part of the framework of accountability and transparency. The Government and Bank are required to reply to them and the resulting dialogue then acts as a mechanism to permit the framework to evolve and respond to new circumstances in a flexible way.

In addition the Bank of England has instituted mechanisms to evaluate and improve the performance of the MPC. Responsibility for appraisal of the procedures of the MPC, including ensuring the appropriate collection of information to conduct monetary policy, lies with the Bank of England's Court of Directors. Recent appraisals include the commissioning of a report into MPC procedure and monetary analysis (Kohn 2000), which was published by the Bank. Many of the suggestions, including greater allocation of resources to external members of the MPC have already been implemented. This combination of scrutiny by parliamentary committees, as well as the Court of Directors, can help to ensure that the MPC's good performance continues.

One of the most important benefits of the enhanced transparency and accountability of the new monetary policy framework is that it has greatly improved the awareness of the aims and objectives of monetary policy. Financial markets, businesses, trade unions, and the general public now have a greater understanding of how and what policy makers are trying to achieve. As a result, the monetary policy framework has established considerable credibility, with people increasingly expecting that price stability will be maintained.

Four important quantitative measures of the credibility of monetary policy are:

- long-term interest rate differentials
- inflation expectations derived from index-linked and conventional gilts
- independent forecasts of inflation
- the public's perception of inflation.

Differentials between countries' bond rates reflect market expectations of inflation and other risk premia. In the past, yields on UK government bonds have typically exceeded those of other major countries, primarily because of the UK's poor inflation record. Figure 19.4 compares the five-year forward rates for UK and German government bonds.

Figure 19.4 shows that the spread between UK and German bonds dropped sharply after the introduction of the new monetary policy framework and has since trended down to a historically low level. This outcome reflects greater market confidence in the ability of the framework to deliver low inflation in the future.

Figure 19.5 shows the yield curve in April 1997, just before the new framework was introduced and September 2001 for both the UK and

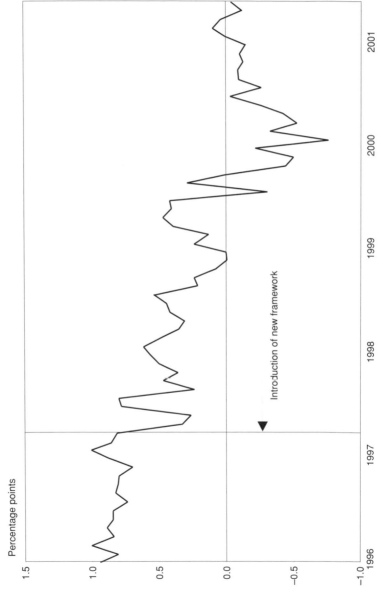

Figure 19.4 UK–German 5-year forward rate differential

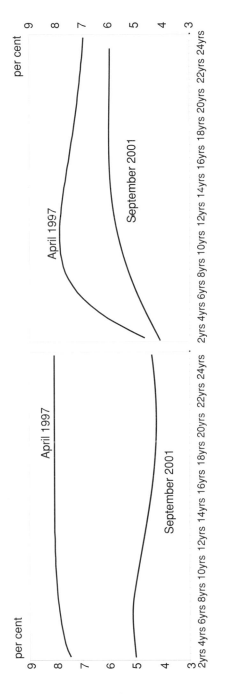

Figure 19.5(a) UK forward nominal interest rates

Figure 19.5(b) German forward nominal interest rates

Germany. It shows that there has been a marked fall in UK interest rates across all maturities since April 1997. While there has also been an overall fall in German rates, the magnitude of this fall is much smaller, particularly at longer maturities. While other factors lie behind some of these changes, the data suggest that there has been a marked fall in long-term inflation expectations for the UK compared with Germany. Although rates have fallen in Germany, they have fallen by substantially more in the UK.

Inflation expectations derived from index-linked and conventional gilts

Lower inflation expectations help to reduce the costs of maintaining low inflation. One way to derive inflation expectations from financial markets is to compare the yield curves for conventional and index-linked gilts. As Figure 19.6 shows, market expectations of inflation ten years ahead immediately fell sharply from over 4 per cent on the introduction of the new framework, and have since fallen to a level close to the target, indicating that markets are confident that price stability will be maintained over the longer term.

Independent forecasts of inflation

An indication of the credibility of the inflation target over the medium-term is given by the expectation of independent forecasters. Each month, HM Treasury surveys more than 30 independent organisations. Figure 19.7 plots the average forecast for RPIX inflation one year ahead made each month by those independent forecasters surveyed. It shows that the average inflation forecast has fallen substantially since the new framework was introduced, with forecasts remaining very close to the target for most of this time. This suggests that independent observers are confident in the ability of the MPC to act quickly to ensure that inflation is kept close to target.

The public's perception of inflation

An important goal of the new framework is to reduce the public's expectations of future inflation. This is particularly relevant for the wage bargaining process. If those involved expect inflation will be low, this will help to moderate wage growth which is, in turn, one of the key factors that influence inflation.

Barclay's Basix survey provides a quarterly indication of the inflation expectations of a range of groups. Table 19.1 shows that the inflation expectations of several key groups have both fallen and narrowed since the new framework was introduced, and have converged on 2½ per cent.

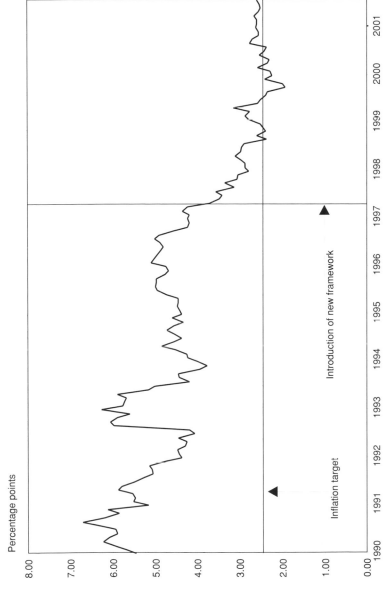

Figure 19.6 Inflation expectations 10 years ahead

The inflation expectations of the general public have shown a greater stickiness, but have also fallen. Their expectation of inflation two years ahead has fallen from 4.7 per cent just before the new framework was introduced to 4.0 per cent in March 2001. However the public's expectation of inflation one year ahead is closer to the target level with the latest figure (March 2001) at 3.5 per cent.

Table 19.1   Range of inflation expectations

Inflation	1997		2001	
	One year ahead	Two years ahead	One year ahead	Two years ahead
Public Expectations	4.0	4.7	3.5	4.0
Professional Expectations				
Maximum	3.3	4.7	2.4	2.8
Minimum	3.0	3.4	2.3	2.6

Note: Professional expectations includes business economists, academic economists, trade unions, finance directors and investment analysts.

Source: Barclays Basix survey.

On balance the evidence clearly suggests that the government has made a decisive step forward to a credible model of macroeconomic policy making in the UK. And largely because of the sound and forward-looking judgements of the MPC, the economy remained stable with growth close to trend during a period when most outside forecasters were forecasting greater instability.

Flexibility in response to shocks

The UK economy and the new monetary policy framework have faced difficult periods. Starting from a point in early 1997 when inflation pressures were rising sharply, policy makers have also had to face challenges posed by substantial global instability, including a number of major financial crises, large swings in oil prices and recessions in several countries. The implications of these factors have all had to be considered by the MPC when setting interest rates. As discussed earlier, monetary policy has reacted sensibly to these shocks, thus avoiding past volatility. This has been recognised by the Treasury Committee, which noted that

the MPC has had initial success in ... helping to manage the consequences for Britain of instability in the world economy. (Treasury Committee 1999)

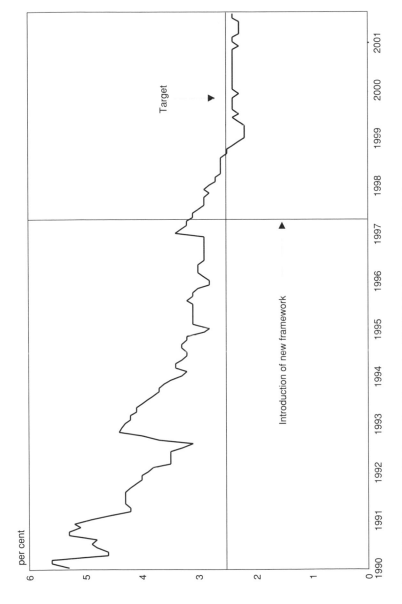

Figure 19.7 Average of independent forecasts of RPIX inflation one year ahead

The Treasury Committee also noted that:

> Witnesses told us that survey evidence of the type seen in the second half of 1998 had in the past always been a strong indicator of an economic recession. In light of this, the actions of the MPC have helped to stave off recession. (ibid.)

The evidence so far is that this new model based on constrained discretion has produced the flexibility required to respond to economic events without sacrificing long-term credibility.

The response of the MPC to the uncertainty created by the terrorist attacks on the US on 11 September 2001 demonstrated the flexibility of the framework in dealing with such extraordinary circumstances. The Governor of the Bank convened an unscheduled meeting of the MPC on 18 September 18, in accordance with the Bank of England Act 1998. At this meeting the MPC considered the impact of the attacks on the global economy and on UK consumer and business confidence. It decided to cut rates by a quarter of a percentage point. This demonstrated that the MPC was prepared to take immediate action, but it also allowed time to consider fully the true impact of the attacks before the next scheduled meeting. In the words of the MPC minutes:

> Although a 25bp reduction would be less than the cuts made by the Federal Reserve, the ECB and some other central banks, both current economic conditions and the impact of the recent shock differed across countries. That needed to be taken into account when judging the appropriate policy response for the UK.

At the next scheduled meeting on 7 October rates were cut by a further quarter of a point. Necessary action was thus combined with maintaining credibility.

From a Treasury perspective the new system has produced a much more effective coordination of monetary and fiscal policy than in the past. Fiscal policy has been set in a predictable medium-term context. The ratio of net debt has fallen to historically low levels.

It is too early to make a definitive judgement. Four years is not a long time in economic policy making. Some argue that this new UK model has not yet been tested against a severe national or world economic shock. An Open Letter has yet to be received by the Chancellor, although this is in itself a tribute to the MPC's success in delivering inflation to target. And the new system has yet to experience a change of government.

Legitimacy

In Chapter 6 it was suggested that the new monetary framework should be judged against three objectives: credibility, flexibility and legitimacy. The first two have been discussed above.

Legitimacy is difficult to measure. However, it is reasonable to claim that there is a new consensus in the UK both about the need for stability and the operational framework to achieve it. Any decision to raise interest rates is bound to be unpopular. Nevertheless, there is now an all-party consensus in favour of an independent MPC setting interest rates.[1]

Ultimately, that consensus depends on what the new framework achieves for the UK economy. Support for a long-term approach can only be sustained if stability is combined with faster growth and sustained low unemployment. The new macroeconomic framework provides a sound basis for policies to close the productivity gap and promote full employment. These are now the next challenge. The credibility and legitimacy of the new macroeconomic framework will in the end be judged by results in terms of growth and employment.

The public finances under the new fiscal policy framework

The fiscal framework has enhanced the credibility of the Government's fiscal policy and has promoted a constituency of support for stability orientated policies, enabling and encouraging people and businesses to plan for the long term. It has ensured that the highest standards of transparency, responsibility and accountability apply to fiscal policy decisions.

Within the framework, the Government's cautious management of the public finances has restored them to a healthy and stable position. This has given the Government the opportunity to increase spending on its key priorities, while still remaining on track to meet its two fiscal rules even in the cautious case (see below).

The golden rule

The Government remains well on course to meet the golden rule (which is met when, over a complete economic cycle, the current budget is in balance or surplus). The surplus on current budget was equivalent to 2.6 per cent of GDP in 2000–01. It is then projected to decline to 0.8 per cent of GDP by 2003–04 because of the increased current spending provided by Spending Review 2000, and then to remain stable. On a cyclically adjusted basis, the current surplus remains positive throughout this period. The average surplus since 1999–2000, which on the Government's provisional judgement is the start of the current cycle, also stays positive, remaining at more than 1 per cent of GDP over the next five years.

The sustainable investment rule

The sustainable investment rule is comfortably on track to be met. The fiscal rules state that net debt must be maintained at a stable and prudent level. The Government has stated that, other things being equal, it would be desirable to keep net debt below 40 per cent of GDP. Net debt has declined continuously as a proportion of GDP since 1996–97, when it stood at over 44 per cent of GDP. With the benefits of sound public finances, lower interest rate expectations and the proceeds from the auction of radio spectrum licences, the ratio of net debt to GDP is projected to fall to 30 per cent in 2002–03, remaining broadly stable at this level thereafter, well within the 40 per cent target.

Sustainable long-term public finances

The new fiscal framework has restored the public finances to a healthy and sustainable position, making possible the investment in public services announced in the Spending Review 2000 announced in July 2000 (see Chapter 12 for details of the public spending regime). While the economic forecast is based on a neutral estimate of trend growth of 2.5 per cent per annum, the public finance projections continue to be based on the deliberately cautious assumption for trend growth of 2¼ per cent per annum.

Projections of the public finances necessarily involve a significant degree of uncertainty. Revenue and spending projections depend heavily on forecasts of economic growth and, in particular, on assumptions made about the position of the economy in relation to its long-term trend. This means that projections of strong growth in the medium term can quickly deteriorate if most of the strength was cyclical and the economy slows to below trend over the forecast horizon. The Government therefore builds in a safety margin and stress tests its performance against a cautious case in which the level of trend output is presumed to be 1 percentage point lower than in the central case. This increases the probability of meeting the fiscal rules and also creates a buffer against fiscal risks. By creating a safety margin, it minimises the need for unexpected changes of direction and so allows a smoother path for public spending.

Stabilisation of the net asset position

In addition to PSNB and public sector net debt, several other fiscal indicators such as net worth[2] have a role to play in assessing the long-term sustainability of the public finances. Public sector net worth measures the difference between total assets, including non-financial assets (such as roads), and liabilities of the government. Changes in net worth provide an indication of the extent to which the net assets of the public sector are changing. Net worth is no longer declining after a prolonged period in which the poor state of the public finances led to net worth falling below 15 per cent of GDP. Budget 2001 projections of net worth show net worth improving and stabilising in coming years (see Chapter 15 for more details on this issue).

Monetary–fiscal coordination

An important element in the evaluation of the macroeconomic framework is the extent to which the coordination between monetary and fiscal policy has improved. One way to look at this question is to present some stylised facts about macroeconomic policy coordination. Evidence from previous economic cycles suggests that policy coordination in the UK has not always been optimal. An example is the late 1980s, when monetary and fiscal policies were both loosened as the economy was overheating (see Chapters 1 and 2 for a more detailed discussion of this point).

Between 1985–86 and 1987–88, the Treasury now estimates that the output gap increased by 4 percentage points and inflationary pressures in the economy increased.[3] During the same period, however, interest rates were cut by 2¾ percentage points, while structural PSNB moved from an estimated small deficit of 0.6 per cent of GDP in 1985–86 to a larger deficit of 2.1 per cent of GDP in 1987–88. Both fiscal and monetary policies were pro-cyclical, contributing to increased volatility of output during the late 1980s and early 1990s. When monetary policy was finally tightened, interest rates had to be increased by more than would otherwise have been necessary to offset the cumulative loosening of fiscal policy.

One possible explanation for these pro-cyclical changes in both fiscal and monetary policy is that the Treasury's estimates of the structural improvement in output growth implied by its medium-term growth projections were too optimistic. There is some evidence of this in the *Financial Statement and Budget Reports* (FSBR) – the assumed growth of GDP (excluding North Sea oil) underpinning the five-year medium-term

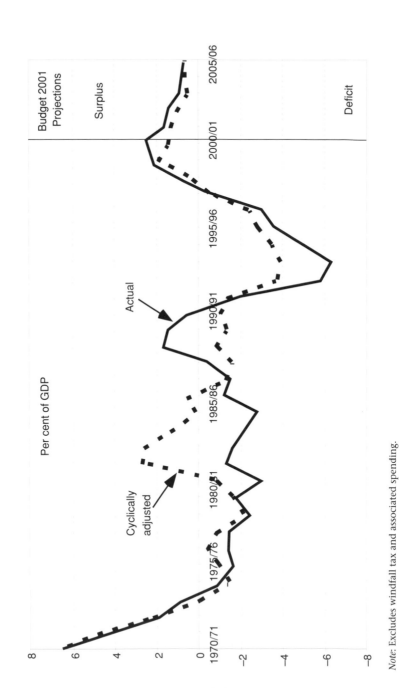

Note: Excludes windfall tax and associated spending.

Figure 19.8 Surplus on current budget – actual and cyclically adjusted

economic projections was revised up incrementally from 2¼ per cent in the 1986 FSBR to 3 per cent in the 1989 FSBR. Consequently, at that time, inflationary pressures as measured by an implied output gap would have been significantly underestimated. The implied structural improvement in output growth turned out to be too optimistic.

During this current economic cycle, monetary and fiscal policy have worked in tandem to help deliver greater stability. Unlike in the last cycle, the tightening of the fiscal stance during 1997–98 supported monetary policy in containing the inflationary pressures which were emerging when the economy was above trend, as well as restoring the public finances to a sound position. This was another factor that enabled interest rates to peak at a much lower level and subsequently to fall more quickly.

A similar role has been played by fiscal policy as the economy has moved into the above trend phase of the cycle. Here, the automatic stabilisers have been allowed to play their role in supporting monetary policy, while ensuring the structural fiscal position has remained sound, supporting longer-term stability.

Comments made by both the Governor and the Chancellor illustrate that monetary and fiscal policy makers are very satisfied with the degree of coordination that has occurred under the new framework. As the Governor said when appearing before the Lords Committee on 26 January 1999:

> I do not believe that the worry that there is not enough co-ordination between the monetary and fiscal side is a real one. I do not feel any discomfort on that score at all. (Governor of the Bank of England 1999)

This view was reiterated by the Chancellor in his Mansion House speech on 10 June 1999, when he said:

> I am convinced that today there is a much more informed discussion of the interaction of monetary and fiscal policy – and as a result much better coordination. (Chancellor of the Exchequer 1999b)

Conclusions

Much of the poor inflation record of the UK over the last 30 years can be attributed to policy mistakes that were the result of numerous short-comings in the framework governing monetary policy. Taking account of the lessons of these policy mistakes has been an important step forward.

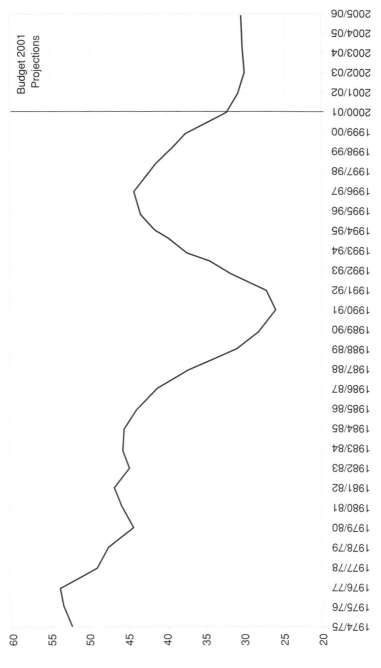

Figure 19.9 Net public debt (per cent of GDP)

The monetary policy framework established by the Government was specifically designed to address these problems. The new framework is based on a better understanding of the proper role of monetary policy and also recognises the need for clear objectives and procedures and for greater openness and transparency.

The fiscal policy framework has been built on the principles of transparency, accountability and responsibility. It recognises the dangers of being over-optimistic about economic performance and past biases against investment. It also provides outsiders with an objective means of judging the Government's performance against long-term targets.

To date, there is evidence to suggest that together the monetary and fiscal frameworks have done a good job not only in delivering price stability but also in supporting the objective of high and stable levels of growth and employment. In contrast with the past, the UK economy has enjoyed a period of stability and steady growth. This has taken place despite severe instability in the global economy and has also been contrary to the expectations of many independent observers who forecasted a boom in 1997 and a recession in 1999.

The framework has been praised internationally. A typical comment is the following from the International Monetary Fund Article IV review of the UK for 2000:

> Strengthened macroeconomic and structural policies, underpinned by improved monetary and fiscal policy frameworks, have contributed importantly to the United Kingdom's achievements. The tightening of fiscal policy in the late 1990s and a fiscal policy framework that has improved transparency and provided a medium-term orientation to policy have helped increase private sector confidence. The credibility of monetary policy has been enhanced with the adoption of a framework that provided for the operational independence of the Bank of England, a clear inflation target, and increased transparency of monetary policy decisions. (IMF 2001)

The new framework has delivered good results. Inflation has been low, stable and close to target, while the economy has recorded solid growth and rising employment. The proactive and forward-looking nature of the MPC combined with a sustainable fiscal policy has helped the UK to steer a course of stability and steady growth.

While the success so far has been encouraging, the MPC must continue to be vigilant and forward-looking in its decision making if inflation is to remain on target. Communicating the aims and rationale of monetary policy to those sectors of society – such as households – whose inflation expectations, while lower than in the past, remain above the inflation target could be stepped up. Equally, the maintenance of a credible and sustainable fiscal policy will be fundamental to allowing monetary policy to pursue these goals.

A proactive monetary policy focussed on a symmetric inflation target, together with a sustainable fiscal policy, provides the foundation for economic stability. The MPC's record so far in meeting the inflation target, and supporting a more stable path for output and employment than in previous cycles, is a good one. The discipline of the fiscal framework will enable the authorities to take decisions of long-term benefit to society, even in an adverse external climate. Nonetheless, both the Government and the MPC recognise that it is important not to be complacent.

Notes

Chapter 1

1. Two former Chancellors, Nigel Lawson and Norman Lamont, indicated in their memoirs that they had become convinced of the merits of depoliticising interest rate decisions through independence for the Bank of England as a result of their experience (see Lawson 1992, Lamont 1999). Norman Lamont commented that 'Experience with the PM over interest rates convinced me that politicians would always want to interfere with decisions for political reasons.' Another former Chancellor, Kenneth Clarke, was initially sceptical about independence on the grounds that it might introduce a deflationary bias to monetary policy. He too has now accepted that independence has benefited the conduct of monetary policy (see Hansard, 13 March 2001).
2. The Chancellor of the time, Nigel Lawson, attributed the failure to raise interest rates earlier to a number of factors, including statistics which at the time underestimated the expansion of the economy, but also to the fact that bank lending was increasing far faster than would have been expected on the basis of historical relationships. However, he also recognises that although in retrospect sharp rate rises might have been required he would have been isolated politically had he moved pre-emptively. His account of the period emphasises the intensely political nature of interest rate decisions and how these were strongly influenced by the political relationship between the Chancellor and the Prime Minister (see Lawson 1992, pp. 844–59).

Chapter 3

1. The only exception to this rule is the power given to the Governor of the Bank of England to call an extraordinary meeting if the circumstances require it. At the time of writing this power had only been used once, following the terrorist attacks on the US on 11 September 2001.

Chapter 4

1. This approach may generate biased results as single-country time series may be picking up the results of authorities' policy reactions. In almost all countries there is a positive relation between inflation and growth in the short-run, with the direction of causation running from higher growth (at least relative to productive potential) to higher inflation.
2. This contrasts with earlier views on the costs of anticipated inflation, reflected in Tobin's famous quote, 'it takes a heap of Harberger triangles to fill an Okun gap'.

Chapter 5

1. The ECB's monetary policy strategy is based on a system of 'two pillars', of which money is the first pillar. It is expressed as a reference range which is deemed to be consistent with the second pillar, the price stability objective.
2. As explained below, measurement bias means that the true price level will multiply less rapidly than implied by this table. For example, if the true inflation rate is 1.5 per cent when the measured inflation rate is 2.5 per cent, the true price level will double every 47 years rather than every 28 years.
3. The target price level could be specified so as to build in an allowance for the estimated level of measurement bias.

Chapter 6

1. This implies that the cost of reneging on their plans for the FA and MA must be trivial or zero and that this is common knowledge.
2. If the cost of reneging on plans is low or zero, then the ex post return on reneging is higher than the return from sticking to the pre-commitment plan.
3. Although under the Bank of England Act 1998 the Treasury can take control of monetary policy, it is clear that circumstances to justify this would be exceptional.
4. The remit states that the inflation target is 2.5 per cent RPIX inflation at all times. It is clear from reading the minutes of meetings and the inflation report that the MPC does not translate this to mean that it should attempt to bring inflation back to target in a very short period as this would result in undesirably high output volatility (and possibly instrument volatility).
5. Bean notes that Batini and Haldane (1998) also find the same general shape for the policy frontier suggesting that the result may not be model dependent.
6. The Treasury representative on the MPC is usually Gus O'Donnell. Around twice a year the Treasury's Permanent Secretary, Sir Andrew Turnbull, fulfils the role.
7. See for example *Goldman Sachs UK Weekly Analyst*, 10 March, 2000.

Chapter 7

1. We can only address this subject very briefly here. It is tackled in more detail by, for example, Llewellyn (1999). Dow (1996) is one of many papers looking at the case for banking regulation. Benston (1998) and Simpson (1996) are examples of economists who dispute the case for extensive regulation.
2. As a result of the Bank of England Act 1998.
3. Financial Services Authority website <http:/www.fsa.gov.uk>
4. Financial Services Authority website <http:/www.fsa.gov.uk>
5. The excess of assets over liabilities in insurance terminology is broadly equivalent to capital in banking terminology.
6. Financial Services Act 1986, Sch. 4.
7. Briault (1999) has a more extensive discussion of the case for a single regulator.

8. Money purchase personal pension type arrangements have been available much longer than that, notably for the self-employed, but it is only since 1988 that employees have had the option of 'contracting out' of SERPS into a personal pension.
9. Details of the proposed arrangements for stakeholder pensions are set out in six consultation briefs (DSS 1999a–f) and a subsequent Government announcement (DSS 2000).
10. Calculations based on Inland Revenue (2000) indicate that slightly less than 40 per cent of earners earn between £9000 and £18 000.

Chapter 9

1. Part of the decline can also be explained by falling land prices and the effect of privatisations whereby public corporations' tangible assets were transferred to the private sector at a price less than the previously recorded book value.
2. By way of further example, the level of net public debt in the US – measured in cash terms – poses few difficulties to a very large economy like that of the US, but would jeopardise economic stability if such levels were repeated in a smaller economy such as that of Britain.
3. A deadweight cost reflects the efficiency loss incurred when the imposition of taxes drives the economy away from its free market equilibrium.
4. The primary balance is equal to:

   PB = – PSNB – financial trasactions + net interest payments

   where PSNB is public sector net borrowing. Thus it reflects the budgetary position including financial transactions but excluding the impact of past cumulated deficits. In 1999/2000, the primary surplus in Britain was 4.3 per cent of GDP.
5. Data on a gross general government and net public sector basis are only available from 1970 onwards, and share the same general trend over this latter period.

Chapter 10

1. The formula to calculate the primary balance required to stabilise the net debt ratio is given in the appendix to Chapter 10.
2. Financial transactions include net lending to the private sector and the rest of the world, net acquisition of UK company securities, accounts receivable and payable, adjustment for interest on gilts, and other financial transactions.
3. The balancing item includes: the capital uplift on index-linked gilts, fluctuations in exchange rates which affect the sterling value of the official reserves, and an amount to cover the discrepancy caused when gilts are issued at discount or premia, which means that the level of debt changes by the nominal value of gilts issued whereas the net cash requirement is financed by the actual cash amount received.
4. The methodology for the cyclical adjustment of the public finances is described in more detail in HM Treasury (1999b).

Chapter 11

1. As output above its sustainable trend level is assumed to lead to inflation, it is clear that potential output is closely related to the concept of the sustainable level of unemployment or NAIRU (Non-Accelerating Inflation Rate of Unemployment). However, there are likely to be short-run differences since cyclical movements in unemployment tend to lag behind the GDP cycle.
2. LFS measure of employment.
3. The same applies to the ratio of public sector net cash requirement to GDP, as financial transactions are not expected to be cyclical, and also the Maastricht definition of deficit, GGFD (general government financial deficit).
4. These include the November 1997 *Pre-Budget Report* (HM Treasury 1997c) and the accompanying paper, *Fiscal Policy: Lessons from the Last Economic Cycle* (HM Treasury 1997b); the March 1998 *Financial Statement and Budget Report* (HM Treasury 1998b); the June 1998 *Economic and Fiscal Strategy Report* (HM Treasury 1998c); the November 1998 *Pre-Budget Report* (HM TReasury 1998f), and the March 1999 Budget.
5. The picture for the public sector net cash requirement looks very similar to net borrowing, with the exception of the late 1980s when privatisations contribute to a cyclically adjusted surplus on PSNCR.

Chapter 14

1. The OECD used both the number of elderly and the number of deaths as a basis for costs. Where the number of elderly was used, health care costs rose from 6.0 per cent of GDP in 1995 to 7.0 per cent of GDP in 2030. Where the number of deaths was used, health costs rose to 6.2 per cent in 2030 (OECD 1996).

Chapter 15

1. The information is typically published in the *Blue Book*. The latest balance sheet data were published in ONS (2000). The compilation of the data is described in Bryant (1987).
2. The way in which the public sector balance sheet is built up from separate balance sheets for central government, local authorities and public corporations means that central government's holdings of local authority and public corporation debt appears as an asset in the balance sheet, cancelling out much of the local authority and public corporation debt shown on the liability side.
3. The IMF and the OECD have been amongst those drawing attention to the potential problems: see IMF (1996) and OECD (1995).

Chapter 16

1. Most countries use the multi-price or discriminatory format where each bidder pays their own bid. However, in a uniform-price auction, all bidders pay the market clearing price. This reduces the risk of winning the auction by paying too much for the bond. Theoretically, this should encourage bidders to increase their bid.

2. However, even if they are not directly accounted for, changes in market returns will be taken into account implicitly because they will be reflected in debt servicing costs whenever debt is rolled over and new debt is issued.
3. This example is taken from Alesina et al. (1990). See also Cole and Kehoe (1998). The experience of Mexico in 1994 provides a real-time example of how issuing short-term foreign debt can contribute to a liquidity crisis.

Chapter 17

1. Hong Kong, Australia, Singapore and the Netherlands.

Chapter 18

1. For price stability the average rate of inflation, observed over a period of one year before the examination, should not exceed by more than 1½ percentage points that of the three best-performing member states in terms of price stability. For the budgetary position, at the time of examination, the member state should not be the subject of a Council decision under Article 104c(6) that an Excessive deficit exists. For the exchange rate criterion, the member state must have respected the normal fluctuations of the ERM without severe tensions for at least two years before the examination. In particular, the member state should not have devalued its currency's bilateral rate against any other member state on its own initiative over the same period. Finally, for the interest rate criterion, the member state should not have an average long-term interest rate more than 2 percentage points above that of the best-performing member states in terms of price stability.
2. As third stage EMU began with 11 member states, and not all 15 countries, the ECB has adopted the term 'the Eurosystem' to describe the ECB plus the 11 national central banks of the participating countries. If all 15 countries joined the third stage EMU, the term 'Eurosystem' would be synonymous with the term 'ESCB'.
3. Article 108 of the Treaty (ex Article 107) and Article 7 of the ESCB Statute.
4. Article 112 of the Treaty (ex Article 109a).
5. Article 15 of the ESCB Statute.
6. Article 112(3) (ex Article 109b).
7. Article 105(1) of the Treaty.

Chapter 19

1. The Conservative Party commissioned a report to review the workings of the monetary framework and the MPC. While it made a number of proposals to improve transparency and appointments procedures, its central conclusion was:

> It is right to delegate the operation of monetary policy to a technical agency. We also recognise that stability in the monetary policy framework is important for the continued success of the UK economy. We therefore recommend that the Monetary Policy Committee of the Bank of England should retain operational independence within an improved, more transparent set of arrangements. (Portillo 2000)

2. Net worth was previously referred to as net wealth. However, due to changes to the presentation of the national accounts as a result of ESA 95, it is now called net worth.

3. At the time, the Treasury did not publish output gap estimates. It is certainly true that the official data were subsequently revised up somewhat. It is to avoid such errors in the future that fiscal policy is now based on a cautious case, which assumes that trend growth is lower than its central estimate.

Glossary of Monetary and Fiscal Policy Terms

actual   (See *unadjusted*).

Annually Managed Expenditure (AME)   Spending that is managed on an annual basis. AME represents around half of *Total Managed Expenditure* (TME), and includes programmes such as social security benefits and debt interest payments that are subject to volatilities that make them difficult to budget for sensibly over a three-year horizon (the period covered by *Departmental Expenditure Limits* (DEL)).

AME margin   A provision for uncertainty in the forecast of AME components. It represents an unallocated margin built into the total forecast of AME spending.

automatic stabilisers   Various features of the tax and spending regime which act to stabilise the economy. As the economy strengthens, private incomes and expenditure tend to rise, resulting in higher tax receipts, while falling unemployment reduces social security spending. As the economy weakens, the opposite effect occurs. So government borrowing will tend to be relatively low when the economy is operating above trend and relatively high when the economy is below trend. This helps to reduce the swings in output over the *economic cycle*.

average surplus on current budget   The average of the differences between current receipts (or *current revenue*) and *current expenditure* including depreciation in each year of the cycle. The *golden rule* is met when the average surplus as a proportion of gross domestic product (GDP) over the *economic cycle* is in balance or surplus.

Balance sheet   A statement of assets and liabilities. Balance sheets can be constructed for the *public sector* in a similar manner to those for companies. The difference between assets and liabilities shows the net asset position of the *public sector* (see *net worth*).

balanced budget   A situation where total government revenue is approximately equal to total spending. This contrasts with the *golden rule*, whereby the government seeks to balance the current component of the budget over the *economic cycle* while permitting borrowing to fund capital spending.

baseline projection   Refers to the outlook for the public finances based on an assumption of unchanged policy (including *pipeline measures*). A baseline projection provides an indication of the extent of policy changes necessary to meet the government's fiscal objectives.

capital expenditure   (See *net investment* and *gross investment*).

cautious case   An additional public finance projection published by the government under which trend output is assumed to be 1 per cent lower than in the central projection. This scenario models the implications of assuming that a greater proportion of the projected surplus on the *current budget* is due to the cyclical strength of the economy.

central bank   The institution responsible for the conduct of monetary policy such as the Bank of England.

central government   Comprises predominantly government departments as well as other bodies subject to ministerial or departmental control, and extra-budgetary funds and accounts controlled by departments.

central government net cash requirement (CGNCR)   Equal to net borrowing by central government, plus financial transactions. This is a cash measure of central government's *short-term* net financing requirement (after refinancing of maturing debt).

Code for Fiscal Stability   Statement of the broad parameters of the *fiscal framework* issued pursuant to the Finance Act 1998. Approved by Parliament in December 1998, the purpose of the Code is to improve the conduct of *fiscal policy* by specifying the principles that guide the formulation and implementation of fiscal policy and strengthening the reporting requirements on government. The Code does this by requiring the government to commit to, among other things, five principles of fiscal management, more transparent financial reporting and the use of best practice accounting methods.

Comprehensive Spending Review (CSR)   The *Comprehensive Spending Review*, completed in July 1998, set out new departmental spending plans for the *medium term*, to cover the three years to 2001–02. These spending plans were arrived at after a root and branch examination of *public sector* expenditure to ensure that departmental spending contributes effectively to meeting the government's objectives.

current budget   The difference between *current revenue* and *current expenditure* including *depreciation*. A current budget which is positive is termed a current surplus; that which is negative, a current deficit.

current expenditure   Spending on items that are 'consumed' in the year of purchase (as opposed to *investment* which is 'consumed' in future years), such as *public sector* salaries and *transfers*.

current revenue (also termed **current receipts**)   Revenue relating to activities in the current year, comprising mainly *direct* and *indirect taxes*, but also including social security contributions, interest, dividends, capital taxes and profits from trading activities. Proceeds from the sale of assets are not included.

cyclical adjustment   The method of adjusting public finance indicators by subtracting an estimate of the impact of the *economic cycle* so that the underlying or *structural* trend can be seen more easily. This is particularly important when assessing fiscal prospects. The economic cycle can have a large *short-term* impact on the public finances through the operation of the *automatic stabilisers*. Experience has shown that in the past serious policy errors can occur if purely cyclical – and thus temporary – improvements in the public finances are treated as though they represented *structural* improvements. The *Code for Fiscal Stability* commits the government to publishing cyclically adjusted *fiscal indicators*.

Debt and Reserves Management Report   One of the four annual documents required under the *Code for Fiscal Stability* (see also the *Pre-Budget Report* (PBR), the *Financial Statement and Budget Report* (FSBR), and the *Economic and Fiscal Strategy Report* (EFSR)). The *Debt and Reserves Management Report* reviews developments in debt management over the past financial year, and sets out the details of the UK government's borrowing programme for the forthcoming financial year.

Departmental Expenditure Limits (DEL)   Multi-year spending plans for government departments fixed in cash terms and representing around half of *Total Managed Expenditure* (TME). Within DEL, current and capital spending are planned and managed separately to reduce any bias against spending on investment.

depreciation   A measure of the reduction in the value of an asset over its life. Depreciation can be thought of as the consumption of capital and is a component of the *current budget*.

direct taxation   Taxes levied on income and wealth; for example, income tax, corporation tax and inheritance tax.

discretionary change in the fiscal stance   Changes in the *fiscal stance* that occur through one or both of (i) discretionary Budget measures to achieve the desired change in the fiscal stance (for example, additional expenditure); (ii) a decision to accommodate or offset the impact of non-discretionary factors that are expected to alter the fiscal stance.

Economic and Fiscal Strategy Report (EFSR)   One of the four annual documents required under the *Code for Fiscal Stability* (see also the *Pre-Budget Report* (PBR), the *Financial Statement and Budget Report* (FSBR), and the *Debt and Reserves Management Report*). Published each year with the FSBR at the time of the Budget, the EFSR sets out the government's *long-term* economic and fiscal strategy and objectives.

economic cycle   Output has both a trend and a cyclical component. Trend growth is a function of employment and advances in labour productivity. But over the *shorter term* the economy is likely to move through periods above and below the trend growth path – the resulting movements in output give rise to the *economic cycle*.

excessive deficit   First defined in the Maastricht (European Communities) Treaty. Compliance with budgetary discipline is examined in relation to reference values of 3 per cent of GDP for the general government financial deficit and 60 per cent for general government gross debt. In practice, with certain exceptions, a deficit of more than 3 per cent of GDP is regarded as excessive.

Financial Statement and Budget Report (FSBR)   One of the four annual documents required under the *Code for Fiscal Stability* (see also the *Pre-Budget Report* (PBR), the *Economic and Fiscal Strategy Report* (EFSR), and the *Debt and Reserves Management Report*). Published each year with the EFSR at the time of the Budget, the FSBR sets out the Budget measures, and presents the economic background to the Budget and the fiscal position.

fiscal code   (See *Code for Fiscal Stability*).

fiscal drag   The tendency for tax receipts as a percentage of GDP to increase over time. This is due to the progressive nature of the tax system, whereby the average tax rate increases the more income is earned. Nominal fiscal drag occurs when inflation pushes incomes up; real fiscal drag occurs when wages rise faster than inflation due to productivity growth.

fiscal framework   The framework within which the government operates fiscal and debt management policy. The framework is underpinned by the *Code for Fiscal Stability*.

fiscal indicators   Indicators used to assess *fiscal policy*. There are a variety of indicators or aggregates, such as the *surplus on the current budget*, *public sector net borrowing* (PSNB), *net debt* and *net worth*, each of which can be helpful in analysing the impact, sustainability or generational fairness of fiscal policy.

fiscal loosening   The term used to describe the *fiscal stance* when *structural* (cyclically adjusted) *public sector net borrowing* (PSNB) is rising.

fiscal policy   The combination of spending and tax policies which a government uses to achieve its objectives.

fiscal principles   The five principles of transparency, stability, responsibility, fairness and efficiency enshrined in the Finance Act 1998 and the *Code for Fiscal Stability*. The Code explains how these principles are to be reflected in the formulation and implementation of *fiscal policy*.

fiscal stance   The term used to describe the change in *structural* (cyclically adjusted) *public sector net borrowing* (PSNB).

fiscal tightening   The term used to describe the *fiscal stance* when *structural* (cyclically adjusted) *public sector net borrowing* (PSNB) is falling.

general government   A measure of government incorporating both *central government* and *local authorities*.

general government financial deficit   (See *Maastricht deficit*).

generational accounts   Provide a comparison of the net burden of tax and *transfer* payments on present and future generations, assuming current policies are maintained.

generational fairness   The principle that those generations who benefit from specific items of spending should meet the cost.

golden rule   One of the government's two fiscal rules (see also the *sustainable investment rule*). States that, on average over the *economic cycle*, the government will borrow only to invest and not to fund current spending.

gross investment   Total expenditure on capital goods, before taking into account *depreciation*.

indirect taxation   Taxes levied on expenditure, such as excise duties or VAT.

inflation target   The rate of inflation targeted by a central bank's monetary policy. Not all central banks have an inflation target.

investment   (See *net investment*).

liquid financial assets   Assets which can be redeemed readily for cash; for example, bank deposits.

local authorities   Public authorities of limited geographical scope, having power to raise funds by certain forms of local taxation.

long term   Often taken to mean at least ten years ahead, and a period in which *economic cycles* cease to be relevant to policy analysis.

long-term fiscal projections   Projections of the public finances for a period of ten years or more. Under the *Code for Fiscal Stability* the government is required to publish illustrative long-term fiscal projections each year in the *Economic and Fiscal Strategy Report* (EFSR). These projections incorporate the effects of demographic trends and other influences on long-term spending and taxation levels.

M0   The narrowest measure of the money stock, comprising the notes and coins in circulation outside the Bank of England, and banks' operational deposits with the Bank of England.

M3   A broader measure of money including *M0* plus cheque accounts and deposits for terms of up to two years by individuals and non-financial corporations with banks and other financial institutions.

M4   Broad money – includes *M3* plus longer-term deposits, held at banks and building societies in the UK. For more details on the definitions of these monetary aggregates see the most recent edition of *Bank of England Monetary and Financial Statistics*.

Maastricht deficit   Also known as the *general government* financial deficit, this is equivalent to *public sector net borrowing* less borrowing by *public corporations* and excluding financial transactions. It therefore measures general government net borrowing. Described as the 'Maastricht deficit', as it is the measure of government borrowing used for the purposes of the Stability and Growth Pact.

medium term   Often taken to mean at least three to ten years ahead.

monetary policy   The tool of macroeconomic policy that seeks to control inflation by influencing aggregate demand through movements in interest rates.

net debt   Gross debt minus *liquid financial assets*. *Public sector net debt*, expressed as a percentage of GDP, is the key indicator by which progress against the *sustainable investment rule* is measured.

net investment   Gross spending on *investment* less *depreciation*. It measures the extent to which public spending is adding to the country's stock of physical capital.

net worth   The difference between total assets and liabilities (including debt) held by the government. It represents a more comprehensive measure of the overall worth position of the government than *net debt*, as it includes non-financial assets (such as roads). The stock equivalent of the surplus on *current budget* (although also affected by revaluations), changes in net worth reflect the extent to which the net assets of the *public sector* are changing.

neutral fiscal stance   The term used to describe the *fiscal stance* when *structural* (cyclically adjusted) *public sector net borrowing* (PSNB) is unchanged.

nominal variable   One from which the effects of inflation have not been excluded (see *real variable*).

non-accelerating inflation rate of unemployment (NAIRU)   The rate of unemployment which is consistent with a constant rate of inflation. If unemployment is lower than the NAIRU, pressure on wages will tend to increase inflation, while unemployment above the NAIRU will exert downwards pressure on wage and price inflation.

Okun coefficient   The ratio of the change of *output gap* to change in the unemployment rate at a constant *non-accelerating inflation rate of unemployment* (NAIRU).

output gap   The difference between observed GDP and *potential GDP*. A positive output gap implies inflationary pressures in the economy and a negative output gap implies disinflationary pressures. The output gap is often used as a measure of the position of the economy in the *economic cycle*.

overall fiscal impact   A term used to describe the change in actual *public sector net borrowing* (PSNB). The overall fiscal impact is the sum of the change in the *fiscal stance* plus the effect of the *automatic stabilisers* stemming from the cyclical position of the economy.

pipeline measures   Measures announced in previous Budgets, yet to come into effect, but which nevertheless will have an impact on the fiscal position. Pipeline measures are included in the *baseline projections*. Therefore they are taken account of when decisions are made about the *discretionary* Budget *measures* required to bring those projections into line with desired outcomes. The *fiscal indicators* published in the *Economic and Fiscal Strategy Report* (EFSR), the *Financial Statement and Budgetary Report* (FSBR) and the *Pre-Budget Report* (PBR) include the full effects of pipeline measures.

policy mix The combination of *fiscal* and *monetary policy* settings at any given time.

potential GDP The sustainable maximum output of the economy, determined by the availability of factors of production and technology. If observed GDP rises temporarily above *potential GDP*, bottlenecks and other forces will soon reduce GDP to or below potential.

Pre-Budget Report (PBR) One of the four annual documents required under the *Code for Fiscal Stability* (see also the *Financial Statement and Budget Report* (FSBR), the *Economic and Fiscal Strategy Report* (ESFR), and the *Debt and Reserves Management Report*). Published at least three months prior to the Budget (usually in the preceding November), the PBR provides a progress report on what has been achieved so far, updates forecasts on the economy and the public finances, and sets out the direction of government policy and further measures that are under consideration in the run-up to the next Budget, for information and consultation purposes.

primary balance *Public sector net borrowing* (PSNB) excluding *net debt* interest payments. It measures the current fiscal position excluding the interest costs of accumulated net debt from previous years, and is used to assess whether current policy is consistent with stabilising the ratio of net debt to national income, given assumptions about future interest rates and economic growth.

prospective net worth A forward-looking measure of the government's net assets, it represents *net worth* plus the discounted value of all future spending and receipts that the government will face as a result of its current policies. In practice these future cash flows are difficult to measure.

public corporations Publicly owned and controlled organisations which manage publicly owned industries.

public sector The widest measure of government incorporating *central government, local authorities* and *public corporations*. Focusing on the whole of the public sector removes incentives to reclassify activities to avoid constraints on borrowing.

public sector net borrowing (PSNB)   The sum of current spending (including *depreciation*) and net *investment*, less total revenues.

public sector net cash requirement (PSNCR)   Formerly known as the public sector borrowing requirement (PSBR), and equal to *public sector net borrowing* (PSNB) plus financing requirements that come from financial transactions (for example, net asset sales, lending to the private sector and abroad, and accruals adjustments). This is a cash measure of the public sector's *short-term* net financing requirement (after refinancing of maturing debt).

public sector net debt (PSND)   (See *net debt*).

real variable   One that is adjusted to remove the impact of inflation. Examining real variables is useful since it provides a better indication of the resources actually consumed.

remit to MPC   In accordance with section 12 of the Bank of England Act 1998, this is the annual written notice given to the Bank of England MPC by the Treasury specifying what is to be the operational target for monetary policy over the coming year and the economic policy of HM Government.

retail prices index (RPI)   The principal measure of the cost of living. The rate of growth of the index is the main measure of consumer price inflation in the UK.

RPIX   The *retail prices index* excluding mortgage interest payments. This is the measure of inflation which the Bank of England targets with its *monetary policy*.

short term   Often taken to mean the next one to two years.

sound public finances   (See *sustainability*).

Stability and Growth Pact (SGP)   An agreement among participants in the euro to maintain sustainable *fiscal policies*, reduce debt and avoid excessive deficits (normally greater than 3 per cent of GDP).

structural   (See *cyclical adjustment*).

surplus on current budget   The difference between *current revenue* and *current expenditure* including *depreciation*.

sustainability   At a basic level, *fiscal policy* can be said to be sustainable if the government can maintain indefinitely its current spending and taxation policies while continuing to meet its debt interest obligations. The costs to an economy of fiscal policy becoming unsustainable can be extremely large.

sustainable investment rule   The second of the Government's two fiscal rules (see also the *golden rule*), the sustainable investment rule states that *public sector net debt* (PSND) as a proportion of GDP will be held over the *economic cycle* at a stable and prudent level. The government believes that, other things being equal, it is desirable that PSND be reduced to below 40 per cent of GDP over the economic cycle.

Total Managed Expenditure (TME)   The sum of *Annually Managed Expenditure* (AME) and *Departmental Expenditure Limits* (DEL). Or equivalently, total current and capital spending by the *public sector*.

transfers   A form of government expenditure, such as unemployment benefits, which involves a transfer of money from taxpayers to individuals, as opposed to a payment for a good or service.

unadjusted   A *fiscal indicator* which has not been adjusted to take into account the effect of the *economic cycle*. Also referred to as actual.

Bibliography

Akerlof, G., Dickens, W. and Perry, G. (1996) 'The Macroeconomics of Low Inflation', *Brookings Papers on Economic Activity* 1 (July).

Alesina, A. (1988) 'Macroeconomics and Politics', in NBER, *Macroeconomics Annual*. Cambridge, MA: MIT Press.

Alesina, A. (1989) 'Politics and Business Cycles in Industrial Democracies', *Economic Policy* 8, pp. 55–98.

Alesina, A. and Gatti, R. (1995) 'Independent Central Banks: Low Inflation at No Cost?', *American Economic Review, Papers and Proceedings* 85, pp. 196–200.

Alesina, A. and Roubini, R. (1992) 'Political Cycles in OECD Economies', *Review of Economic Studies* 59(4), pp. 663–90.

Alesina, A. and Summers, L.H. (1993) 'Central Bank Independence and Macroeconomic Performance: Some Comparative Evidence', *Journal of Money, Credit and Banking* 25, pp. 151–62.

Alesina, A. and Tabellini, G. (1987) 'Rules and Discretion with Non-coordinated Fiscal and Monetary Policies', *Economic Enquiry*.

Alesina, A., Prati, A. and Tabellini, G. (1990) 'Public Confidence and Debt Management: A Model and a Case Study of Italy', in R. Dornbusch and M. Draghi (eds), *Public Debt Management: Theory and History*. Cambridge, New York and Melbourne: Cambridge University Press, pp. 94–118.

Al-Marhubi, F. (1997) 'A Note on the Link between Income Inequality and Inflation', *Economic Letters* 55 (September), pp. 317–19.

Anderson, N., Breedon, F., Deacon, M., Derry, A. and Murphy, G. (1996) *Estimating and Interpreting the Yield Curve*. Chichester: John Wiley and Sons Ltd.

Anderson, N., Emerson, R. and Price, S. (1998) 'The Objectives of Debt Management'. Bank of England Working Paper, April.

Andrés, J. and Hernando, I. (1997) 'Does Inflation Harm Economic Growth? Evidence for the OECD'. NBER Working Paper No. 6062.

Asilis, C.M. (1994) 'The US Public Debt – Implications for Growth'. IMF Working Paper No. WP/94/4.

Ausubel, L.M. and Cramton, P. (1998) 'Auctioning Securities'. University of Maryland Working Paper, March.

Bakhshi, H., Haldane, A.G. and Hatch, N. (1998) 'Some Costs and Benefits of Price Stability in the United Kingdom'. Bank of England Working Paper No. 78/NBER Working Paper No. 6660.

Ball, L. (1993) 'What Determines the Sacrifice Ratio?' NBER Working Paper No. 4306.

Ball, L. (1994) 'What Determines the Sacrifice Ratio?', in G. Mankiw (ed.), *Monetary Policy*. Illinois: University of Chicago Press.

Ball, L. (1996) 'Disinflation and the NAIRU'. NBER Working Paper No. 5520.

Balls, E. (1998) 'Open Macroeconomics in an Open Economy', *Scottish Journal of Political Economy*, pp. 113–32.

Balls, E. (2001) 'Delivering Economic Stability'. Speech delivered to Oxford Business School Alumni Association Annual Lecture, Merchant Taylor's Hall, 12 June.

Barro, R. (1979) 'On the Determination of the Public Debt', *Journal of Political Economy* 87(5) (October), pp. 940–91.

Barro, R. (1995) 'Inflation and Economic Growth', *Bank of England Quarterly Bulletin* (May).

Barro, R. (1996) 'Determinants of Economic Growth: A Cross-Country Empirical Study'. NBER Working Paper No. 5698.

Barro, R.J. (1998) 'Optimal Funding Policy', in G.A. Calvo and M. King (eds), *The Debt Burden and its Consequences for Monetary Policy: Proceedings of a Conference Held by the International Economic Association at the Deutsche Bundesbank, Frankfurt, Germany.* Basingstoke: Macmillan.

Barro, R.J. and Gordon, D. (1983) 'Rules, Discretion and Reputation in a Model of Monetary Policy', *Journal of Monetary Economics* 12, pp. 101–21.

Bean, C. (1998) 'The New UK Monetary Arrangements: A View from the Literature'. Treasury Academic Panel Paper AP(98)2.

Benston, G.J. (1998) *Regulating Financial Markets: A Critique and Some Proposals.* Hobart Paper No. 135. London: Institute of Economic Affairs.

Black, R., Coletti, D. and Monnier, S. (1998) 'On the Costs and Benefits of Price Stability', in *Price Stability, Inflation Targets, and Monetary Policy.* Proceedings of a conference held by the Bank of Canada, May 1997.

Black, R., Macklem, T. and Ploz, S. (1994) 'Non-Superneutralities and some Benefits of Disinflation: A Qualitative General Equilibrium Analysis', in Bank of Canada (ed.) *Economic Behaviour and Policy Choice Under Price Stability.* Canada: Bank of Canada, pp. 477–516.

Blanchard, O.J. and Summers, L.H. (1990) 'Hysteresis and the European Unemployment Problem', in L.H. Summers (ed.), *Understanding Unemployment.* Cambridge, MA: MIT Press.

Bleaney, M. (1996) 'Central Bank Independence, Wage Bargaining Structure, and Macroeconomic Performance in OECD Countries', *Oxford Economic Papers* 48, pp. 20–8.

Blinder, A.S. (1997) 'What Central Bankers could Learn from Academics – and Vice Versa' (Distinguished Lecture on Economics in Government), *Journal of Economic Perspectives* 11(2), pp. 3–19.

Bohn, H. (1988) 'Why Do We Have Nominal Government Debt?', *Journal of Monetary Economics* 21(1) (January), pp. 127–40.

Bohn, H. (1990) 'Tax Smoothing with Financial Instruments', *American Economic Review* 80(5) (December), pp. 1217–30.

Boltho, A. and Holtham, G. (1992) 'The Assessment: New Approaches to Economic Growth', *Oxford Review of Economic Policy* 8(4) (Winter).

Bonato, L. (1998) 'Price Stability: Some Costs and Benefits in New Zealand'. Reserve Bank of New Zealand Discussion Paper 98/10.

Boskin et al. (1996) 'Toward a More Accurate Measure of the Cost of Living'. Final Report to the Senate Finance Committee from the Advisory Commission to Study the Consumer Price Index.

Bouthevillain, C. et al. (2001) 'Cyclically-Adjusted Budget Balances: An Alternative Approach'. ECB Working Paper No. 77.

Bowden, R.J. (1995) 'Government Debt and the Value of Government', *New Zealand Economic Papers* 29(2), pp. 215–30.

Briault, C. (1995) 'The Costs of Inflation', *Bank of England Quarterly Bulletin* (February).

Briault, C. (1999) 'The Rationale for a Single National Financial Services Regulator'. FSA Occasional Paper No. 2.

British Invisibles (2000) *International Financial Markets in the UK, October 2000*.

Britton, A. (1991) *Macroeconomic Policy in Britain 1974–1987*. Cambridge: Cambridge University Press.

Brown, G. (2001) 'The Conditions for High and Stable Employment', *Economic Journal* 111 (May).

Bruno, M. and Easterly, W. (1996) 'Inflation and Growth: In Search of a Stable Relationship', *Federal Reserve Bank of St Louis Review* 78(3), pp. 139–46.

Bryant, C. (1987) 'National and Sector Balance Sheets', *Economic Trends* (May).

Buiter, W. (1985) 'A Guide to Public Sector Debt and Deficits', *Economic Policy* (November).

Buti, M., Franco, D. and Ongena, H. (1997) 'Budgetary Policies During Recessions', *European Commission Economic Papers* (May).

Calvo, G.A. and Guidotti, P.E. (1990) 'Indexation and Maturity of Government Bonds: An Exploratory Model', in R. Dornbusch and M. Draghi (eds), *Public Debt Management: Theory and History*. Cambridge, New York and Melbourne: Cambridge University Press, pp. 52–82.

Calvo, G.A. and Guidotti, P.E. (1992) 'Optimal Maturity of Nominal Government Debt: An Infinite-Horizon Model', *International Economic Review* 33(4) (November), pp. 895–919.

Calvo, G.A. and Guidotti, P.E. (1993) 'Management of the Nominal Public Debt: Theory and Applications', in H.A.A. Verbon and F.A.A.M. van Winden (eds), *The Political Economy of Government Debt*. Amsterdam, London, New York and Tokyo: North Holland, pp. 207–32.

Campbell, J.Y. (1998) 'Asset Prices, Consumption, and the Business Cycle'. NBER Working Paper No. 6485, March.

Campbell, J.Y. and Shiller, R.J. (1996) 'A Scorecard for Indexed Government Debt'. NBER Working Paper No. 1125, May.

Card, D. and Hyslop, D. (1996) 'Does Inflation 'Grease the Wheels of the Labor Market'?'. NBER Working Paper No. 5538, April.

Card, D. and Hyslop, D. (1997) 'Does Inflation "Grease the Wheels of the Labor Market"?' in D. Card, D. Hyslop, C.D. Romer and D.H. Romer (eds) *Reducing Inflation: Motivation and Strategy*. NBER Studies in Business Cycles, Vol. 30. Chicago and London: University of Chicago Press, pp. 71–114.

Cardarelli, R., Sefton, J. and Kotlikoff, L.J. (1998) *Generational Accounting in the UK*. London: National Institute for Economic and Social Research, November.

Cardarelli, R., Sefton, J. and Kotlikoff, L.J. (2000) 'Generational Accounting in the UK', *Economic Journal* (November).

Cassard, M. and Folkerts-Landau, D. (1997) 'Risk Management of Sovereign Assets and Liabilities'. IMF Working Paper No. WP/97/166, December.

Chancellor of the Exchequer (1997a) Letter to the Governor of the Bank of England, 6 May.

Chancellor of the Exchequer (1997b) Speech at the Mansion House, 12 June.

Chancellor of the Exchequer (1997c) Budget Speech, 2 July.

Chancellor of the Exchequer (1997d) Statement to the IMF Interim Committee meeting, Hong Kong, 21 September.

Chancellor of the Exchequer (1999a) Speech to the EBRD Annual Meetings, April.

Chancellor of the Exchequer (1999b) Speech at the Mansion House, 10 June.

Chancellor of the Exchequer (1999c) Mais Lecture at City University, 19 October.

Chancellor of the Exchequer (2000) Speech to the Commonwealth Finance Ministers' Meeting, Malta.

Chapple, S. (1996) 'Sticky Money Wages'. New Zealand Institute of Economic Research Working Paper 96/13 (July).

Chari, V.V. and Kehoe, P.J. (1998) 'Optimal Fiscal and Monetary Policy'. Federal Reserve Bank of Minneapolis Research Department Staff Report No. 251, July.

Chari, V.V. and Weber, R.J. (1992) 'How the US Treasury Should Auction its Debt', *Federal Reserve Bank of Minneapolis Quarterly Review* 16(4) (Fall), pp. 3–12.

Chote, R. (1997) 'An Expensive Lunch: The Political Economy of Britain's New Monetary Framework'. Social Market Foundation Memorandum.

Chowdhury, A.R. (1991) 'The Relationship between the Inflation Rate and its Variability: The Issues Reconsidered', *Applied Economics* 23, pp. 993–1003.

Clark, P., Laxton, D. and Rose, D. (1996) 'Asymmetry in the US Output–Inflation Nexus', *IMF Staff Papers* 43 (March), pp. 216–51.

Cole, H.L. and Kehoe, P.J. (1998) 'Models of Sovereign Debt: Partial versus General Reputations', *International Economic Review* 39(1) (February), pp. 55–70.

Cooley, T.F. and Hansen, G.D. (1991) 'The Welfare Costs of Moderate Inflation', *Journal of Money, Credit and Banking* 23(3), Part 2, pp. 483–503.

Crawford, A. (1993) 'Measurement Biases in the Canadian CPI'. Bank of Canada Technical Report No. 64.

Crawford, A. and Harrison, A. (1997) 'Testing for Downward Rigidity in Nominal Wages'. Bank of Canada Working Paper.

Cruickshank, D. (1999) 'Competition and Regulation: An Interim Report'.

Cukierman, A. (1995) 'The Economics of Central Banking'. Paper presented at the Eleventh World Congress of the International Economic Association, Tunis, December.

Cukierman, A., Webb, S.B. and Neyapti, B. (1992) 'Measuring the Independence of Central Banks and its Effectiveness on Policy Outcomes', *World Bank Economic Review* 6, pp. 353–98.

Cunningham, A. (1996) 'Measurement Bias in the Price Indices: An Application to the UK's RPI'. Bank of England Working Paper No. 47.

Dale, S., Mongiardino, A. and Quah, D.T. (1987) 'A Modest Proposal for Setting the Public Debt Structure'. CEPR/ESRC Workshop on Optimal Fiscal Policy, April.

Das, S.R. and Sundaram, R.K. (1996) 'Auction Theory: A Survey with Applications to Treasury Markets', *Financial Markets, Institutions and Instruments* 5(5) (December), pp. 1–36.

Debelle, G. and Fischer, S. (1994) 'How Independent Should a Central Bank Be?'. CEPR Publication No. 392 (Stanford University).

Debelle, G. and Laxton, D. (1996) 'Is the Phillips Curve Really a Curve? Some Evidence for Canada, the United Kingdom, and the United States'. IMF Working Paper 111 (October).

De Cecco, M., Pecchi, L. and Piga, G. (1997) *Managing Public Debt: Index-Linked Bonds in Theory and Practice*. Cheltenham, and Brookfield, WI: Edward Elgar.

De Fontenay, P., Milesi-Ferretti, G.M. and Pill, H. (1995) 'The Role of Foreign Currency Debt in Public Debt Management'. IMF Working Paper No. WP/95/21, February.

De Haan, J. and Sturm, J.-E.E. (1992) 'The Case for Central Bank Independence', *Banca Nazionale del Lavoro Quarterly Review* 182, pp. 305–27. Reprinted in M. Parkin (ed.) (1994) *The Theory of Inflation*. Aldershot: Edward Elgar.

De-Long, J. and Summers, L.H. (1992) 'Macroeconomic Policy and Long-Run Growth', *Federal Reserve Bank of Kansas City Economic Review* 77(4).

Department of Social Security (1998) *A New Contract for Welfare: Partnership in Pensions*. London: The Stationery Office.

Department of Social Security (1999a) 'Stakeholder Pensions: Minimum Standards – The Government's Proposals'. Consultation Brief No. 1.

Department of Social Security (1999b) 'Stakeholder Pensions: Employer Access – The Government's Proposals'. Consultation Brief No. 2.

Department of Social Security (1999c) 'Stakeholder Pensions: Clearing Arrangements – The Government's Proposals'. Consultation Brief No. 3.

Department of Social Security (1999d) 'Stakeholder Pensions: Regulation, Advice and Information – The Government's Proposals'. Consultation Brief No. 4.

Department of Social Security (1999e) 'Stakeholder Pensions: Governance – The Government's Proposals'. Consultation Brief No. 5.

Department of Social Security (1999f) 'Stakeholder Pensions: Tax Regime – The Government's Proposals'. Consultation Brief No. 6.

Department of Social Security (2000) 'Darling Announces Key Decisions on Stakeholder Pensions'. DSS press release 00/001.

Dolado, J.J., Gonzalez-Paramo, J.M. and Vinals, J. (1997) 'A Cost-Benefit Analysis of Going from Low Inflation to Price Stability'. Paper presented at the NBER conference on the Costs and Benefits of Achieving Price Stability, Federal Reserve Bank of New York.

Dornbusch, R. (1998) 'Debt and Monetary Policy: The Policy Issues', in G.A. Calvo and M. King (eds), *The Debt Burden and its Consequences for Monetary Policy: Proceedings of a Conference Held by the International Economic Association at the Deutsche Bundesbank, Frankfurt, Germany*. Basingstoke: Macmillan.

Dornbusch, R. and Draghi, M. (eds) (1990) *Public Debt Management: Theory and History*. Cambridge, New York and Melbourne: Cambridge University Press.

Dotsey, M. and Sarte, P.-D. (1997) 'Inflation Uncertainty and Growth in a Simple Monetary Model'. Working Paper No. 97–5, Federal Reserve Bank of Richmond.

Dow, S.C. (1996) 'Why the Banking System Should be Regulated', *Economic Journal* 106, pp. 698–707.

Dupasquier, C. and Ricketts, R. (1997) 'Non-Linearities in the Output–Inflation Relationship – Some More Empirical Evidence'. Bank of Canada Working Paper 98/14.

Economic Policy Committee (2000) 'Progress Report to the ECOFIN Council on the Impact of Aging Populations on Public Pension Systems'. <http://europa.eu.int/comm/economy-finance>

Edey, M. (1994) 'Costs and Benefits of Moving from Low Inflation to Price Stability', *OECD Economic Studies* 23 (Winter).

Eijffinger, S.C.W. and De Haan, J. (1996) 'The Political Economy of Central Bank Independence'. Special Papers in International Economics No. 19, Princeton University.

Eijffinger, S.C.W. and Schaling, E. (1992) 'Central Bank Independence: Criteria and Indices'. Research Memorandum No. 548, Department of Economics, Tilburg University.

Eijffinger, S.C.W. and Schaling, E. (1993) 'Central Bank Independence in Twelve Industrial Countries', *Banca Nazionale del Lavoro Quarterly Review* 184, pp. 1–41.

Englander, A. and Gurney, A. (1994) 'Medium-Term Determinants of OECD Productivity', *OECD Economic Studies* 22.

Feldstein, M. (1996) 'The Costs and Benefits of Going from Low Inflation to Price Stability'. NBER Working Paper No. 5469.

Feldstein, M. (1997) 'The Costs and Benefits of Going from Low Inflation to Price Stability', in C.H. Romer and D.H. Romer (eds), *Reducing Inflation*. Illinois: University of Chicago Press.

Fillion, J.-F. and Tetlow, R. (1994) 'Zero Inflation or Price Level Targeting? Some Answers from Stochastic Simulations on a Small Open-Economy Macro Model', in *Economic Behaviour and Policy Choice Under Price Stability*. Proceedings of a conference held by the Bank of Canada, 1993.

Fischer, S. (1981) 'Towards an Understanding of the Costs of Inflation: II', in *The Costs and Consequences of Inflation*, Carnegie-Rochester Conference Series on Public Policy, North Holland, vol. 15, pp. 5–41.

Fischer, S. (1983) 'Welfare Aspects of Government Issue of Indexed Bonds', in R. Dornbusch and M.H. Simonsen (eds), *Inflation, Debt and Indexation*. Cambridge, MA, and London: MIT Press.

Fischer, S. (1990) 'Rules versus Discretion in Monetary Policy', in B. Friedman and F. Hahn (eds), *Handbook of Monetary Economics*, vol. II. Amsterdam: North-Holland.

Fischer, S. (1993) 'The Role of Macroeconomic Factors in Growth', *Journal of Monetary Economics* 32(3).

Fischer, S. (1994a) 'Modern Central Banking'. Paper prepared for the tercentenary of the Bank of England.

Fischer, S. (1994b) 'Modern Central Banking', in F. Capie, C.A.E. Goodhart and N. Schandt (eds), *The Future of Central Banking*. Cambridge: Cambridge University Press.

Fischer, S. (1996) 'Why are Central Banks Pursuing Long-Run Price Stability?', in *Achieving Price Stability*, Federal Reserve Bank of Kansas City.

Forder, J. (1998) 'Central Bank Independence – Conceptual Clarification and Interim Assessment', *Oxford Economic Papers* 50(3) (July), pp. 307–34.

Fortin, P. (1996) 'The Great Canadian Slump', *Canadian Journal of Economics* 29(4) (November), pp. 761–87.

Fudenberg, D. and Tirole, J. (1991) *Game Theory*. Cambridge, MA: MIT Press.

Fuhrer, J. and Madigan, B. (1997) 'Monetary Policy when Interest Rates are Bounded at Zero', *Review of Economics and Statistics* (November).

Friedman, M. (1968) American Economic Association Presidential Lecture.

Friedman, M. (1977) 'Nobel Lecture: Inflation and Unemployment', *Journal of Political Economy* 85, pp. 451–72.

Fry, M., Goodhart, C. and Almeida, A. (1996) 'Central Banking in Developing Countries: Objectives, Activities and Independence', in M. Fry, C. Goodhart and A. Almeida (eds) *Central Banking in Developing Countries*. London and New York: Routledge, Chapter 2.

Gale, D. (1990) 'The Efficient Design of Public Debt', in R. Dornbusch and M. Draghi (eds), *Public Debt management: Theory and History*. Cambridge, New York and Melbourne: Cambridge University Press, pp. 14–47.

George, E. (1998) Speech to the TUC Congress, 15 September. <http://www.bankofengland.co.uk/speeches/speech23.htm>

George, E. (1999) Speech at the Mansion House, 10 June.

Ghosh, A. and Phillips, S. (1998) 'Warning: Inflation may be Harmful to your Growth', *IMF Staff Papers* 45(4), pp. 672–710.

Giavazzi, F. and Pagano, M. (1990) 'Confidence Crises and Public Debt Management', in R. Dornbusch and M. Draghi (eds), *Public Debt Management: Theory and History*. Cambridge, New York and Melbourne: Cambridge University Press, pp. 125–43.

Giorno et al. (1995) 'Estimating Potential Output, Output Gaps and Structural Budget Balances'. OECD Economic Department Working Papers.

Giovannini, A. (1997) 'Government Debt Management', *Oxford Review of Economic Policy* 13(4) (Winter), pp. 43–52.

Golob, J. (1993) 'Inflation, Inflation Uncertainty, and Relative Price Variability: A Survey'. Research Working Paper 93–15, Federal Reserve Bank of Kansas City.

Government Actuary's Department (1995) 'National Insurance Fund Long-Term Financial Estimates'. Report by the Government Actuary on the Third Quinquennial Review under Section 137 of the Social Security Act 1975.

Gower, L.C.B. (1982) *Review of Investor Protection: A Discussion Document*. London: HMSO.

Gower, L.C.B. (1984) *Review of Investor Protection: Part 1*. London: HMSO.

Grilli, V., Masciandaro, D. and Tabellini, G. (1991) 'Political and Monetary Institutions and Public Financial Policies in the Industrial Countries', *Economic Policy* 13, pp. 341–92.

Grimes, A. (1991) 'The Effects of Inflation on Growth: Some International Evidence', *Weltwirtschaftliches Archive* 127.

Groshen, E.L. and Schweitzer, M.E. (1997) 'Inflation Goals: Guidance from the Labour Market?', *Current Issues in Economics and Finance* 3(15) (December), Federal Reserve Bank of New York.

Group of Seven (1998) 'Statement of G7 Finance Ministers and Central Bank Governors', 3 October, Washington DC, Group of Seven.

Group of Seven (1999a) 'Statement of G7 Finance Ministers and Central Bank Governors', 20 February, Bonn, Group of Seven.

Group of Seven (1999b) 'Strengthening the International Financial Architecture: Report of the G7 Finance Ministers to the Cologne Economic Summit', 20 June, Cologne, Group of Seven.

Group of Seven (2000) 'Poverty Reduction and Economic Development: Report from the G7 Finance Ministers to the Heads of State and Government', 21 July, Okinawa, Group of Seven.

Hadri, K., Lockwood, B. and Maloney, J. (1998) 'Does Central Bank Independence Smooth the Political Business Cycle in Inflation? Some OECD Evidence', *The Manchester School* 66(4), pp. 377–95.

Hall, S. and Yates, A. (1999) 'Fiscal and Monetary Policy: Is There Really a Co-ordination Failure?'. Mimeo, Bank of England.

Havrilesky, T. and Granato, J. (1993) 'Determinants of Inflationary Performance: Corporatist Structures vs Central Bank Autonomy', *Public Choice* 76, pp. 249–61.

Henry, S.G.B., Hall, S.G. and Nixon, J. (1999) 'Inflation Targeting: The Delegation and Coordination of Monetary Policy'. Centre for International Macro-economics Discussion Paper No. 2000-08, University of Oxford.

Hess, G.D. and Morris, C.S. (1996) 'The Long-Run Costs of Moderate Inflation', *Federal Reserve Bank of Kansas City Economic Review* 81(2), pp. 71–88.

HM Treasury (1994) *Better Accounting for the Taxpayer's Money: Resource Accounting and Budgeting in Government*, Cm 2622, July.

HM Treasury (1995a) 'Public Finances and the Cycle'. Occasional Paper.

HM Treasury (1995b) *Better Accounting for the Taxpayer's Money: The Government's Proposals*, Cm 2929, July.

HM Treasury (1997a) *Financial Statement and Budget Report*, July.

HM Treasury (1997b) *Fiscal Policy: Lessons from the Last Economic Cycle*, November.

HM Treasury (1997c) *Pre-Budget Report*, November.

HM Treasury (1997d) *The Public Sector Balance Sheet*, December.

HM Treasury (1998a) *The Code for Fiscal Stability*.

HM Treasury (1998b) *Financial Statement and Budget Report*, March.

HM Treasury (1998c) *Economic and Fiscal Strategy Report*, June.

HM Treasury (1998d) *Fiscal Policy: Current and Capital Spending*, June.

HM Treasury (1998e) *Delivering Economic Stability. Lessons from Macroeconomic Policy Experience*, November.

HM Treasury (1998f) *Pre-Budget Report*, November.

HM Treasury (1998g) *Making Saving Easy*.

HM Treasury (1998h) *Whole of Government Accounts*.

HM Treasury (1999a) *Economic and Fiscal Strategy Report*, 'Budget 99: Building a Stronger Economic Future for Britain', March.

HM Treasury (1999b) *Public Finances and the Cycle*, March.

HM Treasury (2000a) *Debt Management Report* 1999–2000.

HM Treasury (2000b) *Pre-Budget Report 2000*.

HM Treasury (2000c) *Economic and Fiscal Strategy Report*, 'Budget 2000: Prudent for a Purpose: Working for a Stronger and Fairer Britain', March.

HM Treasury (2000d) *Planning Sustainable Public Spending: Lessons from Previous Policy Experience*, November.

HM Treasury (2001) *Economic and Fiscal Strategy Report*, 'Budget 2001: Investing for the Long Term: Building Opportunity and Prosperity for All'.

Holmstrom, B. and Tirole, J. (1998) 'Private and Public Supply of Liquidity, *Journal of Political Economy* 106(1) (February), pp. 1–40.

Inland Revenue (2000) *Inland Revenue Statistics 2000*.

International Monetary Fund (1993) *World Economic Outlook*. Washington, DC: IMF, October.

International Monetary Fund (1996) *World Economic Outlook*. Washington, DC: IMF, May.

International Monetary Fund (1998a) *Code of Good Practices on Fiscal Transparency*. Washington, DC: IMF.

International Monetary Fund (1998b) *Manual on Fiscal Transparency*. Washington, DC: IMF.

International Monetary Fund (1999a) 'IMF Concludes Article IV Consultation with the United Kingdom'. Public Information Notice 99/17.

International Monetary Fund (1999b) 'United Kingdom: Selected Issues'. IMF Staff Country Report No. 99/44.

International Monetary Fund (1999c) *Experimental Report On Transparency Practices: United Kingdom*. Washington DC: IMF.

International Monetary Fund (2001) 'United Kingdom: 2000' Article IV Consultation.

Jarrett, P. and Selody, J. (1982) 'The Productivity–Inflation Nexus in Canada, 1963–79', *Review of Economics and Statistics* 64(3) (August), pp. 361–7.

Jenkins, M. (1996) 'Central Bank Independence and Inflation Performance: Panacea or Placebo?'. Hull Economic Research Paper No. 241, University of Hull.

Johnson, K., Small, D. and Tryon, R. (1999) 'Monetary Policy and Price Stability'. Paper prepared for a conference at the Austrian National Bank, June.

Jordan, T.J. (1997) 'Disinflation Costs, Accelerating Inflation Gains and Central Bank Independence', *Weltwirtschaftliches Archive* 133(1), pp. 1–21.

Judson, R. and Orphanides, A. (1996) 'Inflation, Volatility and Growth'. Federal Reserve Board, Finance and Economics Discussion Series 96–19 (May).

Kahn, S. (1997) 'Evidence of Nominal Wage Stickiness from Microdata', *American Economic Review* 87(5) (December).

Keech, W.R. (1985) 'A Theoretical Analysis of the Case for a Balanced Budget Amendment', *Policy Sciences* 18, pp. 157–68.

Keynes, J.M. (1978) *The Collected Writings of John Maynard Keynes*, vol. XXII, ed. D. Moggridge. Cambridge: Cambridge University Press/Macmillan.

King, M. (1995) 'Credibility and Monetary Policy: Theory and Evidence', *Scottish Journal of Political Economy* 42(1) (February).

King, M. (1999a) Speech given at the Queen's University, Belfast, 17 May. Printed in *Bank of England Quarterly Review* (August).

King, M. (1999b) 'Challenges for Monetary Policy: New and Old'. Paper presented at the symposium 'New Challenges for Monetary Policy' sponsored by the Federal Reserve Bank of Kansas City.

Kohler, H. and Wolfensohn, J. (2000) 'The International Monetary Fund and the World Bank Group: An Enhanced Partnership for Sustainable Growth and Poverty Reduction'. Washington DC: IMF and World Bank, 20 September.

Kohn, D. (2000) 'Report to Non-Executive Directors of the Court of the Bank of England', October.

Krozner, R.S. (1998) 'Global Government Securities Markets: Economics and Politics of Recent Market Microstructure Reforms', in G.A. Calvo and M. King (eds), *The Debt Burden and its Consequences for Monetary Policy: Proceedings of a Conference Held by the International Economic Association at the Deutsche Bundesbank, Frankfurt, Germany*. Basingstoke: Macmillan.

Kydland, F.E. and Prescott, E.C. (1977) 'Rules rather than Discretion: The Inconsistency of Optimal Plans', *Journal of Political Economy* 85(3) (June), pp. 473–92.

Laidler, D. (1997) 'Monetary Policy and Inflation Control in Canada: Editor's Introduction', in D. Laidler (ed.) *Where We Go From Here: Inflation Targets in Canada's Monetary Policy Regime*. Toronto: C.D. Howe Institute.

Lamont, N. (1992) Letter to John Watts, MP, Chairman of the Treasury and Civil Service Select Committee, 8 October.

Lamont, N. (1999) *In Office*. London: Little, Brown and Co.

Laurens, B. and de la Piedra, E.G. (1998) 'Coordination of Monetary and Fiscal Policies'. IMF Working Paper 98/25 (Washington, DC: IMF).

Lawson, N. (1992), *The View from No. 11*. London: Bantam Press.

Laxton, D., Meredith, G. and Rose, D. (1995) 'Asymmetric Effects of Economic Activity on Inflation', *IMF Staff Papers* 42(2).

Layard, R., Nickell, S. and Jackman, P. (1991) *Unemployment: Macroeconomic Performance and the Labour Market*. Oxford: Oxford University Press.

Lebow, D., Roberts, J. and Stockton, D. (1992) 'Understanding the Goal of Price Stability'. Internal Paper, Federal Reserve.

Lee, K. and Ni, S. (1995) 'Inflation Uncertainty and Real Economic Activities', *Applied Economics Letters* 2(11).

Lee, R. and Skinner, J. (1999) 'Will Aging Baby Boomers Bust the Federal Budget?', *Journal of Economic Perspectives* 13(1) (Winter), pp. 117–40.

Levhari, D. and Liviatan, N. (1976) 'Government Intermediation in the Indexed Bonds Market', *American Economic Review* 66(2) (May), pp. 186–92.

Levine, R. and Zervos, S.J. (1993) 'What have we Learned about Policy and Growth from Cross-Country Regressions?', *American Economic Review* 83(2), pp. 426–30.

Llewellyn, D. (1999) 'The Economic Rationale for Financial Regulation'. FSA Occasional Paper No. 1.

Lohmann, S. (1992) 'Optimal Commitment in Monetary Policy: Credibility versus Flexibility', *American Economic Review* 82, pp. 273–86.

Lords Select Committee (1999) Report, July.

Lords Select Committee on the Monetary Policy Committee of the Bank of England (2001) *Report*. House of Lords.

Lucas, R.E. (1976) 'Econometric Policy Evaluation: A Critique'. Carnegie-Rochester Conference Series on Public Policy 1(2).

Lucas, R.E., Jr (1981) 'Discussion of Fischer Paper', in *The Costs and Consequences of Inflation*, Carnegie-Rochester Conference Series on Public Policy, North Holland, vol. 15, pp. 43–52.

Lucas, R.E. and Stokey, N.L. (1983) 'Optimal Fiscal and Monetary Policy in an Economy Without Capital', *Journal of Monetary Economics* 12(1) (July), pp. 55–93.

McCallum, B.T. (1995) 'Two Fallacies Concerning Central Bank Independence', *American Economic Review, Papers and Proceedings* 85, pp. 207–11.

McCallum, B.T. (1997) 'Crucial Issues Concerning Central Bank Independence', *Journal of Monetary Economics* 39(1), pp. 99–112.

McLaughlin, K. (1994) 'Rigid Wages?', *Journal of Monetary Economics* 34, pp. 383–414.

Malvey, P., Archibald, C. and Flynn, S.T. (1995) 'Uniform Price Auctions: Evaluation of the Treasury Experience'. Department of the Treasury photocopy, October.

Mankiw, N.G. (1990) 'A Quick Refresher Course in Macroeconomics'. NBER Working Paper No. 3256.

Marcet, A. (1997) 'Recent Developments on Economic Policy Evaluation: Incomplete Markets and Heterogeneous Agents. Possible Applications to Government Debt Policy'.Department of the Treasury photocopy, April.

Marcet, A., Sargent, T.J. and Seppälä, J. (1997) 'Optimal Taxation without State-Contingent Debt'. CEPR/ESRC Workshop on Optimal Fiscal Policy, April.

Marcet, A. and Scott, A. (1999) 'Debt Limits, Deficit Ceilings and Debt Management'. Department of the Treasury photocopy.

Marr, A. (1995) *Ruling Britannia: The Failure and Future of British Democracy*. London: Michael Joseph.

Miles, D. and Scott, A. (2002). *Macroeconomics*. New York: John Wiley & Sons.

Minford, P. (1995) 'Time-Inconsistency, Democracy and Optimal Contingent Rules', *Oxford Economic Papers* 47, pp. 195–210.

Missale, A. (1997a) 'Managing the Public Debt: The Optimal Taxation Approach', *Journal of Economic Surveys* 11(3) (September), pp. 235–65.

Missale, A. (1997b) 'Tax Smoothing with Index-Linked Bonds: A Case Study of Italy and the United Kingdom', In M. de Cecco, L. Pecchi and G. Piga (eds), *Managing Public Debt: Index-Linked Bonds in Theory and Practice*. Cheltenham, and Brookfield, WI: Edward Elgar.

Missale, A. (1999) *Public Debt Mangement*. Oxford: Oxford University Press.

Missale, A. and Blanchard, O.J. (1994) 'The Debt Burden and Debt Maturity', *American Economic Review* 84(1) (March), pp. 309–19.

Modigliani, F. and Sutch, R. (1966) 'Innovations in Interest Rate Policy', *American Economic Review* 56 (May), pp. 178–97.

Mosley, L. (1997) 'International Financial Markets and Government Economic Policy: The Importance of Financial Market Operations'. Unpublished paper prepared for the 1997 Annual Meeting of the American Political Science Association, Duke University, Durham, NC, August.

Nandi, S. (1997) 'Treasury Auctions: What do the Recent Models and Results Tell Us?', *Federal Reserve Bank of Atlanta Economic Review*, pp. 4–15.

Nars, K. (1997) *Excellence in Debt Management: The Strategies of Leading International Borrowers*. London: Euromoney Publications.

Nordhaus, W.D. (1994) 'Policy Games: Coordination and Independence in Monetary and Fiscal Policies', *Brookings Papers on Economic Activity* 2, pp. 139–216.

Oatley, T. (1999) 'Central Bank Independence and Inflation: Corporatism, Partisanship, and Alternative Indices of Central Bank Independence', *Public Choice* 98(3–4) (March), pp. 399–413.

Odling-Smee, J. and Riley, C. (1985) 'Approaches to the PSBR', *National Institute Economic Review* (August).

O'Donnell, G. and Bhundia, A. (forthcoming) 'UK Policy Coordination: The Importance of Institutional Design', *Fiscal Studies*.

Office for National Statistics (1998) *National Accounts: Concepts, Sources and Methods*. London: ONS.

Office for National Statistics (2000) *United Kingdom National Accounts: The Blue Book 2000*. London: ONS.

Organisation for Economic Cooperation and Development (1995) *Economic Outlook*. Paris: OECD, June.

Organisation for Economic Cooperation and Development (1996) 'Ageing Populations, Pension Systems and Government Budgets: Simulations for 20 OECD Countries'. Economics Department Working Paper No. 168.

Organisation for Economic Cooperation and Development (2000) *OECD Economic Surveys: United Kingdom*. Paris: OECD (June).

Orphanides, A. and Wieland, V. (1998) 'Price Stability and Monetary Policy Effectiveness when Nominal Interest Rates are Bounded at Zero'. Finance and Economics Discussion Series 98–3, Board of Governors of the Federal Reserve System.

Parkin, M. (1994) *The Theory of Inflation*. Aldershot: Edward Elgar.

Parkin, M. (1997) 'Monetary Policy and the Future of Inflation Control in Canada: An Overview of the Issues', in D. Laidler (ed.) *Where We Go From Here: Inflation Targets in Canada's Monetary Policy Regime*. Toronto: C.D. Howe Institute.

Pecchi, L. and Piga, G. (1995) 'Does Debt Management Matter? A Market-Oriented Response from the Italian Case', *Economic and Financial Review* 2(1) (Spring), pp. 29–36.

Peled, D. (1985) 'Stochastic Inflation and Government Provision of Indexed Bonds', *Journal of Monetary Economics* 15(3) (May), pp. 291–308.

Persson, M. (1997) 'Index-Linked Bonds: The Swedish Experience', in M. de Cecco, L. Pecchi and G. Piga (eds), *Managing Public Debt: Index-Linked Bonds in Theory and Practice*. Cheltenham, and Brookfield, WI: Edward Elgar.

Persson, T. and Tabellini, G. (1993) 'Designing Institutions for Monetary Stability', Carnegie-Rochester Conference Series on Public Policy 39, pp. 53–84.

Piga, G. (1998) 'In Search of an Independent Province for the Treasuries: How Should Public Debt be Managed?', *Journal of Economics and Business* 50, pp. 257–75.

Portillo, M. (2000) *Bank of England Commission Report*. http://www.conservatives.com/pdf/bankofengland.pdf

Posen, A. (1995) 'Declarations Are Not Enough: Financial Sector Sources of Central Bank Independence', in NBER, *Macroeconomics Annual*. Cambridge, MA: MIT Press.

Public Service Agreement (PSA). White Paper, Cm 4808, July 2000.

Red Book (1997) July.

Reifschneider, D. and Williams, J. (1998) 'Three Lessons for Monetary Policy in a Low Inflation Era'. Finance and Economics Discussion Paper No. 44. Board of Governors of the Federal Reserve System.

Rickets, N. and Rose, D. (1995) 'Inflation, Learning and Monetary Policy Regimes in G7 Countries'. Bank of Canada Working Paper No. 95–6.

Robson, W.B.P. and Scarth, W.M. (1997) *Out Front on Federal Debt Reduction: Programs and Payoffs*. Toronto: C.D. Howe Institute.

Rogoff, K. (1985) 'The Optimal Degree of Commitment to an Intermediate Monetary Target', *Quarterly Journal of Economics* 110, pp. 1169–90.

Romer, C.D. and Romer, D.H. (1998) 'Monetary Policy and the Well-Being of the Poor'. NBER Working Paper No. 6793.

Romer, D. (2001) *Advanced Macroeconomics*, 2nd edition. New York: McGraw-Hill.

Romer, P. (1986) 'Increasing Returns and Long-Run Growth', *Journal of Political Economy* (October).

Sachs, J. (1989) 'Social Conflict and Populist Policies in Latin America'. NBER Working Paper No. 2897.

Sarel, M. (1996) 'Non-Linear Effects of Inflation on Economic Growth', *IMF Staff Papers* 43 (March), pp. 199–215.

Scott, A. (1997) 'Does Tax Smoothing Imply Smooth Taxes?'. CEPR/ESRC Workshop on Optimal Fiscal Policy, April.

Sill, D.K. (1994) 'Managing the Public Debt', *Federal Reserve Bank of Philadelphia Business Review* 0(4) (July–August), pp. 3–13.

Simpson, D. (1996) *Regulating Pensions: Too Many Rules, Too Little Competition.* Hobart Paper No. 131. London: Institute of Economic Affairs.

Smith, J. (1998) 'The Cost of Low Inflation? Nominal Wage Rigidity in the UK'. Warwick University.

Smyth, D.J. and Hsing, Y. (1995) 'In Search of an Optimal Debt Ratio for Economic Growth', *Contemporary Economic Policy* 13, pp. 51–9.

Spiegel, M.M. (1998) 'Central Bank Independence and Inflation Expectations: Evidence from British Index-Linked Gilts', *Federal Reserve Bank of San Francisco Economic Review*, pp. 3–14.

Stanners, W. (1993) 'Is Low Inflation an Important Condition of High Growth?', *Cambridge Journal of Economics* 17.

Stiglitz, J.E. (1994) *Whither Socialism?* Cambridge, MA: MIT Press.

Stiglitz, J. and Weiss, A. (1981) 'Credit Rationing in Markets with Imperfect Information', *American Economic Review* 71(3) (June).

Summers, L. (1991) 'How Should Long-Term Monetary Policy be Determined?', *Journal of Money, Credit and Banking* 23(3), Part 2.

Svensson, L.E.O. (1995) 'Optimal Inflation Targets, Conservative Central Banks, and Linear Inflation Contracts'. Working Paper, Stockholm University.

Swinburne, M. and Castello-Branco, M. (1991) 'Central Bank Independence: Issues and Experience'. IMF Working Paper No. 58.

Tavelli, H., Tullio, G. and Spinelli, F. (1998) 'The Evolution of European Central Bank Independence: An Updating of the Masciandaro and Spinelli Index', *Scottish Journal of Political Economy* 45(3), pp. 341–4.

Tobin, J. (1963) 'An Essay on Principles of Debt Management', in *Fiscal and Debt Management Policies.* Englewood Cliffs, NJ: Prentice-Hall, pp. 143–218.

Tödter, K.H. and Ziebarth, G. (1997) 'Price Stability vs Low Inflation in Germany: An Analysis of Costs and Benefits'. NBER Working Paper No. 6170.

Townend, J. (1997) 'Index-Linked Government Securities: The UK Experience', in M. de Cecco, L. Pecchi and G. Piga (eds), *Managing Public Debt: Index-Linked Bonds in Theory and Practice.* Cheltenham, and Brookfield, WI: Edward Elgar.

Treasury Committee (1998) *Sixth Report*, June.

Treasury Committee (1999) *Eighth Report*, July.

Treasury Committee (2001) *Ninth Report: The Monetary Policy Committee – an End of Term Report.* House of Commons.

Turner, D. (1995) 'Speed Limit and Asymmetric Inflation Effects from the Output Gap in the Major Seven Economies', *OECD Economic Studies*.

Vahey, S.P. (1994) 'The Optimal Structure of Government Debt.' Bank of England photocopy, December.

Van den Noord, P. (2000) 'The Size and Role of Automatic Fiscal Stabilizers in the 1990s and Beyond'. OECD Working Paper 230, January.

Viard, A.D. (1993) 'The Welfare Gain from the Introduction of Indexed Bonds', *Journal of Money, Credit and Banking* 25(3) (August), Part 2, pp. 612–28.

Vickrey, W. (1961) 'Counterspeculation, Auctions and Competitive Sealed Tenders', *Journal of Finance* (March), pp. 8–37.

Virley, S. and Hurst, M. (1995) 'Public Finances and the Cycle'. HM Treasury Occasional Paper No. 4, September.

Walsh, C.E. (1995) 'Central Bank Independence and the Costs of Disinflation in the EC', in B. Eichengreen, J. Frieden and J. von Haged (eds), *Monetary and Fiscal Policy in an Integrated Europe*. Berlin, Heidelberg and New York: Springer-Verlag, pp. 12–37.

West, P. (1998) 'Improving the Non-Financial Balance Sheets', ONS *Economic Trends* (November).

West, P. and Clifton-Fearnside, A. (1999) 'Improving the Non-Financial Balance Sheets and Capital Stock Estimates', ONS *Economic Trends* (November).

Yates, A. (1998) 'Downward Nominal Rigidity and Monetary Policy'. Bank of England Working Paper No. 83 (August).

Zee, H.H. (1988) 'The Sustainability and Optimality of Government Debt', *IMF Staff Papers* 35(4), pp. 658–85.

Index

Compiled by Sue Carlton

Action Against Illegal Drugs 238
Ahluwalia, Montek Singh 312–13
Akerloff, G. 79
Al-Marhubi, F. 69
Alesina, A. 9, 101
Annually Managed Expenditure
    (AME) 191, 236, 241, 246, 247
assets and liabilities 263–4, 265–6,
    270, 271–2, 278
    changes in value 272, 274
    valuation of 275
Australia
    balancing budget 166
    fiscal policy 137
    government debt 180
automatic stabilisers 158, 186, 187,
    188, 196, 218–19

Bakhshi, H. 65, 78, 80, 81
balance sheets 263–4
    see also public sector balance sheet
Ball, L. 78, 80
Balls, Ed 27, 85
Bank of England 18, 28, 117, 340
    built-in flexibility 96, 100
    Court of Directors 54, 55
    expert independent decisions 96,
        99–100
    flexibility 97
    generational accounts 162
    independence 85, 91–3, 96–100,
        103–8, 295, 338
    and inflation targets 347
    relationship with Treasury 91–2,
        96, 97–8, 105
    role of 17, 45, 50
    single symmetric inflation target
        96, 97–9, 105
    strategic ownership 96, 97
    transparency and accountability
        57, 97, 100, 105
    see also central bank independence;
        Monetary Policy Committee
Bank of England Act 44, 55, 71, 105

banks
    failure 112–13
    regulation of 113–14, 117
Barclay's Basix survey 342
Barro, R.J. 41, 65, 88
benchmark bonds 285, 286, 297
Bhundia, Ashok 85
Black, R. 81
Blanchard, O.J. 294
Blinder, A.S. 88
Bohn, H. 293
Bonato, L. 65
boom-bust cycles 10, 19, 31, 45
    see also economic cycle; recession
Boskin Report 76–7
Brazil 301
Bretton Woods system 35, 315, 318
British Chambers of Commerce
    Survey 208
British Household Panel Study 80
Broad Economic Policy Guidelines
    (BEPG) 322, 327, 329
Brown, Gordon, Chancellor of the
    Exchequer
    on financial crises 307
    on financial product standards 126
    on IMF and World Bank 314
    and independence of Bank of
        England 85, 91, 338
    on policy coordination 351
    remit to MPC 55–7
    on stability 29
Bruno, M. 64
Budget
    baseline projections 190
    Budget 2000 195
    Budget 2001 182, 183, 195
    fiscal policy decisions 189–92, 199
    and fiscal stance 186–7, 190
    and interest rate changes 25, 26
    pipeline measures 190
    see also Budget projections; *Pre-
        Budget Report*

budget deficits 166, 192, 198, 222
Budget projections 19, 20, 106–7, 187,
    188, 350–1
  cautious approach 200
  and debt management 198
  and net debt and net worth 195–6,
    349
  and uncertainty 189, 199
  see also Pre-Budget Report,
    projections
building societies, regulation of 114
Buiter, W. 167, 278
Bundesbank 37, 42, 86, 94–5, 97
Bureau of Labor Statistics, US 77

Canada
  Debt Reduction Plan 180
  nominal rigidities 81
capital market liberalisation 35, 306–7
Capital Markets Consultative Group
    (CMCG) 305
Capital Modernisation Fund 236
capital spending, bias against 160,
    181, 183, 231, 233, 236–7, 240
Card, D. 79
Cardarelli, R. 258
Cardiff Process 322
CAT standards 126–7, 128, 130, 131
central bank
  and interest rates 82
  see also Bank of England; European
    Central Bank; Monetary Policy
    Committee
central bank independence 40–2, 49,
    295, 319
  arguments for 86–91
  and inflation 88–91, 96
  models of 94–100
  and policy coordination 101–8
  UK model 96–100
Chowdhury, A.R. 60
Clarke, Kenneth 355n
Code for Fiscal Stability 105, 132, 133,
    144–52, 153–4
  and accounting practice 140–1,
    147, 151, 242
  and cyclical adjustment 203, 218
  debt management 143–4, 146, 147,
    151
  and distribution of reports 144, 152

and economic and fiscal
    projections 142–3, 148, 149–51
  and fiscal principles 135, 138–40,
    145–8, 162
  and fiscal reporting 141–2, 147–9,
    191
  and fiscal rules 155, 158
  and intergenerational equity 249
  key provisions 138
  and long-term fiscal projections
    185, 253
  and National Audit Office 143
  purpose of 144–5
  rationale for 136–7
  and referral to Select Committee
    144, 151
  setting objectives 140, 146–7
Code of Good Practices on Fiscal
    Transparency, IMF 137
Colletti, D. 81
Cologne Process 322
compensation, and moral hazard 113,
    117
Comprehensive Spending Review
    (CSR) 233, 236–7, 244, 247, 363
Comptroller and Auditor General 151,
    154
Confederation of British Industry
    (CBI) 205, 208
consumer spending
  changes in 186
  and sustainability 10
Contingent Credit Lines (CCLs) 306
Convergence Programmes 329
corporation tax 219, 221
CPI (US consumer price index) 76
Crawford, A. 80
credibility 4, 27, 34–43, 93, 96, 136
  definition of 34
  discretion 34, 39
  and inflation expectations 8, 9, 12
  loss of 36–7
  and sound long-term policies 27,
    35–8
  and suspicion 39, 41
  through fixed rules 34–5
  through maximum transparency
    38–40, 42
  through pre-commitment 40–3
  see also transparency

credit unions, regulation of 114
Criminal Justice System 238
crises *see* financial crises
Cruickshank, Don 122
Cukierman, A. 88
current and capital spending 159–60,
    162, 183, 231, 240, 241, 246
    defining 166–7
current spending and revenue 169,
    193, 195
    and depreciation 185
CWN index 88, 89
cyclical adjustment 22, 199, 201, 203
    and fiscal indicators 23, 222–4
    methodology 219–22; new 'ready
        reckoners' 220, 221

Dale, S. 291
Davies, Sir Howard 311
De Haan, J. 88
debt management 152, 153, 199, 272,
    280–98
    asymmetric information 282–3
    auctions 285, 286, 287, 296
    cost minimisation 281–7; and risk
        281–6, 295, 296
    debt maturity 290, 294
    debt servicing costs 281–93, 294,
        296
    and fiscal rules 292
    gains from liquidity 297
    imperfect financial markets 284–6
    improving policy 296–8
    index linked debt 289, 291, 292–9
    and investor confidence 294, 296
    issuance policy 287, 296
    liquid secondary market 285, 295
    and missing markets 283–4
    and monetary and fiscal policy
        282–3, 285
    nominal debt 289, 291, 294, 295
    'preferred habitats' 284, 287
    reducing uncertainty 285
    refinancing 294, 297
    and risk 288–93, 294, 297; defini-
        tions of 291–2; optimal taxation
        approach 288–91, 292, 295
    segmented markets 284
    state-contingent debt 288–9

and tax smoothing 169, 282, 291,
    293
and time consistency 293–1
transaction costs 297–8
and transparency 287, 295
see also public debt; public sector
    net borrowing (PSNB)
Debt Management Office (DMO) 50,
    52, 287
Debt and Reserves Management Report
    138, 143–4, 151, 153, 363
defence spending 258
Delors Report 218, 318
Denmark 108
Departmental Expenditure Limits
    (DEL) 235, 236, 241, 246, 247, 364
Departmental Investment Strategies
    (DIS) 236, 241, 247
deposit insurance, and moral hazard
    113
depreciation 185, 239, 247
deregulation 31
discretion 35, 36, 158
    and cheating 41, 42
    private 33, 34
    and transparency 39
disinflation costs 65, 73, 78–80, 81–2
Dupasquier, C. 79
dynamic efficiency 174–5

Easterly, W. 64
ECOFIN 318, 319, 322, 324, 325,
    327–31
economic cycle
    and debt interest 226
    defining 164
    estimating 219, 220–2
    estimation results 225–9
    and fiscal rules 218, 219
    Government expenditure and
        revenue 205
    measuring 204–18
    negative impact of 29, 92–3
    and policy coordination 349
    and setting fiscal policy 18–19, 135
    short-term effects of 203–4, 218
    symmetry and asymmetry of 164
    see also boom-bust cycle; cyclical
        adjustment

Economic and Fiscal Strategy Report (EFSR) 133, 135, 153, 185, 252
  long-term projections 142, 148–9, 253–8
economic growth
  and Budget decisions 189
  forecasting errors 18, 19
  and price stability 45
  stable levels of 4, 10, 25, 28–9, 139, 353
  and sustainability 14, 19, 22, 182, 261
Economic and Monetary Union (EMU) 37, 76, 159, 318
  and central bank independence 86
  characteristics of euro-area 321–2
  convergence criteria 319
  Convergence Programmes 329
  and current macroeconomic environment 322
  Eurogroup 330
  and exchange rate policy 330–1
  and fiscal policy 327–30; excessive deficit procedure 327–8, 329
  Maastricht criteria 318–20, 321
  and member states' national legislation 320
  and monetary policy 323–7
  progress towards 318–22
  timetable 319–20
  UK policy on 320
economic policy
  and accountability 18, 28, 49
  and, institutional changes 28, 30, 41–2
  and clear objectives 12–13, 23, 41
  decision making 17–8, 28
  employment and economic opportunities 27, 28–9, 30, 35, 44
  fixed rules 28, 32–3, 34–5
  and globalisation 35
  governments cheating 33–4, 35, 40, 41
  and imperfect information 38–40
  role of government 29, 32
  and stability 27, 28–9, 30
  supply-side barriers to growth 27, 29–30

  see also fiscal policy; macroeconomic policy; monetary policy
economic shocks *see* shocks
Ecuador 309
education
  and ageing population 258
  and labour productivity 215
  spending on 167, 258, 259
Eijffinger, S.C.W. 88
employment
  and inflation 10–12, 28–9, 32, 47–8
  and labour productivity 215, 217, 250
  and monetary policy 68
  and population growth 212–14
  and potential output 212–15, 217, 218
  stable levels of 4, 10, 28–9
  working-age population 212, 213, 215, 250
  see also labour market participation; unemployment
End-Year Flexibility (EYF) system 232, 247
Eurogroup 330
Europe
  interest rates 37
  variations in economic policy 36
  see also European Union
European Central Bank (ECB) 76, 86, 95, 317, 319, 321
  exchange rate policy 330–1
  functions of 324–5
  and monetary policy within EMU 326
  organisational structure 323–5
  reporting requirements 325
  see also European System of Central Banks (ESCB)
European Commission 318, 325, 326, 327–8, 329
European Investment Bank 328
European Monetary Institute (EMI) 318, 319–20
European System of Accounts (ESA) 204, 219, 264
European System of Central Banks (ESCB) 319, 320, 323–5
  objectives 325–7, 331

European Union
  Broad Economic Policy Guidelines
    (BEPG) 322, 327, 329
  HICP (Harmonised Index of
    Consumer Prices) 75–6, 83, 322
  macroeconomic policy framework
    317–31; objectives 317–18
  old-age dependency ratio 250
  see also Economic and Monetary
    Union (EMU); Stability and
    Growth Pact (SGP)
Eurostat 75
Eurosystem 323, 324
excessive deficit procedure 327–8, 329
  sanctions 329–30
Exchange Rate Mechanism (ERM) 31,
    34, 37, 318
  departure from 5, 41
exchange rates
  and German reunification 34
  targets 31–3
  Thailand 37

Feldstein, M. 65
Fillion, J.-F. 73–4
Finance Act (1998) 132, 133, 135,
    152–4
financial crises 36, 300–1
  bail-out by financial institutions 40
  crisis management 307–9; role of
    official sector 307; role of private
    sector 308–9
  crisis prevention 302–7
  debt reduction 309
  debt restructuring 309
  effects of 36–7, 301
  factors 301–2
  see also international financial
    architecture reform
financial deregulation 31
financial regulation 110–31
  appeals tribunal 124
  bank failures 112–13
  compensation schemes 116–17, 124
  and competition 122, 125
  economic rationale for 111
  employees and controllers 124
  fines for market abuse 124

  history of 117–20
  and information to consumers
    111–13, 114
  objectives of 120–2
  ombudsman 124
  polarisation 116
  product standards 126–30
  scope of 113–17, 123
  single regulator 120–1, 123, 132
  whistle-blowing 125
  see also financial services; Financial
    Services Authority (FSA)
Financial Reporting Advisory Board
    (FRAB) 244
Financial Sector Assessment
    Programme (FSAP) 304, 315
financial services
  commission 129
  consumer advice 129
  consumers' problems 128–30
  and market confidence 121, 122
  product charges 129
  promotion 125
  public awareness 120, 121
  see also financial regulation
Financial Services Act (1988) 118
Financial Services Authority (FSA) 50,
    55, 110, 111, 113–15, 117
  as banking supervisor 113–14, 120
  and collective investment schemes
    116
  and employees and controllers 124
  flexible rule-making powers 120,
    123, 131
  and insolvency 125
  listing authority 125
  and Lloyd's insurance market 125
  and mortgage loans 123
  objectives 121–5
  and SROs 115
Financial Services and Markets Act
    (FSMA) 110, 114, 115, 116,
    120–5
Financial Stability Forum (FSF) 309–11
*Financial Statement and Budget Report
    (FSBR)* 19, 138, 140, 141–2, 148,
    153, 222, 364
  pipeline measures 190

fiscal code *see* Code for Fiscal
  Stability
fiscal indicators 270–1
  cyclically adjusted 222–4
  see also fiscal policy, key fiscal
    aggregates; public sector net
    borrowing (PSNB); surplus on
    current budget
fiscal loosening 25, 135, 156, 187, 188
fiscal policy
  abbreviations 200
  accountability 136, 157
  accounting practice 140–1
  analysing performance 192–9
  cautious approach to 199, 217
  choices and trade-offs 42
  and clear objectives 23
  coordination with monetary policy
    4, 23–5, 49–50, 101–8, 349, *see
    also* policy coordination
  credibility 136, 156–7, 181
  cyclical adjustment 201, 203
  debt management 138, 139, 140,
    198, 272, 289
  and economic cycle 19, 22–3, 142,
    149, 185, 189
  and efficiency 135, 139–40, 145,
    146
  European commitments 142, 149,
    150, 159, 178, 193, 198–9
  external scrutiny 182
  and fairness 135, 139, 145, 146,
    162, 192–5
  financing 196–8
  fiscal reporting 141–2, 153–4, 183
  and fiscal rules 189
  flow measures 201
  forecasting expenditures and
    revenues 22, 150
  and Government's financing
    requirement 193, 196, 198
  history of 18–26
  impact on economy 185–6, 196,
    270
  and instability 18–19, 25
  and institutional mechanisms 42–3
  inter-generational impact 134, 142,
    146, 149, 270

key fiscal aggregates 182–8, 189,
    204
  long-term strategy 142, 149
  and long-term sustainability
    249–62
  and medium-term objectives 183–5
  and Monetary Policy Committee
    (MPC) 190
  and net worth 272, 277
  new framework 132–54, 157,
    182–202, 242, 347, 353
  objectives 5, 132, 133–5, 140
  past failure of 156
  principles 133, 135, 138–40, 152–3
  and public sector balance sheet
    270–4, 278–9
  and responsibility 135, 139, 143,
    145, 146
  rules 30, 132, 135–3, 140
  short-term outlook 137, 138, 141,
    142, 149
  short-term political pressures 157
  short-term stance 185–8, 193
  solvency 170
  and stability 134–6, 139, 145, 146,
    152–4, 182
  stock measures 201
  supporting monetary policy 135,
    158, 188, 196
  sustainability 162, 170–3, 185, 193,
    195–6, 249–62, 270–1
  and transparency 135, 136–7,
    138–9, 143, 145, 199
  and uncertainty 22
  see also economic policy
fiscal rules 155–81
  and bias against capital spending
    160, 181
  and Budget decisions 189, 199
  current and capital spending
    159–60
  and debt management 292
  and economic cycle 218, 219
  and European commitments 159
  and flexibility 93–4, 157–8
  and long-term projections 254
  and public spending 230, 233
  rationale 156–9

and Resource Accounting and
  Budgeting (RAB) 248
and sound public finances 181
and whole public sector 158
see also golden rule; sustainable
  investment rule
fiscal stance 185–8
  and Budget 186–7, 190
  changes in 134, 186, 187
fiscal tightening 108, 158, 160, 183,
  187–8, 349
Fischer, S. 41, 103
flow measures 201
foreign-currency debt 198, 289–90,
  291, 294, 296
France
  and ageing population 262
  real interest rates 83
Friedman, Milton 30, 31, 33, 34
friendly societies, regulation of 114
Fuhrer, J. 81

G7 303, 304, 310
  1998 Declaration 299, 300
  Cologne Report (1999) 305, 307,
    308
  Okinawa report (2000) 313–14
G20 314
Gale, D. 284
GDP
  and low inflation 65–7
  projections 20, 149
GDP deflator 75
general government debt 168
  gross 150, 159, 193
general government financial balance
  159
general government financial deficit
  150, 193
Generally Accepted Accounting
  Practice (GAAP) 244
generational accounts 162, 185, 193,
  258–9
generational fairness 162, 169, 181,
  185, 249
  and public borrowing 169, 178,
    181, 192
  see also golden rule

George, Eddie, Governor of Bank of
  England 47–8, 55, 98–9, 351
Germany
  and ageing population 262
  and budget targets 166
  generational policy 259
  interest rates 83, 340–2
  old-age dependency ratio 250
  pensions 253
  reunification 34, 37, 94–5
Ghosh, A. 64
gilts 144, 151, 198, 286, 287, 344
Gini coefficients 69
global capital markets, power of 35–6
global economy
  crisis management 307–5
  crisis prevention 302–7
  and domestic policy 302
  financial crises 300–1
  and free capital movement 306–7
  global economic governance 311–15
  and IFIs 311–12
  instability of 299, 353
  international cooperation 309–11
  and need for reform 300–1
  see also globalisation; international
    financial architecture reform
global fixed exchange rates 35
globalisation 35, 309
  growth of international trade 35
  and labour markets 35
  see also global economy
GMT index 88, 90
goal independence 103
golden rule 135, 140, 159–67, 170,
  181, 184, 347
  and cautious approach 200
  current and capital spending
    159–60
  and depreciation 248
  and economic cycle 160, 169
  and generational fairness 162, 181,
    185
  implementing 164
  and net worth 272, 279
  and sound public finances 195
  Surplus on Current Budget 204
  see also sustainable investment rule
Gordon, D. 41, 88

Gower, L.C.B. 118
Greece, and single currency 322
Greenspan, Alan 86, 94
Grilli, V. 88
Grimes, A. 63

Hall, S. 104
Harmonised Index of Consumer
    Prices *see* HICP
Harrison, A. 80
health services 249, 252, 258, 259,
    262
    and ageing population 252, 258,
        260, 261
    reforms 266
    see also public services; public
        spending
Heavily Indebted Poor Countries
    (HIPC) Initiative 315
heritage assets 265
Hess, G.D. 64
HICP (Harmonised Index of
    Consumer Prices) 75–6, 83, 322
    exclusions 76
Highly Leveraged Institutions (HLIs)
    311
HP filter (Hodrick Prescott) 207
Hsing, Y. 175
Hyslop, D. 79
hysteresis effects 31, 78–80

Individual Savings Accounts (ISAs)
    110, 126, 127
Indonesia 300
inequality, and inflation 68–70
inflation 5–14
    anticipated 59–60
    and central bank independence
        88–91, 96
    costs of 60–1, 67, 73
    and ECB monetary policy 326
    expectations 8, 9, 12, 46, 342–4
    'front-end loading' 59
    and growth and employment
        10–12, 28–9, 32, 47–8, 63–7
    high 4, 5, 6, 10, 45
    independent forecast of 344, 345

low 28–9, 31–2, 45, 86–8; benefits
    of 58–70, 73, 78; disinflation
    costs 65, 73, 77–80, 81–2; and
    GDP 65–7; menu cost savings
    65; and poverty 67–70; and real
    interest rates 80–1; welfare gains
    60, 65, 67
'menu' costs 59, 65
and money supply 32
and new monetary policy
    framework 332–49
and output gap 205–6, 337
and potential output 204–6
and prices 65, 72–4
public perception of 344, 347
'shoe-leather' costs 59, 66
and 'speed limits' 206
and tax 59–60, 65, 66
UK's record 4, 5, 6, 8–12, 353
unanticipated 60
and unemployment 10–12, 31, 33,
    42, 80, 87–8, 98, 215
variable 4, 5, 7, 45, 48; and
    inflation rate levels 5, 7, 60–1,
    62
and wages 80–1
Inflation Report 41, 51, 52, 54, 55, 57,
    107
inflation targets 31–2, 44–8, 56–7, 70,
    71–84
    and credibility 47, 79
    deviation from 48, 78
    and economic shocks 46, 48, 78
    and intermediate targets 32, 46, 72
    international comparison of 84
    and low inflation 78–83
    need for 72–4
    performance against 333, 338
    point targets *v.* ranges 77–8
    price index measurement bias 76–7
    and price indices 74–6
    and price level targets 72–3
    setting 76–83, 105–6
    symmetric 47–8, 78, 83, 96, 97, 105
    see also Monetary Policy
        Committee; price stability
Information and Communications
    Technology (ICT) 215
instrument independence 103

insurance companies, regulation of
   114–15, 117
interest rates
   and Bank of England independence
      86
   and debt management 281, 286, 290
   and economic cycles 29
   Europe 37
   and fiscal policy 25
   long-term differentials 340–2, 344
   and monetary policy 12, 18, 19
   and output gap 14, 15, 19, 25, 335,
      336
   post-budget changes 25, 26
   real 82–3
   risk premium 173
   set by Monetary Policy Committee
      49
   UK base rates 16
   variable 14
   see also Monetary Policy
      Committee
international exchange rate system
      330
international financial architecture
      reform 299–316
   and capital flows 306–7, 309–10,
      311, 314
   contingent credit line 305–2
   crisis management 307–9
   crisis prevention 302–7, 310
   enhanced international surveil-
      lance 302–5
   Financial Stability Forum (FSF)
      309–11
   and global economic governance
      311–15
   and Highly Leveraged Institutions
      (HLIs) 311
   international codes and standards
      303–5, 306
   international cooperation in
      financial sector 309–11
   market-based approaches 305
   Multilateral Development Banks
      (MDBs) 313–14
   need for 300–2
   objectives 300
   and offshore financial centres 311

   and poverty reduction 313–14
   and stability 299, 309–11
   and transparency 302, 303–4, 305
   see also financial crises
International Financial Institutions
      (IFIs) 311–15
   bail-out role 40
   cooperation between IMF and
      World Bank 314–15
   transparency and accountability
      312–13
International Monetary and Financial
      Committee (IMFC) 303, 309
International Monetary Fund (IMF)
      49, 121, 299
   bailing-out role 40
   cooperation with World Bank
      313–15
   and financial crises 300–1, 302,
      307, 309
   Independent Evaluation Office
      312–13
   and international financial archi-
      tecture reform 304–5, 306, 307,
      310
   International Monetary and
      Financial Committee (IMFC)
      303, 309
   and public debt 178
   safeguarding use of resources 313
   and transparency 28, 137, 312–13
   on UK monetary policy 353
investment 161, 215, 231
   and economic cycles 29
   and inflation 45
   long-term projections 255
   risk sharing between generations
      284
   see also debt management
investment business
   appointed representatives 116
   collective schemes 116
   compensation schemes 116
   failure of 118
   information to consumers 116,
      129–30
   regulation of 115–18, 124
   self-regulating organisations 115,
      116, 118–19, 125

investment exchanges 117
Investment Management Regulatory
    Organisation (IMRO) 115, 118
Ireland 108
Italy, pensions 253

Japan
    and ageing population 262
    and budget targets 166
    generational policy 259
    old-age dependency ratio 250

Kalman filter 207
Keech, W.R. 157
Keynes, J.M. 67–8
King, M. 73
King, Mervyn 17, 33
Kohler, Horst 314
Kohn, Don 107–8
Korea 300
Kydland, F.E. 86, 88

labour costs 81
    see also nominal rigidities; wages
labour market participation
    effects of 257
    long-term projections 255, 258
    raising 261
    see also employment
labour productivity
    and employment rate 215, 217
    outlook for 215–14
    raising 261
Laidler, D. 80
Lamont, Norman 355n
Lawson, Nigel 355n
Laxton, D. 79
Lee, R. 252
Levine, R. 64
liquid financial assets 271
Lloyd's insurance market 125
Local Authorities
    balance sheets 275
    net worth 266
    and PSAs 234
London International Financial
    Futures and Options Exchange
    (LIFFE) 117
London Stock Exchange (LSE) 117, 125

long-term fiscal projections 142, 162,
    185, 196, 253–8, 348
    baseline projections 190, 255, 256
    economic parameters 254–5
    and uncertainty 170, 189
    see also Budget projections; genera-
        tional accounts; *Pre-Budget
        Report*, projections
Lucas, R.E. 288
Luxembourg Process 322

Maastricht deficit 198
Maastricht Treaty 86, 95, 159
McCallum, B.T. 88
McLaughlin, K. 80
macroeconomic policy 25, 156
    credibility 28, 34–43, 93, 109
    and economic shocks 32–3, 37
    excessive expansion 31
    flexibility 93–4, 109
    four principles 27, 30–43
    and imperfect information 38–40
    legitimacy 94, 109, 347
    long-term policies 28, 92–3
    new framework 332–56
    and poverty reduction 68
    reforms 28
Madigan, B. 81
Malaysia 300
Masciandrao, D. 88
medical technology 249, 252
Meredith, G. 79
Mexico, financial crisis 37
Minford, P. 88
MIRAS (mortgage interest relief at
    source) 65
Missale, A. 291, 292
monetarism 33–4
monetary policy
    accountability 18, 49, 339–40
    constrained by rules 87–8
    coordination with fiscal policy 4,
        23–5, 49–50, 101–8, 349, *see also*
        policy coordination
    credibility 18, 339–47
    decision making process 17–18, 338
    and employment 68
    and exchange rate 12

expansionary 68, 70
flexibility 41–2, 48, 93–4, 347–8
Government responsibility 14, 17,
    49–50
Government's objectives 44–50
history of 4–18
inappropriate objectives 10–12
and inflation targets 31–2, 44, 45,
    46, 86–7
and instability 25
and institutional mechanisms 41–2
and interest rates 12, 13–14, 18, 19,
    31, 86–7
legitimacy 94, 109, 347
and moderate inflation 61
new framework 5–10, 44–57,
    332–49, 353
and poverty and inequality 68
and price stability 10, 12, 18, 45–6,
    50, 56
roles and responsibilities 14, 17
short-term political pressures
    17–18, 33, 42, 49
specifying objectives 12–13, 45
supported by fiscal policy 135, 158,
    188, 196
transparency 18, 49, 339–40
see also economic policy
Monetary Policy Committee (MPC)
    50–7, 96–100, 103–8, 338–9
accountability 48, 49, 50, 54–5, 57
annual report 54
composition of 50–1
and financial markets 52–3
and fiscal policy 190
and independent experts 18, 335–9
and inflation targets 44–8, 49, 51,
    54, 56–7, 70–1
and interest rates 49, 52, 74, 334–5,
    346, 347
meetings 52; minutes 53, 54, 57
Open Letter system 48, 56–7, 96,
    100, 334, 348
and Parliament 54–5
proactive policy making 334–5,
    356
procedure 51–2
relationship with government
    49–50, 54–5

remit 55–7, 71
reporting requirements on 49, 53–4
and research 51–2
and stability 334–5, 348, 356
and transparency 49, 52, 53–5, 190,
    339–40
and Treasury representative 105,
    106–8
see also Bank of England; central
    bank independence
Mongiardino, A. 291
Monnier, S. 81
moral hazard 113, 117
Morris, C.S. 64
mortgages
Cat standard 127
financial regulation 110
interest payments 74, 76
regulation 123
see also financial regulation
Multilateral Development Banks
    (MDBs) 313–14

NAIRU (non-accelerating inflation
    rate of unemployment) 78–9,
    215, 368
National Asset Register 237, 240, 241,
    275
National Audit Office (NAO) 138, 143,
    151, 199, 244
National Debt 175–7
see also debt management; public
    debt
National Debt Management Agency
    of Ireland 291
National Health Service Trusts 266
National Institute for Economic and
    Social Research (NIESR) 162,
    185, 258, 259
National Savings 144, 151, 198
negative and non-negative real
    interest rates 82–3
net debt 150, 183–4, 195, 352
as fiscal indicator 271
and gross debt 167, 184, 271
long-term projections 150
and net worth 172
primary balance 184, 199, 202
see also golden rule; sustainable
    investment rule

net debt ratio 184, 195, 199, 204, 272
net financial assets 271
net worth/wealth 184, 195, 264,
    265–7, 349
  by level of government 268
  changes in 274
  determining 275
  fall in 164, 165, 196
  as fiscal indicator 271–2, 277, 278
  and golden rule 272, 279
  prospective 184–5
  recent trends 266, 267
  tangible assets 269, 270
  v. net debt 273
New Deal Programmes 214
New Zealand
  budget targets 166
  fiscal policy 137
  Fiscal Responsibility Act 272
Neyapti, B. 88
nominal rigidities 35, 79, 80–2
  see also prices; wages
Nordhaus, W.D. 101–3, 104, 105
North Sea revenues 186, 278
Norton Warburg 118
nuclear decommissioning 249, 261

Occupational Pensions Regulatory
    Authority (OPRA) 117
Odling-Smee, J. 278
Office for National Statistics (ONS) 74,
    184, 264, 275
offshore financial centres 311
oil price rises 186
Okun coefficient 80
old-age dependency ratio 250
Open Letter system 48, 56–7, 96, 100,
    334, 348
Organisation for Economic
    Cooperation and Development
    (OECD) 100, 217, 253, 260, 335,
    338
Orphanides, A. 81
output gap 14–15, 19, 25, 204–18,
    221–2
  historical estimates of 210–12
  and inflation 205–6, 337, 349
  and interest rates 14, 15, 19, 25,
    335, 336
  see also potential output

Pakistan 309
pensions 252–9, 260, 276, 278
  personal pensions (PPs) 127, 130
  regulation 117
  stakeholder pensions 111, 127,
    130, 261
  State Second Pension (SSP) 261
  unfunded liabilities 265, 276, 277,
    278
Personal Equity Plans (PEPs) 126
Personal Investment Authority (PIA)
    115, 118
personal pensions (PPs), complexity
    of 127, 130
Philippines 300
Phillips, S. 64
Phillips curve 31, 35, 80, 81, 205, 207
policy coordination
  and game theory 101–3
  improvement in 349
  Nordhaus model 101–3, 104, 105
  and policy mix 108
  pre-commitment to 104–5
population, ageing 250–2, 258, 260,
    261–2
post-war monetary policy regimes 7
potential output 204–18
  estimating 206–10; across full and
    half cycles 208, 210; CBI survey
    208; trend extraction methods
    206–8
  historical estimates of 210–12
  and inflation 204–6
  and oil component of GDP 210
  predicting trend growth 212–18;
    employment 212–15, 217, 218;
    labour productivity 215–17, 218
  see also output gap
Poverty Reduction Strategy Paper
    (PRSP) 315
Pre-Budget Report (PBR) 138, 141,
    142–3, 147–8, 153, 164
  projections 106–7, 191–2, 199, 211,
    212, 223, 224
  transparency 191
Prescott, E.C. 86, 88
Prevention of Fraud Act (1958) 117
price indices 74–6, 84
  GDP deflator 75
  measurement bias 76–7

price stability 10, 12, 18, 45–7, 50
and entry to EMU 318, 319, 326
and index-linked debt 293
and MPC 71
see also inflation; inflation targets;
stability
prices, nominal rigidities 35, 80–2
primary balance 170–3, 184, 193, 196
and net debt ratio 199, 202
and pensions 260
privatisation 266, 270
prospective net worth 184–5, 276–7
public borrowing 42
and automatic stabilisers 186, 219
for current spending 192
motives for 169–70
to finance investment 272
see also public sector net borrowing
(PSNB)
public corporations 264–9
balance sheets 275
and fiscal rules 158
net worth 266
public debt
concepts of 167–8
and current spending and revenue
169, 192
dynamic efficiency tests 174–5
and economic growth 175, 178
and economic shocks 173, 178
effects of high levels of 173–4, 181
and external debt 168
and fiscal policy 177–80, 181, 184
and generational fairness 181, 192
increases in 5, 23
international comparison 177, 180
Maastricht reference level 178, 180
and national income (GDP) 168
net debt v. gross debt 167
optimal level of 174–5, 178
private sector benchmarks 174
and risk premium in interest rates
173
and sustainability and solvency
171
upper limit on 170
and war 169, 175, 177
see also debt management; public
sector net borrowing (PSNB)

Public Expenditure Surveys 231
public finance initiatives 235
public sector balance sheet 263–79
bottom line measure 264
and fiscal policy 270–4, 278–9
and future cash flows 276, 277
future developments 276–7
negative balance sheets 264
prospective net worth 276
and quality of data 274–5, 279
valuing assets and liabilities 275
public sector current expenditure
(PSCE) 220, 226
public sector current receipts (PSCR)
220
public sector net borrowing (PSNB)
24, 150, 183, 184, 186–8, 197,
224
current spending and revenue 195
fall in 196
as fiscal indicator 220, 222
public sector net cash requirement
(PSNCR) 21, 150, 160, 183, 196
public sector net debt (PSND) see net
debt
public sector net investment 161
public sector net wealth see net
worth/wealth
Public Service Agreements (PSAs) 234,
238, 241, 261
Public Service Productivity Panel 235,
261
public services 178
and demographic trends 250–2
long-term sustainability 261
modernisation 261
raising productivity 261
Public Services and Public
Expenditure (PSX), Cabinet
Committee 235
public spending 230–8
and ageing population 260, 261–2
annual negotiation 231, 235
and asset management 231–2, 233,
236, 240, 241–2
and capital spending 233, 236–7,
240
departmental boundaries 232, 233,
237–8
and fiscal rules 233, 234–2

public spending *continued*
  and investment 231, 236, 241
  long-term planning 233, 235
  long-term projections 255
  new control framework 230–8, 241;
    principles 232–3
  old control system 230–2
  three-year process 233, 235, 240,
    241, 246
  transparency 233, 234
  and working capital 241
  see also education; health services;
    Resource Accounting and
    Budgeting (RAB)
public–private partnerships 235

Quah, D.T. 291

recession 8, 14, 19, 29, 31
  and negative interest rates 82
  see also boom-bust cycles
recognised investment exchanges
  (RIEs) 117
recognised professional bodies (RPBs)
  116, 119
Reifschneider, D. 81
'repo' markets 285, 296
Reports on the Observance of
    Standards and Codes (ROSCs)
    304
Requests for Resources (RfRs) 245
Resource Accounting and Budgeting
    (RAB) 140–1, 147, 149, 236–7,
    239–48
  and balance sheets 264, 275
  benefits of 240–2
  and capital stock 241
  and fiscal framework 242
  and fiscal rules 248
  and government departments 243
  implementation 243–4
  in-year control 247
  non-cash costs 239, 247
  and non-departmental public
    bodies 246
  resource accounts 244–5
  resource budgeting 246–7
  resource estimates 245–6

and spending control framework
    241–2
  trigger point strategy 243–4
Resource Accounting Manual (RAM) 244
retail prices index excluding mortgage
    payments (RPIX), inflation 5, 46,
    47, 74, 84
retail prices index (RPI) 46, 74–5
Ricketts, R. 79
Riley, C. 278
Robson, W.B.P. 175
Romer, C.D. and Romer, D.H. 68–9
Romer, Paul 29
Rose, D. 79
RPIY 74–5
Russia 301

Sachs, J. 70
sacrifice ratio 79, 80
Sarel, M. 64
Scarth, W.M. 175
Securities and Futures Authority (SFA)
    115, 118
Securities and Investments Board (SIB)
    118–19, 120
self-regulating organisations (SROs)
    115, 116, 118–9, 125
Service Delivery Agreements (SDAs)
    241
shocks 46, 101, 297
  and debt management 288, 289,
    290–7
  demand shocks 32, 207, 289, 339
  and fiscal policy 158
  and inflation rate 48, 56
  and interest rates 171
  and labour costs 81
  and macroeconomic policy 32–3,
    37
  responding to 41–2, 107, 158, 339,
    347–8
  supply shocks 32, 34, 35, 37, 39,
    207, 289, 339
  to incomes 281, 284
single currency *see* Economic and
    Monetary Union
Skinner, J. 252
Smith, J. 80
Smyth, D.J. 175

social security
    and ageing population 252–3
    benefits linked to prices 253, 255
    long-term projections 255
    pensions 252–3, 260
sound public finances 5, 28–9, 30,
    134, 159, 328, 348
    see also Stability and Growth Pact;
    sustainability
stability
    and central bank independence 86,
    92–3, 94
    and credibility 93, 94–5
    and employment 214
    sustained 29, 30
    through constrained discretion 27,
    32–5, 95
    see also price stability
Stability and Growth Pact (SGP) 142,
    148, 149, 150, 159, 328–30
    Convergence Programmes 329
    excessive deficits procedure 166,
    198, 317, 327, 329–30
    requirements of 198
    and Stability Programmes 321, 329
stakeholder pensions (SHPs) 110, 111,
    127, 130, 261
state pensions 276, 278
State Second Pension (S2P) 261
statistical filters 207
Stiglitz, Joseph 38
stock measures 201
Stokey, N.L. 288
'strips' 285, 296
structural deficit 25
Summers, L.H. 80–1
Sure Start 238
surplus on current budget 163, 193,
    195, 272
    cyclical adjustment 220, 222, 223,
    350
    as fiscal indicator 204, 220, 222, 279
    long-term projections 150, 191–2,
    199, 347
    and net worth 279
    and public sector balance sheet 278
sustainability
    and ageing population 250–2, 258
    see also sound public finances

sustainable investment rule 135, 155,
    167–80, 181, 184, 204, 272
    and economic cycle 160
    and new fiscal policy framework 348
    public debt concepts 167–8
    and sound public finances 195
    see also golden rule
Sweden, and single currency 322

Tabellini, G. 88, 101
tax
    aggregate tax burden 227
    and debt management 281, 282,
    288–91
    fall in effective rate 191
    generational accounts 259
    and inflation 59–60, 65, 66
    long-term projections 254–5
    and prospective net worth 276–7
    and public borrowing 169
    receipts and tax base 229
    tax bases 228
    tax cuts 23
Tax Exempt Special Savings Accounts
    (TESSAs) 126
technological change 30, 32, 35, 215
Tetlow, R. 73–4
Thailand 37, 300
Tietmeyer, Hans 310
time inconsistency problem 33–4, 35,
    38, 40
    and central bank independence 41,
    86, 88
    and debt management 293–4
Tobin, J. 281–2
Total Managed Expenditure (TME)
    220, 225
transfer payments 254, 255, 256, 257,
    259
transparency 135, 136
    and credibility 27, 28, 38–40, 42,
    95–6
    and democracy 138–9
    economic and fiscal projections 143
    exceptions 139, 145
    and fiscal policy 135, 136–7, 138–9,
    143, 145, 199
    and Monetary Policy Committee
    49, 52, 53–5, 190

transparency *continued*
Pre-Budget Report 191
public spending 233
see also credibility
Treasury, powers of 123, 125, 131
Treasury Bills 52, 198
Treasury Select Committee 138, 141,
151, 338, 339, 347–8
trend output *see* potential output

UK
financial markets crisis 36
and international financial architecture reform 302, 303–4, 310,
316
labour productivity 217
real interest rates 83
and transparency in economic
policy 95–6, 105
Ukraine 309
unemployment 29, 30, 31, 35, 38
'hysteresis' effect 31
and inflation 10–12, 31, 33, 42, 80,
87–8, 98, 215
see also employment; Phillips curve
unit trusts 116, 118
US
and ageing population 262
Balanced Budget Act 166, 180
consumer price index (CPI) 76
generational policy 259
real interest rates 83

US Federal Reserve 42, 82, 86, 94, 97
utilities, privatised 266

wages
nominal rigidities 80–2
non-wage compensation 81
Webb, S.B. 88
welfare state, reform of 30, 261
Welfare to Work 238
Werner Report 318
Whole of Government Accounts
(WGA) 242, 275
Wieland, V. 81
Williams, J. 81
women, retirement age 261
Working Families Tax Credit (WFTC)
190
working-age population 212, 213,
215, 250
World Bank 299, 304, 310
cooperation with IMF 314–15
Independent Inspection Panel
312
and transparency 312
world economy 35, 299
see also globalisation

Yates, A. 80, 104

Zee, H.H. 175
zero inflation 60, 65, 70, 73–4, 78, 82
Zervos, S.J. 64